Foundations of Agnostic Statistics

Reflecting a sea change in how empirical research has been conducted over the past three decades, *Foundations of Agnostic Statistics* presents an innovative treatment of modern statistical theory for the social and health sciences. This book develops the fundamentals of what the authors call agnostic statistics, which considers what can be learned about the world without assuming that there exists a simple generative model that can be known to be true. Aronow and Miller provide the foundations for statistical inference for researchers unwilling to make assumptions beyond what they or their audience would find credible. Building from first principles, the book covers topics including estimation theory, regression, maximum likelihood, missing data, and causal inference. Using these principles, readers will be able to formally articulate their targets of inquiry, distinguish substantive assumptions from statistical assumptions, and ultimately engage in cutting-edge quantitative empirical research that contributes to human knowledge.

Peter M. Aronow is an associate professor of Political Science, Public Health (Biostatistics), and Statistics and Data Science at Yale University and is affiliated with the university's Institution for Social and Policy Studies, Center for the Study of American Politics, Institute for Network Science, and Operations Research Doctoral Program.

Benjamin T. Miller is a doctoral candidate in Political Science at Yale University. Mr. Miller holds a BA in Economics and Mathematics from Amherst College (2012).

Foundations of Agnostic Statistics

PETER M. ARONOW
Yale University

BENJAMIN T. MILLER
Yale University

CAMBRIDGE
UNIVERSITY PRESS

CAMBRIDGE
UNIVERSITY PRESS

University Printing House, Cambridge CB2 8BS, United Kingdom

One Liberty Plaza, 20th Floor, New York, NY 10006, USA

477 Williamstown Road, Port Melbourne, VIC 3207, Australia

314–321, 3rd Floor, Plot 3, Splendor Forum, Jasola District Centre, New Delhi – 110025, India

79 Anson Road, #06-04/06, Singapore 079906

Cambridge University Press is part of the University of Cambridge.

It furthers the University's mission by disseminating knowledge in the pursuit of education, learning, and research at the highest international levels of excellence.

www.cambridge.org
Information on this title: www.cambridge.org/9781107178915
DOI: 10.1017/9781316831762

First published 2019
3rd printing 2021

Printed in Singapore by Markono Print Media Pte Ltd

A catalogue record for this publication is available from the British Library.

Library of Congress Cataloging-in-Publication Data
Names: Aronow, Peter M., author. | Miller, Benjamin T., author.
Title: Foundations of agnostic statistics / Peter M. Aronow, Benjamin T. Miller.
Description: New York : Cambridge University Press, 2019.
Identifiers: LCCN 2018039877 | ISBN 9781107178915 (hardback) |
ISBN 9781316631140 (paperback)
Subjects: LCSH: Quantitative research. | Statistics. |
BISAC: POLITICAL SCIENCE / General.
Classification: LCC QA76.9.Q36 A76 2019 |
DDC 001.4/2–dc23 LC record available at https://lccn.loc.gov/2018039877

ISBN 978-1-107-17891-5 Hardback
ISBN 978-1-316-63114-0 Paperback

For Our Parents

I do not pretend to know where many ignorant men are sure—that is all that agnosticism means.

— Clarence Darrow

Contents

List of Tables and Figures — *page* xii
Introduction — xv

PART I PROBABILITY — 1

1 Probability Theory — 3
- 1.1 *Random Events* — 4
  - 1.1.1 *What Is Probability?* — 4
  - 1.1.2 *Fundamentals of Probability Theory* — 5
  - 1.1.3 *Joint and Conditional Probabilities* — 9
  - 1.1.4 *Independence of Events* — 14
- 1.2 *Random Variables* — 15
  - 1.2.1 *What Is a Random Variable?* — 16
  - 1.2.2 *Discrete Random Variables* — 18
  - 1.2.3 *Cumulative Distribution Functions* — 21
  - 1.2.4 *Continuous Random Variables* — 24
  - 1.2.5 *Support* — 30
- 1.3 *Bivariate Relationships* — 31
  - 1.3.1 *Discrete Bivariate Distributions* — 32
  - 1.3.2 *Discrete Marginal and Conditional Distributions* — 33
  - 1.3.3 *Jointly Continuous Random Variables* — 36
  - 1.3.4 *Independence of Random Variables* — 38
- 1.4 *Multivariate Generalizations* — 39
- 1.5 *Further Readings* — 43

2 Summarizing Distributions 44
2.1 *Summary Features of Random Variables* 45
2.1.1 *Expected Values* 45
2.1.2 *Moments, Variances, and Standard Deviations* 50
2.1.3 *Mean Squared Error* 56
2.2 *Summary Features of Joint Distributions* 59
2.2.1 *Covariance and Correlation* 59
2.2.2 *Covariance, Correlation, and Independence* 64
2.2.3 *Conditional Expectations and Conditional Expectation Functions* 67
2.2.4 *Best Predictors and Best Linear Predictors* 75
2.2.5 *CEFs and BLPs under Independence* 82
2.3 *Multivariate Generalizations* 84
2.4 *Further Readings* 88

PART II STATISTICS 89
3 Learning from Random Samples 91
3.1 *I.I.D. Random Variables* 91
3.1.1 *Random Sampling* 92
3.1.2 *I.I.D. as Approximation* 94
3.2 *Estimation* 96
3.2.1 *Sample Means* 96
3.2.2 *Estimation Theory* 102
3.2.3 *Variance Estimators* 105
3.2.4 *The Central Limit Theorem for Sample Means* 108
3.2.5 *Asymptotic Estimation Theory* 111
3.2.6 *Estimating Standard Errors of Sample Means* 114
3.3 *The Plug-In Principle* 116
3.3.1 *The Usual Plug-In Regularity Conditions* 120
3.3.2 *Kernel Estimation* 121
3.4 *Inference* 124
3.4.1 *Confidence Intervals* 124
3.4.2 *Hypothesis Testing* 128
3.4.3 *The Bootstrap* 130
3.4.4 *Micronumerosity* 132
3.5 *Cluster Samples* 135

3.5.1 Estimation with Clustering 136
3.5.2 Inference with Clustering 140
3.6 Further Readings 141
4 Regression 143
4.1 Regression Estimation 143
4.1.1 Bivariate Case 144
4.1.2 OLS Regression 145
4.1.3 Regression with Matrix Algebra 147
4.2 Inference 151
4.2.1 Standard Errors and Inference 151
4.2.2 Inference with Robust Standard Errors and the Bootstrap 152
4.2.3 Classical Standard Errors 155
4.3 Estimation of Nonlinear Conditional Expectation Functions 156
4.3.1 Polynomials 158
4.3.2 Overfitting 161
4.3.3 Interactions 164
4.3.4 Summarizing Partial Derivatives of the CEF 165
4.3.5 Sieve Estimation 168
4.3.6 Penalized Regression 169
4.4 Application: Access to Clean Water and Infant Mortality 170
4.5 Further Readings 177
5 Parametric Models 178
5.1 Models and Parameters 178
5.1.1 The Classical Linear Model 180
5.1.2 Binary Choice Models 182
5.2 Maximum Likelihood Estimation 185
5.2.1 The Logic of Maximum Likelihood Estimation 185
5.2.2 Maximum Likelihood Estimation when the Parametric Model Is True 193
5.2.3 Maximum Likelihood Estimation when the Parametric Model Is Not True 194
5.2.4 Maximum Likelihood Plug-In Estimation 197
5.2.5 Mixture Models 198
5.2.6 Penalized Maximum Likelihood Regression 201
5.2.7 Inference 202

5.3 *A Note on Models as Approximations* 203
5.4 *Further Readings* 204

PART III IDENTIFICATION 205

6 Missing Data 207
6.1 *Identification with Missing Data [7.1]* 208
6.1.1 *Bounds [7.1.3]* 209
6.1.2 *Missing Completely at Random [7.1.4]* 213
6.1.3 *Missing at Random [7.1.5]* 215
6.1.4 *The Role of the Propensity Score for Missing Data [7.1.6]* 217
6.2 *Estimation with Missing Data under MAR [7.2]* 219
6.2.1 *Plug-In Estimation [7.2.1]* 219
6.2.2 *Regression Estimation [7.2.2]* 222
6.2.3 *Hot Deck Imputation [7.2.4]* 224
6.2.4 *Maximum Likelihood Plug-In Estimation of Propensity Scores [7.2.5]* 225
6.2.5 *Weighting Estimators [7.2.6]* 226
6.2.6 *Doubly Robust Estimators [7.2.7]* 228
6.3 *Application: Estimating the Cross-National Average of Clean Energy Use* 231
6.4 *Further Readings* 234

7 Causal Inference 235
7.1 *Identification with Potential Outcomes [6.1]* 236
7.1.1 *Framework* 236
7.1.2 *Ties to Missing Data* 238
7.1.3 *Bounds [6.1.1]* 240
7.1.4 *Random Assignment [6.1.2]* 244
7.1.5 *Ignorability [6.1.3]* 247
7.1.6 *The Role of the Propensity Score for Causal Inference [6.1.4]* 250
7.1.7 *Post-Treatment Variables* 252
7.1.8 *Generalizing Beyond Binary Treatments* 254
7.2 *Estimation of Causal Effects under Ignorability [6.2]* 256
7.2.1 *Plug-In Estimation [6.2.1]* 256
7.2.2 *Regression Estimation [6.2.2]* 258
7.2.3 *Maximum Likelihood Plug-In Estimation of Causal Effects* 261

7.2.4 *Matching [6.2.3]* 262

7.2.5 *Maximum Likelihood Plug-In Estimation of Propensity Scores [6.2.4]* 264

7.2.6 *Weighting Estimators [6.2.5]* 264

7.2.7 *Doubly Robust Estimators [6.2.6]* 267

7.2.8 *Placebo Testing* 270

7.3 *Overlap and Positivity* 271

7.3.1 *Changing the Target Population* 273

7.3.2 *Empirical Overlap, Micronumerosity, and Weighting Estimators* 273

7.4 *Further Extensions* 276

7.5 *Application: The Effect of Gender on Swiss Citizenship Approval Votes* 276

7.6 *Further Readings* 280

Glossary of Mathematical Notation 282

Glossary of Common Abbreviations 286

References 288

Index 293

Tables and Figures

TABLES

3.4.1 Implications of Micronumerosity (Standard Uniform Distribution) *page* 134
3.4.2 Implications of Micronumerosity (Bernoulli Distribution with $p = 0.5$) 134
4.1.1 Sample of $n = 15$ Draws from (X, Y) 145
4.4.5 Regression Table for Cross-National Infant Mortality 173
6.3.1 Estimates of the Cross-National Average of Clean Energy Usage with Missing Data 233
7.5.1 Estimates for Effect of Gender on Percentage "No" Votes 280

FIGURES

1.2.1 Die Roll CDF 23
1.2.2 PDF of the Standard Uniform Distribution 29
1.2.3 CDF of the Standard Uniform Distribution 29
1.2.4 PDF of the Standard Normal Distribution 30
1.2.5 CDF of the Standard Normal Distribution 30
2.1.1 Minimum MSE Solution for a Fair Coin Flip 59
2.2.1 Plotting the CEF and BLP 82
2.2.2 Plotting the CEF and the BLP over Different Distributions of X 83
3.2.1 Weak Law of Large Numbers 101
3.2.2 Simulated Sampling Distributions of the Sample Mean 111

3.3.1 CDF of a Continuous Random Variable, and Illustrative Empirical CDF 117
3.3.2 Visualization of Different Kernels 122
4.1.2 Illustration of $n = 15$ Sample of Draws from (X, Y) 146
4.3.1 Plotting the CEF and BLP 157
4.3.2 A Nonlinear CEF 159
4.3.3 Polynomial Approximations of a Nonlinear CEF 160
4.3.4 Overfitting with a Linear CEF 162
4.3.5 Overfitting with a Nonlinear CEF 163
4.4.1 Plotting Cross-National Infant Mortality Against Access to Clean Water 171
4.4.2 Estimates of the CEF of Infant Mortality with Respect to Access to Clean Water 172
4.4.3 Plotting Cross-National Infant Mortality Against Access to Clean Water and Electricity 175
4.4.4 Estimates of the CEF of Infant Mortality with Respect to Access to Clean Water and Electricity 176
5.1.1 Logit and Probit Functions 184
5.2.1 A Likelihood Function for Three Coin Tosses 190
5.2.2 Minimum KL Divergence Approximation of an Unusual Distribution 197
5.2.3 Unusual Distribution 199
5.2.4 Normal, Log-Normal, and Exponential Maximum Likelihood Approximations 200
5.2.5 Mixture Model Maximum Likelihood Approximation 201
7.3.1 Limited Population Overlap Illustration 272
7.3.2 Empirical Overlap Illustration 274

Introduction

> *Humans are allergic to change. They love to say, "We've always done it this way." I try to fight that. That's why I have a clock on my wall that runs counter-clockwise.*
>
> —GRACE HOPPER

The last three decades have seen a marked change in the manner in which quantitative empirical inquiry in the social and health sciences is conducted. Sometimes dubbed the "credibility revolution," this change has been characterized by a growing acknowledgment that the evidence that researchers adduce for their claims is often predicated on unsustainable assumptions. Our understanding of statistical and econometric tools has needed to change accordingly. We have found that conventional textbooks, which often begin with incredible modeling assumptions, are not well suited as a starting point for credible research.

We designed this book as a first course in statistical inquiry to accommodate the needs of this evolving approach to quantitative empirical research. Our book develops the fundamentals of what we call *agnostic statistics*. With agnostic statistics, we attempt to consider what can be learned about the world without assuming that there exists a simple generative model that can be known to be true. We provide the foundations for statistical inference for researchers unwilling to make assumptions beyond what they or their audience would find credible.

Under the agnostic paradigm, there is little magic required for statistical inquiry. Armed with the tools developed in this book, readers will be able to critically evaluate the credibility of both applied work and statistical methods under the assumptions warranted by their substantive context. Additionally, building from the principles established in the book, readers will be able to formally articulate their targets of inquiry, distinguish substantive assumptions from statistical assumptions, and ultimately engage in cutting-edge quantitative empirical research that contributes to human knowledge.

WHAT IS IN THIS BOOK?

In Part I (Probability, Chapters 1 and 2), we begin by presenting a canonical mathematical formulation of randomness: the notion of probability. We can neatly describe random events using a set-theoretic formalization that largely agrees with our intuitions. Furthermore, when events can be quantified, we can represent random generative processes with *random variables*. We show that probability theory provides us with a clear language for describing features of random generative processes, even when the structure of those processes is not fully known.

In Part II (Statistics, Chapters 3, 4, and 5), we engage with data. If the researcher can collect data produced by repeated, independent draws from some random generative process, we can learn about some of the characteristics of the process that generated them without any further assumptions. We can estimate features of this random generative process (for example, "our guess of the average height in this population is 5.6 feet"), and we can even make probabilistic statements describing the uncertainty of our estimates (for example, "we can state with 95% confidence that our guess lies within 0.2 feet of the true average height"). Simple statistical methods for estimation and inference (based on the *plug-in principle*), including standard tools such as ordinary least squares regression and maximum likelihood estimation, allow us to approximate these features without assuming the validity of a restrictive model.

In Part III (Identification, Chapters 6 and 7), we show how the statistical foundations of an agnostic approach to statistics naturally allow us to draw ties between features of a probability distribution and substantive processes. This task, of course, necessitates detailed knowledge of the process at hand. We discuss assumptions with clear substantive interpretations that allow us to generalize from the statistical model to broader phenomena, including missing data and causal inference. These *identification* assumptions can be viewed as separable from those embedded in the agnostic approach to statistical inference, thus laying bare the sources of our inferential leverage.

WHAT DO I NEED TO KNOW TO READ THIS BOOK?

We expect that the readers of this book will have had some exposure to the ideas of probability and statistics at the undergraduate level; while not required, it will significantly ease the readers' experience with the book. Some mild calculus will be used—nothing much beyond partial derivatives and integrals, and even then, numerical methods will typically suffice for anything more complicated than a polynomial. Some elementary set theory will also be required for our exposition of probability theory. Notably, we avoid the gratuitous use of linear algebra, and readers need not have prior training in order to engage with the text. Concepts from more advanced areas of mathematics (such as measure theory) appear in some technical footnotes, but these can be safely ignored by readers not yet fully comfortable with these subjects. We try to include the proofs of as many of the theorems and principles in this book as possible, though we omit those that would be tedious or require advanced mathematics not covered here.

HOW SHOULD I READ THIS BOOK?

This book is intended to serve as an introductory graduate-level course in statistics as well as a reference work for more experienced researchers. We have therefore attempted to write this book in a manner that is both accessible to readers with minimal background in statistics and useful to those with more advanced training. One way in which we attempt to strike this balance is through extensive use of footnotes to provide clarification and commentary on technical points. These are provided mainly to answer questions that some sophisticated readers might raise and to note how certain concepts and theorems can be extended. Some readers may find these notes useful, but in general, they can be safely ignored by readers new to the subject. Similarly, we provide references at the end of each chapter to other texts that discuss the subjects we cover in greater detail.

Though this is not primarily a book on probability theory, it does make extensive and rigorous use of the concepts and theorems of this foundational area of mathematics. Thus, our treatment of probability in Part I is abbreviated but mathematically dense. Mathematically sophisticated readers (that is, those comfortable with the concepts and notation of calculus, basic set theory, and proofs) should have little difficulty learning the essentials of probability theory from these chapters. For readers who have already been exposed to mathematical probability theory, these chapters should serve as a review of the concepts that will be important for the rest of this book. Once we have laid this technical groundwork, the mathematics ease in Parts II and III.

Many of the ideas in Part I are essential for understanding the fundamentals of this book, and our treatment of them may be somewhat unfamiliar for readers whose prior training is in applied econometrics or data analysis. We therefore recommend that even relatively statistically sophisticated readers (and also readers otherwise uninterested in probability theory) read the contents of these chapters, as their presentation will inform our discussion of more advanced and applied topics in subsequent chapters. For readers with neither previous exposure to probability theory nor fluency in college-level mathematics, we strongly recommend consulting an undergraduate textbook on probability theory.[1]

[1] We recommend Chapter 1 of Wasserman (2004) for a concise treatment, though we are also fond of Part IV of Freedman, Pisani, and Purves (1998) as a very friendly introduction to the basics of probability theory. For a more thorough treatment of mathematical probability theory, we recommend Blitzstein and Hwang (2014) and Wackerly, Mendenhall, and Scheaffer (2008).

Finally, some common mathematical notation used in this book will not be defined in the main text. However, definitions of many of these notations are included in the Glossary of Mathematical Notation. Readers with little background in advanced mathematics or statistics may want to begin by reviewing and familiarizing themselves with the concepts and notation in this appendix. In addition, we provide a Glossary of Common Abbreviations, which gives the meanings of all common abbreviations used in this book, along with references to where they are defined in the text.

WHO HELPED TO WRITE THIS BOOK?

We thank the following readers and research assistants for their valuable contributions to this book: Ellen Alpert, Laura Balzer, Tommaso Bardelli, Jonathon Baron, Paul C. Bauer, Kassandra Birchler, Xiaoxuan Cai, Alex Coppock, Forrest Crawford, Naoki Egami, Germán Feierherd, Robin Gomila, Don Green, Anand Gupta, Josh Kalla, Sarah Hamerling, Erin Hartman, Jennifer Hill, Will Hunt, Jun Hwang, Donald Lee, Daniel Masterson, Mary McGrath, Adelaide McNamara, Joel Middleton, Avi Nuri, Lilla Orr, Betsy Levy Paluck, Raja Panjwani, Kyle Peyton, Thomas Richardson, Jamie Robins, Cyrus Samii, Fredrik Sävje, Collin Schumock, Matt Shafer, Vivien Shotwell, Pavita Singh, Brandon Stewart, Eric Tchetgen-Tchetgen, Dustin Tingley, Teppei Yamamoto, the participants of the *Theory of Agnostic Statistics: A Discussion* conference at Yale University, and the reviewers and editorial staff at *Cambridge University Press*. We thank Jens Hainmueller and Dominik Hangartner for generous data sharing. We owe a special debt of gratitude to Winston Lin, whose comments and insights guided us at every stage of the book—from conception to development to completion. In fact, our book's title is an homage to Lin (2013), itself referencing the "agnostic regression" of Angrist and Imbens (2002). We would also be remiss not to specially acknowledge the many contributions of Molly Offer-Westort, which included coding, technical edits, figures, and important guidance on framing. We thank our editor, Robert Dreesen, whose patience, encouragement, and wisdom helped us turn an idea into a manuscript and a manuscript into a book.

We also thank our classes, the Yale students in the first year graduate quantitative methods sequence for political science (PLSC 500 and PLSC 503), who were invaluable in shaping the contents of this book. In fact, this book originated from the lecture notes for these courses, in which one of us (Aronow) was the instructor and the other (Miller) was a student and later a teaching fellow. We began work on the book in earnest during the summer of 2014, and it quickly became a fully collaborative effort. We view our contributions to this book as equal and inseparable.

PART I

PROBABILITY

1

Probability Theory

Though there be no such thing as chance in the world, our ignorance of the real cause of any event has the same influence on the understanding.

—David Hume

Our book begins by providing a formalization of probability theory, establishing some basic theorems that will allow us to formally describe random generative processes and quantify relevant features of these processes. We believe that it is important for researchers to understand the assumptions embedded in mathematical probability theory before attempting to make statistical claims. In keeping with the agnostic paradigm, we will attempt to draw attention to the relevant intricacies involved, and highlight where mathematical constructions serve as approximations. The foundation of probability theory allows researchers to precisely define the scope of their research questions and to rigorously quantify their uncertainty about the conclusions they draw from their findings. Our approach is somewhat unconventional, in that we focus on describing random variables *before* we consider data, so as to have well-defined inferential targets. This is sometimes referred to as the "population first" approach.[1] This approach will enable us to engage with the more complex topics in Parts II and III with relative ease and rigor.

We begin this chapter with a discussion of how random generative processes assign probabilities to random events. We can then describe probabilities of individual events and how the probability of one event relates to the probability of another. We proceed to consider random variables, which take on real number values determined by the outcomes of random generative processes. We describe several types of functions that characterize the probability *distributions* of random variables; these distribution functions allow us to characterize the probability that the random variable takes on any given value

1 See Angrist and Pischke (2009).

or values. When we have two or more random variables whose values are determined simultaneously, we can describe their joint distributions, which also allows us to describe their marginal and conditional distributions. Here, we primarily focus on bivariate relationships (between two random variables), but we outline multivariate generalizations. At the end of the chapter, we provide suggestions for readers interested in a more technical treatment of the material or alternative approaches.

1.1 RANDOM EVENTS

Probability theory is a *mathematical construct* used to represent processes involving randomness, unpredictability, or intrinsic uncertainty. In a setting in which there are several possible outcomes, each with some probability of occurring, we refer to the process by which the outcome is determined as a *random generative process*. In this section, we present the basic principles of probability theory used to describe random generative processes.

1.1.1 What Is Probability?

We can think of a random generative process as a mechanism that selects an *outcome* from among multiple possible outcomes. This mechanism could be flipping a coin or rolling a die, drawing a ball from an urn, selecting a person at random from a group of people, or any other process in which the outcome is in some sense uncertain. A single instance of selecting an outcome is known as a *draw* from or *realization* of the random generative process. The term *experiment* is also commonly used, but we shall refrain from this usage to avoid confusion with experiments in the ordinary sense of the term.

The probability of an event describes the proportion of times that event can be expected to occur among many realizations of a random generative process. This interpretation of probability is known as *frequentist probability* or *frequentism*: the probability of an event A is interpreted as representing how frequently A would occur among many, many draws from a random generative process. It is the long-run average or limiting value of the frequency of observing event A among repeated realizations of the generative process.[2]

Probability theory is a *model*, which is an approximation of reality. Everyday macrophysical processes are not actually characterized by fundamental randomness. Consider, for example, a coin flip. In principle, if we could know the exact mass, shape, and position of the coin at the moment it was flipped and the exact magnitude and direction of the force imparted to it by the flipper

2 There are other interpretations of probability, most notably the *Bayesian* interpretation, which treats probability as representing a degree of belief or confidence in a proposition. We do not discuss these alternative interpretations and will be operating under the frequentist paradigm throughout this book.

and of all other forces acting on it, we could predict *with certainty* whether it would land on heads or tails.[3]

The mathematical construct of randomness is, therefore, a *modeling assumption*, not necessarily a fundamental feature of reality.[4] It allows us to model the outcomes of the coin flip given our uncertainty about the exact nature of the forces that will act on the coin in any particular instance. Similarly, in the social and health sciences, the assumption of randomness allows us to model various outcomes that we might care about, given our uncertainty about the precise features of complex social or biological processes.

1.1.2 Fundamentals of Probability Theory

We now introduce the formal definitions and notation used to represent the basic elements of random generative processes. There are three formal components that together fully describe a random generative process. The first is the *sample space*, denoted by Ω. The sample space is the set of all possible[5] outcomes of the random generative process. Individual outcomes (sometimes known as *sample points*) are denoted by $\omega \in \Omega$. Outcomes can be represented by numbers, letters, words, or other symbols—whatever is most convenient for describing every distinct possible outcome of the random generative process. For example, if we wanted to describe a single roll of a six-sided die, we could let $\Omega = \{1,2,3,4,5,6\}$. To describe a roll of two six-sided dice, we could let Ω be the set of all ordered pairs of integers between 1 and 6, that is, $\Omega = \{(x,y) \in \mathbb{Z}^2 : 1 \leq x \leq 6, 1 \leq y \leq 6\}$. To describe a fair coin flip, we could let $\Omega = \{\text{Heads}, \text{Tails}\}$ or $\Omega = \{H,T\}$. To describe choosing a random person in the United States and measuring their height in inches, we could let Ω be the set of all positive real numbers, $\Omega = \mathbb{R}^+$.

The second component of a random generative process is the *event space*. Events are subsets of Ω and are denoted by capital Roman letters, for example, $A \subseteq \Omega$. Whereas Ω describes all distinguishable states of the world that could result from the generative process, an event may occur in multiple states of the world, so we represent it as a set containing all states of the world in which it occurs. For example, in the case of rolling a single six-sided die, we could represent the event of rolling an even number by the set $A = \{\omega \in \Omega : \omega \text{ is even}\} = \{2,4,6\}$. Of course, an event can also correspond to a single state of the world, for instance, the event of rolling a 3, which we might represent by

3 See Diaconis, Holmes, and Montgomery (2007).

4 Current thinking in physics suggests that randomness *is* a fundamental feature of quantum-mechanical processes rather than merely a representation of unknown underlying variables determining individual outcomes. We are not considering quantum mechanics in this book. Suffice it to say that quantum randomness is probably not relevant to the social or health sciences.

5 We use the word "possible" here loosely, as the probability of a given outcome occurring may be zero.

the set $B = \{3\}$; such events are variously known as *atomic events* , *elementary events*, or *simple events*. For a given random generative process, a set of events is called an event space if it satisfies certain properties, which we state in the following definition. (We use the notation A^C to refer to the *complement* of the event A with respect to the sample space: $A^C = \Omega \backslash A = \{\omega \in \Omega : \omega \notin A\}$.)

Definition 1.1.1. *Event Space*
A set S of subsets of Ω is an *event space* if it satisfies the following:

- Nonempty: $S \neq \emptyset$.
- Closed under complements: if $A \in S$, then $A^C \in S$.
- Closed under countable unions: if $A_1, A_2, A_3, ... \in S$, then $A_1 \cup A_2 \cup A_3 \cup ... \in S$.[6]

Since each event in an event space will have an associated probability of occurring, these properties ensure that certain types of events will always have well-defined probabilities. Consider, again, a single roll of a six-sided die. Suppose A is the event of rolling an even number. If we can assign a probability to this event occurring, then we will also be able to assign a probability to this event *not* occurring, that is, A^C, the event of rolling an odd number. Similarly, suppose B is the event of rolling a number greater than 4. If we can assign probabilities to A and B, then we will also be able to assign a probability to the event of *at least one* of these occurring, that is, $A \cup B$, the event of rolling a 2, 4, 5, or 6.

This brings us to the final component needed to mathematically describe a random generative process: the *probability measure*. A probability measure is a function $P : S \to \mathbb{R}$ that assigns a probability to every event in the event space.[7] To ensure that P assigns probabilities to events in a manner that is coherent and in accord with basic intuitions about probabilities, we must place some conditions on P. Such conditions are provided by the *Kolmogorov probability axioms*, which serve as the foundation of probability theory. These axioms define a *probability space*, a construct that both accords with basic intuitions about probabilities and lends itself to rigorous and useful mathematics.

[6] A set S of subsets of another set Ω that satisfies these properties is formally known as a σ-*algebra* or σ-*field* on Ω. Some readers well versed in set theory may wonder why we do not simply let $S = \mathcal{P}(\Omega)$, the power set (that is, the set of all subsets) of Ω. For reasons that we will not discuss in this book, this does not always work; for some sample spaces Ω, it is impossible to define the probability of every subset of Ω in a manner consistent with the axioms of probability (see Definition 1.1.2). We need not worry too much about this point, though; in practice we will be able to define the probability of any event of interest without much difficulty. For this reason, we suggest that readers not worry too much about σ-algebras on their first read.

[7] Note: we do not make the stronger assumption that $P : S \to [0,1]$, since we prove this in Theorem 1.1.4.

Definition 1.1.2. *Kolmogorov Axioms*
Let Ω be a sample space, S be an event space, and P be a probability measure. Then (Ω, S, P) is a *probability space* if it satisfies the following:

- Non-negativity: $\forall A \in S$, $P(A) \geq 0$, where $P(A)$ is finite and real.
- Unitarity: $P(\Omega) = 1$.
- Countable additivity: if $A_1, A_2, A_3, \ldots \in S$ are pairwise disjoint,[8] then

$$P(A_1 \cup A_2 \cup A_3 \cup \ldots) = P(A_1) + P(A_2) + P(A_3) + \ldots = \sum_i P(A_i).$$

The intuition behind each of these axioms is as follows: The first axiom states that the probability of any event is a non-negative number; there cannot be a less-than-zero chance of an event occurring. The second axiom states that the probability measure of the entire sample space is one.[9] In other words, it is certain that *some* outcome will occur. Finally, the third axiom states that, given any number of *mutually exclusive* events, the probability that one of those events will occur is the sum of their individual probabilities. Together, these axioms are sufficient to rule out any probability statements that would be nonsensical, and they provide the building blocks that will allow us to derive other useful properties (as we will see in Theorem 1.1.4, *Basic Properties of Probability*).

We can represent any random generative process as a probability space (Ω, S, P), as illustrated by the following simple example.

Example 1.1.3. *A Fair Coin Flip*
Consider a fair coin flip. Let H represent the outcome "heads" and T represent the outcome "tails." Let $\Omega = \{H, T\}$ and $S = \{\emptyset, \{H\}, \{T\}, \{H, T\}\}$. Then we can define the probability measure as follows:

$$P(A) = \frac{1}{2}|A|, \forall A \in S.$$

The notation $|A|$ denotes the *cardinality* of the set A, that is, the number of elements in A. So this means

- $P(\emptyset) = \frac{1}{2}|\emptyset| = \frac{1}{2} \cdot 0 = 0$. The probability of nothing happening is zero.
- $P(\{H\}) = \frac{1}{2}\left|\{H\}\right| = \frac{1}{2} \cdot 1 = \frac{1}{2}$. The probability of getting heads is $\frac{1}{2}$.
- $P(\{T\}) = \frac{1}{2}\left|\{T\}\right| = \frac{1}{2} \cdot 1 = \frac{1}{2}$. The probability of getting tails is $\frac{1}{2}$.

8 Recall that sets A and B are disjoint if $A \cap B = \emptyset$. We say that $A_1, A_2, A_3, \ldots$ are pairwise disjoint if each of them is disjoint from every other, that is, $\forall i \neq j$, $A_i \cap A_j = \emptyset$.

9 Notice that Definition 1.1.1 implies that any event space must contain Ω: S is nonempty, so $\exists A \in S$. Since S is closed under complements, $A^C \in S$, and so since S is closed under countable unions, $A \cup A^C = \Omega \in S$. Likewise, $\Omega^C = \emptyset \in S$.

- $P(\{H,T\}) = \frac{1}{2}|\{H,T\}| = \frac{1}{2}\cdot 2 = 1$. The probability of getting either heads or tails is one.

The reader can verify that S is a proper event space (that is, it is nonempty and closed under complements and countable unions) and that P satisfies the Kolmogorov axioms, so (Ω, S, P) is a probability space. $\triangle$[10]

Several other fundamental properties of probability follow directly from the Kolmogorov axioms.

Theorem 1.1.4. *Basic Properties of Probability*
Let (Ω, S, P) be a probability space.[11] Then

- Monotonicity: $\forall A, B \in S$, if $A \subseteq B$, then $P(A) \leq P(B)$.
- Subtraction rule: $\forall A, B \in S$, if $A \subseteq B$, then $P(B \backslash A) = P(B) - P(A)$.
- Zero probability of the empty set: $P(\emptyset) = 0$.
- Probability bounds: $\forall A \in S$, $0 \leq P(A) \leq 1$.
- Complement rule: $\forall A \in S$, $P(A^C) = 1 - P(A)$.

Proof: Let $A, B \in S$ with $A \subseteq B$. Since $B = A \cup (B \backslash A)$, and A and $(B \backslash A)$ are disjoint, countable additivity implies

$$P(B) = P(A) + P(B \backslash A).$$

Rearranging this equation, non-negative probabilities then imply monotonicity: $P(B \backslash A) \geq 0$, so

$$P(A) = P(B) - P(B \backslash A) \leq P(B).$$

Rearranging again yields the subtraction rule:

$$P(B \backslash A) = P(B) - P(A).$$

The subtraction rule, in turn, implies zero probability of the empty set: $A \subseteq A$, so

$$P(\emptyset) = P(A \backslash A) = P(A) - P(A) = 0.$$

Monotonicity and unitarity (and non-negativity) imply the probability bounds: since $A \subseteq \Omega$,

$$0 \leq P(A) \leq P(\Omega) = 1.$$

Finally, the subtraction rule and unitarity imply the complement rule:

$$P(A^C) = P(\Omega \backslash A) = P(\Omega) - P(A) = 1 - P(A). \quad \square$$

10 Note that we use the $\triangle$ symbol to denote the end of an example.
11 This assumption shall henceforth be implicit in all definitions and theorems referring to Ω, S, and/or P.

We can put each of these properties in simple terms. Monotonicity implies that, if one event is a subset of another (so that the former always occurs whenever the latter does), then the probability of the former occurring is no greater than that of the latter. The subtraction rule implies that the probability that the second event occurs but not the first is equal to the probability of the second event minus the probability of the first event. Zero probability of the empty set means that *some* event in our event space must occur, and probability bounds mean that each of these events has some probability of occurring between zero and one. Finally, the complement rule implies that the probability of any of these events *not* occurring is one minus the probability of the event occurring—so that the probability that a given event either occurs or does not occur is one.

1.1.3 Joint and Conditional Probabilities

We often want to describe how the probability of one event relates to the probability of another. We begin by establishing the *joint probability* of events A and B, or the probability that events A and B will both occur in a single draw from (Ω, S, P).

Definition 1.1.5. *Joint Probability*
For $A, B \in S$, the *joint probability* of A and B is $P(A \cap B)$.

In other words, the joint probability of two events A and B is the probability of the intersection of A and B (which is itself an event in S), that is, the set of all states of the world in which both A and B occur. We illustrate this point with the following example.

Example 1.1.6. *A Fair Die Roll*
Consider a roll of one fair (six-sided) die. Let $\Omega = \{1,2,3,4,5,6\}$, $S = \mathcal{P}(\Omega)$ (the power set—that is, the set of all subsets—of Ω), and $P(A) = \frac{1}{6}|A|$, $\forall A \in S$. Let $A = \{\omega \in \Omega : \omega \geq 4\} = \{4,5,6\}$ and $B = \{\omega \in \Omega : \omega \text{ is even}\} = \{2,4,6\}$. Then

$$P(A \cap B) = P\big(\{4,5,6\} \cap \{2,4,6\}\big) = P\big(\{4,6\}\big) = \frac{1}{6}\big|\{4,6\}\big| = \frac{2}{6} = \frac{1}{3}. \quad \triangle$$

Just as $P(A \cap B)$ is the probability that both A *and* B will occur in a single draw from (Ω, S, P), $P(A \cup B)$ is the probability that A *or* B (or both) will occur in a single draw from (Ω, S, P). The following theorem allows us to relate these two probabilities.

Theorem 1.1.7. *Addition Rule*
For $A, B \in S$,

$$P(A \cup B) = P(A) + P(B) - P(A \cap B).$$

Proof: Note that $(A\backslash B)$, $(B\backslash A)$, and $(A \cap B)$ are pairwise disjoint and

$$(A \cup B) = (A\backslash B) \cup (B\backslash A) \cup (A \cap B),$$

so by countable additivity,

$$\begin{aligned} P(A \cup B) &= P(A\backslash B) + P(B\backslash A) + P(A \cap B) \\ &= P\big(A\backslash(A \cap B)\big) + P\big(B\backslash(A \cap B)\big) + P(A \cap B) \\ &= P(A) - P(A \cap B) + P(B) - P(A \cap B) + P(A \cap B) \\ &= P(A) + P(B) - P(A \cap B), \end{aligned}$$

where the second equality holds because

$$\begin{aligned} A\backslash B &= \emptyset \cup (A\backslash B) \\ &= \left(A \cap A^C\right) \cup \left(A \cap B^C\right) \\ &= A \cap \left(A^C \cup B^C\right) \\ &= A \cap (A \cap B)^C \\ &= A\backslash(A \cap B), \end{aligned}$$

and likewise $B\backslash A = B\backslash(A \cap B)$, while the third equality follows from the subtraction rule, since $A \cap B \subseteq A$ and $A \cap B \subseteq B$. □

In other words, the probability of *at least one* of two events occurring is equal to the sum of the probabilities of *each* occurring minus the probability of *both* occurring. Of course, if A and B are disjoint, this reduces to $P(A \cup B) = P(A) + P(B)$, which is just a special case of countable additivity.

We might also want to describe the probability of observing event A *given* that we observe event B. This is known as *conditional probability.*

Definition 1.1.8. *Conditional Probability*
For $A, B \in S$ with $P(B) > 0$, the *conditional probability* of A given B is

$$P(A|B) = \frac{P(A \cap B)}{P(B)}.$$

We can rearrange this definition to obtain another useful formula: the *Multiplicative Law of Probability.*

Theorem 1.1.9. *Multiplicative Law of Probability*
For $A, B \in S$ with $P(B) > 0$,

$$P(A|B)P(B) = P(A \cap B).$$

Proof: Rearrange Definition 1.1.8. □

One of the most important theorems regarding conditional probability is *Bayes' Rule* (also known as *Bayes' Theorem* or *Bayes' Law*). Bayes' Rule relates the conditional probability of A given B to the conditional probability of B given A. Suppose we have a hypothesis about the probability that some event A will occur, and we then observe event B. We can update the probability that we predict A will occur, using information about the frequency with which B occurs given A. This kind of deduction constitutes a key element of probabilistic reasoning and thus has many applications in the social sciences.

Theorem 1.1.10. *Bayes' Rule*
For $A, B \in S$ with $P(A) > 0$ and $P(B) > 0$,

$$P(A|B) = \frac{P(B|A)P(A)}{P(B)}.$$

Proof: By the Multiplicative Law of Probability, $P(A \cap B) = P(B|A)P(A)$. So, by the definition of conditional probability,

$$P(A|B) = \frac{P(A \cap B)}{P(B)} = \frac{P(B|A)P(A)}{P(B)}. \quad \square$$

Although we will not be making use of Bayes' Rule in this book, we would be remiss to neglect it entirely. The following example illustrates the above concepts, including the utility of Bayes' Rule, by combining the previous examples of fair coins and fair dice.

Example 1.1.11. *Flipping a Coin and Rolling a Die*
Consider the following generative process. An experimenter flips a fair coin. If the coin comes up heads, the experimenter rolls a fair four-sided die. If the coin comes up tails, the experimenter rolls a fair six-sided die. The sample space can thus be represented by

$$\Omega = \{(H,1),(H,2),(H,3),(H,4),(T,1),(T,2),(T,3),(T,4),(T,5),(T,6)\}.$$

Let A denote the event of observing heads, B denote the event of observing 3, and C denote the event of observing 6. Formally, $A = \{(H,1),(H,2),(H,3),(H,4)\}$, $B = \{(H,3),(T,3)\}$, and $C = \{(T,6)\}$. What is the (joint) probability of observing heads and 3? The probability of observing heads is $P(A) = \frac{1}{2}$. Additionally, if heads is observed, then the experimenter rolls a fair four-sided die, so the probability of observing 3 *given that heads has been observed* is $P(B|A) = \frac{1}{4}$. So, by the Multiplicative Law of Probability,

$$P(A \cap B) = P(B|A)P(A) = \frac{1}{4} \cdot \frac{1}{2} = \frac{1}{8}.$$

Likewise, the probability of observing tails and 3 is

$$P(A^C \cap B) = P(B|A^C)P(A^C) = \frac{1}{6} \cdot \frac{1}{2} = \frac{1}{12}.$$

Since the experimenter can never roll a 6, if the coin comes up heads, the probability of observing heads and 6 is

$$P(A \cap C) = P(\emptyset) = 0.$$

The conditional probability of observing 3 given that heads (or tails) was observed is relatively straightforward, as we see above. But suppose we wanted to know the conditional probability that heads was observed given that 3 is observed. This is where Bayes' Rule is useful. We want to know $P(A|B)$. We know $P(B|A)$ and $P(A)$. What is $P(B)$? From countable additivity,

$$P(B) = P(A \cap B) + P\left(A^C \cap B\right) = \frac{1}{8} + \frac{1}{12} = \frac{5}{24}.$$

Thus, by Bayes' Rule,

$$P(A|B) = \frac{P(B|A)P(A)}{P(B)} = \frac{\frac{1}{4} \cdot \frac{1}{2}}{\frac{5}{24}} = \frac{3}{5}. \ \triangle$$

The "trick" used above to calculate $P(B)$ is actually a special case of another important theorem, the *Law of Total Probability*. To state this theorem, we require the following definition.

Definition 1.1.12. *Partition*
If $A_1, A_2, A_3, ... \in S$ are nonempty and pairwise disjoint, and $\Omega = A_1 \cup A_2 \cup A_3 \cup ...$, then $\{A_1, A_2, A_3, ...\}$ is a *partition* of Ω.

A partition divides the sample space into mutually exclusive and exhaustive categories or "bins."[12] Every outcome in Ω is contained in exactly one A_i, so exactly one event A_i in the partition occurs for any draw from (Ω, S, P).

Theorem 1.1.13. *Law of Total Probability*
If $\{A_1, A_2, A_3, ...\}$ is a partition of Ω and $B \in S$, then

$$P(B) = \sum_i P(B \cap A_i).$$

If we also have $P(A_i) > 0$ for $i = 1, 2, 3, ...$, then this can also be stated as

$$P(B) = \sum_i P(B|A_i)P(A_i).$$

Proof: If $\{A_1, A_2, A_3, ...\}$ is a partition of Ω, then $\forall i \neq j$,

$$(B \cap A_i) \cap (B \cap A_j) = (B \cap B) \cap (A_i \cap A_j) = B \cap (A_i \cap A_j) = B \cap \emptyset = \emptyset.$$

12 The number of bins may be finite or countably infinite.

So $(B \cap A_1), (B \cap A_2), (B \cap A_3), \ldots$ are pairwise disjoint. Thus,

$$\begin{aligned} P(B) &= P(B \cap \Omega) \\ &= P\big(B \cap (A_1 \cup A_2 \cup A_3 \cup \ldots)\big) \\ &= P\big((B \cap A_1) \cup (B \cap A_2) \cup (B \cap A_3) \cup \ldots\big) \\ &= \sum_i P(B \cap A_i), \end{aligned}$$

where the last equality follows from countable additivity.

Additionally, if $P(A_i) \geq 0$ for $i = 1, 2, 3, \ldots$, then we can apply the Multiplicative Law of Probability to each term in the summation to obtain

$$P(B) = \sum_i P(B|A_i)P(A_i). \ \square$$

The probability of an event B is effectively a weighted average of the conditional probabilities of that event (B), where the weights are determined by the probabilities of the events that are being conditioned on ($A_1, A_2, A_3, \ldots$). Notice that for any event A, $\{A, A^C\}$ is a partition of Ω, so the method we used to calculate $P(B)$ above was indeed a special case of the Law of Total Probability. In fact, this "trick" is so often necessary for the application of Bayes' Rule that it is frequently incorporated directly into the statement of the theorem.

Theorem 1.1.14. *Alternative Forms of Bayes' Rule*
If $\{A_1, A_2, A_3, \ldots\}$ is a partition of Ω with $P(A_i) > 0$ for $i = 1, 2, 3, \ldots$, and $B \in S$ with $P(B) > 0$, then

$$P(A_j|B) = \frac{P(B|A_j)P(A_j)}{\sum_i P(B \cap A_i)},$$

or equivalently,

$$P(A_j|B) = \frac{P(B|A_j)P(A_j)}{\sum_i P(B|A_i)P(A_i)}.$$

Proof: Apply each form of the Law of Total Probability to the denominator in Theorem 1.1.10 (*Bayes' Rule*). $\square$

As we can see from Bayes' Rule, sometimes knowing whether one event has occurred gives us more information about whether another event has occurred. When the events are *independent*, this is not the case.

1.1.4 Independence of Events

We now define *independence* of events under a random generative process (sometimes referred to as *statistical independence* or *stochastic independence*). Independence is important because it codifies the idea that events are unrelated. Independence will be central to ideas in Sections 1.3.4 (*Independence of Random Variables*), 2.2 (*Summary Features of Joint Distributions*), 2.2.5 (*CEFs and BLPs under Independence*), and 3.1 (*I.I.D. Random Variables*), as well as identification results in Chapters 6 and 7.

Definition 1.1.15. *Independence of Events*
Events $A, B \in S$ are *independent* if $P(A \cap B) = P(A)P(B)$.

In Example 1.1.11 (*Flipping a Coin and Rolling a Die*), events A (observing heads) and B (observing 3) are *not* independent, since $P(A \cap B) = \frac{1}{8}$, but $P(A)P(B) = \frac{1}{2} \cdot \frac{5}{24} = \frac{5}{48}$. However, if we changed the example so that the experimenter rolled a six-sided die regardless of the outcome of the coin flip, then A and B would be independent.

The following useful theorem follows immediately from this definition and the definition of conditional probability.

Theorem 1.1.16. *Conditional Probability and Independence*
For $A, B \in S$ with $P(B) > 0$, A and B are independent if and only if $P(A|B) = P(A)$.[13]

Proof: By Definition 1.1.15,

$$A \text{ and } B \text{ are independent} \iff P(A \cap B) = P(A)P(B).$$

By Theorem 1.1.9 (*Multiplicative Law of Probability*), $P(A \cap B) = P(A|B)P(B)$. Thus,

$$\begin{aligned} A \text{ and } B \text{ are independent} &\iff P(A|B)P(B) = P(A)P(B) \\ &\iff P(A|B) = P(A). \quad \square \end{aligned}$$

Loosely speaking, this theorem tells us that when A and B are independent, knowing whether or not B has occurred gives us *no information* about the probability that A has occurred. Referring again to Example 1.1.11 (*Flipping a Coin and Rolling a Die*), events A (observing heads) and B (observing 3) are *not* independent, since $P(A) = \frac{1}{2}$, but $P(A|B) = \frac{3}{5}$. The fact that B occurred tells

13 Some texts give this as the definition of independence and then prove as a theorem that A and B are independent if and only if $P(A \cap B) = P(A)P(B)$. This formulation is equivalent, and the proof is virtually identical.

us that it is more likely that A occurred, since, overall, we expect to observe A (heads) half of the time, but among instances in which B (a die roll of 3) is observed, we expect that A will have occurred in three fifths of those instances. More extremely, A (heads) and C (a die roll of 6) are not independent, since $P(A) = \frac{1}{2}$, but

$$P(A \mid C) = \frac{P(A \cap C)}{P(C)} = \frac{P(\emptyset)}{P(C)} = 0.$$

Overall, the probability of observing heads is one half, but if we know that a 6 was rolled, we can be *certain* that the coin came up tails.

Similarly, $P(B) = \frac{5}{24}$, but $P(B \mid A) = \frac{1}{4}$. Among all realizations of this random generative process, we expect to observe B (a die roll of 3) five twenty-fourths of the time, but among just those instances in which A (heads) is observed, we expect to observe B one quarter of the time. So, the fact that the coin came up heads increases the probability of observing a die roll of 3. Finally, by the Law of Total Probability,

$$P(C) = P(C \cap A) + P(C \cap A^C) = 0 + P(C \mid A^C)P(A^C) = \frac{1}{6} \cdot \frac{1}{2} = \frac{1}{12}.$$

In other words, we can only observe C (a die roll of 6) when we observe A^C (not heads, that is, tails), so since tails will come up half the time, and then among those instances a 6 will be rolled one sixth of the time, overall we will observe C one twelfth of the time. But when we know A has occurred, C is not possible, so

$$P(C \mid A) = \frac{P(C \cap A)}{P(A)} = \frac{P(\emptyset)}{P(A)} = 0.$$

When the coin comes up heads, we know for sure that the experimenter will not roll a 6.

Again, if we were to change the example so that the experimenter rolled a six-sided die regardless of the outcome of the coin flip, then A and B would be independent. Knowing the outcome of the coin flip would then tell us nothing about the probability of observing any outcome of the die roll, and vice versa.

1.2 RANDOM VARIABLES

Many aspects of the world can be quantified. When a random generative process has outcomes that can be assigned real number values, its properties can more easily be described mathematically. A *random variable* is a variable that takes on a real value that is determined by a random generative process. In other words, random variables allow us to neatly represent random events by mapping those events to plain numbers. They are remarkable mathematical objects that will allow us to characterize probabilities in concise mathematical terms. We begin by providing a formal definition in the next section.

1.2.1 What Is a Random Variable?

Informally, we can think of a random variable as a container or placeholder for a quantity that has yet to be determined by a random generative process, just as ordinary algebraic variables represent unknown or unspecified quantities. However, the technical definition of a random variable is less intuitive and requires some careful discussion. Formally, a random variable is a real-valued function of the outcome of a random generative process.

Definition 1.2.1. *Random Variable*
A *random variable* is a function $X : \Omega \to \mathbb{R}$ such that, $\forall r \in \mathbb{R}$, $\{\omega \in \Omega : X(\omega) \leq r\} \in S$.[14]

Recall that each $\omega \in \Omega$ denotes a state of the world, which may be represented by anything: numbers, letters, words, or other symbols, whatever notation is most convenient to describe all the distinct possible outcomes that could occur. A random variable maps each of these states of the world to a real number. Thus, it is often remarked that, technically, a random variable is neither random nor a variable, as it is merely a function. However, we can still informally think of a random variable as a variable that takes on a value determined by a random generative process; when the state of the world is ω, the random variable takes on the value $X(\omega)$. Indeed, the dependence on ω is typically suppressed, so X is understood to mean $X(\omega)$. Thus, for example, the event $\{X = 1\}$ should be understood to mean the set of states $\{\omega \in \Omega : X(\omega) = 1\}$.

There are two ways one can apply functions to random variables. The first is to use the value of $X(\omega)$ as input into another function g, with the result being another random variable. The second is to operate on the function $X(\cdot)$ itself, returning a value characterizing some feature of the function. We provide two formal definitions that we will delineate notationally.

Definition 1.2.2. *Function of a Random Variable*
Let $g : U \to \mathbb{R}$ be a function, where $X(\Omega) \subseteq U \subseteq \mathbb{R}$. Then, if $g \circ X : \Omega \to \mathbb{R}$ is a random variable, we say that g is a *function of* X, and write $g(X)$ to denote the random variable $g \circ X$.[15]

14 This regularity condition is necessary and sufficient to ensure that X is a measurable function. In particular, it ensures that we can define the cumulative distribution function of X (see Definition 1.2.11, *Cumulative Distribution Function*).

15 Though this definition might seem superfluous, it is necessary because not every function $g : U \to \mathbb{R}$ is sufficiently well behaved that $g(X)$ is a random variable. So when we refer to a function g of X, we implicitly mean that g satisfies the regularity conditions necessary for $g(X)$ to be a random variable. Also, note that $X(\Omega)$ is the *range* of the function X (see Glossary of Mathematical Notation).

Examples of functions of a random variable include $g(X) = X^2$ and

$$g(X) = \begin{cases} 1 & : \quad X > 0 \\ 0 & : \quad \text{otherwise.} \end{cases}$$

It is a rather general definition, and allows us to formally work with transformations of random variables as random variables in their own right.

Definition 1.2.3. *Operator on a Random Variable*
An *operator* A on a random variable maps the function $X(\cdot)$ to a real number, denoted by $A[X]$.[16]

We will use operators to summarize random variables; Chapter 2 is devoted to describing and defining certain types of operators that may be of scientific interest. Since $g(X)$ is itself a random variable, it is possible to define $A[g(X)]$ (see, e.g., Section 2.1.5, *Expectation of a Function of a Random Variable*). We will not formally generalize these definitions later when we consider random vectors (Section 1.3, *Bivariate Relationships*), but the logic carries through.

We can define events in S in terms of a random variable X. For example, we could let

- $A = \{\omega \in \Omega : X(\omega) = 1\}$.
- $B = \{\omega \in \Omega : X(\omega) \geq 0\}$.
- $C = \{\omega \in \Omega : X(\omega)^2 < 10, X(\omega) \neq 3\}$.

Or, stated in words, A is the event that X takes on the value of one, B is the event that X takes on a value greater than or equal to zero, and C is the event that X takes on a value such that X^2 is less than 10 *and* X is not 3.[17] As shorthand, we typically drop the $\omega \in \Omega$ and denote events by their defining conditions on X. So, for the above examples, we would write

- $A = \{X = 1\}$.
- $B = \{X \geq 0\}$.
- $C = \{X^2 < 10, X \neq 3\}$.

Furthermore, we use $\Pr[\cdot]$ to denote the probability that some condition(s) on a random variable[18] will hold, or, equivalently, the probability that the event defined by those conditions will occur. So, for the above examples,

16 Everything we say about random variables is implicitly in the context of a probability space (Ω, S, P). A random variable $X(\cdot)$ is endowed with its probabilistic properties by the probability measure. Operators will summarize these properties, so they implicitly embed information from (Ω, S, P).

17 When we list conditions separated by commas, the commas implicitly mean "and."

18 Or variables; see Section 1.3 (*Bivariate Relationships*).

- $\Pr[X = 1] = P(A)$.
- $\Pr[X \geq 0] = P(B)$.
- $\Pr[X^2 < 10, X \neq 3] = P(C)$.

We use uppercase letters (for example, X, Y, Z, W) to denote random variables and lowercase letters (for example, x, y, z, w) to denote generic outcome[19] values, in other words, as variables in the regular, algebraic sense. Thus, when we say $X = x$, this can be read as "the random variable X takes on the value x."

1.2.2 Discrete Random Variables

It will be useful to delineate different types of random variables based on their mathematical properties. We will begin by providing a formal definition for one of the simplest types of random variables: the *discrete random variable*.

Definition 1.2.4. *Discrete Random Variable*
A random variable X is *discrete* if its range, $X(\Omega)$, is a countable set.

A discrete random variable is a random variable that only can take on a finite or countably infinite number of different values. As a result, the mathematics for discrete random variables tend to be relatively simple. However, although all real-world measurements are in practice discrete, when we have relatively fine-grained measurements, it becomes mathematically simpler to represent them as random variables that can take on a continuum of possible values and use calculus to describe their properties. In Section 1.2.4 (*Continuous Random Variables*), we will consider random variables of this kind, which have an uncountably large number of possible values.

Given a discrete random variable X, we can summarize the probability of each outcome x occurring with a *probability mass function (PMF)*.

Definition 1.2.5. *Probability Mass Function (PMF)*
For a discrete random variable X, the *probability mass function* of X is

$$f(x) = \Pr[X = x], \forall x \in \mathbb{R}.$$

We can apply the definition of the PMF to our familiar die roll example, showing the simplicity of the mathematical representation.

Example 1.2.6. *A Fair Die Roll*
Consider again a roll of one fair (six-sided) die. Let X take on the value of the

[19] We will informally refer to elements $x \in X(\Omega)$ as outcomes, even though, strictly speaking, they are not necessarily elements of the sample space Ω, and, indeed, there may be more than one $\omega \in \Omega$ such that $X(\omega) = x$.

outcome of the die roll; that is, let $\Omega = \{1,2,3,4,5,6\}$ and $X(\omega) = \omega$, $\forall \omega \in \Omega$. Then $\Pr[X = 1] = \Pr[X = 2] = ... = \Pr[X = 6] = \frac{1}{6}$. Out of many die rolls, we expect each of the values 1 through 6 to come up one sixth of the time. Thus, the PMF of X is

$$f(x) = \begin{cases} \frac{1}{6} & : \; x \in \{1,2,3,4,5,6\} \\ 0 & : \; \text{otherwise.} \end{cases} \qquad \triangle$$

We can also highlight a generalization of our coin flip example: a biased coin flip. The resulting random variable is known as a *Bernoulli* random variable.

Example 1.2.7. *A Biased Coin Flip (Bernoulli Distribution)*
Consider a coin flip with a (potentially) biased coin—that is, a coin that comes up tails with some unknown probability. Let $X = 0$ if the coin comes up heads and $X = 1$ if the coin comes up tails; that is, let $\Omega = \{H, T\}$ and let $X(H) = 0$ and $X(T) = 1$. Let p be the probability that the coin comes up tails: $\Pr[X = 1] = p$. Then $\Pr[X = 0] = 1 - \Pr[X = 1] = 1 - p$. Out of many coin flips, we expect that the proportion of times the coin comes up tails will be p and the proportion of times the coin comes up heads will be $1 - p$. The random variable X thus has the PMF

$$f(x) = \begin{cases} 1-p & : \; x = 0 \\ p & : \; x = 1 \\ 0 & : \; \text{otherwise.} \end{cases} \qquad \triangle$$

One further example illustrates how a discrete random variable can have a countably infinite number of possible values.

Example 1.2.8. *Flipping a Biased Coin Until It Comes Up Tails (Geometric Distribution)* Suppose we flipped a (potentially) biased coin repeatedly until the first time it came up tails. Let p be the probability that the coin comes up tails, and assume $0 < p < 1$. Let X be the number of flips it takes to get tails. For any given positive integer x, getting the first tails on exactly the xth flip requires getting heads on each of the first $x - 1$ flips and then tails on the xth. The probability of this happening is $(1-p)^{x-1}p$, or the product of the probabilities of the desired outcome on each flip (since the flips are independent). So the PMF of X is

$$f(x) = \begin{cases} (1-p)^{x-1}p & : \; x \in \mathbb{N} \\ 0 & : \; \text{otherwise.} \end{cases}$$

So, for example, if it is a fair coin (that is, $p = 1 - p = \frac{1}{2}$) then $\forall x \in \mathbb{N}$, $\Pr[X = x] = (\frac{1}{2})^x$; the first tails will be obtained on the first flip with probability $\frac{1}{2}$, on the second flip with probability $\frac{1}{4}$, on the third flip with probability $\frac{1}{8}$, and so on. Thus, X can take on *any* positive integer value, albeit with vanishingly small probability for large values. $\triangle$

For a discrete random variable X, the PMF tells us everything about its *distribution*, which is loosely defined as the collection of probabilities assigned to events that can be defined just in terms of X. To illustrate how the PMF can fully describe a discrete random variable, consider a random variable X such that $f(x) = 0$ for all $x \notin \mathbb{Z}$ (that is, X takes on only integer values). Then

- $\Pr[X \geq 3] = \sum_{x=3}^{\infty} f(x)$.
- $\Pr[X \geq 3 \text{ or } X = 1] = f(1) + \sum_{x=3}^{\infty} f(x)$.
- $\Pr[X < 4] = \sum_{x=1}^{3} f(x)$.

For example, for the die roll (Example 1.2.6),

- $\Pr[X \geq 3] = \sum_{x=3}^{6} f(x) = \frac{4}{6} = \frac{2}{3}$.
- $\Pr[X \geq 3 \text{ or } X = 1] = f(1) + \sum_{x=3}^{6} f(x) = \frac{1}{6} + \frac{4}{6} = \frac{5}{6}$.
- $\Pr[X < 4] = \sum_{x=1}^{3} f(x) = \frac{3}{6} = \frac{1}{2}$.

We now note some important properties of PMFs that accord with our general intuitions about probabilities.

Theorem 1.2.9. *Properties of PMFs*
For a discrete random variable X with PMF f,

- $\forall x \in \mathbb{R}, f(x) \geq 0$.
- $\sum_{x \in X(\Omega)} f(x) = 1$.

We omit the proof of this theorem, but the intuition follows directly from the Kolmogorov axioms (Definition 1.1.2): none of the probabilities are negative, and all probabilities add up to one. More generally, the following theorem gives the formula for using the PMF to compute the probability of *any* event defined in terms of a discrete random variable X.

Theorem 1.2.10. *Event Probabilities for Discrete Random Variables*
For a discrete random variable X with PMF f, if $D \subseteq \mathbb{R}$ and $A = \{X \in D\}$, then

$$P(A) = \Pr[X \in D] = \sum_{x \in X(A)} f(x).$$

We also omit the proof of this theorem, though again, it follows directly from the Kolmogorov axioms. Note that any condition on X can be expressed as $X \in D$ for some set $D \subseteq \mathbb{R}$, so this theorem allows us to compute the probability of any event defined in terms of a discrete random variable X. Theorem 1.2.10 thus establishes the link between our results on event probabilities from Section 1.1.2 (*Fundamentals of Probability Theory*) and random variables.

1.2.3 Cumulative Distribution Functions

In the previous section, we defined the concept of a PMF, which describes the distribution of a discrete random variable. We now define an alternative (and, as we will see, more general) way of describing the distribution of a random variable, the *cumulative distribution function (CDF)*. All random variables (such as the *continuous* random variables we will consider in Section 1.2.4, *Continuous Random Variables*), not just discrete ones, have CDFs.

Definition 1.2.11. *Cumulative Distribution Function (CDF)*
For a random variable X, the *cumulative distribution function* of X is

$$F(x) = \Pr[X \leq x], \forall x \in \mathbb{R}.$$

The CDF returns the probability that an outcome for a random variable will be less than or equal to a given value. Importantly, given any random variable X, the CDF of X tells us *everything* there is to know about the behavior of X. For any event A that can be described just in terms of X, we can derive the probability of A from the CDF of X alone. (This, again, is what we mean when we talk about the distribution of a random variable X: the complete collection of probabilities assigned to events defined in terms of X.) The following important properties of CDFs follow immediately from the axioms and basic properties of probability.

Theorem 1.2.12. *Properties of CDFs*
For a random variable X with CDF F,

- F is nondecreasing: $\forall x_1, x_2 \in \mathbb{R}$, if $x_1 < x_2$, then $F(x_1) \leq F(x_2)$.
- $\lim_{x \to -\infty} F(x) = 0$.
- $\lim_{x \to \infty} F(x) = 1$.
- $\forall x \in \mathbb{R}$, $1 - F(x) = \Pr[X > x]$.

Proof: Let $x_1, x_2 \in \mathbb{R}$ with $x_1 < x_2$. Then, since $\{X \leq x_1\} \subseteq \{X \leq x_2\}$, monotonicity implies that F is nondecreasing:

$$F(x_1) = \Pr[X \leq x_1] = P(\{X \leq x_1\}) \leq P(\{X \leq x_2\}) = \Pr[X \leq x_2] = F(x_2).$$

P is continuous,[20] and $\lim_{x \to -\infty}\{X \leq x\} = \{X \in \emptyset\} = \emptyset$, so

$$\begin{aligned}
\lim_{x \to -\infty} F(x) &= \lim_{x \to -\infty} \Pr[X \leq x] \\
&= \lim_{x \to -\infty} P(\{X \leq x\}) \\
&= P\left(\lim_{x \to -\infty} \{X \leq x\}\right) \\
&= P(\emptyset) = 0.
\end{aligned}$$

Similarly, $\lim_{x \to \infty}\{X \leq x\} = \{X \in \mathbb{R}\} = \Omega$, so

$$\lim_{x \to \infty} F(x) = \lim_{x \to \infty} \Pr[X \leq x] = \lim_{x \to \infty} P(\{X \leq x\}) = P\left(\lim_{x \to \infty} \{X \leq x\}\right) = P(\Omega) = 1.$$

Finally, by the complement rule, $\forall x \in \mathbb{R}$,

$$\begin{aligned}
1 - F(x) &= 1 - \Pr[X \leq x] \\
&= 1 - P(\{X \leq x\}) \\
&= P(\{X \leq x\}^C) \\
&= P(\{X > x\}) \\
&= \Pr[X > x]. \quad \square
\end{aligned}$$

[20] More precisely, for any sequence of sets $A_1, A_2, A_3, \ldots \in S$, if $A_1 \subseteq A_2 \subseteq A_3 \subseteq \ldots$ and $A_1 \cup A_2 \cup A_3 \cup \ldots = A$, then

$$\lim_{i \to \infty} P(A_1 \cup A_2 \cup \ldots \cup A_i) = P(A),$$

and for any sequence of sets $B_1, B_2, B_3, \ldots \in S$, if $B_1 \supseteq B_2 \supseteq B_3 \supseteq \ldots$ and $B_1 \cap B_2 \cap B_3 \cap \ldots = B$, then

$$\lim_{i \to \infty} P(B_1 \cap B_2 \cap \ldots \cap B_i) = P(B).$$

This property allows us to "pass" the limit into $P(\cdot)$. We omit the proof of this fact.

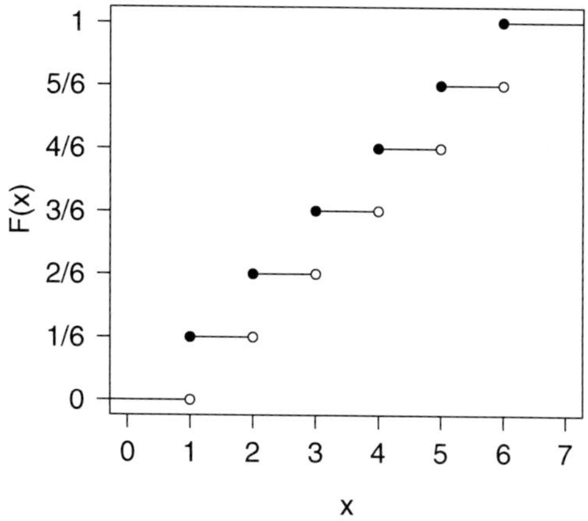

FIGURE 1.2.1. *Die Roll CDF*

Returning again to the die roll example, we can illustrate how the CDF characterizes the distribution of a random variable.

Example 1.2.13. *CDF of a Fair Die Roll*
For discrete random variables such as a die roll, the CDF is necessarily a step function, that is, a function that is flat everywhere except where it "jumps" from one value to another. Figure 1.2.1 shows the CDF for the die roll, which illustrates that the CDF increases by $\frac{1}{6}$ at each value in $\{1,2,3,4,5,6\}$. We can evaluate the CDF at any real value, for example,

- $F(-1) = 0$.
- $F(1) = \frac{1}{6}$.
- $F(1.5) = \frac{1}{6}$.
- $F(2) = \frac{2}{6} = \frac{1}{3}$.
- $F(6) = 1$.
- $F(7) = 1$.
- $F(24{,}603) = 1$.

Note that, in this example, the value of the CDF for any x greater than or equal to 6 will be one; since any outcome we get is guaranteed to be less than or equal to 6, it follows that any outcome we get is guaranteed to be less than or equal to 7 or 24,603.

Additonally, as usual, we can use the CDF to compute event probabilities:

- $\Pr[X < 2] = \Pr[X \leq 1] = F(1) = \frac{1}{6}$,
- $\Pr[X \geq 3] = 1 - \Pr[X < 3] = 1 - \Pr[X \leq 2] = 1 - F(2) = \frac{4}{6} = \frac{2}{3}$,
- $\Pr[2 \leq X \leq 4] = \Pr[X \leq 4] - \Pr[X < 2] = F(4) - F(1) = \frac{4}{6} - \frac{1}{6} = \frac{3}{6} = \frac{1}{2}$,

where the second line applies the complement rule and the third applies the subtraction rule (see Theorem 1.1.4, *Basic Properties of Probability*). △

However, there are other types of random variables that are more complex than discrete random variables. But regardless of type, every random variable has a CDF. We take up one important special case in the following section, where we consider random variables that have continuous CDFs.

1.2.4 Continuous Random Variables

Sometimes we are interested in quantities that can be measured to essentially any degree of precision, such as height, weight, or time. When a random variable represents the outcome of such a measurement, the number of possible values it could take on is limited only by the precision of our measuring instruments. For reasons of mathematical convenience, such a random variable can be treated as having a continuum of possible values, and is thus known as a *continuous random variable*.[21]

Loosely speaking, a random variable is continuous if its CDF is a continuous function.[22] This implies that a continuous random variable X can take on an uncountably infinite number of different values; that is, $X(\Omega)$ is an uncountable set (and therefore, so is Ω). More specifically, $X(\Omega)$ must include some interval or union of intervals of the real line. Formally, a continuous random variable is defined as follows:

Definition 1.2.14. *Continuous Random Variable*
A random variable X is *continuous* if there exists a non-negative function $f: \mathbb{R} \to \mathbb{R}$ such that the CDF of X is

$$F(x) = \Pr[X \leq x] = \int_{-\infty}^{x} f(u)du, \forall x \in \mathbb{R}.$$

The function f is called the *probability density function (PDF)*. The Fundamental Theorem of Calculus implies that, for any continuous random variable, the PDF is unique and can be defined as follows:

21 There are also random variables with distributions that share features of both discrete and continuous random variables. In practice, we can treat any distribution as continuous and use generalized integration. Since this requires measure theory, we do not discuss such distributions explicitly in this book. Nevertheless, while we often state definitions and theorems in this book only in terms of discrete and/or continuous distributions, readers should bear in mind that these can almost always be generalized to all probability distributions using the appropriate measure theory.

22 Technically, this is a necessary but not sufficient condition for a random variable to be continuous. The sufficient condition is that the corresponding probability measure be absolutely continuous with respect to the Lebesgue measure. This is a technical measure-theoretic condition that need not concern us, as it is implied by Definition 1.2.14.

Definition 1.2.15. *Probability Density Function (PDF)*
For a continuous random variable X with CDF F, the *probability density function* of X is

$$f(x) = \left.\frac{dF(u)}{du}\right|_{u=x}, \forall x \in \mathbb{R}.$$

Conceptually, the PDF is the continuous analog to the PMF in that it describes how the CDF changes with x. The difference is that, whereas a PMF specifies the size of the "jump" in the CDF at a point x, a PDF gives the instantaneous slope (derivative) of the CDF at a point x. That is, for a very small number $\epsilon > 0$, if we moved from x to $x + \epsilon$, the CDF would change by approximately $\epsilon f(x)$.

We now establish some basic properties of PDFs, which are analogous to those of PMFs (Theorem 1.2.9).

Theorem 1.2.16. *Properties of PDFs*
For a continuous random variable X with PDF f,

- $\forall x \in \mathbb{R}, f(x) \geq 0.$
- $\int_{-\infty}^{\infty} f(x)dx = 1.$

Proof: Let F be the CDF of X. F is nondecreasing, so, $\forall x \in \mathbb{R}$,

$$f(x) = \left.\frac{dF(u)}{du}\right|_{u=x} \geq 0,$$

and

$$\int_{-\infty}^{\infty} f(x)dx = \lim_{x\to\infty} \int_{-\infty}^{x} f(u)du = \lim_{x\to\infty} F(x) = 1. \ \square$$

Using these properties, we can relate continuous random variables to events, much as we did in Theorem 1.2.10 (*Event Probabilities for Discrete Random Variables*). The following theorem establishes that we can express any event of the form $\{X \in I\}$, where I is an interval in $\mathbb{R}$, in terms of integrals of the PDF.

Theorem 1.2.17. *Event Probabilities for Continuous Random Variables*
For a continuous random variable X with PDF f,

- $\forall x \in \mathbb{R}, \Pr[X = x] = 0.$
- $\forall x \in \mathbb{R}, \Pr[X < x] = \Pr[X \leq x] = F(x) = \int_{-\infty}^{x} f(u)du.$
- $\forall x \in \mathbb{R}, \Pr[X > x] = \Pr[X \geq x] = 1 - F(x) = \int_{x}^{\infty} f(u)du.$

- $\forall a, b \in \mathbb{R}$ with $a \le b$,

$$\begin{aligned}\Pr[a < X < b] &= \Pr[a \le X < b] = \Pr[a < X \le b] \\ &= \Pr[a \le X \le b] = F(b) - F(a) = \int_a^b f(x)dx.\end{aligned}$$

Proof: Let F be the CDF of X. To establish that, $\forall x \in \mathbb{R}, \Pr[X = x] = 0$, we will proceed with a proof by contradiction. Let $x \in \mathbb{R}$, and suppose that $\Pr[X = x] = P(\{X = x\}) > 0$. Then, since P is continuous and $\lim_{u \to x^-} \{X \le u\} = \{X < x\}$,

$$\begin{aligned}\lim_{u \to x^-} F(u) &= \lim_{u \to x^-} \Pr[X \le u] \\ &= \lim_{u \to x^-} P(\{X \le u\}) \\ &= P\left(\lim_{u \to x^-} \{X \le u\}\right) \\ &= P(\{X < x\}) \\ &< P(\{X < x\}) + P(\{X = x\}) \\ &= P(\{X \le x\}) \\ &= \Pr[X \le x] \\ &= F(x).\end{aligned}$$

Thus, F has a discontinuity at x, contradicting the assumption that X is continuous. So $\Pr[X = x] \le 0$, and thus, by non-negativity of probability, $\Pr[X = x] = 0$. Then, $\forall x \in \mathbb{R}$,

$$\begin{aligned}\Pr[X < x] &= P(\{X < x\}) \\ &= P(\{X < x\}) + P(\{X = x\}) \\ &= P(\{X \le x\}) \\ &= \Pr[X \le x] \\ &= F(x) \\ &= \int_{-\infty}^{x} f(u)du.\end{aligned}$$

Similarly, $\forall x \in \mathbb{R}$,

$$\begin{aligned}\Pr[X \ge x] &= P(\{X \ge x\}) \\ &= P(\{X > x\}) + P(\{X = x\})\end{aligned}$$

$$
\begin{aligned}
&= P(\{X > x\}) \\
&= \Pr[X > x] \\
&= 1 - F(x) \\
&= 1 - \int_{-\infty}^{x} f(u)du \\
&= \int_{-\infty}^{\infty} f(u)du - \int_{-\infty}^{x} f(u)du \\
&= \int_{x}^{\infty} f(u)du.
\end{aligned}
$$

Finally, by the same logic as above, $\forall a, b \in \mathbb{R}$ with $a < b$,

$$\Pr[a < X < b] = \Pr[a \leq X < b] = \Pr[a < X \leq b] = \Pr[a \leq X \leq b].$$

Furthermore, since

$$\{X < a\} \cup \{a \leq X \leq b\} = \{X \leq b\} \text{ and } \{X < a\} \cap \{a \leq X \leq b\} = \emptyset,$$

by countable additivity,

$$P(\{X < a\}) + P(\{a \leq X \leq b\}) = P(\{X \leq b\}).$$

Therefore,

$$P(\{a \leq X \leq b\}) = P(\{X \leq b\}) - P(\{X < a\}),$$

and thus

$$
\begin{aligned}
\Pr[a \leq X \leq b] &= P(\{a \leq X \leq b\}) \\
&= P(\{X \leq b\}) - P(\{X < a\}) \\
&= \Pr[X \leq b] - \Pr[X < a] \\
&= F(b) - F(a) \\
&= \int_{a}^{b} f(x)dx,
\end{aligned}
$$

where the final equality follows from the Fundamental Theorem of Calculus. □

Note that by applying countable additivity, we can use Theorem 1.2.17 (*Event Probabilities for Continuous Random Variables*) to compute the probability of any event of the form $\{X \in D\}$, where D is a countable union of disjoint intervals in $\mathbb{R}$.[23]

[23] In measure theory terms, for any Lebesgue-measurable set $D \subseteq \mathbb{R}$, $\Pr[X \in D] = \int_D f(x)dx$.

It may seem strange that, for a continuous random variable X, any specific outcome $x \in \mathbb{R}$ has probability $\Pr[X = x] = 0$. There is not necessarily a physical interpretation of this property; it is a consequence of the mathematical construct. In practice, our measurements are discrete because we do not have infinite precision of measurement. Nevertheless, continuous random variables can be thought of as mathematical approximations to random variables that are measured with sufficiently fine granularity that the gaps between possible outcome values are very small, and the probability of observing any one *exact* outcome is negligible.

Theorem 1.2.17 provides us with a clearer intuition for the meaning of the PDF: the area under the PDF over an interval is equal to the probability that the random variable takes on a value in that interval. Formally, this theorem implies that we need not worry about strict versus weak inequalities when describing the probability that a continuous random variable falls within a certain interval.

We now discuss two important examples of continuous distributions:[24] the *standard uniform distribution* and *standard normal distribution*.[25] We begin with the standard uniform distribution because of its simplicity.

Example 1.2.18. *Standard Uniform Distribution*
Consider the standard uniform distribution, denoted by $U(0,1)$. Informally, if a random variable X follows the standard uniform distribution, X takes on a random real value from the interval $[0,1]$, with all values in this interval equally likely to occur. We write $X \sim U(0,1)$ to denote that X follows the standard uniform distribution. The standard uniform distribution has the PDF

$$f(x) = \begin{cases} 1 & : \quad 0 \leq x \leq 1 \\ 0 & : \quad \text{otherwise.} \end{cases}$$

Figure 1.2.2 plots the PDF of the standard uniform distribution.

The CDF of $U(0,1)$ is thus

$$F(x) = \Pr[X \leq x] = \int_{-\infty}^{x} f(u)du = \begin{cases} 0 & : \quad x < 0 \\ x & : \quad 0 \leq x \leq 1 \\ 1 & : \quad x > 1. \end{cases}$$

Figure 1.2.3 shows the CDF of the standard uniform distribution. △

Example 1.2.19. *Standard Normal Distribution*
The reader may be familiar with the standard normal (or Gaussian) distribution. We will discuss some of the reasons why this distribution is important

[24] By *continuous distribution*, we simply mean the distribution of a continuous random variable.
[25] We will discuss other families of distributions in Chapter 5 (*Parametric Models*), but we do not need to establish the properties of, say, the Poisson or Gamma distribution to proceed. For a discussion of such distributions, see, e.g., Wackerly, Mendenhall, and Scheaffer (2008).

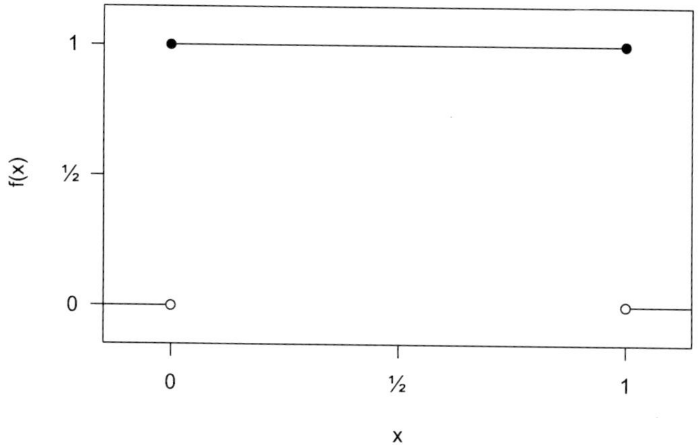

FIGURE 1.2.2. *PDF of the Standard Uniform Distribution*

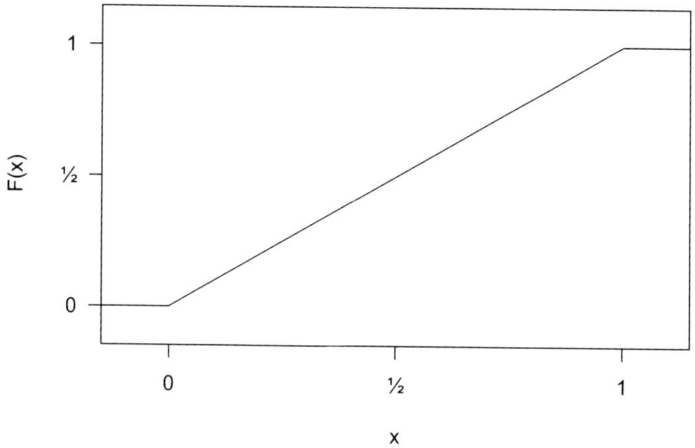

FIGURE 1.2.3. *CDF of the Standard Uniform Distribution*

to statistical inference later in this book (see, e.g., Section 3.2.4, *The Central Limit Theorem for Sample Means*). The standard normal distribution, denoted by $N(0,1)$, has PDF

$$\phi(x) = \frac{1}{\sqrt{2\pi}} e^{-\frac{x^2}{2}},$$

and CDF

$$\Phi(x) = \int_{-\infty}^{x} \frac{1}{\sqrt{2\pi}} e^{-\frac{u^2}{2}} \, du.$$

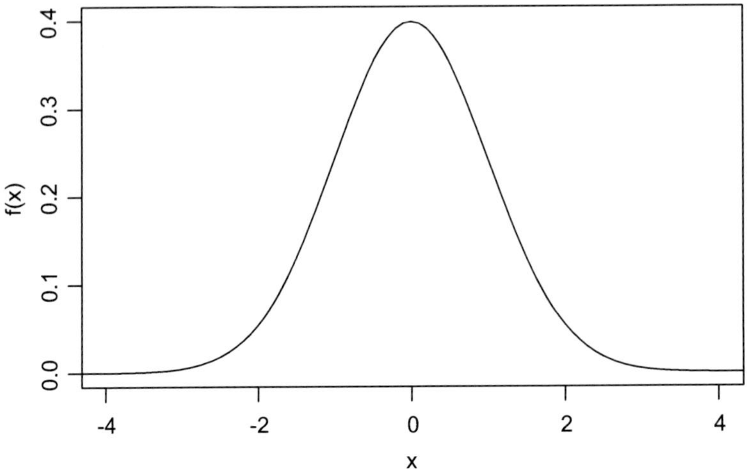

FIGURE 1.2.4. *PDF of the Standard Normal Distribution*

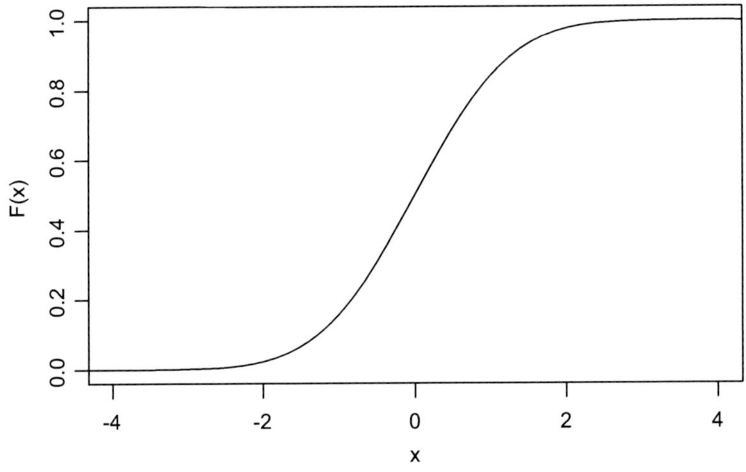

FIGURE 1.2.5. *CDF of the Standard Normal Distribution*

By convention, $\phi(x)$ and $\Phi(x)$ denote the PDF and CDF of the standard normal distribution, respectively. These are shown in Figures 1.2.4 and 1.2.5. $\triangle$

1.2.5 Support

We will often be interested in the subset of outcomes that could actually be observed for a given random variable. The set of values at which the PMF or PDF of a random variable is positive is called its *support*. In practice, we will use this term to restrict the values under consideration from those on the real line to only those that could possibly be observed.

Definition 1.2.20. *Support*
For a random variable X with PMF/PDF f, the *support* of X is

$$\text{Supp}[X] = \{x \in \mathbb{R} : f(x) > 0\}.$$

For discrete X, Supp[X] is the set of values that X takes on with nonzero probability. For example, if X is the outcome of a die roll, then Supp[X] = $\{1,2,3,4,5,6\}$. For continuous X, Supp[X] is the set of values over which X has nonzero probability density.[26] For example, if $X \sim U(0,1)$, then $\text{Supp}[X] = [0,1] = \{x \in \mathbb{R} : 0 \leq x \leq 1\}$. The notion of the support of a random variable will be particularly important in Section 2.2.3, when we define conditional expectations, and in Part III, in which assumptions about support will comprise key elements of our approach to identification.

1.3 BIVARIATE RELATIONSHIPS

As with random events, we often want to describe how multiple random variables are related. We therefore generalize the concepts presented above to the bivariate case. (Further generalization to the case of three or more random variables can be done analogously—see Section 1.4, *Multivariate Generalizations.*) We can have multiple random variables whose values are determined simultaneously by a single generative process: $X : \Omega \to \mathbb{R}$ and $Y : \Omega \to \mathbb{R}$, with X and Y each satisfying the regularity condition in Definition 1.2.1 (*Random Variable*).[27] Functions of and operators on multiple random variables are also defined analogously.

The following fundamental definition will be important going forward: when we say two random variables are equal, we mean that they are equal *as functions*; they assign the same value to every state of the world.

Definition 1.3.1. *Equality of Random Variables*
Let X and Y be random variables. Then $X = Y$ if, $\forall \omega \in \Omega$, $X(\omega) = Y(\omega)$.[28]

[26] As Manski (1999, p. 15) intuitively describes it, "A value x_0 is said to be on the *support* of the probability distribution of x if there is a positive probability of observing x arbitrarily close to x_0."

[27] Whenever we have multiple random variables in a given setting, we always have a single probability space in the background.

[28] It is not technically equivalent, however, to say that $\Pr[X = Y] = 1$. Although $X = Y$ implies $\Pr[X = Y] = 1$, the converse is not strictly true in general, as there could be "measure zero" events for which $X \neq Y$. Consider, for example, a coin that always comes up heads. Let $\Omega = \{H, T\}$. Let $X(H) = 0$, $X(T) = 1$, $Y(H) = 0$, and $Y(T) = 2$. Then $\Pr[X = Y] = 1$, but $X \neq Y$. When $\Pr[X = Y] = 1$, X and Y are said to be *equal almost surely*.

From this definition, it follows that two functions of a random variable, $g(X)$ and $h(X)$, are equal as random variables if and only if they are equal as functions on $X(\Omega)$.

Theorem 1.3.2. *Equality of Functions of a Random Variable*
Let X be a random variable, and let f and g be functions of X. Then

$$g(X) = h(X) \iff \forall x \in X(\Omega), g(x) = h(x).$$

Proof: Suppose that $\forall x \in X(\Omega)$, $g(x) = h(x)$. Let $\omega \in \Omega$. Then $X(\omega) \in X(\Omega)$, so $g(X(\omega)) = h(X(\omega))$. Thus, $\forall \omega \in \Omega$, $g(X(\omega)) = h(X(\omega))$, so $g(X) = h(X)$.

Now suppose that $g(X) = h(X)$, so $\forall \omega \in \Omega$, $g(X(\omega)) = h(X(\omega))$. Let $x \in X(\Omega)$. Then $\exists \omega \in \Omega$ such that $X(\omega) = x$, so $g(x) = h(x)$. Thus, $\forall x \in X(\Omega)$, $g(x) = h(x)$. □

This theorem will be especially important in Section 2.2.3, where it will allow us to make concise statements about conditional expectation functions.

1.3.1 Discrete Bivariate Distributions

Just as univariate random variables can be completely described by their PMF or PDF, bivariate distributions can be completely described by their joint PMF or PDF. To ground intuitions, we begin with the discrete case. In the case where X and Y are both discrete random variables, we can define the *joint PMF* of X and Y. The joint PMF at (x,y) is the probability that $X = x$ *and* $Y = y$ in a single realization of the generative process.

Definition 1.3.3. *Joint PMF*
For discrete random variables X and Y, the *joint PMF* of X and Y is

$$f(x,y) = \Pr[X = x, Y = y], \forall x,y \in \mathbb{R}.$$

Likewise, for any random variables X and Y, we can define their *joint CDF*. The joint CDF at (x,y) gives the probability of observing $X \leq x$ and $Y \leq y$ in a single realization of the generative process.

Definition 1.3.4. *Joint CDF*
For random variables X and Y, the *joint CDF* of X and Y is

$$F(x,y) = \Pr[X \leq x, Y \leq y], \forall x,y \in \mathbb{R}.$$

As with univariate distributions, *every* bivariate distribution, whether discrete or continuous, is characterized by a CDF. Furthermore, as in the univariate case, the joint CDF tells us everything about the behavior of X and Y.

Given any event A that can be described just in terms of X and Y, the probability of A can be derived from the joint CDF of X and Y. The following example returns to the coinflip and die roll to illustrate concepts in the discrete case.

Example 1.3.5. *Flipping a Coin and Rolling a Die*
Consider the generative process from Example 1.1.11, in which the experimenter flips a coin and then rolls either a four-sided or six-sided die depending on the outcome of the coin flip. Let $X = 0$ if the coin comes up heads and $X = 1$ if the coin comes up tails, and let Y be the value of the outcome of the die roll. Then the joint PMF of X and Y is

$$f(x,y) = \begin{cases} \frac{1}{8} & : \quad x = 0, y \in \{1,2,3,4\} \\ \frac{1}{12} & : \quad x = 1, y \in \{1,2,3,4,5,6\} \\ 0 & : \quad \text{otherwise.} \end{cases}$$

For discrete random variables, the joint CDF is constructed by summing over the appropriate values of X and Y. For example,

$$\begin{aligned} F(1,3) &= \sum_{x \leq 1} \sum_{y \leq 3} f(x,y) \\ &= f(0,1) + f(0,2) + f(0,3) + f(1,1) + f(1,2) + f(1,3) \\ &= \frac{1}{8} + \frac{1}{8} + \frac{1}{8} + \frac{1}{12} + \frac{1}{12} + \frac{1}{12} = \frac{5}{8}. \ \triangle \end{aligned}$$

1.3.2 Discrete Marginal and Conditional Distributions

In addition to the joint PMF and joint CDF, we can also describe the distribution of X and Y in terms of their marginal and conditional PMFs. The marginal distribution of a variable tells us only information about that variable, irrespective of its relationship with other variables. Accordingly, the *marginal PMF* of Y is simply the PMF of Y, ignoring the existence of X. The following theorem shows how a marginal PMF can be derived from a joint PMF.

Theorem 1.3.6. *Marginal PMF*
For discrete random variables X and Y with joint PMF f, the *marginal PMF* of Y is

$$f_Y(y) = \Pr[Y = y] = \sum_{x \in \text{Supp}[X]} f(x,y), \forall y \in \mathbb{R}.$$

(Henceforth we shall abbreviate $\sum_{x \in \text{Supp}[X]}$ as $\sum_x$.) We omit the proof, but it follows directly from the Law of Total Probability (Theorem 1.1.13): we sum the joint probabilities of $X = x$ and $Y = y$ for every possible outcome for X to get the overall probability that $Y = y$. We can also compute the marginal PMF of X analogously.

The conditional distribution, by contrast, tells us the distribution of a given variable when we know another variable has a specific value. The *conditional PMF* of Y given X tells us the probability that a given value of Y will occur, *given that* a certain value of X occurs. That is, the conditional PMF of Y given $X = x$ tells us what the PMF of Y would be if we "threw out" all realizations of the generative process except those in which $X = x$.

Definition 1.3.7. *Conditional PMF*
For discrete random variables X and Y with joint PMF f, the *conditional PMF* of Y given $X = x$ is

$$f_{Y|X}(y|x) = \Pr[Y = y | X = x] = \frac{\Pr[X = x, Y = y]}{\Pr[X = x]} = \frac{f(x,y)}{f_X(x)},$$

$\forall y \in \mathbb{R}$ and $\forall x \in \text{Supp}[X]$.

Since $x \in \text{Supp}[X]$ is equivalent to $f_X(x) > 0$, this domain condition ensures that the denominator is nonzero. The conditional PMF of X given Y is defined analogously. Note that the definition of the conditional PMF is directly analogous to that of conditional probability. To illustrate the concept of the conditional PMF, we return to the example of flipping a coin and rolling a die.

Example 1.3.8. *Flipping a Coin and Rolling a Die*
In the coin flip and die roll example (Example 1.1.11), the marginal PMFs are

$$f_X(x) = \begin{cases} \frac{1}{2} & : \; x = 0 \\ \frac{1}{2} & : \; x = 1 \\ 0 & : \; \text{otherwise} \end{cases}$$

and

$$f_Y(y) = \begin{cases} \frac{5}{24} & : \; y \in \{1,2,3,4\} \\ \frac{1}{12} & : \; y \in \{5,6\} \\ 0 & : \; \text{otherwise,} \end{cases}$$

and the conditional PMFs are

$$f_{X|Y}(x|y) = \begin{cases} \frac{3}{5} & : & x = 0, y \in \{1,2,3,4\} \\ \frac{2}{5} & : & x = 1, y \in \{1,2,3,4\} \\ 1 & : & x = 1, y \in \{5,6\} \\ 0 & : & \text{otherwise} \end{cases}$$

and

$$f_{Y|X}(y|x) = \begin{cases} \frac{1}{4} & : & x = 0, y \in \{1,2,3,4\} \\ \frac{1}{6} & : & x = 1, y \in \{1,2,3,4,5,6\} \\ 0 & : & \text{otherwise.} \end{cases}$$

Note that we can operate on marginal PMFs in the same way that we would on univariate PMFs, since they *are* univariate PMFs. Similarly, conditional PMFs are univariate PMFs given any fixed value for the conditioning variable. So, in this example,

$$f_{X|Y}(x|3) = \begin{cases} \frac{3}{5} & : & x = 0 \\ \frac{2}{5} & : & x = 1 \\ 0 & : & \text{otherwise} \end{cases}$$

is a univariate PMF. △

Notice that we can rearrange Definition 1.3.7 (*Conditional PMF*) to obtain an analog to Theorem 1.1.9 (*Multiplicative Law of Probability*) for PMFs.

Theorem 1.3.9. *Multiplicative Law for PMFs*
Let X and Y be two discrete random variables with joint PMF f. Then, $\forall x \in \mathbb{R}$ and $\forall y \in \text{Supp}[Y]$,

$$f_{X|Y}(x|y) f_Y(y) = f(x,y).$$

Proof: Rearrange Definition 1.3.7. □

1.3.3 Jointly Continuous Random Variables

We can extend the definitions of marginal and conditional distributions to the case where both random variables are continuous, and define marginal and conditional PDFs analogously. To do this, however, it is not technically sufficient to simply have X and Y be continuous. Instead, we require a slightly stronger condition: X and Y must be *jointly continuous*.

Definition 1.3.10. *Jointly Continuous Random Variables*
Two random variables X and Y are jointly continuous if there exists a non-negative function $f: \mathbb{R}^2 \to \mathbb{R}$ such that the joint CDF of X and Y is

$$F(x,y) = \Pr[X \leq x, Y \leq y] = \int_{-\infty}^{x} \int_{-\infty}^{y} f(u,v)\,dv\,du, \forall x,y \in \mathbb{R}.$$

The function f is called the *joint probability density function (joint PDF)*. Just as a single continuous random variable is characterized by a continuous CDF, two jointly continuous random variables are characterized by a continuous joint CDF. Additionally, just as taking the derivative of the CDF of a continuous random variable yields the PDF, taking the mixed second-order partial derivative of the joint CDF of two jointly continuous random variables yields the joint PDF.

Definition 1.3.11. *Joint PDF*
For jointly continuous random variables X and Y with joint CDF F, the *joint PDF* of X and Y is

$$f(x,y) = \left.\frac{\partial^2 F(u,v)}{\partial u \partial v}\right|_{u=x,v=y}, \forall x,y \in \mathbb{R}.$$

Without going into too much detail regarding partial derivatives, the joint PDF has roughly the same interpretation as the univariate PDF: if we perturb x or y a little bit, how much does the CDF change? Perhaps more intuitively, as with univariate continuous distributions, event probabilities are computed by integration: $\forall a,b,c,d \in \mathbb{R}$ with $a \leq b$ and $c \leq d$,

$$\Pr[a \leq X \leq b, c \leq Y \leq d] = \int_{a}^{b} \int_{c}^{d} f(x,y)\,dy\,dx.$$

That is, the volume under the PDF over a region equals the probability that X and Y take on values such that (X,Y) is a point in that region. Indeed, the probability of *any* event (not just those represented by rectangular regions) can be computed by integration.

Theorem 1.3.12. *Event Probabilities for Bivariate Continuous Distributions*
For jointly continuous random variables X and Y with joint PDF f, if $D \subseteq \mathbb{R}^2$, then

$$\Pr\left[(X,Y) \in D\right] = \iint_D f(x,y)dydx.$$[29]

We omit the proof of this theorem. So, for example, the probability that (X, Y) will fall within the triangular region $\{0 \leq X \leq 1, Y \leq X\}$ is

$$\Pr[0 \leq X \leq 1, Y \leq X] = \int_0^1 \int_0^x f(x,y)dydx.$$

Consequently, properties analogous to those in Theorem 1.2.16 (*Properties of PDFs*) and Theorem 1.2.17 (*Event Probabilities for Continuous Random Variables*) apply to bivariate continuous distributions: the joint PDF is non-negative everywhere and integrates to one; exact outcomes have probability zero,[30] and therefore strict versus weak inequalities in event specifications make no difference; for example, $\Pr[X \geq 7, 3 \leq Y < 6] = \Pr[X > 7, 3 < Y \leq 6]$ if X and Y are jointly continuous.

We can now define marginal and conditional PDFs analogously to marginal and conditional PMFs. As in the discrete case, the *marginal PDF* of Y is just the PDF of Y, ignoring the existence of X. The following theorem shows how a marginal PDF can be derived from a joint PDF.

Theorem 1.3.13. *Marginal PDF*
For jointly continuous random variables X and Y with joint PDF f, the *marginal PDF* of Y is

$$f_Y(y) = \int_{-\infty}^{\infty} f(x,y)dx, \forall y \in \mathbb{R}.$$

We omit the proof, but the intuition is analogous to the discrete case: we use integration to "sum" the joint density of X and Y over all values of x to get the overall density for Y at a given y. As before, the marginal PDF of X is computed analogously.

By contrast, the *conditional PDF* of X given Y is the PDF of X *given that* a certain value of Y occurs.

29 As in the univariate case, D must be Lebesgue-measurable, or the integral does not exist.

30 For bivariate continuous distributions, this means not only that $\Pr[X = x, Y = y] = 0$, but also that any event that specifies *either* $X = x$ *or* $Y = y$ has probability zero, for example, $\Pr[X > x, Y = y] = 0$. Indeed, for any $D \subseteq \mathbb{R}^2$ that has zero area (that is, Lebesgue measure zero), $\Pr[(X,Y) \in D] = 0$, for example, $\Pr[X = Y] = 0$, since the set $\{(x,y) \in \mathbb{R}^2 : x = y\}$ is a line.

Definition 1.3.14. *Conditional PDF*
For jointly continuous random variables X and Y with joint PDF f, the *conditional PDF* of Y given $X = x$ is

$$f_{Y|X}(y|x) = \frac{f(x,y)}{f_X(x)}, \forall y \in \mathbb{R} \text{ and } \forall x \in \text{Supp}[X].$$

Again, the domain condition $\mathbf{x} \in \text{Supp}[X]$ ensures that the denominator is nonzero. The conditional PDF of X given $Y = y$ is again defined analogously. As in the discrete case, marginal PDFs are univariate PDFs, and conditional PDFs are univariate PDFs given any fixed value for the conditioning variable. Theorem 1.2.16 (*Properties of PDFs*) thus applies to all marginal PDFs and to all conditional PDFs given any fixed value of the conditioning variable.

Just as with PMFs (see Theorem 1.3.9, *Multiplicative Law for PMFs*), we can rearrange Definition 1.3.14 to obtain an analog to Theorem 1.1.9 (*Multiplicative Law of Probability*) for PDFs.

Theorem 1.3.15. *Multiplicative Law for PDFs*
Let X and Y be two jointly continuous random variables with joint PDF f. Then, $\forall x \in \mathbb{R}$ and $\forall y \in \text{Supp}[Y]$,

$$f_{X|Y}(x|y)f_Y(y) = f(x,y).$$

Proof: Rearrange Definition 1.3.14. □

1.3.4 Independence of Random Variables

Like random events, random variables can be statistically independent, since random variables are just real-valued functions of outcomes. The intuitions are analogous. We conclude this section by defining independence of random variables and noting some important implications of independence.

Definition 1.3.16. *Independence of Random Variables*
Let X and Y be either two discrete random variables with joint PMF f or two jointly continuous random variables with joint PDF f. Then X and Y are *independent* if, $\forall x, y \in \mathbb{R}$,

$$f(x,y) = f_X(x)f_Y(y).$$

We write $X \perp\!\!\!\perp Y$ to denote that X and Y are independent.

Note the similarity to the definition of independence of events (Definition 1.1.15). Returning again to the coin flip and die roll example, we see that X (the outcome of the coin flip, where $X = 0$ for heads and $X = 1$ for tails) and Y (the outcome of the die roll) clearly are *not* independent, since, as we have already shown, $f(0,3) = \frac{1}{8} \neq \frac{1}{2} \cdot \frac{5}{24} = f_X(0)f_Y(3)$.

The following theorem states some properties that hold if and only if X and Y are independent.

Theorem 1.3.17. *Implications of Independence (Part I)*
Let X and Y be either two discrete random variables with joint PMF f or two jointly continuous random variables with joint PDF f. Then the following statements are equivalent (that is, each one implies all the others):

- $X \perp\!\!\!\perp Y$.
- $\forall x, y \in \mathbb{R}$, $f(x,y) = f_X(x)f_Y(y)$.
- $\forall x \in \mathbb{R}$ and $\forall y \in \text{Supp}[Y]$, $f_{X|Y}(x|y) = f_X(x)$.
- $\forall D, E \subseteq \mathbb{R}$, the events $\{X \in D\}$ and $\{Y \in E\}$ are independent.
- For all functions g of X and h of Y, $g(X) \perp\!\!\!\perp h(Y)$.

We omit the proof of this theorem. Notice that the third statement is analogous to Theorem 1.1.16 (*Conditional Probability and Independence*); if X and Y are independent, knowing the outcome for Y gives us *no information* about the probability of any outcome for X, as the conditional distribution of X remains the same regardless of the value that Y takes on.

1.4 MULTIVARIATE GENERALIZATIONS

We conclude this chapter by briefly outlining the generalizations of some of the above concepts to the case where we have more than two random variables. We provide no examples or proofs in this section, as our goal is simply to illustrate that the concepts we have presented in detail in the bivariate case are easily extended. Essentially all omitted definitions, properties, and theorems can be generalized analogously.

We begin by defining a natural way to characterize a collection of multiple random variables: a *random vector* is a vector whose components are random variables. Beginning in Chapter 2, we will use this notation frequently when we are considering the relationships between multiple random variables.

Definition 1.4.1. *Random Vector*
A *random vector* (of length K) is a function $\mathbf{X} : \Omega \to \mathbb{R}^K$ such that, $\forall \omega \in \Omega$,

$$\mathbf{X}(\omega) = \left(X_{[1]}(\omega), X_{[2]}(\omega), \ldots, X_{[K]}(\omega)\right),$$

where $\forall k \in \{1, 2, \ldots, K\}$, $X_{[k]}$ is a random variable.

Here we must pause to provide some remarks on notation. All vectors (random or otherwise) in this book shall be denoted by boldface letters, and all vectors are row vectors unless otherwise indicated. Importantly, we use bracketed subscripts to denote distinct random variables or components of a random vector, as we will use plain subscripts to denote multiple, independent realizations of a single random variable beginning in Chapter 3. As usual, we will suppress the ω notation, so we will write, for instance, $\mathbf{X} = (X_{[1]}, X_{[2]}, ..., X_{[K]})$. In some cases, components of a random vector may be represented by distinct letters for notational convenience, for example, (X, Y) or $(X_{[1]}, X_{[2]}, ..., X_{[K]}, Y)$, the latter of which may also be denoted by $(\mathbf{X}, Y)$.

As in the bivariate case, the joint CDF of $X_{[1]}, X_{[2]}, ..., X_{[K]}$ tells us everything about the behavior of these random variables. Importantly, it makes no difference whether we think of $X_{[1]}, X_{[2]}, ..., X_{[K]}$ as separate random variables or as components of a random vector $\mathbf{X}$. They still have a joint distribution characterized by a joint CDF, which thus also fully characterizes the distribution of $\mathbf{X}$.

Definition 1.4.2. *Joint CDF (Multivariate Case)*
For random variables $X_{[1]}$, $X_{[2]}$, ..., $X_{[K]}$, the *joint CDF* of $X_{[1]}$, $X_{[2]}$, ..., $X_{[K]}$ is

$$F(x_{[1]}, x_{[2]}, ..., x_{[K]}) = \Pr\left[X_{[1]} \le x_{[1]}, X_{[2]} \le x_{[2]}, ..., X_{[K]} \le x_{[K]}\right],$$

$\forall x_{[1]}, x_{[2]}, ..., x_{[K]} \in \mathbb{R}$.

As before, the joint CDF at $(x_{[1]}, x_{[2]}, ..., x_{[K]})$ gives the probability of observing $X_{[1]} \le x_{[1]}$, $X_{[2]} \le x_{[2]}$, ..., $X_{[K]} \le x_{[K]}$, in a single realization of the generative process. This can equivalently be written as $F(\mathbf{x}) = \Pr[\mathbf{X} \le \mathbf{x}]$, $\forall \mathbf{x} \in \mathbb{R}^K$.

In the case where $X_{[1]}$, $X_{[2]}$, ..., $X_{[K]}$ are all discrete random variables, we can define the joint PMF of $X_{[1]}$, $X_{[2]}$, ..., $X_{[K]}$ just as before.

Definition 1.4.3. *Joint PMF (Multivariate Case)*
For discrete random variables $X_{[1]}$, $X_{[2]}$, ..., $X_{[K]}$, the *joint PMF* of $X_{[1]}$, $X_{[2]}$, ..., $X_{[K]}$ is

$$f(x_{[1]}, x_{[2]}, ..., x_{[K]}) = \Pr\left[X_{[1]} = x_{[1]}, X_{[2]} = x_{[2]}, ..., X_{[K]} = x_{[K]}\right],$$

$\forall x_{[1]}, x_{[2]}, ..., x_{[K]} \in \mathbb{R}$.

Again, as before, the joint PMF at $(x_{[1]}, x_{[2]}, ..., x_{[K]})$ is the probability that $X_{[1]} = x_{[1]}$, $X_{[2]} = x_{[2]}$, ..., $X_{[K]} = x_{[K]}$ in a single realization of the generative process. This can equivalently be written as $f(\mathbf{x}) = \Pr[\mathbf{X} = \mathbf{x}]$, $\forall \mathbf{x} \in \mathbb{R}^K$. In the case where $X_{[1]}$, $X_{[2]}$, ..., $X_{[K]}$ are all continuous random variables, we must first define joint continuity before we can define the joint PDF.

Definition 1.4.4. *Jointly Continuous Random Variables (Multivariate Case)*
The random variables $X_{[1]}$, $X_{[2]}$, ..., $X_{[K]}$, are *jointly continuous* if there exists a non-negative function $f: \mathbb{R}^K \to \mathbb{R}$ such that the joint CDF F of $X_{[1]}$, $X_{[2]}$, ..., $X_{[K]}$ is

$$F(x_{[1]}, x_{[2]}, ..., x_{[K]}) = \int_{-\infty}^{x_{[1]}} \int_{-\infty}^{x_{[2]}} \cdots \int_{-\infty}^{x_{[K]}} f(u_{[1]}, u_{[2]}, ..., u_{[K]}) du_{[K]} ... du_{[2]} du_{[1]},$$

$\forall x_{[1]}, x_{[2]}, ..., x_{[K]} \in \mathbb{R}$.

The function f is the joint PDF. As in the bivariate case, we define the joint PDF more explicitly as follows:

Definition 1.4.5. *Joint PDF (Multivariate Case)*
For jointly continuous random variables $X_{[1]}$, $X_{[2]}$, ..., $X_{[K]}$ with joint CDF F, the *joint PDF* of $X_{[1]}$, $X_{[2]}$, ..., $X_{[K]}$ is

$$f(x_{[1]}, x_{[2]}, ..., x_{[K]}) = \left. \frac{\partial^K F(u_{[1]}, u_{[2]}, ..., u_{[K]})}{\partial u_{[1]} \partial u_{[2]} \cdots \partial u_{[K]}} \right|_{u_{[1]}=x_{[1]}, u_{[2]}=x_{[2]}, ..., u_{[K]}=x_{[K]}},$$

$\forall x_{[1]}, x_{[2]}, ..., x_{[K]} \in \mathbb{R}$.

The intuition is the same as in the bivariate case, and event probabilities are again obtained by integrating the PDF over the region that corresponds to that event.

We can also define marginal and conditional PMFs/PDFs in the multivariate case. Here it will be useful to distinguish one of the random variables from the others, so we state the following definitions for random variables denoted by $X_{[1]}$, $X_{[2]}$, ..., $X_{[K]}$, and Y—which, again, could also be combined into the random vector $(\mathbf{X}, Y)$. The notational distinction between the Xs and Y will also be important in later chapters for distinguishing between random variables that are used to predict (the Xs) and the random variable that we seek to predict (Y).

Definition 1.4.6. *Marginal PMF/PDF (Multivariate Case)*
For discrete random variables $X_{[1]}$, $X_{[2]}$, ..., $X_{[K]}$, and Y with joint PMF f, the *marginal PMF* of Y is

$$f_Y(y) = \Pr[Y = y] = \sum_{x_{[1]}} \sum_{x_{[2]}} \cdots \sum_{x_{[K]}} f(x_{[1]}, x_{[2]}, ..., x_{[K]}, y), \forall y \in \mathbb{R}.$$

For jointly continuous random variables $X_{[1]}, X_{[2]}, \ldots, X_{[K]}$, and Y with joint PDF f, the *marginal PDF* of Y is

$$f_Y(y) = \int_{-\infty}^{\infty}\int_{-\infty}^{\infty}\cdots\int_{-\infty}^{\infty} f\big(x_{[1]}, x_{[2]}, \ldots, x_{[K]}, y\big)\,dx_{[1]}dx_{[2]}\ldots dx_{[K]}, \forall y \in \mathbb{R}.$$

The idea behind the marginal PMF/PDF is as before: we sum (or integrate) over all possible outcomes for the X variables to obtain the univariate PMF/PDF of Y, that is, the PMF/PDF of Y ignoring the existence of the Xs. This is actually just one of many types of marginal distributions we can obtain in the multivariate case. We could similarly sum (or integrate) over just Y to obtain the marginal (joint) distribution of the Xs, ignoring the existence of Y. Let $f_{\mathbf{X}}(\mathbf{x})$ denote the marginal (joint) distribution of $\mathbf{X}$. Then, in the discrete case,

$$f_{\mathbf{X}}(\mathbf{x}) = \sum_y f(\mathbf{x}, y),$$

and in the continuous case,

$$f_{\mathbf{X}}(\mathbf{x}) = \int_{-\infty}^{\infty} f(\mathbf{x}, y)dy,$$

where $f(\mathbf{x}, y)$ is just another way of denoting the joint PMF/PDF. Indeed, we could choose any arbitrary $k \leq K$ of these random variables to "marginalize out," thereby obtaining the marginal (joint) distribution of the remaining variables.

As in the bivariate case, whereas a marginal PMF/PDF describes the distribution of a random variable (or vector) ignoring the existence of other random variables, a conditional PMF/PDF describes the distribution of a random variable (or vector) given that other random variables take on certain values.

Definition 1.4.7. *Conditional PMF/PDF (Multivariate Case)*
For discrete random variables $X_{[1]}, X_{[2]}, \ldots, X_{[K]}$, and Y with joint PMF f, the *conditional PMF* of Y given $\mathbf{X} = \mathbf{x}$ is

$$f_{Y|\mathbf{X}}(y|\mathbf{x}) = \Pr[Y = y|\mathbf{X} = \mathbf{x}] = \frac{\Pr[Y = y, \mathbf{X} = \mathbf{x}]}{\Pr[\mathbf{X} = \mathbf{x}]} = \frac{f(\mathbf{x}, y)}{f_{\mathbf{X}}(\mathbf{x})},$$

$\forall y \in \mathbb{R}$ and $\forall \mathbf{x} \in \text{Supp}[X]$.

For jointly continuous random variables $X_{[1]}, X_{[2]}, \ldots, X_{[K]}$, and Y with joint PDF f, the *conditional PDF* of Y given $\mathbf{X} = \mathbf{x}$ is

$$f_{Y|\mathbf{X}}(y|\mathbf{x}) = \frac{f(\mathbf{x}, y)}{f_{\mathbf{X}}(\mathbf{x})}, \forall y \in \mathbb{R} \text{ and } \forall \mathbf{x} \in \text{Supp}[X].$$

Similar to marginal distributions, we can in fact condition on any $k \leq K$ of the variables and obtain the conditional distribution of the others, for example, $f_{\mathbf{X}|Y}$, the conditional (joint) distribution of $\mathbf{X}$ given Y.

1.5 FURTHER READINGS

Alternative readings covering much of our Chapter 1 are available at varying levels of technicality. We recommend Blitzstein and Hwang (2014) and Freedman, Pisani, and Purves (1998), both of which provide rigorous, but reader-friendly, introductions to probability theory. Freedman, Pisani, and Purves (1998) is especially recommended for readers without prior exposure to undergraduate-level probability or mathematics. Freedman and Stark (2003) is a highly accessible article that discusses the fundamentals and interpretation of probabilistic statements (with application to earthquake forecasts). For more traditional and in-depth introductions to mathematical statistics and probability, we recommend Rice (2007), Casella and Berger (2001), Wackerly, Mendenhall, and Scheaffer (2008), and Pitman (1993). Wasserman (2004) provides a clear and concise treatment of the materials covered here. Billingsley (1995) is a measure-theoretic treatment of probability theory that comes highly recommended for readers with previous exposure to real analysis at the advanced undergraduate level or above.

2

Summarizing Distributions

Probability is expectation founded upon partial knowledge. A perfect acquaintance with all the circumstances affecting the occurrence of an event would change expectation into certainty, and leave neither room nor demand for a theory of probabilities.

—George Boole

In this chapter, we discuss some important summary features of random variables. Summarizing distributions is a key aspect of an agnostic approach to statistical inference—it allows us to precisely describe features of potentially infinitely complex objects without making further assumptions about the data generating process. Thus, this chapter will be foundational to defining inferential targets that will guide our approach to estimation as the book proceeds.

We begin by defining measures of the "center" and "spread" of the distribution of a single random variable, which will be central to our discussion of estimation in Chapter 3. In the remainder of the chapter, we will discuss summary features of joint distributions, which allow us to describe the relationships between random variables. We will focus on two primary ways of characterizing the relationship between two variables: the conditional expectation function and best linear predictor.[1] These concepts will be central to our treatment of regression in Chapter 4. As with Chapter 1, we conclude by considering multivariate generalizations.

1 We are fond of an anonymous reviewer's characterization that "we are building the tools needed to relate two variables to one another, which is something we might want to do if we wish to describe general patterns in data. With these tools and these tools only, we have a powerful way to describe what might in principle be very complicated things."

2.1 SUMMARY FEATURES OF RANDOM VARIABLES

In Chapter 1, we presented some examples of simple probability distributions (such as Bernoulli, uniform, and normal). In the real world, the full probability distribution of a random variable may be highly complex and therefore may not have a simple mathematical representation. Thus, we will want to be able to describe at least certain key features of such distributions *nonparametrically*, that is, without assuming that these distributions can be fully characterized by a distribution function with a finite number of parameters. (Chapter 5 contains details on the promise, and perils, of parametric models.) Even for very complex distributions, these characteristics have substantive meaning and practical applications. We begin with perhaps the simplest of these summary features: the *expected value*.

2.1.1 Expected Values

The expected value (also known as the *expectation* or *mean*) of a random variable can be thought of as the value we would obtain if we took the average over many, many realizations of that random variable. It is the most commonly used measure of the "center" of a probability distribution. The expected value will be very important as we proceed, since our inferential targets can very often be written in terms of expectations. (See, e.g., Sections 3.1, 3.2.2, and 3.2.3.)

Definition 2.1.1. *Expected Value*
For a discrete random variable X with probability mass function (PMF) f, if $\sum_x |x| f(x) < \infty$,[2] then the *expected value* of X is

$$\mathrm{E}[X] = \sum_x x f(x).$$

For a continuous random variable X with probability density function (PDF) f, if $\int_{-\infty}^{\infty} |x| f(x) dx < \infty$, then the *expected value* of X is

$$\mathrm{E}[X] = \int_{-\infty}^{\infty} x f(x) dx.$$

The expected value is an operator (hence the $[\cdot]$ notation—see Definition 1.2.3, *Operator on a Random Variable*); it takes as an input a random variable and returns a number. So when we compute the expected value of a random variable, we are applying the *expectation operator*. The following examples illustrate how the expectation operator works in practice.

[2] This regularity condition (and the corresponding one in the continuous case) is known as *absolute convergence*. It is virtually always satisfied in practice, so we omit this technical condition from all subsequent discussion of expectations.

Example 2.1.2. *A Fair Die Roll*
Consider, again, a roll of one fair (six-sided) die. Let X be the value of the outcome of the die roll. Then the expected value of X is

$$\mathrm{E}[X] = \sum_{x=1}^{6} xf(x) = 1 \cdot \frac{1}{6} + 2 \cdot \frac{1}{6} + 3 \cdot \frac{1}{6} + 4 \cdot \frac{1}{6} + 5 \cdot \frac{1}{6} + 6 \cdot \frac{1}{6} = \frac{7}{2}.$$

Note that a random variable does not necessarily take on its expected value with positive probability. In this example, $\Pr[X = \mathrm{E}[X]] = \Pr[X = \frac{7}{2}] = f(\frac{7}{2}) = f(3.5) = 0$. △

The example of a Bernoulli distribution is particularly helpful here, and will be used frequently when discussing binary data (see, e.g., Sections 5.1.2, 6.1.4, and 7.1.6).

Example 2.1.3. *Bernoulli Distribution*
Let X be a Bernoulli random variable with probability p. (Recall that, as shown in Example 1.2.7, we can think of such a random variable as a potentially biased coin flip.) Then

$$\mathrm{E}[X] = \sum_{x=0}^{1} xf(x) = 0 \cdot (1-p) + 1 \cdot p = p.$$

Notice that this implies a convenient feature of Bernoulli random variables: $\mathrm{E}[X] = \Pr[X = 1]$. △

Finally, we can show that another important distribution, the standard normal distribution, has the property of being centered on zero.

Example 2.1.4. *Standard Normal Distribution*
Let $X \sim N(0,1)$. Then the expected value of X is

$$\begin{aligned}
\mathrm{E}[X] &= \int_{-\infty}^{\infty} x \frac{1}{\sqrt{2\pi}} e^{-\frac{x^2}{2}} dx \\
&= \frac{1}{\sqrt{2\pi}} \int_{-\infty}^{\infty} x e^{-\frac{x^2}{2}} dx \\
&= \frac{1}{\sqrt{2\pi}} \left(-e^{-\frac{x^2}{2}} \right) \Bigg|_{-\infty}^{\infty} = 0. \ \triangle
\end{aligned}$$

Since functions of random variables are themselves random variables, they too have expected values. The following theorem establishes how we can compute the expectation of a function of a random variable $g(X)$ without actually deriving the PMF or PDF of $g(X)$.

Theorem 2.1.5. *Expectation of a Function of a Random Variable*

- If X is a discrete random variable with PMF f and g is a function of X, then

$$\mathrm{E}\big[g(X)\big] = \sum_x g(x)f(x).$$

- If X is a continuous random variable with PDF f and g is a function of X then

$$\mathrm{E}\big[g(X)\big] = \int_{-\infty}^{\infty} g(x)f(x)dx.$$

We omit the proof of this theorem, but it highlights how an operator can be applied to a function of a random variable.

When dealing with functions of a random variable, we will often simply write, for instance, $X^2 + 3X$ to denote the random variable $g(X)$, where $g(X) = X^2 + 3X$. In general, any mathematical expression containing a random variable X denotes the function of X (itself a random variable) defined by that expression.

The following theorem states two basic properties of the expectation operator, the proofs of which will be helpful for understanding what it means to apply operators more generally.

Theorem 2.1.6. *Properties of Expected Values*
For a random variable X,

- $\forall c \in \mathbb{R}, \mathrm{E}[c] = c.$
- $\forall a \in \mathbb{R}, \mathrm{E}[aX] = a\mathrm{E}[X].$

Proof: A constant c can be considered as a discrete random variable X with the PMF

$$f(x) = \begin{cases} 1 & : \quad x = c \\ 0 & : \quad \text{otherwise.} \end{cases}$$

(This is known as a *degenerate distribution* or *degenerate random variable.*) Thus, $\forall c \in \mathbb{R}$,

$$\mathrm{E}[c] = \sum_x xf(x) = cf(c) = c \cdot 1 = c.$$

Now, let $a \in \mathbb{R}$, and let $g(X) = aX$. If X is discrete with PMF f, then by Theorem 2.1.5,

$$E[aX] = E\big[g(X)\big] = \sum_x g(x)f(x) = \sum_x axf(x) = a\sum_x xf(x) = aE[X].$$

Likewise, if X is continuous with PDF f, then by Theorem 2.1.5,

$$\begin{aligned} E[aX] &= E\big[g(X)\big] \\ &= \int_{-\infty}^{\infty} g(x)f(x)dx \\ &= \int_{-\infty}^{\infty} axf(x)dx \\ &= a\int_{-\infty}^{\infty} xf(x)dx \\ &= aE[X]. \ \square \end{aligned}$$

These results will be fundamental when dealing with expectations going forward.

We need not stop with the univariate case. We can generalize the concept of expected value to the bivariate case in a couple of ways. (Again, further generalization to the case of three or more random variables can be done analogously.) Since each of the elements of a random vector is just a random variable, the expected value of a random vector (X, Y) is defined as the vector of expected values of its components.

Definition 2.1.7. *Expectation of a Bivariate Random Vector*
For a random vector (X, Y), the *expected value* of (X, Y) is

$$E\big[(X, Y)\big] = \big(E[X], E[Y]\big).$$

This definition is rarely used, but it illustrates how an operator can be applied to a random vector. More importantly, we can compute the expected value of a function of two random variables, since a function of random variables is itself a random variable.

Theorem 2.1.8. *Expectation of a Function of Two Random Variables*

- For discrete random variables X and Y with joint PMF f, if h is a function of X and Y, then

$$E[h(X,Y)] = \sum_x \sum_y h(x,y)f(x,y).$$

- For jointly continuous random variables X and Y with joint PDF f, if h is a function of X and Y, then

$$E[h(X,Y)] = \int_{-\infty}^{\infty}\int_{-\infty}^{\infty} h(x,y)f(x,y)dydx.$$

We omit the proof of this theorem. As in the univariate case, we will often simply write, for instance, $X^2 + 3Y + XY$ to denote the random variable $h(X,Y)$, where $h(X,Y) = X^2 + 3Y + XY$. So we might therefore write $E[X^2 + 3Y + XY]$ to denote $E[h(X,Y)]$. In general, any mathematical expression containing one or more random variables denotes the function of random variables (itself a random variable) defined by that expression.

A consequence of Theorem 2.1.8 is the following generalization of Theorem 2.1.6 (*Properties of Expected Values*).

Theorem 2.1.9. *Linearity of Expectations*
Let X and Y be random variables. Then, $\forall a,b,c \in \mathbb{R}$,

$$E[aX + bY + c] = aE[X] + bE[Y] + c.$$

Proof: Let X and Y be either discrete random variables with joint PMF f or jointly continuous random variables with joint PDF f,[3] and let $a,b,c \in \mathbb{R}$. Let $h(X,Y) = aX + bY + c$. If X and Y are discrete, then by Theorem 2.1.8,

$$\begin{aligned}
E[aX + bY + c] &= E[h(X,Y)] \\
&= \sum_x \sum_y h(x,y)f(x,y) \\
&= \sum_x \sum_y (ax + by + c)f(x,y) \\
&= a\sum_x \sum_y xf(x,y) + b\sum_x \sum_y yf(x,y) + c\sum_x \sum_y f(x,y)
\end{aligned}$$

[3] This theorem, and every subsequent theorem that we only prove for these two cases, also holds when one random variable is discrete and the other continuous. We omit the formal proofs for the mixed case because they require measure theory.

$$= a\sum_x x\sum_y f(x,y) + b\sum_y y\sum_x f(x,y) + c\sum_x\sum_y f(x,y)$$

$$= a\sum_x xf_X(x) + b\sum_y yf_Y(y) + c\sum_x f_X(x)$$

$$= a\mathrm{E}[X] + b\mathrm{E}[Y] + c\cdot 1$$

$$= a\mathrm{E}[X] + b\mathrm{E}[Y] + c.$$

Likewise, if X and Y are jointly continuous, then by Theorem 2.1.8,

$$\begin{aligned}
\mathrm{E}[aX+bY+c] &= \mathrm{E}\big[h(X,Y)\big] \\
&= \int_{-\infty}^{\infty}\int_{-\infty}^{\infty} h(x,y)f(x,y)dydx \\
&= \int_{-\infty}^{\infty}\int_{-\infty}^{\infty} (ax+by+c)f(x,y)dydx \\
&= a\int_{-\infty}^{\infty}\int_{-\infty}^{\infty} xf(x,y)dydx + b\int_{-\infty}^{\infty}\int_{-\infty}^{\infty} yf(x,y)dydx \\
&\quad + c\int_{-\infty}^{\infty}\int_{-\infty}^{\infty} f(x,y)dydx \\
&= a\int_{-\infty}^{\infty} x\left(\int_{-\infty}^{\infty} f(x,y)dy\right)dx + b\int_{-\infty}^{\infty} y\left(\int_{-\infty}^{\infty} f(x,y)dx\right)dy \\
&\quad + c\int_{-\infty}^{\infty}\int_{-\infty}^{\infty} f(x,y)dydx \\
&= a\int_{-\infty}^{\infty} xf_X(x)dx + b\int_{-\infty}^{\infty} yf_Y(y)dy + c\int_{-\infty}^{\infty} f_X(x)dx \\
&= a\mathrm{E}[X] + b\mathrm{E}[Y] + c\cdot 1 \\
&= a\mathrm{E}[X] + b\mathrm{E}[Y] + c. \quad \square
\end{aligned}$$

Linearity of expectations is a useful implementation of the properties of expected values (Theorem 2.1.6) and will be key in how we define our primary inferential target in Section 7.1 (*Identification with Potential Outcomes*).

2.1.2 Moments, Variances, and Standard Deviations

The expected value is one of the most commonly used summary features of a random variable. We can generalize this concept to further characterize the features of a distribution. We begin with a simple case: *raw moments*, which include the expected value as a special case.

Definition 2.1.10. *j^{th} Raw Moment*
For a random variable X and $j \in \mathbb{N}$, the jth *raw moment* of X is

$$\mu_j' = \mathrm{E}\left[X^j\right].$$

The jth raw moment of a random variable X is the expected value of X^j. The expected value is therefore the first raw moment. Raw moments provide summary information about a distribution, describing elements of its shape and location. Sometimes, however, we might seek to have a summary measure that purely reflects the shape and spread of a distribution, and does not depend on its expected value.[4] For $j > 1$, the jth *central moment* generally provides more useful information about the spread and shape of a distribution than the regular j^{th} moment.

Definition 2.1.11. *j^{th} Central Moment*
For a random variable X and $j \in \mathbb{N}$, the jth *central moment* of X is

$$\mu_j = \mathrm{E}\left[(X - \mathrm{E}[X])^j\right].$$

This is referred to as a central moment because it is centered on $\mathrm{E}[X]$.

Note that $\mathrm{E}[X]$ is the first raw moment, *not* the first central moment. The first central moment of any distribution is $\mathrm{E}\big[X - \mathrm{E}[X]\big] = \mathrm{E}[X] - \mathrm{E}[X] = 0$. Note that, when $\mathrm{E}[X] = 0$, then all raw and central moments agree. The sole distinction between raw and central moments lies in whether or not the expected value of X is subtracted before calculations. One of the most frequently employed central moments is the second central moment, also known as the *variance*. Whereas the expected value of a distribution characterizes its location or center, variance characterizes its variability or spread. Formally, variance measures the expected value of the squared difference between the observed value of X and its mean. Consequently, higher variance implies greater unpredictability.[5]

4 In other words, suppose that $Y = X + c$. Then any given raw moment for X and Y may differ, even though the distribution of Y is identical to that of X, just shifted to the right by c. So we may want summary measures that reflect the fact that the distributions of X and Y have the same shape.

5 There are also an infinite number of higher moments, from which one can compute additional features of the shape of a distribution: skewness, kurtosis, etc. In practice, we are very unlikely to make use of moments higher than the second moment of a distribution (unless we need

Definition 2.1.12. *Variance*
The *variance* of a random variable X is

$$\mathrm{V}[X] = \mathrm{E}\left[(X - \mathrm{E}[X])^2\right].$$

In words, the variance is the average squared deviation from the expected value. The following theorem gives an alternative formula for the variance that is often easier to compute in practice.

Theorem 2.1.13. *Alternative Formula for Variance*
For a random variable X,

$$\mathrm{V}[X] = \mathrm{E}\left[X^2\right] - \mathrm{E}[X]^2.$$

Proof:

$$\begin{aligned}
\mathrm{V}[X] &= \mathrm{E}\left[(X - \mathrm{E}[X])^2\right] \\
&= \mathrm{E}\left[X^2 - 2X\mathrm{E}[X] + \mathrm{E}[X]^2\right] \\
&= \mathrm{E}\left[X^2\right] - 2\mathrm{E}\left[X\mathrm{E}[X]\right] + \mathrm{E}\left[\mathrm{E}[X]^2\right] \\
&= \mathrm{E}\left[X^2\right] - 2\mathrm{E}[X]\mathrm{E}[X] + \mathrm{E}[X]^2 \\
&= \mathrm{E}\left[X^2\right] - 2\mathrm{E}[X]^2 + \mathrm{E}[X]^2 \\
&= \mathrm{E}\left[X^2\right] - \mathrm{E}[X]^2. \quad \square
\end{aligned}$$

Notice that $\mathrm{E}[X]$ is a *constant* and is therefore treated as such each time we apply linearity of expectations above. The same holds for the variance operator, $\mathrm{V}[\cdot]$. The following theorem states some basic properties of the variance operator. Note carefully how these differ from the properties of expected values (Theorem 2.1.6).

Theorem 2.1.14. *Properties of Variance*
For a random variable X,

- $\forall c \in \mathbb{R}, \mathrm{V}[X + c] = \mathrm{V}[X]$.
- $\forall a \in \mathbb{R}, \mathrm{V}[aX] = a^2\mathrm{V}[X]$.

conditions for asymptotics). Counterexamples presented to us by readers will be met with prompt, but perhaps insincere, apologies.

Proof: Let $a, c \in \mathbb{R}$. Then

$$\begin{aligned} \mathrm{V}[X+c] &= \mathrm{E}\Big[\big(X+c-\mathrm{E}[X+c]\big)^2\Big] \\ &= \mathrm{E}\Big[\big(X+c-\mathrm{E}[X]-c\big)^2\Big] \\ &= \mathrm{E}\Big[\big(X-\mathrm{E}[X]\big)^2\Big] \\ &= \mathrm{V}[X], \end{aligned}$$

and

$$\begin{aligned} \mathrm{V}[aX] &= \mathrm{E}\Big[\big(aX-\mathrm{E}[aX]\big)^2\Big] \\ &= \mathrm{E}\Big[\big(aX-a\mathrm{E}[X]\big)^2\Big] \\ &= \mathrm{E}\Big[a^2\big(X-\mathrm{E}[X]\big)^2\Big] \\ &= a^2\mathrm{E}\Big[\big(X-\mathrm{E}[X]\big)^2\Big] \\ &= a^2\mathrm{V}[X]. \quad \square \end{aligned}$$

While the variance is one of the most common measures of the "spread" of a distribution, perhaps even more common is the *standard deviation*, which is the square root of the variance.

Definition 2.1.15. *Standard Deviation*
The *standard deviation* of a random variable X is

$$\sigma[X] = \sqrt{\mathrm{V}[X]}.$$

We can begin to see why the standard deviation might be preferred when we consider the basic properties of this operator, which are stated in the following theorem.

Theorem 2.1.16. *Properties of Standard Deviation*
For a random variable X,

- $\forall c \in \mathbb{R}, \sigma[X+c] = \sigma[X]$.
- $\forall a \in \mathbb{R}, \sigma[aX] = |a|\sigma[X]$.

Proof: Take the square root of both sides of each equation from Theorem 2.1.14. □

The standard deviation is often preferable to the variance, since it is on the same scale as the random variable of interest. We illustrate this with an example.

Example 2.1.17. *A Fair Die Roll*
Consider, again, a roll of one fair (six-sided) die. Let X be the value of the outcome of the die roll. Then

$$\begin{aligned} \mathrm{V}[X] &= \mathrm{E}\left[X^2\right] - \mathrm{E}[X]^2 \\ &= \sum_{x=1}^{6}\left(x^2 \cdot \frac{1}{6}\right) - \left(\sum_{x=1}^{6} x \cdot \frac{1}{6}\right)^2 \\ &= \frac{91}{6} - \left(\frac{21}{6}\right)^2 \\ &= \frac{35}{12} \approx 2.92. \end{aligned}$$

So

$$\sigma[X] = \sqrt{\mathrm{V}[X]} = \frac{\sqrt{105}}{6} \approx 1.71.$$

Now let $Z = 100X$, which is equivalent to rolling a fair six-sided die with faces labeled 100, 200, 300, 400, 500, and 600. Then

$$\mathrm{V}[Z] = \mathrm{V}[100X] = 100^2\mathrm{V}[X] = 10{,}000\mathrm{V}[X] = \frac{87{,}500}{3} \approx 29{,}200,$$

and

$$\sigma[Z] = \sigma[100X] = |100|\sigma[X] = \frac{50\sqrt{105}}{3} \approx 171. \ \triangle$$

When we scale up the random variable, the standard deviation remains in the same order of magnitude as the spread of outcomes. By contrast, the variance of a random variable can "blow up" when we rescale the random variable. Variance is thus more difficult to interpret than standard deviation, since its magnitude does not clearly correspond to the magnitude of the spread of the distribution.

We can infer some other features of a distribution just by knowing its mean and standard deviation. For example, *Chebyshev's*[6] *Inequality* allows us to put

[6] Also sometimes spelled Chebychev, Chebysheff, Chebychov, Chebyshov, Tchebychev, Tchebycheff, Tschebyschev, Tschebyschef, or Tschebyscheff.

an upper bound on the probability that a draw from the distribution will be more than a given number of standard deviations from the mean.

Theorem 2.1.18. *Chebyshev's Inequality*
Let X be a random variable with finite[7] $\sigma[X] > 0$. Then, $\forall \epsilon > 0$,

$$\Pr\Big[|X - \mathrm{E}[X]| \geq \epsilon\sigma[X]\Big] \leq \frac{1}{\epsilon^2}.$$

We omit the proof here, but see Goldberger (1968, p. 31) for a simple proof via Markov's Inequality. This theorem will be important later for showing that estimators converge to the "right" value (see Theorem 3.2.5, *Chebyshev's Inequality for the Sample Mean*, and Definition 3.2.17, *Consistency*). Notice that what we learn about the distribution from Chebyshev's Inequality is driven by $\sigma[X]$ rather than $\mathrm{V}[X]$.

While useful for theoretical reasons, the bounds provided by Chebyshev's Inequality are somewhat limited in their practical applicability. When we know more about the distribution, knowledge of its expected value and standard deviation can be even more informative. For example, in the case of the *normal distribution*, knowing just these two quantities tells us *everything*.

Definition 2.1.19. *Normal Distribution*
A continuous random variable X follows a *normal distribution* if it has PDF

$$f(x) = \frac{1}{\sigma\sqrt{2\pi}} e^{-\frac{(x-\mu)^2}{2\sigma^2}}, \forall x \in \mathbb{R},$$

for some constants $\mu, \sigma \in \mathbb{R}$ with $\sigma > 0$. We write $X \sim N(\mu, \sigma^2)$ to denote that X follows a normal distribution with parameters μ and σ.

The following theorem implies that knowing the mean and standard deviation of a normal distribution tells us everything about the distribution. Recall that the standard normal distribution, introduced in Example 1.2.19, has a PDF with the same form, but with mean, μ, specified as zero and standard deviation, σ, specified as one.

[7] Moments, including the expected value, can be infinite or undefined; this is why we invoked the condition of absolute convergence in Definition 2.1.1 (Expected Value). To see this, try taking the expected value of $\frac{1}{X}$, where $X \sim U(0,1)$. Note also that, if the jth moment of a random variable X is non-finite, then all higher moments (that is, all k^{th} moments where $k > j$) are also non-finite.

Theorem 2.1.20. *Mean and Standard Deviation of the Normal Distribution*
If $X \sim N(\mu, \sigma^2)$, then

- $\mathrm{E}[X] = \mu$.
- $\sigma[X] = \sigma$.

We omit the proof of this theorem. The parameters μ and σ of a normal distribution are its mean and standard deviation, respectively. A normal distribution is thus uniquely specified by its mean and standard deviation.[8] Furthermore, this is why $N(0,1)$ is the *standard* normal distribution: it has the "nice" properties of being centered on zero ($\mu = 0$) and having a standard deviation (and variance) of 1 ($\sigma = \sigma^2 = 1$).

The normal distribution has many nice properties, two of which we state in the following theorem.

Theorem 2.1.21. *Properties of the Normal Distribution*
Suppose $X \sim N(\mu_X, \sigma_X^2)$ and $Y \sim N(\mu_Y, \sigma_Y^2)$. Then

- $\forall a, b \in \mathbb{R}$ with $a \neq 0$, if $W = aX + b$, then $W \sim N(a\mu_X + b, a^2\sigma_X^2)$.
- If $X \perp\!\!\!\perp Y$ and $Z = X + Y$, then $Z \sim N(\mu_X + \mu_Y, \sigma_X^2 + \sigma_Y^2)$.

We omit the proof. This theorem has an interesting and immediate implication: any linear combination of any number of mutually independent normal random variables must itself be normal.[9]

2.1.3 Mean Squared Error

We often want to characterize how well a random variable X approximates a certain value c. In order to do so, we will need a metric for how far off X is from c, on average. The most commonly used metric is the *mean squared error (MSE)*, which is the expected value of the squared difference between the observed value of X and c.[10] As we proceed, we will see that MSE has a

8 Caution: when we see, for example, $X \sim N(2, 9)$, this means X is normally distributed with mean $\mu = 2$ and *variance* $\sigma^2 = 9$, so $\sigma = \sqrt{9} = 3$. This convention is used because a multivariate normal distribution is characterized by its mean and covariance matrix (see Definition 2.3.1).

9 This result, implying that the normal distribution is a "stable distribution," is closely related to the Central Limit Theorem (Theorem 3.2.24). We refer interested readers to DasGupta (2008, Ch. 5).

10 MSE is most commonly used as a term to quantify the precision of an estimator; as we will discuss in Chapter 3, this is in fact the same definition in a different context (see Definition 3.2.14, *MSE of an Estimator*). There are alternative metrics, such as *mean absolute error* (MAE), which is the expected value of the absolute difference between the observed value of X and c.

number of appealing properties for the applied researcher. Notice that the MSE is closely related to other concepts we have introduced in this chapter. The MSE about zero is the same as the second raw moment, and the MSE about E[X] is the same as the second central moment, which is also the variance.

Definition 2.1.22. *Mean Squared Error (MSE) about c*
For a random variable X and $c \in \mathbb{R}$, the *mean squared error* of X about c is $\mathrm{E}[(X-c)^2]$.

A closely related quantity is the *root mean squared error* about c, $\sqrt{\mathrm{E}[(X-c)^2]}$. Much as the standard deviation rescales the variance in a way that ensures that it remains on the same scale as the range of outcomes for X, root MSE rescales the MSE so that it remains on the same scale as $X-c$. For these reasons, researchers often prefer to report the root MSE rather than the MSE.

We can apply Theorem 2.1.13 (*Alternative Formula for Variance*) to derive an alternative formula for MSE, which will help elucidate how MSE relates to the expected value and variance of X.

Theorem 2.1.23. *Alternative Formula for MSE*
For a random variable X and $c \in \mathbb{R}$,

$$\mathrm{E}\left[(X-c)^2\right] = \mathrm{V}[X] + \left(\mathrm{E}[X]-c\right)^2.$$

Proof:

$$\begin{aligned}
\mathrm{E}\left[(X-c)^2\right] &= \mathrm{E}\left[X^2 - 2cX + c^2\right] \\
&= \mathrm{E}\left[X^2\right] - 2c\mathrm{E}[X] + c^2 \\
&= \mathrm{E}\left[X^2\right] - \mathrm{E}[X]^2 + \mathrm{E}[X]^2 - 2c\mathrm{E}[X] + c^2 \\
&= \left(\mathrm{E}\left[X^2\right] - \mathrm{E}[X]^2\right) + \left(\mathrm{E}[X]^2 - 2c\mathrm{E}[X] + c^2\right) \\
&= \mathrm{V}[X] + \left(\mathrm{E}[X]-c\right)^2. \quad \square
\end{aligned}$$

Our decomposition also gives some insight into the utility of the expected value for approximating a random variable X. Theorem 2.1.23 directly implies that the expected value, E[X], has an interpretation as the best predictor of X in terms of MSE:

Theorem 2.1.24. *The Expected Value Minimizes MSE*
For a random variable X, the value of c that minimizes the MSE of X about c is $c = \mathrm{E}[X]$.

Proof:

$$\begin{aligned}\underset{c \in \mathbb{R}}{\arg\min}\, \mathrm{E}\left[(X-c)^2\right] &= \underset{c \in \mathbb{R}}{\arg\min}\left(\mathrm{V}[X] + \left(\mathrm{E}[X]-c\right)^2\right) \\ &= \underset{c \in \mathbb{R}}{\arg\min}\left(\mathrm{E}[X]-c\right)^2 \\ &= \mathrm{E}[X]. \;\square\end{aligned}$$

In other words, if we had to pick one number as a prediction of the value of X, the "best" choice (in terms of minimizing MSE) would be $\mathrm{E}[X]$. We illustrate Theorem 2.1.24 by minimizing MSE for a fair coin flip in the example below.

Example 2.1.25. *A Fair Coin Flip*
Consider, again, a fair coin flip. Let $X = 0$ if the coin comes up heads and $X = 1$ if the coin comes up tails. What is the *minimum MSE* guess for the value of X? The PMF of X is

$$f(x) = \begin{cases} \frac{1}{2} & : \; x \in \{0, 1\} \\ 0 & : \; \text{otherwise,} \end{cases}$$

so the MSE about c is

$$\begin{aligned}\mathrm{E}\left[(X-c)^2\right] &= \frac{1}{2}(0-c)^2 + \frac{1}{2}(1-c)^2 \\ &= \frac{1}{2}(c^2 + 1 + c^2 - 2c) \\ &= \frac{1}{2}(1 + 2c^2 - 2c) \\ &= \frac{1}{2} + c^2 - c.\end{aligned}$$

The first-order condition is thus

$$0 = \frac{d}{dc}\mathrm{E}\left[(X-c)^2\right] = \frac{d}{dc}\left(\frac{1}{2} + c^2 - c\right) = 2c - 1,$$

which is solved by $c = \frac{1}{2}$. This is $\mathrm{E}[X]$ (see Example 2.1.3, *Bernoulli Distribution*). $\triangle$

Figure 2.1.1 illustrates this solution: the value that minimizes MSE is, as expected, $c = \mathrm{E}[X] = \frac{1}{2}$.

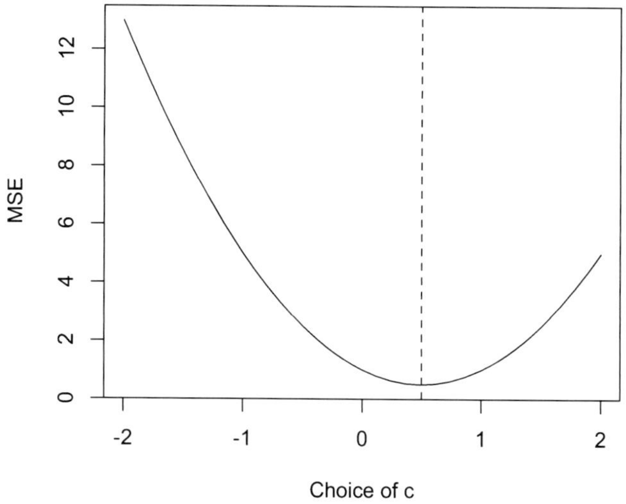

FIGURE 2.1.1. *Minimum MSE Solution for a Fair Coin Flip*

2.2 SUMMARY FEATURES OF JOINT DISTRIBUTIONS

One of the primary uses of statistics in the social and health sciences is to describe relationships between random variables. For example, we often want to know: if one quantity, X, is high, is another, Y, more or less likely to be high? There exist many useful summary features of the joint distribution of two or more random variables. The simplest of these are covariance and correlation.

2.2.1 Covariance and Correlation

We will show that a natural generalization of variance to the bivariate case is the *covariance*. Covariance measures the extent to which two random variables "move together." If X and Y have positive covariance, that means that the value of X tends to be large when the value of Y is large and small when the value of Y is small. If X and Y have negative covariance, then the opposite is true: the value of X tends to be small when the value of Y is large and large when the value of Y is small.

Definition 2.2.1. *Covariance*
The *covariance* of two random variables X and Y is

$$\text{Cov}[X, Y] = \text{E}\Big[\big(X - \text{E}[X]\big)\big(Y - \text{E}[Y]\big)\Big].$$

As with expected value and variance, $\text{Cov}[\cdot,\cdot]$ is an operator, not a function of the values its arguments take on, so $\text{Cov}[X, Y]$ is a constant, not a random variable. As with variance, there is an alternative formula for covariance that is generally easier to compute in practice.

Theorem 2.2.2. *Alternative Formula for Covariance*
For random variables X and Y,

$$\mathrm{Cov}[X,Y]=\mathrm{E}[XY]-\mathrm{E}[X]\mathrm{E}[Y].$$

Proof:

$$\begin{aligned}\mathrm{Cov}[X,Y]&=\mathrm{E}\Big[\big(X-\mathrm{E}[X]\big)\big(Y-\mathrm{E}[Y]\big)\Big]\\&=\mathrm{E}\big[XY-X\mathrm{E}[Y]-Y\mathrm{E}[X]+\mathrm{E}[X]\mathrm{E}[Y]\big]\\&=\mathrm{E}[XY]-\mathrm{E}[X]\mathrm{E}[Y]-\mathrm{E}[X]\mathrm{E}[Y]+\mathrm{E}[X]\mathrm{E}[Y]\\&=\mathrm{E}[XY]-\mathrm{E}[X]\mathrm{E}[Y].\ \square\end{aligned}$$

We will put this representation of the covariance into immediate use in the proof of the following theorem, which generalizes Theorem 2.1.14 (*Properties of Variance*) to the bivariate case, allowing us to draw a fundamental link between variances and covariances.

Theorem 2.2.3. *Variance Rule*
Let X and Y be random variables. Then

$$\mathrm{V}[X+Y]=\mathrm{V}[X]+2\mathrm{Cov}[X,Y]+\mathrm{V}[Y].$$

More generally, $\forall a,b,c\in\mathbb{R}$,

$$\mathrm{V}[aX+bY+c]=a^2\mathrm{V}[X]+2ab\mathrm{Cov}[X,Y]+b^2\mathrm{V}[Y].$$

Proof:

$$\begin{aligned}\mathrm{V}[X+Y]&=\mathrm{E}\big[(X+Y)^2\big]-\mathrm{E}[X+Y]^2\\&=\mathrm{E}\big[X^2+2XY+Y^2\big]-\big(\mathrm{E}[X]+\mathrm{E}[Y]\big)^2\\&=\mathrm{E}\big[X^2\big]+2\mathrm{E}[XY]+\mathrm{E}\big[Y^2\big]-\mathrm{E}[X]^2-2\mathrm{E}[X]\mathrm{E}[Y]-\mathrm{E}[Y]^2\\&=\mathrm{E}\big[X^2\big]-\mathrm{E}[X]^2+2\big(\mathrm{E}[XY]-\mathrm{E}[X]\mathrm{E}[Y]\big)+\mathrm{E}\big[Y^2\big]-\mathrm{E}[Y]^2\\&=\mathrm{V}[X]+2\mathrm{Cov}[X,Y]+\mathrm{V}[Y].\end{aligned}$$

The proof of the more general version is omitted. $\square$

Note that, unlike expected values, we do *not* have linearity of variances: $\mathrm{V}[aX+bY]\neq a\mathrm{V}[X]+b\mathrm{V}[Y]$. To remember the variance rule, it may be helpful to recall the algebraic formula $(x+y)^2 = x^2 + 2xy + y^2$. Indeed, the above proof shows that this similarity is not coincidental.

We now derive a few properties of covariance.

Theorem 2.2.4. *Properties of Covariance*
For random variables X, Y, Z, and W,

- $\forall c, d \in \mathbb{R}, \text{Cov}[c, X] = \text{Cov}[X, c] = \text{Cov}[c, d] = 0$.
- $\text{Cov}[X, Y] = \text{Cov}[Y, X]$.
- $\text{Cov}[X, X] = \text{V}[X]$.
- $\forall a, b, c, d \in \mathbb{R}, \text{Cov}[aX + c, bY + d] = ab\text{Cov}[X, Y]$.
- $\text{Cov}[X + W, Y + Z] = \text{Cov}[X, Y] + \text{Cov}[X, Z] + \text{Cov}[W, Y] + \text{Cov}[W, Z]$.

Proof: Let $a, b, c, d \in \mathbb{R}$. Then

$$\text{Cov}[c, X] = \text{E}[cX] - \text{E}[c]\text{E}[X] = c\text{E}[X] - c\text{E}[X] = 0.$$

$$\text{Cov}[X, c] = \text{E}[Xc] - \text{E}[X]\text{E}[c] = c\text{E}[X] - c\text{E}[X] = 0.$$

$$\text{Cov}[c, d] = \text{E}[cd] - \text{E}[c]\text{E}[d] = cd - cd = 0.$$

$$\begin{aligned}\text{Cov}[X, Y] &= \text{E}[XY] - \text{E}[X]\text{E}[Y] \\ &= \text{E}[YX] - \text{E}[Y]\text{E}[X] \\ &= \text{Cov}[Y, X].\end{aligned}$$

$$\text{Cov}[X, X] = \text{E}[XX] - \text{E}[X]\text{E}[X] = \text{E}\left[X^2\right] - \text{E}[X]^2 = \text{V}[X].$$

$$\begin{aligned}\text{Cov}[aX + c, bY + d] &= \text{E}\Big[\big(aX + c - \text{E}[aX + c]\big)\big(bY + d - \text{E}[bY + d]\big)\Big] \\ &= \text{E}\Big[\big(aX + c - a\text{E}[X] - c\big)\big(bY + d - b\text{E}[Y] - d\big)\Big] \\ &= \text{E}\Big[a\big(X - \text{E}[X]\big)b\big(Y - \text{E}[Y]\big)\Big] \\ &= ab\text{E}\Big[\big(X - \text{E}[X]\big)\big(Y - \text{E}[Y]\big)\Big] \\ &= ab\text{Cov}[X, Y].\end{aligned}$$

$$\begin{aligned}\text{Cov}[X + W, Y + Z] &= \text{E}\big[(X + W)(Y + Z)\big] - \text{E}[X + W]\text{E}[Y + Z] \\ &= \text{E}[XY + XZ + WY + WZ] \\ &\quad - \big(\text{E}[X] + \text{E}[W]\big)\big(\text{E}[Y] + \text{E}[Z]\big) \\ &= \text{E}[XY] + \text{E}[XZ] + \text{E}[WY] + \text{E}[WZ] \\ &\quad - \text{E}[X]\text{E}[Y] - \text{E}[X]\text{E}[Z] - \text{E}[W]\text{E}[Y] - E[W]\text{E}[Z]\end{aligned}$$

$$= \big(\mathrm{E}[XY] - \mathrm{E}[X]\mathrm{E}[Y]\big) + \big(\mathrm{E}[XZ] - \mathrm{E}[X]\mathrm{E}[Z]\big)$$
$$+ \big(\mathrm{E}[WY] - \mathrm{E}[W]\mathrm{E}[Y]\big) + \big(\mathrm{E}[WZ] - \mathrm{E}[W]\mathrm{E}[Z]\big)$$
$$= \mathrm{Cov}[X,Y] + \mathrm{Cov}[X,Z] + \mathrm{Cov}[W,Y] + \mathrm{Cov}[W,Z]. \quad \square$$

Although many of these properties will be helpful for our calculus, perhaps the most noteworthy is the third: $\mathrm{Cov}[X,X] = \mathrm{V}[X]$. Variance is effectively a special case of covariance: the covariance of a random variable with itself is its variance. Thus, covariance is indeed a natural generalization of variance.

Another measure of the relationship between two random variables is their *correlation*. Readers are likely to be familiar with the idea of correlation in conversational use; we provide a formal definition in the statistical setting.

Definition 2.2.5. *Correlation*
The *correlation* of two random variables X and Y with $\sigma[X] > 0$ and $\sigma[Y] > 0$ is

$$\rho[X,Y] = \frac{\mathrm{Cov}[X,Y]}{\sigma[X]\sigma[Y]}.$$

Much like standard deviation rescales variance, correlation rescales covariance to make its interpretation clearer. Importantly, since the denominator of the expression for correlation is positive, correlation is positive when covariance is positive and negative when covariance is negative. (Note that, unlike covariance, correlation is undefined when the variance of either variable is zero.)

Linear dependence describes the relationship between two random variables where one can be written as a linear function of the other; X and Y are linearly dependent if $\exists a, b \in \mathbb{R}$ such that $Y = aX + b$. Even if two random variables are not exactly linearly dependent, they can be more or less nearly so. Correlation measures the degree of linear dependence between two random variables and is bounded in $[-1, 1]$, where a correlation of one represents perfect positive linear dependence, a correlation of -1 represents perfect negative linear dependence, and a correlation of zero implies no linear relationship.[11] We formalize these facts (except for the last one) in the following theorem.

[11] For this reason, some people prefer to call $\rho[\cdot,\cdot]$, the *linear correlation*. Some nonlinear measures of correlation include the Spearman and Kendall rank correlations, discussed in Wackerly, Mendenhall, and Scheaffer (2008, Ch. 15.10).

Theorem 2.2.6. *Correlation and Linear Dependence*
For random variable X and Y,

- $\rho[X,Y] \in [-1,1]$.
- $\rho[X,Y] = 1 \iff \exists a,b \in \mathbb{R}$ with $b > 0$ such that $Y = a + bX$.
- $\rho[X,Y] = -1 \iff \exists a,b \in \mathbb{R}$ with $b > 0$ such that $Y = a - bX$.

We omit the proof of this theorem.[12] The following theorem states some other important properties of correlation.

Theorem 2.2.7. *Properties of Correlation*
For random variables X, Y, and Z,

- $\rho[X,Y] = \rho[Y,X]$.
- $\rho[X,X] = 1$.
- $\rho[aX+c, bY+d] = \rho[X,Y]$, $\forall a,b,c,d \in \mathbb{R}$ such that either $a,b > 0$ or $a,b < 0$.
- $\rho[aX+c, bY+d] = -\rho[X,Y]$, $\forall a,b,c,d \in \mathbb{R}$ such that either $a < 0 < b$ or $b < 0 < a$.

Proof:

$$\rho[X,Y] = \frac{\operatorname{Cov}[X,Y]}{\sigma[X]\sigma[Y]} = \frac{\operatorname{Cov}[Y,X]}{\sigma[Y]\sigma[X]} = \rho[Y,X].$$

$$\rho[X,X] = \frac{\operatorname{Cov}[X,X]}{\sigma[X]\sigma[X]} = \frac{\operatorname{V}[X]}{\sigma[X]^2} = \frac{\operatorname{V}[X]}{\left(\sqrt{\operatorname{V}[X]}\right)^2} = \frac{\operatorname{V}[X]}{\operatorname{V}[X]} = 1.$$

Let $a,b,c,d \in \mathbb{R}$ with $a,b \neq 0$. Then

$$\rho[aX+c, bY+d] = \frac{\operatorname{Cov}[aX+c, bY+d]}{\sigma[aX+c]\sigma[bY+d]} = \frac{ab\operatorname{Cov}[X,Y]}{|a||b|\sigma[X]\sigma[Y]} = \frac{ab}{|ab|}\rho[X,Y].$$

[12] The fact that correlation is bounded in $[-1,1]$ is equivalent to the well-known *Cauchy–Schwarz Inequality*, which, in one form, states that, for random variables X and Y, $\operatorname{Cov}[X,Y]^2 \leq \operatorname{V}[X]\operatorname{V}[Y]$. This equivalence is shown as follows:

$$\operatorname{Cov}[X,Y]^2 \leq \operatorname{V}[X]\operatorname{V}[Y] \iff \frac{\operatorname{Cov}[X,Y]^2}{\operatorname{V}[X]\operatorname{V}[Y]} \leq 1 \iff \sqrt{\frac{\operatorname{Cov}[X,Y]^2}{\operatorname{V}[X]\operatorname{V}[Y]}} \leq 1 \iff \frac{\sqrt{\operatorname{Cov}[X,Y]^2}}{\sqrt{\operatorname{V}[X]}\sqrt{\operatorname{V}[Y]}} \leq 1$$

$$\iff \frac{|\operatorname{Cov}[X,Y]|}{\sigma[X]\sigma[Y]} \leq 1 \iff -1 \leq \frac{\operatorname{Cov}[X,Y]}{\sigma[X]\sigma[Y]} \leq 1 \iff -1 \leq \rho[X,Y] \leq 1.$$

If $a,b > 0$ or $a,b < 0$ (that is, a and b have the same sign), then $\frac{ab}{|ab|} = 1$, so

$$\rho[aX+c, bY+d] = \rho[X,Y],$$

and if $a < 0 < b$ or $b < 0 < a$ (that is, a and b have opposite signs), then $\frac{ab}{|ab|} = -1$, so

$$\rho[aX+c, bY+d] = -\rho[X,Y]. \ \square$$

These results agree with our intuitions. In particular, X is perfectly (positively) correlated with itself, and linear transformations of X or Y do not change their absolute degree of linear dependence.

2.2.2 Covariance, Correlation, and Independence

Independence, covariance, and correlation are tightly connected topics. In this brief section, we show how independence relates to correlation and covariance. We begin by deriving some properties of independent random variables.

Theorem 2.2.8. *Implications of Independence (Part II)*
If X and Y are independent random variables, then

- $\mathrm{E}[XY] = \mathrm{E}[X]\mathrm{E}[Y]$.
- Covariance is zero: $\mathrm{Cov}[X,Y] = 0$.
- Correlation is zero: $\rho[X,Y] = 0$.
- Variances are additive: $\mathrm{V}[X+Y] = \mathrm{V}[X] + \mathrm{V}[Y]$.

Proof: Let X and Y be either two discrete independent random variables with joint PMF $f(x,y)$ or two jointly continuous independent random variables with joint PDF $f(x,y)$. Then, $\forall x,y \in \mathbb{R}$, $f(x,y) = f_X(x)f_Y(y)$. So, if X and Y are discrete, then

$$\begin{aligned}
\mathrm{E}[XY] &= \sum_x \sum_y xyf(x,y) \\
&= \sum_x \sum_y xyf_X(x)f_Y(y) \\
&= \sum_x xf_X(x) \sum_y yf_Y(y) \\
&= \mathrm{E}[X]\mathrm{E}[Y].
\end{aligned}$$

Likewise, if X and Y are jointly continuous, then

$$\begin{aligned}
\mathrm{E}[XY] &= \int_{-\infty}^{\infty}\int_{-\infty}^{\infty} xyf(x,y)dydx \\
&= \int_{-\infty}^{\infty}\int_{-\infty}^{\infty} xyf_X(x)f_Y(y)dydx \\
&= \int_{-\infty}^{\infty} xf_X(x)dx \int_{-\infty}^{\infty} yf_Y(y)dy \\
&= \mathrm{E}[X]\mathrm{E}[Y].
\end{aligned}$$

Thus,

$$\mathrm{Cov}[X,Y] = \mathrm{E}[XY] - \mathrm{E}[X]\mathrm{E}[Y] = \mathrm{E}[X]\mathrm{E}[Y] - \mathrm{E}[X]\mathrm{E}[Y] = 0,$$

and

$$\rho[X,Y] = \frac{\mathrm{Cov}[X,Y]}{\sqrt{\mathrm{V}[X]}\sqrt{\mathrm{V}[Y]}} = \frac{0}{\sqrt{\mathrm{V}[X]}\sqrt{\mathrm{V}[Y]}} = 0.$$

Finally, by Theorem 2.2.3 (*Variance Rule*),

$$\begin{aligned}
\mathrm{V}[X+Y] &= \mathrm{V}[X] + 2\mathrm{Cov}[X,Y] + \mathrm{V}[Y] \\
&= \mathrm{V}[X] + 2\cdot 0 + \mathrm{V}[Y] \\
&= \mathrm{V}[X] + \mathrm{V}[Y]. \quad \square
\end{aligned}$$

Recall that random variables X and Y are independent if and only if knowing the outcome for one provides no information about the probability of any outcome for the other. In other words, independence means there is *no relationship* between the outcome for X and the outcome for Y. Thus, it is not surprising that no relationship implies no linear relationship. However, unlike in Theorem 1.3.17 (*Implications of Independence, Part I*), the converses of the statements in Theorem 2.2.8 do *not* necessarily hold—lack of correlation does *not* imply independence. The following example illustrates this fact.

Example 2.2.9. *Zero Correlation Does Not Imply Independence*
Let X be a discrete random variable with marginal PMF

$$f_X(x) = \begin{cases} \frac{1}{3} & : \ x \in \{-1,0,1\} \\ 0 & : \ \text{otherwise,} \end{cases}$$

and let $Y = X^2$, so Y has marginal PMF

$$f_Y(y) = \begin{cases} \frac{1}{3} & : & y = 0 \\ \frac{2}{3} & : & y = 1 \\ 0 & : & \text{otherwise,} \end{cases}$$

and the joint PMF of X and Y is

$$f(x,y) = \begin{cases} \frac{1}{3} & : & (x,y) \in \{(0,0),(1,1),(-1,1)\} \\ 0 & : & \text{otherwise.} \end{cases}$$

Clearly, X and Y are not independent; for instance, $f(0,1) = 0 \neq \frac{2}{9} = \frac{1}{3} \cdot \frac{2}{3} = f_X(0)f_Y(1)$. Yet

$$\begin{aligned}
\text{Cov}[X,Y] &= \text{E}[XY] - \text{E}[X]E[Y] \\
&= \sum_x \sum_y xyf(x,y) - \sum_x xf_X(x) \sum_y yf_Y(y) \\
&= \left(-1 \cdot 1 \cdot \frac{1}{3} + 0 \cdot 0 \cdot \frac{1}{3} + 1 \cdot 1 \cdot \frac{1}{3}\right) \\
&\quad - \left(-1 \cdot \frac{1}{3} + 0 \cdot \frac{1}{3} + 1 \cdot \frac{1}{3}\right)\left(0 \cdot \frac{1}{3} + 1 \cdot \frac{2}{3}\right) \\
&= 0 - 0 \cdot \frac{2}{3} \\
&= 0.
\end{aligned}$$

Thus, $\rho[X,Y] = \dfrac{\text{Cov}[X,Y]}{\sigma[X]\sigma[Y]} = 0$. So we have $\rho[X,Y] = 0$, but $X \not\perp\!\!\!\perp Y$.[13] △

13 While $\rho(X,Y) = 0$ does not generally imply $X \perp\!\!\!\perp Y$ even when X and Y are both normal, it does in the special case where the joint distribution of X and Y is *bivariate normal*, that is, X and Y have the joint PDF

$$f(x,y) = \frac{1}{2\pi\sigma_X\sigma_Y\sqrt{1-\rho^2}} e^{-\frac{1}{2(1-\rho^2)}\left[\frac{(x-\mu_X)^2}{\sigma_X^2} + \frac{(y-\mu_Y)^2}{\sigma_Y^2} - \frac{2\rho(x-\mu_X)(y-\mu_Y)}{\sigma_X\sigma_Y}\right]}$$

for some $\mu_X, \mu_Y, \sigma_X, \sigma_Y, \rho \in \mathbb{R}$ with $\sigma_X > 0$, $\sigma_Y > 0$, and $-1 \leq \rho \leq 1$. As with the univariate normal distribution, it can be shown that the parameters correspond to the appropriate summary features of the distribution: $\mu_X = \text{E}[X]$, $\mu_Y = \text{E}[Y]$, $\sigma_X = \sigma[X]$, $\sigma_Y = \sigma[Y]$, and $\rho = \rho[X,Y]$.

2.2.3 Conditional Expectations and Conditional Expectation Functions

Just as we were able to compute the conditional probability of an event (Definition 1.1.8) and the conditional PMF (Definition 1.3.7) or PDF (Definition 1.3.14) of a random variable, we can compute the *conditional expectation* of a random variable, that is, the expected value of a random variable given that some other random variable takes on a certain value.

The idea of a conditional expectation is key to how we will characterize the relationship of one distribution to another in this book. Conditional expectations allow us to describe how the "center" of one random variable's distribution changes once we condition on the observed value of another random variable. To calculate a conditional expectation of a random variable, we replace the (marginal) PMF/PDF with the appropriate conditional PMF/PDF in the formula for expected value.

Definition 2.2.10. *Conditional Expectation*
For discrete random variables X and Y with joint PMF f, the *conditional expectation* of Y given $X = x$ is

$$\mathrm{E}[Y|X = x] = \sum_{y} y f_{Y|X}(y|x), \forall x \in \mathrm{Supp}[X].$$

For jointly continuous random variables X and Y with joint PDF f, the *conditional expectation* of Y given $X = x$ is

$$\mathrm{E}[Y|X = x] = \int_{-\infty}^{\infty} y f_{Y|X}(y|x)dy, \forall x \in \mathrm{Supp}[X].$$

Recall that an (unconditional) expected value is an operator, meaning it takes a random variable as an input and returns a number that describes a feature of the distribution of that random variable. In the case of conditional expectations, $\mathrm{E}[Y|X = x]$ is a family of operators on the random vector (X, Y) indexed by x. That is, for every $x \in \mathrm{Supp}[X]$, $\mathrm{E}[Y|X = x]$ is an operator that summarizes a particular cross section of the joint distribution of X and Y, namely, the conditional distribution of Y given $X = x$. So, for example, if X is a Bernoulli random variable, so that $\mathrm{Supp}[X] = \{0, 1\}$, then we have two operators: $\mathrm{E}[Y|X = 0]$ and $\mathrm{E}[Y|X = 1]$, where $\mathrm{E}[Y|X = 0]$ gives the long-run average value of Y among all realizations where $X = 0$, and $\mathrm{E}[Y|X = 1]$ gives the long-run average value of Y among all realizations where $X = 1$. Of course, if X is continuous, then we have an infinite number of operators, each of which describes the center of the conditional distribution of Y given $X = x$ for a particular value of x.

As with regular expectations (see Theorem 2.1.5, *Expectation of a Function of a Random Variable* and Theorem 2.1.8, *Expectation of a Function of Two*

Random Variables), we can apply conditional expectations to functions of one or more random variables.

Theorem 2.2.11. *Conditional Expectation of a Function of Random Variables*
For discrete random variables X and Y with joint PMF f, if h is a function of X and Y, then the conditional expectation of $h(X, Y)$ given $X = x$ is

$$\mathrm{E}\left[h(X,Y)\,|\,X=x\right] = \sum_y h(x,y)f_{Y|X}(y|x), \forall x \in \mathrm{Supp}[X].$$

For jointly continuous random variables X and Y with joint PDF f, if h is a function of X and Y, then the conditional expectation of $h(X, Y)$ given $X = x$ is

$$\mathrm{E}\left[h(X,Y)\,|\,X=x\right] = \int_{-\infty}^{\infty} h(x,y)f_{Y|X}(y|x)dy, \forall x \in \mathrm{Supp}[X].$$

We omit the proof of this theorem. Everything else carries through just as though we were operating on a univariate PMF/PDF. For example, we can define the *conditional variance* of Y given $X = x$.

Definition 2.2.12. *Conditional Variance*
For random variables X and Y, the *conditional variance* of Y given $X = x$ is

$$\mathrm{V}[Y|X=x] = \mathrm{E}\left[\left(Y - \mathrm{E}[Y|X=x]\right)^2 \middle| X=x\right], \forall x \in \mathrm{Supp}[X].$$

As with regular variance, we can derive an alternative formula for conditional variance that is generally easier to work with in practice.

Theorem 2.2.13. *Alternative Formula for Conditional Variance*
For random variables X and Y, $\forall x \in \mathrm{Supp}[X]$,

$$\mathrm{V}[Y|X=x] = \mathrm{E}\left[Y^2\,|\,X=x\right] - \mathrm{E}[Y|X=x]^2.$$

The proof is essentially the same as the proof of Theorem 2.1.13 (*Alternative Formula for Variance*). Additionally, just like unconditional expectations, conditional expectations are linear.

Theorem 2.2.14. *Linearity of Conditional Expectations*
For random variables X and Y, if g and h are functions of X, then $\forall x \in \text{Supp}[X]$,

$$\text{E}\big[g(X)Y + h(X)\,\big|\,X = x\big] = g(x)\text{E}[Y|X = x] + h(x).$$

Proof: Let X and Y be either discrete random variables with joint PMF f or jointly continuous random variables with joint PDF f, and let g and h be functions of X. If X and Y are discrete, then by Theorem 2.2.11, $\forall x \in \text{Supp}[X]$,

$$\begin{aligned}
\text{E}\big[g(X)Y + h(X)\,\big|\,X = x\big] &= \sum_y \big(g(x)y + h(x)\big) f_{Y|X}(y|x) \\
&= g(x)\sum_y y f_{Y|X}(y|x) + h(x)\sum_y f_{Y|X}(y|x) \\
&= g(x)\text{E}[Y|X = x] + h(x)\cdot 1 \\
&= g(x)\text{E}[Y|X = x] + h(x).
\end{aligned}$$

Likewise, if X and Y are jointly continuous, then by Theorem 2.2.11, $\forall x \in \text{Supp}[X]$,

$$\begin{aligned}
\text{E}\big[g(X)Y + h(X)\,\big|\,X = x\big] &= \int_{-\infty}^{\infty} \big(g(x)y + h(x)\big) f_{Y|X}(y|x)dy \\
&= g(x)\int_{-\infty}^{\infty} y f_{Y|X}(y|x)dy + h(x)\int_{-\infty}^{\infty} f_{Y|X}(y|x)dy \\
&= g(x)\text{E}[Y|X = x] + h(x)\cdot 1 \\
&= g(x)\text{E}[Y|X = x] + h(x). \quad \square
\end{aligned}$$

We now turn to a central definition of this book: the *conditional expectation function (CEF)*. The CEF is a function that takes as an input x and returns the conditional expectation of Y given $X = x$. The CEF is extremely useful, since it is a single function that characterizes all possible values of $\text{E}[Y|X = x]$. If we are interested in characterizing the way in which the conditional distribution of Y depends on the value of X, the CEF is a natural summary feature of the joint distribution to target. Furthermore, we will see that the CEF can be closely linked to many topics that this book considers, including regression (Chapter 4), missing data (Chapter 6), and causal inference (Chapter 7).

Definition 2.2.15. *Conditional Expectation Function (CEF)*
For random variables X and Y with joint PMF/PDF f, the *conditional expectation function* of Y given $X = x$ is

$$G_Y(x) = \text{E}[Y|X = x], \forall x \in \text{Supp}[X].$$

A few remarks on notation are in order here. We will generally write $\mathrm{E}[Y|X = x]$ to denote the CEF rather than $G_Y(x)$. The above definition is merely meant to emphasize that, when we use the term CEF, we are referring to the *function* that maps x to $\mathrm{E}[Y|X = x]$, rather than the value of $\mathrm{E}[Y|X = x]$ at some specific x. It is also intended to clarify that the CEF, $\mathrm{E}[Y|X = x]$, is a univariate function of x. It is *not* a function of the random variable Y. So, for example, if X is a Bernoulli random variable, then the CEF of Y given X is

$$G_Y(x) = \mathrm{E}[Y|X = x] = \begin{cases} \mathrm{E}[Y|X = 0] & : \quad x = 0 \\ \mathrm{E}[Y|X = 1] & : \quad x = 1. \end{cases}$$

$G_Y(X)$ is a function of the random variable X and is therefore itself a random variable[14] whose value depends on the value of X. That is, when X takes on the value x, the random variable $G_Y(X)$ takes on the value $G_Y(x) = \mathrm{E}[Y|X = x]$.

We write $\mathrm{E}[Y|X]$ to denote $G_Y(X)$ (since $\mathrm{E}[Y|X = X]$ would be confusing). So, for example, if X is a Bernoulli random variable with $p = \frac{1}{2}$, then $\mathrm{E}[Y|X]$ is a random variable that takes on the value of $\mathrm{E}[Y|X = 0]$ with probability $\frac{1}{2}$ and the value of $\mathrm{E}[Y|X = 1]$ with probability $\frac{1}{2}$. Also note that we can analogously define the *conditional variance function*, $H_Y(x) = \mathrm{V}[Y|X = x]$, which we will generally write as $\mathrm{V}[Y|X = x]$, and write $\mathrm{V}[Y|X]$ to denote the random variable $H_Y(X)$.

Theorem 1.3.2 (*Equality of Functions of a Random Variable*) implies that we can write statements about conditional expectation functions in the more compact $\mathrm{E}[Y|X]$ form. For example, Theorem 2.2.14 can equivalently be stated as follows: for random variables X and Y, if g and h are functions of X, then

$$\mathrm{E}\big[g(X)Y + h(X)\,\big|\,X\big] = g(X)\mathrm{E}[Y|X] + h(X).$$

From this point on, we will generally state theorems involving conditional expectation functions using this more concise notation.

We now illustrate these concepts with our familiar example of flipping a coin and rolling a four- or six-sided die.

Example 2.2.16. *Flipping a Coin and Rolling a Die*
Consider, again, the generative process from Example 1.1.11. Recall from Example 1.3.5 that the conditional PMF of Y given $X = x$ is

$$f_{Y|X}(y|x) = \begin{cases} \frac{1}{4} & : \quad x = 0, y \in \{1,2,3,4\} \\ \frac{1}{6} & : \quad x = 1, y \in \{1,2,3,4,5,6\} \\ 0 & : \quad \text{otherwise.} \end{cases}$$

14 Ignoring some unimportant measure-theoretic regularity conditions, namely $X(\Omega) = \mathrm{Supp}[X]$.

Thus, the CEF of Y given $X=x$ is

$$\mathrm{E}[Y|X=x] = \sum_y y f_{Y|X}(y|x)$$

$$= \begin{cases} \sum_{y=1}^{4} y \cdot \frac{1}{4} & : \quad x=0 \\ \sum_{y=1}^{6} y \cdot \frac{1}{6} & : \quad x=1 \end{cases}$$

$$= \begin{cases} \frac{5}{2} & : \quad x=0 \\ \frac{7}{2} & : \quad x=1. \end{cases}$$

Likewise, the conditional PMF of X given $Y=y$ is

$$f_{X|Y}(x|y) = \begin{cases} \frac{3}{5} & : \quad x=0, y \in \{1,2,3,4\} \\ \frac{2}{5} & : \quad x=1, y \in \{1,2,3,4\} \\ 1 & : \quad x=1, y \in \{5,6\} \\ 0 & : \quad \text{otherwise,} \end{cases}$$

so the CEF of X given $Y=y$ is

$$\mathrm{E}[X|Y=y] = \sum_x x f_{X|Y}(x|y)$$

$$= \begin{cases} 0 \cdot \frac{3}{5} + 1 \cdot \frac{2}{5} & : \quad y \in \{1,2,3,4\} \\ 0 \cdot 0 + 1 \cdot 1 & : \quad y \in \{5,6\} \end{cases}$$

$$= \begin{cases} \frac{2}{5} & : \quad y \in \{1,2,3,4\} \\ 1 & : \quad y \in \{5,6\}. \end{cases} \qquad \triangle$$

We can now state one of the most important theorems in this book: the *Law of Iterated Expectations*. The Law of Iterated Expectations is important because it allows us to move between conditional expectations and unconditional expectations. Very often, conditional expectations are easier to work with—in such cases, we can treat some random variables as fixed, which allows for more tractable calculations. As a result, the Law of Iterated Expectations will be invoked frequently in proofs throughout the remainder of this book, particularly in Part III.

Theorem 2.2.17. *Law of Iterated Expectations*
For random variables X and Y,

$$\mathrm{E}[Y] = \mathrm{E}\big[\mathrm{E}[Y|X]\big].$$[15]

Proof: Let X and Y be either two discrete random variables with joint PMF f or two jointly continuous random variables with joint PDF f. If X and Y are discrete, then

$$\begin{aligned}
\mathrm{E}[Y] &= \sum_y y f_Y(y) \\
&= \sum_y y \sum_x f(x,y) \\
&= \sum_x \sum_y y f(x,y) \\
&= \sum_x \sum_y y f_{Y|X}(y|x) f_X(x) \\
&= \sum_x \left(\sum_y y f_{Y|X}(y|x) \right) f_X(x) \\
&= \sum_x \mathrm{E}[Y|X=x] f_X(x) \\
&= \mathrm{E}\big[\mathrm{E}[Y|X]\big].
\end{aligned}$$

Likewise, if X and Y are jointly continuous, then

$$\begin{aligned}
\mathrm{E}[Y] &= \int_{-\infty}^{\infty} y f_Y(y) dy \\
&= \int_{-\infty}^{\infty} y \left(\int_{-\infty}^{\infty} f(x,y) dx \right) dy \\
&= \int_{-\infty}^{\infty} \int_{-\infty}^{\infty} y f(x,y) dy dx \\
&= \int_{-\infty}^{\infty} \int_{-\infty}^{\infty} y f_{Y|X}(y|x) f_X(x) dy dx
\end{aligned}$$

15 Note that $\mathrm{E}[Y|X]$ is a (univariate) function of the random variable X, so the outer expectation here takes the expected value of this random variable.

$$= \int_{-\infty}^{\infty} \left(\int_{-\infty}^{\infty} y f_{Y|X}(y|x) dy \right) f_X(x) dx$$

$$= \int_{-\infty}^{\infty} \mathrm{E}[Y|X=x] f_X(x) dx$$

$$= \mathrm{E}\big[\mathrm{E}[Y|X]\big]. \ \square$$

Put simply, the Law of Iterated Expectations implies that the unconditional expectation can be represented as a weighted average of conditional expectations, where the weights are proportional to the probability distribution of the variable being conditioned on. The Law of Iterated Expectations also directly yields the *Law of Total Variance.*

Theorem 2.2.18. *Law of Total Variance*
For random variables X and Y,

$$\mathrm{V}[Y] = \mathrm{E}\big[\mathrm{V}[Y|X]\big] + \mathrm{V}\big[\mathrm{E}[Y|X]\big].$$

Proof:

$$\mathrm{V}[Y] = \mathrm{E}\big[Y^2\big] - \mathrm{E}[Y]^2$$

$$= \mathrm{E}\Big[\mathrm{E}\big[Y^2 | X\big]\Big] - \mathrm{E}\big[\mathrm{E}[Y|X]\big]^2$$

$$= \mathrm{E}\Big[\mathrm{E}\big[Y^2 | X\big] - \mathrm{E}[Y|X]^2 + \mathrm{E}[Y|X]^2\Big] - \mathrm{E}\big[\mathrm{E}[Y|X]\big]^2$$

$$= \mathrm{E}\Big[\mathrm{V}[Y|X] + \mathrm{E}[Y|X]^2\Big] - \mathrm{E}\big[\mathrm{E}[Y|X]\big]^2$$

$$= \mathrm{E}\big[\mathrm{V}[Y|X]\big] + \Big(\mathrm{E}\big[\mathrm{E}[Y|X]^2\big] - \mathrm{E}\big[\mathrm{E}[Y|X]\big]^2\Big)$$

$$= \mathrm{E}\big[\mathrm{V}[Y|X]\big] + \mathrm{V}\big[\mathrm{E}[Y|X]\big]. \ \square$$

Practically speaking, this theorem allows us to decompose the variability of a random variable *Y* into the average variability "within" values of *X* and the variability "across" values of *X*.[16]

16 The Law of Total Variance is also referred to as the Analysis of Variance (ANOVA) identity or theorem. ANOVA can be extended to a broader range of models, considering different sources of variance, which can be used to test hypotheses about differences across groups. For more details, see, e.g., Wackerly, Mendenhall, and Scheaffer (2008, Ch. 13).

The Law of Iterated Expectations and the Law of Total Variance reveal the following properties of deviations from the CEF, which will be necessary to demonstrate its significance.

Theorem 2.2.19. *Properties of Deviations from the CEF*
Let X and Y be random variables and let $\varepsilon = Y - \mathrm{E}[Y|X]$. Then

- $\mathrm{E}[\varepsilon|X] = 0$.
- $\mathrm{E}[\varepsilon] = 0$.
- If g is a function of X, then $\mathrm{Cov}[g(X), \varepsilon] = 0$.
- $\mathrm{V}[\varepsilon|X] = \mathrm{V}[Y|X]$.
- $\mathrm{V}[\varepsilon] = \mathrm{E}\big[\mathrm{V}[Y|X]\big]$.

Proof: Noting that $\mathrm{E}[Y|X]$ is a function solely of X and applying Theorem 2.2.14,

$$\mathrm{E}[\varepsilon|X] = \mathrm{E}\big[Y - \mathrm{E}[Y|X]\,\big|\,X\big] = \mathrm{E}[Y|X] - \mathrm{E}[Y|X] = 0.$$

Applying the Law of Iterated Expectations,

$$\mathrm{E}[\varepsilon] = \mathrm{E}\big[\mathrm{E}[\varepsilon|X]\big] = \mathrm{E}[0] = 0.$$

Let g be a function of X. Then

$$\begin{aligned}
\mathrm{Cov}[g(X), \varepsilon] &= \mathrm{E}[g(X)\varepsilon] - \mathrm{E}[g(X)]\mathrm{E}[\varepsilon] \\
&= \mathrm{E}\Big[g(X)\big(Y - \mathrm{E}[Y|X]\big)\Big] - \mathrm{E}[g(X)](0) \\
&= \mathrm{E}\big[g(X)Y - g(X)\mathrm{E}[Y|X]\big] \\
&= \mathrm{E}[g(X)Y] - \mathrm{E}\big[g(X)\mathrm{E}[Y|X]\big] \\
&= \mathrm{E}[g(X)Y] - \mathrm{E}\Big[\mathrm{E}\big[g(X)Y\,\big|\,X\big]\Big] \\
&= \mathrm{E}[g(X)Y] - \mathrm{E}[g(X)Y] \\
&= 0.
\end{aligned}$$

Recalling the definition of conditional variance (Definition 2.2.12),

$$\begin{aligned}
\mathrm{V}[\varepsilon|X] &= \mathrm{E}\Big[\big(\varepsilon - \mathrm{E}[\varepsilon|X]\big)^2\,\Big|\,X\Big] \\
&= \mathrm{E}\big[(\varepsilon - 0)^2\,\big|\,X\big]
\end{aligned}$$

$$= \mathrm{E}\left[\varepsilon^2 \,|\, X\right]$$

$$= \mathrm{E}\left[\left(Y - \mathrm{E}[Y|X]\right)^2 \Big| X\right]$$

$$= \mathrm{V}[Y|X].$$

Finally, by the Law of Total Variance,

$$\mathrm{V}[\varepsilon] = \mathrm{E}\left[\mathrm{V}[\varepsilon \,|\, X]\right] + \mathrm{V}\left[\mathrm{E}[\varepsilon \,|\, X]\right]$$

$$= \mathrm{E}\left[\mathrm{V}[\varepsilon \,|\, X]\right] + \mathrm{V}[0]$$

$$= \mathrm{E}\left[\mathrm{V}[\varepsilon \,|\, X]\right]$$

$$= \mathrm{E}\left[\mathrm{V}[Y|X]\right]. \quad \square$$

This result allows us to derive a key property of the CEF in the following section.

2.2.4 Best Predictors and Best Linear Predictors

The CEF is also of particular importance as a way to summarize the relationship between two random variables because it affords us some theoretical guarantees without having to impose further assumptions.

Suppose we knew the full joint cumulative distribution function (CDF) of X and Y, and then someone gave us a randomly drawn value of X. What would be the guess of Y that would have the lowest MSE? Formally, what function g of X minimizes $\mathrm{E}[(Y - g(X))^2]$? The answer is given by the CEF. The function $g(X)$ that best approximates Y is the CEF.

Theorem 2.2.20. *The CEF is the Best Predictor*
For random variables X and Y, the CEF, $\mathrm{E}[Y|X]$, is the best (minimum MSE) predictor of Y given X.

Proof: Choose any $g(X)$ to approximate Y. Let $U = Y - g(X)$. By the definition of minimum MSE, our goal is to choose $g(X)$ to minimize $\mathrm{E}[U^2]$. Let $\varepsilon = Y - \mathrm{E}[Y|X]$ and $W = \mathrm{E}[Y|X] - g(X)$, so that $U = \varepsilon + W$. (W is a function of X, so we can treat it like a constant in expectations conditioned on X.) Our goal is then to show that, by choosing $g(X) = \mathrm{E}[Y|X]$, we will minimize $\mathrm{E}[U^2]$. Now,

$$\mathrm{E}\left[U^2 \,|\, X\right] = \mathrm{E}\left[(\varepsilon + W)^2 \,|\, X\right]$$

$$= \mathrm{E}\left[\varepsilon^2 + 2\varepsilon W + W^2 \,|\, X\right]$$

$$= \mathrm{E}\left[\varepsilon^2 \middle| X\right] + 2W\mathrm{E}[\varepsilon|X] + W^2$$

$$= \mathrm{E}\left[\varepsilon^2 \middle| X\right] + 0 + W^2$$

$$= \mathrm{E}\left[\varepsilon^2 \middle| X\right] - \mathrm{E}[\varepsilon|X]^2 + W^2$$

$$= \mathrm{V}[Y|X] + W^2,$$

where the third and fifth lines follow from Theorem 2.2.19. Applying the Law of Iterated Expectations,

$$\mathrm{E}\left[U^2\right] = \mathrm{E}\left[\mathrm{E}\left[U^2 \middle| X\right]\right] = \mathrm{E}\left[\mathrm{V}[Y|X] + W^2\right] = \mathrm{E}\left[\mathrm{V}[Y|X]\right] + \mathrm{E}\left[W^2\right].$$

$\mathrm{E}[\mathrm{V}[Y|X]]$ does not depend on the choice of $g(X)$. Additionally, $\mathrm{E}[W^2] \geq 0$, with equality if $g(X) = \mathrm{E}[Y|X]$. Therefore, choosing $g(X) = \mathrm{E}[Y|X]$ minimizes MSE. □

Thus, the CEF yields the best (minimum MSE) approximation of Y, conditional on the observed value of X. There is no better way (in terms of MSE) to approximate Y given X than the CEF. This makes the CEF a natural target of inquiry: if the CEF is known, much is known about how X relates to Y. However, although it is the best predictor, the CEF can be extremely complicated—without further assumptions, the function can take any shape.

What if we were to restrict ourselves to just linear functions? Among functions of the form $g(X) = a + bX$, what function yields the best prediction of Y given X? By choosing the a and b that minimize MSE, we obtain the *best linear predictor (BLP)* of Y given X.[17] This naturally yields a much simpler target that retains much of the same interpretation. The BLP will have great importance for our discussion in Chapter 4 (*Regression*).

Theorem 2.2.21. *Best Linear Predictor (BLP)*
For random variables X and Y, if $\mathrm{V}[X] > 0$,[18] then the best (minimum MSE) linear predictor of Y given X is $g(X) = \alpha + \beta X$, where

$$\alpha = \mathrm{E}[Y] - \frac{\mathrm{Cov}[X,Y]}{\mathrm{V}[X]}\mathrm{E}[X],$$

$$\beta = \frac{\mathrm{Cov}[X,Y]}{\mathrm{V}[X]}.$$

17 As with the CEF, the BLP is a univariate function of x, not a function of the random variable Y. Consequently, the function that provides us with the best linear prediction of Y given X, when inverted, generally will not provide the best linear prediction of X given Y.

18 If $\mathrm{V}[X] = 0$, then any function such that $g(\mathrm{E}[X]) = \mathrm{E}[Y]$ would minimize MSE. Thus, unlike the CEF, the BLP is not necessarily uniquely defined.

Proof: Let $\varepsilon = Y - (a + bX)$. If $g(X) = \alpha + \beta X$ is the best linear predictor of Y given X, then

$$(\alpha, \beta) = \underset{(a,b)\in\mathbb{R}^2}{\arg\min} \, \mathrm{E}\big[\varepsilon^2\big].$$

The first-order conditions yield the system of equations

$$0 = \frac{\partial \mathrm{E}[\varepsilon^2]}{\partial \alpha},$$
$$0 = \frac{\partial \mathrm{E}[\varepsilon^2]}{\partial \beta}.$$

By linearity of expectations and the chain rule, as well as the fact that derivatives pass through expectations (because they pass through sums and integrals), this becomes:

$$0 = \frac{\partial \mathrm{E}[\varepsilon^2]}{\partial \alpha} = \mathrm{E}\left[\frac{\partial \varepsilon^2}{\partial \alpha}\right] = \mathrm{E}\left[2\varepsilon \frac{\partial \varepsilon}{\partial \alpha}\right] = -2\mathrm{E}[\varepsilon],$$
$$0 = \frac{\partial \mathrm{E}[\varepsilon^2]}{\partial \beta} = \mathrm{E}\left[\frac{\partial \varepsilon^2}{\partial \beta}\right] = \mathrm{E}\left[2\varepsilon \frac{\partial \varepsilon}{\partial \beta}\right] = -2\mathrm{E}[\varepsilon X].$$

Now we solve $0 = \mathrm{E}[Y - (\alpha + \beta X)]$ and $0 = \mathrm{E}[(Y - (\alpha + \beta X))X]$.[19] From the first equation,

$$0 = \mathrm{E}\big[Y - (\alpha + \beta X)\big] = \mathrm{E}[Y] - \alpha - \beta \mathrm{E}[X],$$

19 The second-order partial derivatives are

$$\frac{\partial^2 \mathrm{E}[\varepsilon^2]}{\partial \alpha^2} = \frac{\partial}{\partial \alpha}(-2\mathrm{E}[\varepsilon]) = -2\mathrm{E}\left[\frac{\partial \varepsilon}{\partial \alpha}\right] = -2\mathrm{E}[-1] = 2,$$
$$\frac{\partial^2 \mathrm{E}[\varepsilon^2]}{\partial \beta^2} = \frac{\partial}{\partial \beta}(-2\mathrm{E}[\varepsilon \mathrm{X}]) = -2\mathrm{E}\left[\frac{\partial \varepsilon}{\partial \beta}\mathrm{X}\right] = -2\mathrm{E}\left[-\mathrm{X}^2\right] = 2\mathrm{E}\left[\mathrm{X}^2\right],$$
$$\frac{\partial^2 \mathrm{E}[\varepsilon^2]}{\partial \alpha \partial \beta} = \frac{\partial}{\partial \beta}(-2\mathrm{E}[\varepsilon]) = -2\mathrm{E}\left[\frac{\partial \varepsilon}{\partial \beta}\right] = -2\mathrm{E}[-X] = 2\mathrm{E}[X].$$

So, since

$$\frac{\partial^2 \mathrm{E}[\varepsilon^2]}{\partial \alpha^2} = 2 > 0$$

and

$$\frac{\partial^2 \mathrm{E}[\varepsilon^2]}{\partial \alpha^2}\frac{\partial^2 \mathrm{E}[\varepsilon^2]}{\partial \beta^2} - \left(\frac{\partial^2 \mathrm{E}[\varepsilon^2]}{\partial \alpha \partial \beta}\right)^2 = 4\mathrm{E}\left[\mathrm{X}^2\right] - (2\mathrm{E}[\mathrm{X}])^2 = 4\mathrm{E}\left[\mathrm{X}^2\right] - 4\mathrm{E}[\mathrm{X}]^2$$
$$= 4\left(\mathrm{E}\left[\mathrm{X}^2\right] - \mathrm{E}[\mathrm{X}]^2\right) = 4\mathrm{V}[\mathrm{X}] > 0,$$

a unique solution will be an absolute minimum.

so $\alpha = \mathrm{E}[Y] - \beta\mathrm{E}[X]$. Then from the second equation,

$$\begin{aligned}
0 &= \mathrm{E}\big[(Y - (\alpha + \beta X))X\big] \\
&= \mathrm{E}\big[YX - \alpha X - \beta X^2\big] \\
&= \mathrm{E}[XY] - \alpha\mathrm{E}[X] - \beta\mathrm{E}\big[X^2\big] \\
&= \mathrm{E}[XY] - \big(\mathrm{E}[Y] - \beta\mathrm{E}[X]\big)\mathrm{E}[X] - \beta\mathrm{E}\big[X^2\big] \\
&= \mathrm{E}[XY] - \mathrm{E}[X]\mathrm{E}[Y] + \beta\mathrm{E}[X]^2 - \beta\mathrm{E}\big[X^2\big] \\
&= \mathrm{E}[XY] - \mathrm{E}[X]\mathrm{E}[Y] - \beta\Big(\mathrm{E}\big[X^2\big] - \mathrm{E}[X]^2\Big) \\
&= \mathrm{Cov}[X,Y] - \beta\mathrm{V}[X].
\end{aligned}$$

Solving for β, we obtain

$$\beta = \frac{\mathrm{Cov}[X,Y]}{\mathrm{V}[X]}.$$

Finally, substituting this result back into $\alpha = \mathrm{E}[Y] - \beta\mathrm{E}[X]$ yields

$$\alpha = \mathrm{E}[Y] - \frac{\mathrm{Cov}[X,Y]}{\mathrm{V}[X]}\mathrm{E}[X]. \quad \square$$

Note that α is the y-intercept of the BLP, and β is its slope.[20] We note two important corollaries:

- The BLP is also the best linear approximation of the CEF; setting $a = \alpha$ and $b = \beta$ minimizes

$$\mathrm{E}\Big[\big(\mathrm{E}[Y|X] - (a + bX)\big)^2\Big].$$

- If the CEF is linear, then the CEF is the BLP.

Whereas the CEF might be infinitely complex, the BLP is characterized just by two numbers, α and β. The BLP is a simple approximation of the CEF, and one that operates on the same principle—find the function that minimizes MSE—but with the further restriction that the function must be linear.[21]

20 Readers with prior training in statistics or econometrics may recognize the expression for the BLP as resembling the ordinary least squares (OLS) regression solution. This is not an accident. We will explain this similarity in Chapter 4.

21 The BLP also demonstrates that covariance and correlation indeed measure the *linear* relationship between X and Y (as in Section 2.2.2): the BLP is the only linear function that satisfies $\mathrm{Cov}[X, g(X)] = \mathrm{Cov}[X,Y]$. Additionally, the solution to the BLP demonstrates why $\rho[X,Y] = 1$ if and only if Y is a linear function of X with a positive slope.

The CEF and BLP are very important, as each permits a principled and simple summary of the way in which the best prediction of one variable is related to the value of another variable—this is why we will sometimes refer to X as an *explanatory variable* for Y. Additionally, both the CEF and BLP are generalizations of the simple expected value. It is also worth noting that some, but not all, properties of the CEF (Theorem 2.2.19) have analogous properties when speaking of the BLP.

Theorem 2.2.22. *Properties of Deviations from the BLP*
Let X and Y be random variables and let $\varepsilon = Y - g(X)$, where $g(X)$ is the BLP. Then

- $\mathrm{E}[\varepsilon] = 0$.
- $\mathrm{E}[X\varepsilon] = 0$.
- $\mathrm{Cov}[X, \varepsilon] = 0$.

We omit the proof of this theorem, but it is useful for understanding how the BLP's properties as a linear approximation yield linear analogs to the conditions met by the CEF. But whereas we were able to establish that $\mathrm{E}[\varepsilon | X] = 0$ for the CEF, this is not generally true for the BLP; instead, we have only the weaker statement that $\mathrm{E}[\varepsilon] = 0$. Perhaps the most commonly referenced of these properties is that $\mathrm{Cov}[X, \varepsilon] = 0$—there is no covariance between X and the deviations.

We now consider an example to show how the CEF and BLP allow us to summarize bivariate relationships.

Example 2.2.23. *Plotting the CEF and BLP*
Let X and Y be random variables with $X \sim U(0,1)$ and $Y = 10X^2 + W$, where $W \sim N(0,1)$ and $X \perp\!\!\!\perp W$. We derive the CEF of Y given X as follows:

$$\mathrm{E}[Y|X] = \mathrm{E}\left[10X^2 + W \middle| X\right].$$

By linearity of expectations,

$$\mathrm{E}\left[10X^2 + W \middle| X\right] = 10\mathrm{E}\left[X^2 \middle| X\right] + \mathrm{E}[W|X] = 10\mathrm{E}\left[X^2 \middle| X\right] + 0 = 10X^2.$$

Thus, the CEF of Y given X is $\mathrm{E}[Y|X] = 10X^2$.

We now derive the BLP of Y given X. The slope of the BLP is

$$\begin{aligned}\beta &= \frac{\mathrm{Cov}[X, Y]}{\mathrm{V}[X]} \\ &= \frac{\mathrm{E}[XY] - \mathrm{E}[X]\mathrm{E}[Y]}{\mathrm{E}\left[X^2\right] - \mathrm{E}[X]^2}\end{aligned}$$

$$= \frac{\mathrm{E}\left[X(10X^2 + W)\right] - \mathrm{E}[X]\mathrm{E}\left[10X^2 + W\right]}{\mathrm{E}\left[X^2\right] - \mathrm{E}[X]^2}$$

$$= \frac{\mathrm{E}\left[10X^3 + XW\right] - \mathrm{E}[X]\mathrm{E}\left[10X^2 + W\right]}{\mathrm{E}\left[X^2\right] - \mathrm{E}[X]^2}.$$

By linearity of expectations,

$$\beta = \frac{10\mathrm{E}\left[X^3\right] + \mathrm{E}[XW] - \mathrm{E}[X]\left(10\mathrm{E}\left[X^2\right] + \mathrm{E}[W]\right)}{\mathrm{E}\left[X^2\right] - \mathrm{E}[X]^2}$$

$$= \frac{10\mathrm{E}\left[X^3\right] + \mathrm{E}[XW] - 10\mathrm{E}[X]\mathrm{E}\left[X^2\right] - \mathrm{E}[X]\mathrm{E}[W]}{\mathrm{E}\left[X^2\right] - \mathrm{E}[X]^2}$$

$$= \frac{10\left(\mathrm{E}\left[X^3\right] - \mathrm{E}[X]\mathrm{E}\left[X^2\right]\right) + \left(\mathrm{E}[XW] - \mathrm{E}[X]\mathrm{E}[W]\right)}{\mathrm{E}\left[X^2\right] - \mathrm{E}[X]^2}$$

$$= \frac{10\left(\mathrm{E}\left[X^3\right] - \mathrm{E}[X]\mathrm{E}\left[X^2\right]\right) + \mathrm{Cov}[X, W]}{\mathrm{E}\left[X^2\right] - \mathrm{E}[X]^2}.$$

By independence,

$$\beta = \frac{10\left(\mathrm{E}\left[X^3\right] - \mathrm{E}[X]\mathrm{E}\left[X^2\right]\right) + 0}{\mathrm{E}\left[X^2\right] - \mathrm{E}[X]^2}$$

$$= \frac{10\left(\mathrm{E}\left[X^3\right] - \mathrm{E}[X]\mathrm{E}\left[X^2\right]\right)}{\mathrm{E}\left[X^2\right] - \mathrm{E}[X]^2}.$$

$X \sim U(0,1)$, so its PDF is $f_X(x) = 1$, $\forall x \in [0,1]$, and $f(x) = 0$ otherwise, so

$$\beta = \frac{10\left(\int_0^1 (x^3 \cdot 1)dx - \left(\int_0^1 (x \cdot 1)dx\right)\left(\int_0^1 (x^2 \cdot 1)dx\right)\right)}{\int_0^1 (x^2 \cdot 1)dx - \left(\int_0^1 (x \cdot 1)dx\right)^2}$$

$$= \frac{10\left(\frac{1}{4}x^4\Big|_0^1 - \left(\frac{1}{2}x^2\Big|_0^1\right)\left(\frac{1}{3}x^3\Big|_0^1\right)\right)}{\frac{1}{3}x^3\Big|_0^1 - \left(\frac{1}{2}x^2\Big|_0^1\right)^2}$$

$$= \frac{10\left(\frac{1}{4}(1-0) - \frac{1}{2}(1-0)\frac{1}{3}(1-0)\right)}{\frac{1}{3}(1-0) - \left(\frac{1}{2}(1-0)\right)^2}$$

$$= \frac{10\left(\frac{1}{4} - \frac{1}{6}\right)}{\frac{1}{3} - \left(\frac{1}{2}\right)^2}$$

$$= \frac{10\left(\frac{1}{12}\right)}{\frac{1}{12}}$$

$$= 10.$$

Finally, the intercept is

$$\alpha = \mathrm{E}[Y] - \beta\mathrm{E}[X]$$

$$= \mathrm{E}\big[10X^2 + W\big] - \beta\mathrm{E}[X].$$

By linearity of expectations,

$$\alpha = 10\mathrm{E}\big[X^2\big] + \mathrm{E}[W] - \beta\mathrm{E}[X]$$

$$= 10\mathrm{E}\big[X^2\big] + 0 - \beta\mathrm{E}[X]$$

$$= 10\int_0^1 (x^2 \cdot 1)dx - 10\int_0^1 (x \cdot 1)dx$$

$$= 10 \cdot \frac{x^3}{3}\bigg|_0^1 - 10 \cdot \frac{x^2}{2}\bigg|_0^1$$

$$= \frac{10}{3} - \frac{10}{2}$$

$$= -\frac{5}{3}.$$

Thus, the BLP of Y given X is $g(X) = -\frac{5}{3} + 10X$. △

Figure 2.2.1 plots the CEF (in black) and BLP (in red). Here, the BLP approximates the CEF reasonably well over the domain of the data. While this is not always the case, it is very often the case in the social and health sciences. The BLP is thus a good "first approximation" in a very literal sense, in that it is an approximation with a first-order polynomial.[22] However, when the CEF is not linear, one must take care in interpreting the BLP as equivalent to the CEF. In particular, this may pose a problem when attempting to make inferences where X has low probability mass over some parts of the domain of the CEF. This is because under nonlinearity, the BLP depends on the distribution of X. This is illustrated in the following example.

22 We will discuss the approximation of the CEF with higher-order polynomials in Section 4.3.1.

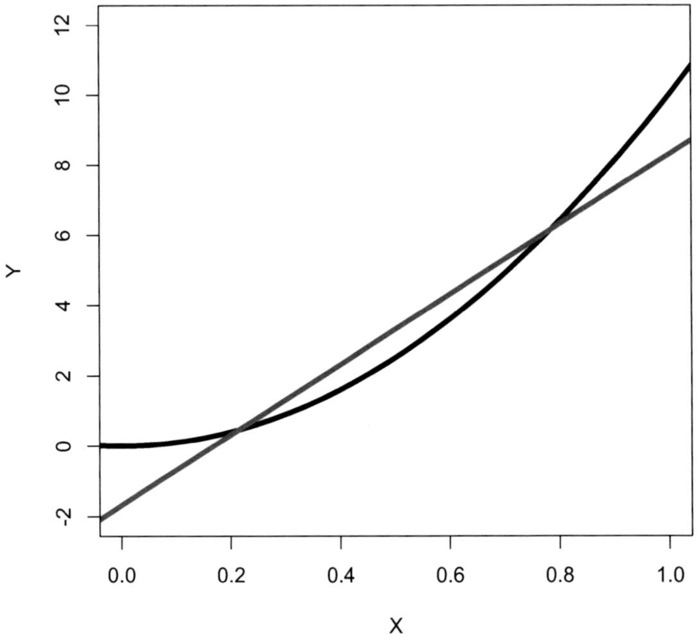

FIGURE 2.2.1. *Plotting the CEF and BLP*

Example 2.2.24. *BLP under Nonlinearity*
Suppose that, as in Example 2.2.23, $Y = 10X^2 + W$, $W \sim N(0,1)$ and $X \perp\!\!\!\perp W$. If X is uniformly distributed between zero and one, the CEF of Y given X is the same as above: $\mathrm{E}[Y|X] = X^2$. However, we see in panel (a) of Figure 2.2.2 that the BLP approximates the CEF reasonably well only over certain areas. Additionally, if the distribution of X changes, the BLP changes. Figure 2.2.2 demonstrates how, with the same (nonlinear) CEF (in black), the BLP (in red) depends on the distribution of X. $\triangle$

2.2.5 CEFs and BLPs under Independence

Although this section is very short, it contains results essential for our calculations in Part III. Here, we derive some additional properties of independent random variables as they relate to conditional expectations, the CEF, and the BLP.

Theorem 2.2.25. *Implications of Independence (Part III)*
If X and Y are independent random variables, then

- $\mathrm{E}[Y|X] = \mathrm{E}[Y]$.
- $\mathrm{V}[Y|X] = \mathrm{V}[Y]$.

- The BLP of Y given X is $\mathrm{E}[Y]$.
- If g is a function of X and h is a function of Y, then
  - $\mathrm{E}\big[g(Y)\,\big|\,h(X)\big] = \mathrm{E}\big[g(Y)\big]$.
  - The BLP of $h(Y)$ given $g(X)$ is $\mathrm{E}\big[h(Y)\big]$.

We omit the proof of Theorem 2.2.25, noting that it directly follows from Theorems 1.3.17 and 2.2.8 (*Implications of Independence, Parts I and II*). These results imply that, when Y and X are independent, the CEF and BLP work as expected: they are both simply equal to $\mathrm{E}[Y]$, regardless of what value X takes on. This is because X provides no information as to

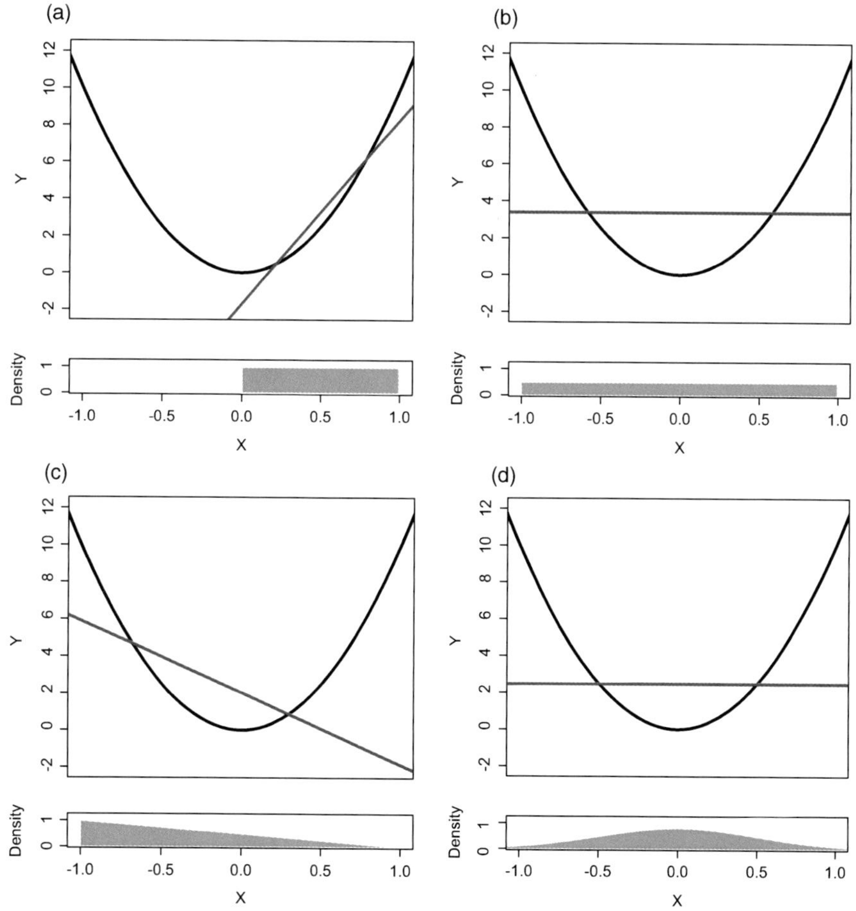

FIGURE 2.2.2. *Plotting the CEF and the BLP over Different Distributions of X*

the distribution of Y, leaving us simply with E[Y] as the best predictor of Y (Theorem 2.1.24).

2.3 MULTIVARIATE GENERALIZATIONS

As in Chapter 1, we conclude by sketching the generalizations of the concepts presented in this chapter to the multivariate case, with the goal of defining the CEF and BLP when we have more than one explanatory variable. We provide no examples and only one small proof in this section, as our goal is to illustrate that the concepts we have presented in detail in the bivariate case are easily extended. Essentially all omitted definitions, properties, and theorems can be generalized analogously.

The multivariate generalization of variance is the *covariance matrix* of a random vector.

Definition 2.3.1. *Covariance Matrix*
For a random vector $\mathbf{X}$ of length K, the *covariance matrix* $\mathrm{V}[\mathbf{X}]$ is a matrix whose $(k,k')^{\text{th}}$ entry is $\mathrm{Cov}[X_{[k]},X_{[k']}]$, $\forall i,j \in \{1,2,...,K\}$. That is,

$$\mathrm{V}[\mathbf{X}] = \begin{pmatrix} \mathrm{V}[X_{[1]}] & \mathrm{Cov}[X_{[1]},X_{[2]}] & \cdots & \mathrm{Cov}[X_{[1]},X_{[K]}] \\ \mathrm{Cov}[X_{[2]},X_{[1]}] & \mathrm{V}[X_{[2]}] & \cdots & \mathrm{Cov}[X_{[2]},X_{[K]}] \\ \vdots & \vdots & \ddots & \vdots \\ \mathrm{Cov}[X_{[K]},X_{[1]}] & \mathrm{Cov}[X_{[K]},X_{[2]}] & \cdots & \mathrm{V}[X_{[K]}] \end{pmatrix}.$$

Note that this is a symmetric matrix (because $\mathrm{Cov}[X_{[k]},X_{[k']}] = \mathrm{Cov}[X_{[k']},X_{[k]}]$, by Theorem 2.2.4, *Properties of Covariance*) and the diagonal entries are variances (because $\mathrm{Cov}[X_{[k]},X_{[k]}] = \mathrm{V}[X_{[k]}]$, again by Theorem 2.2.4). This will be how we describe the variability of the regression estimator in Section 4.2.

We can also state a multivariate version of the variance rule (Theorem 2.2.3).

Theorem 2.3.2. *Multivariate Variance Rule*
For random variables $X_{[1]}$, $X_{[2]}$, ..., $X_{[K]}$,

$$V\big[X_{[1]} + X_{[2]} + \cdots + X_{[K]}\big] = V\left[\sum_{k=1}^{K} X_{[k]}\right] = \sum_{k=1}^{K}\sum_{k'=1}^{K} \mathrm{Cov}\big[X_{[k]},X_{[k']}\big].$$

As in the bivariate case, note how this (not coincidentally) resembles the algebraic identity

$$(x_1 + x_2 + \ldots + x_n)^2 = \sum_{i=1}^{n} \sum_{j=1}^{n} x_i x_j.$$

Theorem 2.3.2 will be key to deriving the variance of the cluster sample mean (see Theorem 3.5.5).

Conditional expectations are defined almost identically in the multivariate case as in the bivariate case (Definition 2.2.10).

Definition 2.3.3. *Conditional Expectation (Multivariate Case)*
For discrete random variables $X_{[1]}$, $X_{[2]}$, ..., $X_{[K]}$, and Y with joint PMF f, the *conditional expectation* of Y given $\mathbf{X} = \mathbf{x}$ is

$$\mathrm{E}[Y|\mathbf{X} = \mathbf{x}] = \sum_{y} y f_{Y|\mathbf{X}}(y|\mathbf{x}), \forall \mathbf{x} \in \mathrm{Supp}[\mathbf{X}].$$

For jointly continuous random variables $X_{[1]}$, $X_{[2]}$, ..., $X_{[K]}$, and Y with joint PDF f, the *conditional expectation* of Y given $\mathbf{X} = \mathbf{x}$ is

$$\mathrm{E}[Y|\mathbf{X} = \mathbf{x}] = \int_{-\infty}^{\infty} y f_{Y|\mathbf{X}}(y|\mathbf{x}) dy, \forall \mathbf{x} \in \mathrm{Supp}[\mathbf{X}].$$

Similarly, the conditional expectation function is analogously defined.

Definition 2.3.4. *CEF (Multivariate Case)*
For random variables $X_{[1]}$, $X_{[2]}$, ..., $X_{[K]}$, and Y with joint PMF/PDF f, the *CEF* of Y given $\mathbf{X} = \mathbf{x}$ is

$$G_Y(\mathbf{x}) = \mathrm{E}[Y|\mathbf{X} = \mathbf{x}], \forall \mathbf{x} \in \mathrm{Supp}[\mathbf{X}].$$

As before, this definition is merely meant to emphasize that the CEF refers to the *function* that maps $\mathbf{x}$ to $\mathrm{E}[Y|\mathbf{X} = \mathbf{x}]$; in general, we will write $\mathrm{E}[Y|\mathbf{X} = \mathbf{x}]$ to denote the CEF. The same notational conventions noted in the bivariate case apply: $\mathrm{E}[Y|\mathbf{X}]$ denotes $G_Y(\mathbf{X})$, which is a function of the random vector $\mathbf{X}$; the conditional variance function is $H_Y(\mathbf{x}) = \mathrm{V}[Y|\mathbf{X} = \mathbf{x}]$, which is generally written as $\mathrm{V}[Y|\mathbf{X} = \mathbf{x}]$; and $\mathrm{V}[Y|\mathbf{X}]$ denotes $H_Y(\mathbf{X})$.

In the multivariate case, the CEF is still the best (minimum MSE) predictor of Y given $X_{[1]}$, $X_{[2]}$, ..., $X_{[K]}$. That is, suppose we knew the full joint CDF of $X_{[1]}$, $X_{[2]}$, ..., $X_{[K]}$, and Y, and then someone gave us a randomly drawn value of $(X_{[1]}, X_{[2]}, \ldots, X_{[K]})$. What would be the guess of Y that would have the lowest MSE? Formally, what function $g : \mathbb{R}^K \to \mathbb{R}$ minimizes $\mathrm{E}[(Y - g(X_{[1]}, X_{[2]}, \ldots, X_{[K]}))^2]$? Again, the answer is given by the CEF.

Theorem 2.3.5. *The CEF Is the Minimum MSE Predictor*
For random variables $X_{[1]}, X_{[2]}, ..., X_{[K]}$, and Y, the CEF, $\mathrm{E}[Y|\mathbf{X}]$, is the best (minimum MSE) predictor of Y given $\mathbf{X}$.

The proof is the same as in the bivariate case.

Finally, we can describe the BLP of Y given $X_{[1]}, X_{[2]}, ..., X_{[K]}$. As before, the BLP is the *linear* function that minimizes MSE.

Definition 2.3.6. *BLP (Multivariate Case)*
For random variables $X_{[1]}, X_{[2]}, ..., X_{[K]}$, and Y, the *best linear predictor* of Y given $\mathbf{X}$ (that is, the minimum MSE predictor of Y given $\mathbf{X}$ among functions of the form $g(\mathbf{X}) = b_0 + b_1X_{[1]} + b_2X_{[2]} ... + b_KX_{[K]}$) is $g(\mathbf{X}) = \beta_0 + \beta_1X_{[1]} + \beta_2X_{[2]} ... + \beta_KX_{[K]}$, where

$$(\beta_0, \beta_1, \beta_2, ..., \beta_K) = \underset{(b_0,b_1,b_2,...,b_K)\in\mathbb{R}^{K+1}}{\operatorname{argmin}} \mathrm{E}\left[\left(Y - \left(b_0 + b_1X_{[1]} + b_2X_{[2]} ... + b_KX_{[K]}\right)\right)^2\right].$$

That is, among functions of the form $g(\mathbf{X}) = b_0 + b_1X_{[1]} + ... + b_KX_{[K]}$, what function yields the best (minimum MSE) prediction of Y given $X_{[1]}, X_{[2]}, ..., X_{[K]}$? Formally, what values of $b_0, b_1, b_2, ..., b_K$ minimize $\mathrm{E}[(Y - (b_0 + b_1X_{[1]} + b_2X_{[2]} + ... + b_KX_{[K]}))^2]$? In the multivariate case, we no longer have the nice, simple formulas $\alpha = \mathrm{E}[Y] - \frac{\mathrm{Cov}[X,Y]}{\mathrm{V}[X]}\mathrm{E}[X]$ and $\beta = \frac{\mathrm{Cov}[X,Y]}{\mathrm{V}[X]}$ for the solution (Theorem 2.2.21). Instead, the full solution is most simply represented using matrix algebra. We shall return to this in Chapter 4.

The BLP has many of the same properties in the multivariate case that it had in the bivariate case. As before:

- The BLP is also the best linear approximation of the CEF; setting $(b_0, b_1, b_2, ..., b_K) = (\beta_0, \beta_1, \beta_2, ..., \beta_K)$ minimizes

$$\mathrm{E}\left[\left(\mathrm{E}[Y|\mathbf{X}] - \left(b_0 + b_1X_{[1]} + b_2X_{[2]} + ... + b_KX_{[K]}\right)\right)^2\right].$$

  The proof is obtained by the same means as above.
- If the CEF is linear, then the CEF is the BLP.

One remarkable feature of the BLP is that it facilitates easy interpretation. The first coefficient, β_0, is the intercept (sometimes known as the constant), and represents the value the BLP would take on if all the variables were held at zero; that is, $g(0,0,...,0) = \beta_0$. To see this, we need only note that $g(0,0,...,0) = \beta_0 + \beta_1 \cdot 0 + \beta_2 \cdot 0 + ... + \beta_K \cdot 0 = \beta_0$.

The remaining coefficients of the BLP represent partial derivatives. For example, β_1 represents how much the BLP of Y would change if we moved one unit on $X_{[1]}$, holding all else equal. This can be demonstrated by considering a set of arbitrary values $(x_{[1]}, x_{[2]}, ..., x_{[K]})$, so that $g(x_{[1]}, x_{[2]}, ..., x_{[K]}) = \beta_0 + \beta_1 x_{[1]} + \beta_2 x_{[2]} ... + \beta_K x_{[k]}$, and $g(x_{[1]} + 1, x_{[2]}, ..., x_{[K]}) = \beta_0 + \beta_1(x_{[1]} + 1) + \beta_2 x_{[2]} ... + \beta_K x_{[k]}$. Therefore, $g(x_{[1]} + 1, x_{[2]}, ..., x_{[K]}) - g(x_{[1]}, x_{[2]}, ..., x_{[K]}) = \beta_1$.

In other words, β_1 is the slope of the BLP with respect to $X_{[1]}$, *conditional* on the values of all the other variables. If we held $X_{[2]}$, $X_{[3]}$, ..., $X_{[K]}$ fixed at some numbers, then how would the BLP change by moving $X_{[1]}$ by one? The same intuition holds for β_2, β_3, and so on. We formalize this in the following theorem.

Theorem 2.3.7. *Coefficients of the BLP Are Partial Derivatives*
For random variables $X_{[1]}$, $X_{[2]}$, ..., $X_{[K]}$, and Y, if $g(\mathbf{X})$ is the best linear predictor of Y given $\mathbf{X}$, then $\forall k \in \{1, 2, ..., K\}$,

$$\beta_k = \frac{\partial g(\mathbf{X})}{\partial X_{[k]}}.$$

Proof: This follows immediately from linearity:

$$\frac{\partial g\left(X_{[1]}, X_{[2]}, ..., X_{[K]}\right)}{\partial X_{[k]}} = \frac{\partial\left(\beta_0 + \beta_1 X_{[1]} + \beta_2 X_{[2]} + ... \beta_K X_{[K]}\right)}{\partial X_{[k]}} = \beta_k. \quad \square$$

When the CEF is well approximated by the BLP, these properties of the BLP afford us a simple way of describing features of the CEF.

Finally, we can state the multivariate generalization of Theorem 2.2.22 (*Properties of Deviations from the BLP*).

Theorem 2.3.8. *Properties of Deviations from the BLP (Multivariate Case)*
For random variables $X_{[1]}$, $X_{[2]}$, ..., $X_{[K]}$, and Y, if $g(\mathbf{X})$ is the best linear predictor of Y given $\mathbf{X}$ and $\varepsilon = Y - g(\mathbf{X})$, then

- $\mathrm{E}[\varepsilon] = 0$.
- $\forall k \in \{1, 2, ..., K\}$, $\mathrm{E}\left[X_{[k]}\varepsilon\right] = 0$.
- $\forall k \in \{1, 2, ..., K\}$, $\mathrm{Cov}\left[X_{[k]}, \varepsilon\right] = 0$.

In Chapter 4, we will see that regression has analogous properties (Theorem 4.1.5, *Properties of Residuals from the OLS Regression Estimator*).

2.4 FURTHER READINGS

The further readings listed in Chapter 1 remain relevant here. Beyond these, we highly recommend Goldberger (1991) and Hansen (2013), which served as key inspiration for our discussion of the topics in Chapter 2. In particular, readers well versed in linear algebra may appreciate Hansen's representation of the BLP using projections. Angrist and Pischke (2009) also contains a concise but highly readable treatment of the topics here.

PART II

STATISTICS

3

Learning from Random Samples

Ignorance gives one a large range of probabilities.

—George Eliot

In Part I, we introduced the concept of random variables, and discussed their properties as a theoretical construct in the context of probability theory. Having established these fundamental concepts, in this chapter, we turn from mathematical probability theory to a canonical motivation of statistics: learning about features of *populations* through random sampling. We first consider the *independent and identically distributed (i.i.d.)* assumption and its ties to random sampling from a population (Section 3.1).

The i.i.d. assumption, if imposed, provides us with a great deal of inferential leverage. We demonstrate how we can estimate features of a random variable and, therefore, features of the population that gives rise to it under random sampling. We pay particular attention to the operating characteristics of estimators as the number of observations grows large (Section 3.2). Furthermore, we show how our degree of uncertainty about these estimates can *itself* be estimated by the same means, and that we can sometimes make probabilistic statements about the statistical uncertainty of a result (Section 3.4). Finally, we consider estimation and uncertainty when there is dependence in the data that can be characterized by discrete clusters (Section 3.5).

3.1 I.I.D. RANDOM VARIABLES

Our treatment of estimation in this book is based on the assumption that the researcher's data consist of *i.i.d.* observations of random variables or vectors. We begin with a formal definition.

Definition 3.1.1. *Independent and Identically Distributed (I.I.D.)*
Let X_1, X_2, ..., X_n be random variables with CDFs F_1, F_2, ..., F_n, respectively. Let F_A denote the joint CDF of the random variables with indices in the set A. Then X_1, X_2, ..., X_n are *independent and identically distributed* if they satisfy the following:

- Mutually independent: $\forall A \subseteq \{1,2,...,n\}$, $\forall (x_1,x_2,...,x_n) \in \mathbb{R}^n$, $F_A\big((x_i)_{i \in A}\big) = \prod_{i \in A} F_i(x_i)$.[1]
- Identically distributed: $\forall i,j \in \{1,2,...,n\}$ and $\forall x \in \mathbb{R}$, $F_i(x) = F_j(x)$.

In other words, we take a draw of the random variable X. Then we take another draw of X in such a manner that our second draw does not depend on the outcome of the first. We repeat this process until we have n draws. So, we have n identical random variables that generate n values. We can subscript each of these n random variables, as shown above, as well as aggregate them to form the random vector $\mathbf{X} = (X_1,...,X_n)^T$.[2] Under the assumption of i.i.d. sampling from X, the collection of values that we see are assumed to be produced by an identical random process. When we have i.i.d. random variables X_1, X_2, ..., X_n, we use the unsubscripted letter X to denote the random variable whose distribution the i.i.d. draws all share. So, for example, $\mathrm{E}[X]$ denotes the expected value common to X_1, X_2, ..., X_n, that is, $\mathrm{E}[X] = \mathrm{E}[X_1] = \mathrm{E}[X_2] = ... = \mathrm{E}[X_n]$.[3]

3.1.1 Random Sampling

We proceed by considering a canonical motivation for the i.i.d. representation of uncertainty: tying the features of random variables to analogous features of populations through the process of *random sampling*. Suppose we have a *finite population* U consisting of N units, indexed $i = 1,2,...N$. The units of analysis may be, for example, people, villages, or countries. Associated with each unit i is a response x_i.[4] We can describe the *finite population mass function*[5] for the responses associated with the finite population U.

1 Mutual independence implies that all observations are pairwise independent: $\forall i \neq j$, $X_i \perp\!\!\!\perp X_j$, but the converse does not generally hold.

2 We are expressing the random vector induced by random sampling as a column vector to clarify that each row represents a separate observation. Later, when we address i.i.d. draws of a random vector, this notational distinction will be helpful.

3 We will sometimes use subscripted variables inside the operator (for example, $\mathrm{E}[X_i]$) when this notation improves clarity.

4 Nothing changes when we have *two* or more features associated with each unit. Suppose we had an ordered pair (x_i, y_i) associated with each unit i. When we randomly draw unit i, we observe and record both values in the pair.

5 This is not a standard term in statistics.

Definition 3.1.2. *Finite Population Mass Function*
Given a finite population U with responses x_1, x_2, ..., x_N, the *finite population mass function*,

$$f_{FP}(x) = \frac{1}{N}\sum_{i=1}^{N} \mathrm{I}(x_i = x).$$

That is, $f_{FP}(x)$ is the proportion of units in U that have $x_i = x$. Let $\mathcal{X}$ denote the set of unique values of x_i, that is, $\mathcal{X} = \{x \in \mathbb{R} : f_{FP}(x) > 0\}$. Let μ denote the population mean of U:

$$\mu = \frac{1}{N}\sum_{i=1}^{N} x_i = \sum_{x\in\mathcal{X}} x f_{FP}(x),$$

and let σ^2 denote the population variance of U:

$$\sigma^2 = \frac{1}{N}\sum_{i=1}^{N}(x_i - \mu)^2 = \sum_{x\in\mathcal{X}}(x-\mu)^2 f_{FP}(x).$$

It will be helpful to have a concrete example to ground these ideas.

Example 3.1.3. *Finite Population Random Sampling* Suppose we have a finite population U consisting of $N = 4$ units. Let $x_1 = 3$, $x_2 = 4$, $x_3 = 3$, and $x_4 = 10$. Then

- $\mathcal{X} = \{3, 4, 10\}$.
- $\mu = \frac{1}{4}(3 + 4 + 3 + 10) = 5$.
- $\sigma^2 = \frac{1}{4}(4 + 1 + 4 + 25) = \frac{17}{2}$.
- $f_{FP}(-1) = 0$.
- $f_{FP}(3) = \frac{1}{2}$.
- $f_{FP}(4) = \frac{1}{4}$.
- $f_{FP}(10) = \frac{1}{4}$.
- $f_{FP}(24603) = 0$.
- $\forall x \notin \{3, 4, 10\}$, $f_{FP}(x) = 0$.

Let us consider a random generative process that selects one unit from U at random (with all units having equal probability of being selected). Let the random variable X take on the value of x_i associated with the unit selected.[6] Each unit is selected with probability $\frac{1}{4}$, so we get $X = 3$ with probability $\frac{2}{4} = \frac{1}{2}$, $X = 4$ with probability $\frac{1}{4}$, and $X = 10$ with probability $\frac{1}{4}$. Note that this is simply a probability mass function. Under random sampling, the distribution

[6] Formally, $\Omega = \{1, 2, 3, 4\}$; $P(\omega) = \frac{1}{4}$, $\forall \omega \in \Omega$; and $X(\omega) = x_\omega$, $\forall \omega \in \Omega$.

of outcomes in the population entirely determines the probability distribution of the random variable. The PMF of X *is* the finite population mass function: $f(x) = f_{FP}(x)$, $\forall x \in \mathbb{R}$, and $\mathcal{X} = \text{Supp}[X]$. Thus,

- $\text{E}[X] = \sum_x x f(x) = \sum_{x \in \mathcal{X}} x f_{FP}(x) = \mu = 5$.
- $\text{V}[X] = \text{E}\Big[\big(x - \text{E}[X]\big)\Big] = \sum_x \big(x - \text{E}[X]\big)^2 f(x) = \sum_{x \in \mathcal{X}} (x - \mu)^2 f_{FP}(x) = \sigma^2 = \frac{17}{2}$. △

So, under random sampling from U,

- $\text{E}[X]$ is the *population mean*, that is, the average of all the x_is.
- $\text{V}[X]$ is the *population variance*, that is, the average squared deviation from the mean of all the x_is.

This allows us to cleanly identify the target of inquiry with respect to a particular set of N units. Consider two types of sampling schemes. The first is "with replacement" sampling: we "return" each unit after we draw it, so that the act of taking a draw does not change the population (and hence the population distribution). Thus, every draw is taken from the same distribution, independently and with its distribution governed by f_{FP}. In the case of "without replacement" sampling from a population, we can only observe each unit once and each draw affects the remaining population. However, if our population is sufficiently large, removing a single unit or a few units changes the distribution of the remaining units by a negligible amount. For example, suppose we had a population of 1,000,000 marbles consisting of 500,000 black marbles and 500,000 white marbles. Suppose we sample n marbles without replacement. Let $X_i = 0$ if marble i in our sample is black and $X_i = 1$ if marble i is white. Then $\Pr[X_2 = 1] = \frac{500{,}000}{1{,}000{,}000} = 0.5$ and $\Pr[X_2 = 1 | X_1 = 1] = \frac{499{,}999}{999{,}999} \approx 0.5$. Similarly, the probability that marble n is black is approximately 0.5 regardless of the colors of marbles 1 through $n - 1$, as long as n is a very small fraction of 1,000,000. Some technical finesse is required to formalize this intuition (e.g., Dubins and Freedman 1979), but it implies that sampling units at random from a hypothetical, infinite *superpopulation* yields data that can be treated as i.i.d.

3.1.2 I.I.D. as Approximation

The i.i.d. assumption need not reflect the manner in which social scientific data are collected in order for it to be a useful approximation. A literal interpretation of the above section as a motivation for the i.i.d. assumption would leave us with only very limited applications for statistical inference. However, for arguments to proceed, frameworks must be set, and the i.i.d. assumption provides one fairly minimal way to do so. The communication of empirical findings often requires some way in which frameworks for inference can be well defined. Accordingly, the superpopulation model can be viewed as a codification of uncertainty about generalizability to broader populations, through the above analogy of random sampling.[7]

The plausibility of the i.i.d. assumption as an approximation depends largely on two elements, namely that the data are approximately *independent* and also approximately *identically distributed*. We first consider settings where the data may not be independent. That is, there may be sources of dependence between units: for example, units 1 and 2 might be intertwined (because they are, say, members of the same household) and so the assumption that $Y_1 \perp\!\!\!\perp Y_2$ would not be a reasonable way to characterize the units under study. In such settings, approaches that erroneously assume the i.i.d. assumption will not generally yield valid inferences. But, assuming that this dependence is not too great between units (loosely speaking, there is relevant information added by new units as we grow in n), then our results will largely carry through—with the caveat that we will be likely to understate uncertainty. Section 3.5 considers one special case, the case where dependence can be represented by discrete clusters, and illustrates some of the consequences of such clustering.

Similarly, we might worry that the data are not identically distributed. When this occurs, the ith observation may have a different distribution than the jth observation. This occurs, for example, when observations are collected over time, and there are changes to the population under study over time. (For example, if collecting survey evidence, opinions may change over time.) In such cases, we are no longer able to neatly describe the distribution of each random variable in terms of a single population distribution. As a statistical matter, most of our results in this chapter will carry through with little modification even if we assume independent but *not* identically distributed data. The primary consequence will lie with interpretation. Instead of being able to make clean statements about features of a single population, our statements are instead about a *pseudopopulation* that aggregates over the different distributions associated with each unit. However, this aggregate pseudopopulation is a moving target, and our statistical claims are circumscribed accordingly. When the data are not identically distributed, predictions for the $(n+1)^{\text{th}}$ unit

[7] Though we do not fully endorse its contents, we are fond of the following quotation from Angrist (2013):

> Some would say all data come from "super-populations," that is, the data we happen to have could have come from other times, other places, or other people, even if we seem to [observe] everyone from a particular scenario. Others take a model-based approach: some kind of stochastic process generates the data at hand; there is always more where they came from. Finally, an approach known as randomization inference recognizes that even in finite populations, counterfactuals remain hidden, and therefore we always require inference. You could spend your life pondering such things. I have to admit I try not to.

generated using the first n units have few guarantees. But as a means for making statements about a (pseudo)population that the data at hand represent, the i.i.d. assumption may nevertheless be a suitable approximation.

3.2 ESTIMATION

If we observed just one draw of a random variable X, we probably could not learn too much about its distribution. Unless X had no variance, any guess about a feature of its distribution (such as its CDF or expected value) would be subject to a great deal of chance variability. We would not be able to *estimate* a feature of the distribution of X with much reliability.

But what if we observed multiple draws of a random variable? As our sample, or collection of observations from the same random variable X, grows larger and larger, we are able to estimate the features of X with more and more precision. We begin here with a rather general definition of a way to summarize the observed data. A *sample statistic* summarizes the values of X_1, X_2, ..., X_n.

Definition 3.2.1. *Sample Statistic*
For i.i.d. random variables X_1, X_2, ..., X_n, a *sample statistic* is a function of X_1, X_2, ..., X_n:

$$T_{(n)} = h_{(n)}(X_1, X_2, ..., X_n),$$

where $h_{(n)} : \mathbb{R}^n \to \mathbb{R}$, $\forall n \in \mathbb{N}$.

Importantly, since a sample statistic is a function of the random variables X_1, X_2, ..., X_n, it is therefore *itself* a random variable. Furthermore, a sample statistic defines a sequence of random variables indexed by the sample size n. (We use parenthetic subscripts to index elements of a sequence, though we often drop the subscript when discussing sample statistics.) This will be important when we discuss the behavior of sample statistics as $n \to \infty$.

3.2.1 Sample Means

We will now focus on the properties of one foundational sample statistic: the sample mean. As we will see in the following sections, many of the intuitions in the case of the sample mean will generalize to other sample statistics. The sample mean of n draws from X can be viewed as an approximation of $\mathrm{E}[X]$. It is the average of all the observed values of X.

Definition 3.2.2. *Sample Mean*
For i.i.d. random variables $X_1, X_2, ..., X_n$, the *sample mean* is

$$\overline{X} = \frac{X_1 + X_2 + ... + X_n}{n} = \frac{1}{n}\sum_{i=1}^{n} X_i.$$

Keep in mind that the sample mean is a sample statistic and thus is itself a random variable. Depending on the outcomes of the random variables $X_1, X_2, ..., X_n$, $\overline{X}$ will take on different values.

We now derive some important properties of $\overline{X}$. First, we will show that the sample mean tends to approximate the population mean, in the sense that "on average" (across hypothetical realizations of the values of $X_1, X_2, ..., X_n$) the value of $\overline{X}$ is $E[X]$.

Theorem 3.2.3. *The Expected Value of the Sample Mean Is the Population Mean*
For i.i.d. random variables $X_1, X_2, ..., X_n$,

$$E\left[\overline{X}\right] = E[X].$$

Proof:

$$\begin{aligned}
E\left[\overline{X}\right] &= E\left[\frac{1}{n}(X_1 + X_2 + ... + X_n)\right] \\
&= \frac{1}{n}E[X_1 + X_2 + ... + X_n] \\
&= \frac{1}{n}\left(E[X_1] + E[X_2] + ... + E[X_n]\right) \\
&= \frac{1}{n}\left(E[X] + E[X] + ... + E[X]\right) \\
&= \frac{1}{n}nE[X] \\
&= E[X]. \quad \square
\end{aligned}$$

As $\overline{X}$ is a random variable, we can describe other features of its distribution. The variance of $\overline{X}$ is known as the *sampling variance* of the sample mean. Much as the variance characterizes the variability of a random variable X, the sampling variance of the sample mean characterizes how much variability we can expect in the sample mean across hypothetical draws of n observations.

Theorem 3.2.4. *Sampling Variance of the Sample Mean*
For i.i.d. random variables $X_1, X_2, \ldots, X_n$ with finite variance $\mathrm{V}[X]$, the *sampling variance* of $\overline{X}$ is

$$\mathrm{V}\left[\overline{X}\right] = \frac{\mathrm{V}[X]}{n}.$$

Proof:

$$\begin{aligned}
\mathrm{V}\left[\overline{X}\right] &= \mathrm{V}\left[\frac{1}{n}(X_1 + X_2 + \ldots + X_n)\right] \\
&= \frac{1}{n^2}\mathrm{V}[X_1 + X_2 + \ldots + X_n] \\
&= \frac{1}{n^2}\big(\mathrm{V}[X_1] + \mathrm{V}[X_2] + \ldots + \mathrm{V}[X_n]\big) \\
&= \frac{1}{n^2}\big(\mathrm{V}[X] + \mathrm{V}[X] + \ldots + \mathrm{V}[X]\big) \\
&= \frac{1}{n^2}n\mathrm{V}[X] \\
&= \frac{\mathrm{V}[X]}{n}. \quad \square
\end{aligned}$$

Notice that the sampling variance $\mathrm{V}[\overline{X}]$ decreases as n increases. This fact, along with Theorem 3.2.3, underlies an important result that we will present shortly. First, however, we must establish the following theorem, which bounds the probability that the sample mean is far from the population mean.

Theorem 3.2.5. *Chebyshev's Inequality for the Sample Mean*
Let $X_1, X_2, \ldots, X_n$ be i.i.d. random variables with finite variance $\mathrm{V}[X] > 0$. Then, $\forall \epsilon > 0$,

$$\Pr\left[\left|\overline{X} - \mathrm{E}[X]\right| \geq \epsilon\right] \leq \frac{\mathrm{V}[X]}{\epsilon^2 n}.$$

Proof: This follows directly from the previous two theorems and Chebyshev's Inequality (Theorem 2.1.18). Let $\epsilon > 0$ and let $\epsilon' = \frac{\epsilon}{\sigma[\overline{X}]}$, so that $\epsilon = \epsilon'\sigma[\overline{X}]$. Then

$$\begin{aligned}
\Pr\left[\left|\overline{X} - \mathrm{E}[X]\right| \geq \epsilon\right] &= \Pr\left[\left|\overline{X} - \mathrm{E}[\overline{X}]\right| \geq \epsilon'\sigma[\overline{X}]\right] \\
&\leq \frac{1}{\epsilon'^2} \\
&= \frac{\sigma[\overline{X}]^2}{\epsilon^2}
\end{aligned}$$

$$= \frac{V[\overline{X}]}{\epsilon^2}$$

$$= \frac{V[X]}{\epsilon^2 n}. \square$$

Theorem 3.2.5 will allow us to prove a crucial theorem in statistics, the *Weak Law of Large Numbers (WLLN)*. To state the WLLN concisely, we will also require the following definition.

Definition 3.2.6. *Convergence in Probability*
Let $(T_{(1)}, T_{(2)}, T_{(3)}, ...)$ be a sequence of random variables and let $c \in \mathbb{R}$. Then $T_{(n)}$ *converges in probability* to c if, $\forall \epsilon > 0$,

$$\lim_{n \to \infty} \Pr\Big[\big| T_{(n)} - c \big| \geq \epsilon \Big] = 0,$$

or equivalently,[8]

$$\lim_{n \to \infty} \Pr\Big[\big| T_{(n)} - c \big| < \epsilon \Big] = 1.$$

We write $T_{(n)} \xrightarrow{p} c$ to denote that $T_{(n)}$ converges in probability to c.[9]

The value c to which a sequence of random variables $T_{(n)}$ converges in probability is referred to as the *probability limit* of $T_{(n)}$. Saying that $T_{(n)}$ converges in probability to c means that as n gets large, it becomes increasingly likely that $T_{(n)}$ will be "close" to c. More specifically, for any $p \in [0,1]$ and any $\epsilon > 0$, there is always an N large enough that, for every $n \geq N$, the probability that $T_{(n)}$ will be within ϵ of c is at least p. As $n \to \infty$, it becomes extremely likely that $T_{(n)}$ will be extremely close to c. This definition can apply to any sequence of random variables, but we use $T_{(n)}$ suggestively, as we will generally discuss convergence in probability of sample statistics.

We briefly digress here to note that convergence in probability of a sequence $T_{(n)}$ implies that any continuous function of $T_{(n)}$ (and potentially other sequences that converge in probability) itself converges in probability to the

[8] The equivalence follows from the complement rule (see Theorem 1.1.4, *Basic Properties of Probability*):

$$\lim_{n \to \infty} \Pr\Big[\big| T_{(n)} - c \big| < \epsilon \Big] = \lim_{n \to \infty} \Big(1 - \Pr\Big[\big| T_{(n)} - c \big| \geq \epsilon \Big] \Big) = 1 - \lim_{n \to \infty} \Pr\Big[\big| T_{(n)} - c \big| \geq \epsilon \Big],$$

so

$$\lim_{n \to \infty} \Pr\Big[\big| T_{(n)} - c \big| \geq \epsilon \Big] = 0 \iff \lim_{n \to \infty} \Pr\Big[\big| T_{(n)} - c \big| < \epsilon \Big] = 1.$$

[9] A more general definition allows for $T_{(n)}$ to converge in probability to a random variable T: for a sequence of random variables $(T_{(1)}, T_{(2)}, T_{(3)}, ...)$ and a random variable T, $T_{(n)} \xrightarrow{p} T$ if $\forall \epsilon > 0$, $\lim_{n \to \infty} \Pr[|T_{(n)} - T| \geq \epsilon] = 0$.

value of the function at the probability limit(s). This result is known as the *Continuous Mapping Theorem (CMT)*, which we state without proof.

Theorem 3.2.7. *Continuous Mapping Theorem (CMT)*
Let $(S_{(1)}, S_{(2)}, S_{(3)}, \ldots)$ and $(T_{(1)}, T_{(2)}, T_{(3)}, \ldots)$ be sequences of random variables. Let $g : \mathbb{R}^2 \to \mathbb{R}$ be a continuous function and let $a, b \in \mathbb{R}$. If $S_{(n)} \xrightarrow{p} a$ and $T_{(n)} \xrightarrow{p} b$, then $g(S_{(n)}, T_{(n)}) \xrightarrow{p} g(a,b)$.

The CMT says that continuous functions preserve convergence in probability. Although Theorem 3.2.7 states the CMT for the case of functions of two random variables, it also applies to functions of a single random variable and functions of more than two random variables. While we will not be using it immediately, the CMT will be useful when we seek to generalize to sample statistics other than the sample mean, and we will invoke it frequently in proofs.

With our definition of convergence in probability, we can now state the Weak Law of Large Numbers.

Theorem 3.2.8. *Weak Law of Large Numbers (WLLN)*
Let X_1, X_2, ..., X_n be i.i.d. random variables with finite variance $V[X] > 0$,[10] and let $\overline{X}_{(n)} = \frac{1}{n}\sum_{i=1}^{n} X_i$. Then

$$\overline{X}_{(n)} \xrightarrow{p} E[X].$$

Proof: By non-negativity of probability and Theorem 3.2.5, $\forall \epsilon > 0$,

$$0 \le \Pr\Big[\,\big|\overline{X}_{(n)} - E[X]\big| \ge \epsilon\Big] \le \frac{V[X]}{\epsilon^2 n},$$

and

$$\lim_{n\to\infty} 0 = \lim_{n\to\infty} \frac{V[X]}{\epsilon^2 n} = 0,$$

so by the Squeeze Theorem for Sequences,[11]

$$\lim_{n\to\infty} \Pr\Big[\,\big|\overline{X}_{(n)} - E[X]\big| \ge \epsilon\Big] = 0. \ \square$$

10 Note that if $V[X] = 0$, the result follows trivially.

11 Squeeze Theorem for Sequences: if $\lim_{n\to\infty} b_{(n)} = \lim_{n\to\infty} c_{(n)} = L$ and there exists an integer N such that $\forall n \ge N$, $b_{(n)} \le a_{(n)} \le c_{(n)}$, then $\lim_{n\to\infty} a_{(n)} = L$.

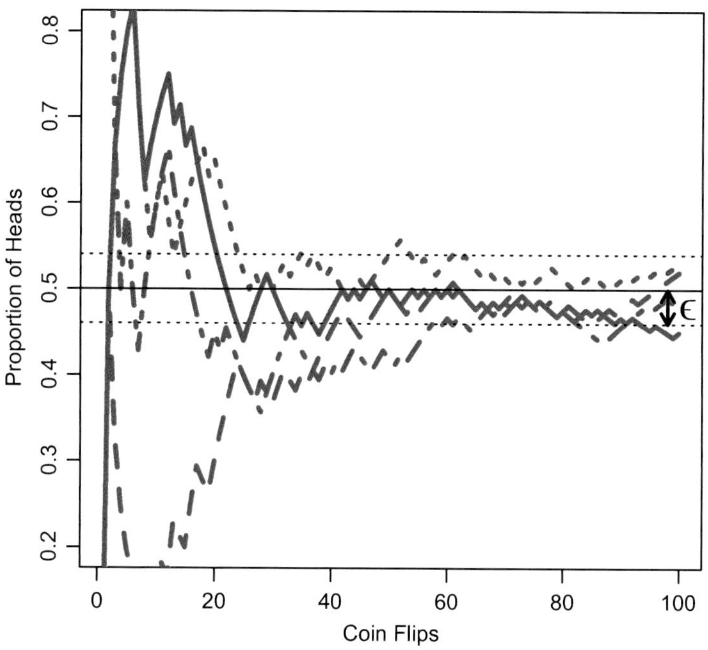

FIGURE 3.2.1. *Weak Law of Large Numbers*

The WLLN is a profound result: as n gets large, the sample mean $\overline{X}$ becomes increasingly likely to approximate E[X] to any arbitrary degree of precision. That is, with a large enough sample, the probability that the sample mean will be far from the population mean will be negligible. (Again, for notational simplicity, we will drop the parenthetic subscript on sample statistics, even when discussing their properties as $n \to \infty$. For example, we will write $\overline{X} \xrightarrow{p} \mathrm{E}[X]$.)

Figure 3.2.1 shows a graphical representation of the WLLN. Each curve in the figure shows the running proportion of heads for a simulated sequence of coin flips. Notice how the cumulative proportion of heads tends to get closer and closer to 0.5. Indeed, for any given distance ϵ from 0.5 (represented by the horizontal dotted lines), there is some number of coin tosses after which it would be virtually certain that the running proportion of heads would be within ϵ of 0.5.

The generality of the WLLN is illustrated in the following theorem, which shows how the sample mean can be used to estimate the CDF at any point. Given that the CDF characterizes everything about the distribution of a random variable (Section 1.2.3, *Cumulative Distribution Functions*), this result is profound. It will also serve as the basis for our general discussion of plug-in estimation in Section 3.3 (*The Plug-In Principle*).

Theorem 3.2.9. *Estimating the CDF*
Let $X_1, X_2, ..., X_n$ be i.i.d. random variables with common CDF F. Let $x \in \mathbb{R}$ and let $Z_i = \mathrm{I}(X_i \leq x)$, $\forall i \in \{1,2,...,n\}$, where $\mathrm{I}(\cdot)$ is the *indicator function*, that is, it takes the value one if its argument is true and zero if it is false.[12] Then

$$\overline{Z} \xrightarrow{p} F(x).$$

Proof: By a generalization of Theorem 1.3.17 (*Implications of Independence, Part I*), $Z_1, Z_2, ..., Z_n$ are i.i.d. random variables with common PMF

$$f_Z(z) = \begin{cases} \Pr[X \leq x] & : \quad z = 1 \\ \Pr[X > x] & : \quad z = 0 \\ 0 & : \quad \text{otherwise.} \end{cases}$$

So, by the definition of the expected value,

$$\mathrm{E}[Z] = \sum_z z f_Z(z) = 1 \cdot \Pr[X \leq x] + 0 \cdot \Pr[X > x] = \Pr[X \leq x] = F(x).$$

Thus, by the WLLN, [13]

$$\overline{Z} \xrightarrow{p} \mathrm{E}[Z] = F(x). \quad \square$$

Note that we could apply this theorem for any or every value of x. Thus, given a sufficient number of observations, we can always approximate the value of the CDF at any point to arbitrary precision. If n is very large, the probability that we are far off from the true value of $F(x)$ is very small.[14] So, since the CDF tells us everything about a random variable, this means that we can estimate features of a random variable to arbitrary precision, given large enough n. We show how this works more generally in Section 3.3, *The Plug-In Principle*. First, though, we must define the general notion of an estimator.

3.2.2 Estimation Theory

Suppose there is some feature θ associated with random variable X. For example, θ could be the expected value of X, $\mathrm{E}[X]$, or it could be something entirely odd, like $\mathrm{V}[(X - \mathrm{E}[X]^3)^2]$. As usual, we observe a sample of n i.i.d. draws of X,

12 Note that for any random variable X, $\forall D \in \mathbb{R}$, $\mathrm{E}[\mathrm{I}(X \in D)] = \Pr[X \in D]$.

13 Technically, if $\Pr[X \leq x] = 0$ or 1, then Z is a degenerate random variable, so $\mathrm{V}[Z] = 0$ and the WLLN is not applicable. But in this case, the result holds trivially. Otherwise, Z has finite $\mathrm{E}[Z]$ and finite $\mathrm{V}[Z] > 0$, so the WLLN applies.

14 Stronger results are possible under weaker assumptions, namely the Strong Law of Large Numbers and the Glivenko–Cantelli Theorem.

which is equivalent to a single draw of the random vector $\mathbf{X} = (X_1, X_2, ..., X_n)^T$. An *estimator* of θ is a random variable $\hat{\theta} = h(\mathbf{X}) = h(X_1, X_2, ..., X_n)$, and the value it takes on is called an *estimate*.[15] Thus, formally, an estimator is nothing more than a sample statistic (see Definition 3.2.1). But we would not refer to just any sample statistic as an estimator. We reserve the term for sample statistics that, in some sense, provide "good" estimates of some population feature θ.

One property often considered to make an estimator "good" is unbiasedness.

Definition 3.2.10. *Unbiasedness*
An estimator $\hat{\theta}$ is *unbiased* for θ if $\mathrm{E}[\hat{\theta}] = \theta$.

An unbiased estimator gets the right answer "on average." Theorem 3.2.3, *The Expected Value of the Sample Mean Is the Population Mean*, can thus be stated as follows: "The sample mean is unbiased for the population mean."

An estimator that is not unbiased is, as one might expect, referred to as *biased*. We can quantify the bias of an estimator as follows:

Definition 3.2.11. *Bias of an Estimator*
For an estimator $\hat{\theta}$, the *bias* of $\hat{\theta}$ in estimating θ is $\mathrm{E}[\hat{\theta}] - \theta$.

The bias tells us the difference between the "average" value of the estimator and the true value of θ. An unbiased estimator, naturally, has bias equal to zero. Unbiasedness is a good property for an estimator to have, though it is less important than it might initially seem. Unbiasedness alone says little about how well we can expect $\hat{\theta}$ to approximate θ. It does not guarantee that our estimate will usually, or even ever, come close to the true value.[16]

Our usual definitions that allow us to characterize random variables also allow to us to characterize the distributions of estimators. (This, of course, is because estimators are themselves random variables.) Some of these properties

[15] For some estimators that we will consider, there may be some positive probability that X_1, X_2, ..., X_n take on values such that $h(\mathbf{X}) = \frac{0}{0}$. In such cases, we will implicitly assume that when this happens, the estimator takes on the value of zero. For well-behaved estimators, this will occur with vanishingly small probability as n grows large.

[16] The fixation on bias of many statisticians results in the following joke (a slightly modified version of Riesbeck N.d., itself a variation on an old joke among statisticians):

> A physicist, an engineer, and a statistician are out hunting. Suddenly, a deer appears 50 yards away. The physicist does some basic ballistic calculations, assuming a vacuum, lifts her rifle to a specific angle, and shoots. The bullet lands 5 yards short. The engineer adds a fudge factor for air resistance, lifts his rifle slightly higher, and shoots. The bullet lands 5 yards long. The statistician yells, "We got 'em!"

have special names in the context of estimators. For example, the variance of an estimator is called the *sampling variance*.

Definition 3.2.12. *Sampling Variance of an Estimator*
For an estimator $\hat{\theta}$, the *sampling variance* of $\hat{\theta}$ is $\mathrm{V}[\hat{\theta}]$.

For example, as in Theorem 3.2.4, we would say that the sampling variance of the sample mean $\overline{X}$ is $\frac{\mathrm{V}[X]}{n}$. The standard deviation of an estimator is similarly important enough to merit its own name: the *standard error*.

Definition 3.2.13. *Standard Error of an Estimator*
For an estimator $\hat{\theta}$, the *standard error* of $\hat{\theta}$ is $\sigma[\hat{\theta}]$.

The standard error has great utility as a metric of variability, and will be central to how we make statistical *inferences* (Section 3.4). Another similarly foundational concept is the *mean squared error (MSE)* of an estimator, or simply the mean squared error of $\hat{\theta}$ about θ.

Definition 3.2.14. *MSE of an Estimator*
For an estimator $\hat{\theta}$, the *mean squared error (MSE)* of $\hat{\theta}$ in estimating θ is $\mathrm{E}\left[(\hat{\theta}-\theta)^2\right]$.

Attentive readers may notice that we have already defined MSE in Section 2.1.3. Indeed, this is the same MSE that we defined it in Definition 2.1.22, just applied to estimators. The MSE of an estimator is the expected squared deviation of the estimate from the true value. As before, we can also write MSE in an alternative form.

Theorem 3.2.15. *Alternative Formula for the MSE of an Estimator*
For an estimator $\hat{\theta}$,

$$\mathrm{E}\left[(\hat{\theta}-\theta)^2\right] = \mathrm{V}[\hat{\theta}] + \left(\mathrm{E}[\hat{\theta}]-\theta\right)^2.$$

Proof: This follows directly from Theorem 2.1.23. □

We can describe the meaning of this formula in words: the MSE of an estimator is equal to its sampling variance plus the square of its bias. We can thus see why unbiasedness alone is insufficient to ensure that an estimator is sensible: an estimator with zero bias but large sampling variance may often, or even always, be very far off from the true value of θ. All else equal, we prefer estimators with a lower MSE, as that implies that our estimates are better approximations. An estimator that has a lower MSE than another is said to be more *efficient*.

Definition 3.2.16. *Relative Efficiency*
Let $\hat{\theta}_A$ and $\hat{\theta}_B$ be estimators of θ. Then $\hat{\theta}_A$ is *more efficient* than $\hat{\theta}_B$ if it has a lower MSE.

We will not explicitly consider efficiency too much in this book, though we may occasionally make reference to the efficiency of one estimator relative to another; these comparisons allow us to evaluate the suitability of estimators for a given problem.

Note that the above properties all implicitly assume some finite sample size n. We can also describe the *asymptotic* properties of an estimator, that is, the properties of $\hat{\theta}$ as $n \to \infty$. The simplest and perhaps most essential of these properties is *consistency*.

Definition 3.2.17. *Consistency*
An estimator $\hat{\theta}$ is *consistent* for θ if $\hat{\theta} \xrightarrow{p} \theta$.

Consistency is a simple notion: if we had enough data, the probability that our estimate $\hat{\theta}$ would be far from the truth θ would be close to zero. The WLLN can thus be stated as follows: "The sample mean is consistent for the population mean." If $\hat{\theta}$ was not in fact consistent, then even infinite data could not give us a high probability of approximating θ well. Consistency can be reasonably considered to be a minimum requirement for an estimator to qualify as reasonable.

Importantly, although unbiased estimators are not necessarily consistent, any unbiased estimator $\hat{\theta}$ with $\lim_{n\to\infty} \mathrm{V}[\hat{\theta}] = 0$ is consistent.[17] (This follows from Theorem 2.1.18, *Chebyshev's Inequality*.) Thus, even when we do not necessarily value unbiasedness, it may be useful in establishing other properties of an estimator. We provide more details on the asymptotic properties of estimators in Section 3.2.5.

3.2.3 Variance Estimators

With these concepts in mind, we can now make our first attempt at proposing an estimator of $\mathrm{V}[X]$, or the *population variance* of a random variable X. Recall from Theorem 2.1.13 (*Alternative Formula for Variance*) that $\mathrm{V}[X] = \mathrm{E}[X^2] - \mathrm{E}[X]^2$. We know from the WLLN that the sample mean converges in probability to the expected value or population mean, so what if we "plug in" sample means for expected values? We will call this the *plug-in sample variance*.[18]

17 The converse, however, does not necessarily hold: an unbiased and consistent estimator may nonetheless have positive (or even infinite) sampling variance (and thus, MSE) even as $n \to \infty$.

18 Plug-in estimators can also be referred to as "analog estimators," based on the "analogy principle of estimation," which encompasses the general use of sample statistics as estimators

Definition 3.2.18. *Plug-In Sample Variance*
For i.i.d. random variables $X_1, X_2, \ldots, X_n$, the *plug-in sample variance* is $\overline{X^2} - \overline{X}^2$.

Note that

$$\overline{X^2} = \frac{1}{n}\sum_{i=1}^{n} X_i^2,$$

that is, the sample mean of X^2, and

$$\overline{X}^2 = \left(\frac{1}{n}\sum_{i=1}^{n} X_i\right)^2,$$

that is, the square of the sample mean of X.

The following theorem describes the key properties of the plug-in sample variance.

Theorem 3.2.19. *Properties of the Plug-In Sample Variance*
For i.i.d. random variables $X_1, X_2, \ldots, X_n$ with finite variance $\text{V}[X] > 0$,

- $\text{E}\left[\overline{X^2} - \overline{X}^2\right] = \frac{n-1}{n}\text{V}[X]$.
- $\overline{X^2} - \overline{X}^2 \xrightarrow{p} \text{V}[X]$.

Proof: Let $Z_i = X_i^2$, $\forall i \in \{1,2,\ldots,n\}$. It follows from a generalization of Theorem 1.3.17 (*Implications of Independence, Part I*) that $Z_1, Z_2, \ldots, Z_n$ are i.i.d., so by Theorem 3.2.3 (*The Expected Value of the Sample Mean is the Population Mean*),

$$\text{E}\left[\overline{X^2}\right] = \text{E}\left[\overline{Z}\right] = \text{E}[Z] = \text{E}\left[X^2\right].$$

Now consider $\overline{X}^2$. Note that $\text{E}[\overline{X}^2] \neq \text{E}[X]^2$. Rather, since $\text{V}[\overline{X}] = \text{E}[\overline{X}^2] - \text{E}[\overline{X}]^2$,

$$\text{E}\left[\overline{X}^2\right] = \text{E}\left[\overline{X}\right]^2 + \text{V}\left[\overline{X}\right] = \text{E}[X]^2 + \frac{\text{V}[X]}{n},$$

for analogous population parameters (Goldberger 1968, Manski 1988). See Section 3.3 (*The Plug-In Principle*).

where the second equality follows from Theorem 3.2.3 and Theorem 3.2.4 (*Sampling Variance of the Sample Mean*). Thus,

$$\begin{aligned}
\mathrm{E}\left[\overline{X^2} - \overline{X}^2\right] &= \mathrm{E}\left[\overline{X^2}\right] - \mathrm{E}\left[\overline{X}^2\right] \\
&= \mathrm{E}\left[X^2\right] - \left(\mathrm{E}[X]^2 + \frac{\mathrm{V}[X]}{n}\right) \\
&= \left(\mathrm{E}\left[X^2\right] - \mathrm{E}[X]^2\right) - \frac{\mathrm{V}[X]}{n} \\
&= \mathrm{V}[X] - \frac{\mathrm{V}[X]}{n} \\
&= \left(1 - \frac{1}{n}\right)\mathrm{V}[X] \\
&= \frac{n-1}{n}\mathrm{V}[X].
\end{aligned}$$

Now, by the WLLN, $\overline{X^2} \xrightarrow{p} \mathrm{E}[X^2]$ and $\overline{X} \xrightarrow{p} \mathrm{E}[X]$. Let $g(u,v) = u - v^2$. Then, by the CMT,

$$\overline{X^2} - \overline{X}^2 = g\left(\overline{X^2}, \overline{X}\right) \xrightarrow{p} g\left(\mathrm{E}\left[X^2\right], \mathrm{E}[X]\right) = \mathrm{E}\left[X^2\right] - \mathrm{E}[X]^2 = \mathrm{V}[X]. \quad \square$$

Theorem 3.2.19 says that the plug-in sample variance is not unbiased but nevertheless converges in probability to the true variance under a mild regularity condition. The size of the bias decreases as n increases (since $\frac{n-1}{n} \to 1$ as $n \to \infty$), so in large samples, it becomes negligible. In this setting, it is also easy to correct for this bias. The *unbiased sample variance* (often referred to simply as the *sample variance*) incorporates this correction.

Definition 3.2.20. *Unbiased Sample Variance*
For i.i.d. random variables $X_1, X_2, \ldots, X_n$, the *unbiased sample variance* is

$$\hat{\mathrm{V}}[X] = \frac{n}{n-1}\left(\overline{X^2} - \overline{X}^2\right).$$

In general, just as we used $\hat{\theta}$ to denote an estimator of θ, we add a "hat" ($\hat{}$) to an expression to denote an estimator of that quantity. The following theorem states that the unbiased sample variance is indeed unbiased, and also consistent.

Theorem 3.2.21. *Properties of the Unbiased Sample Variance*
For i.i.d. random variables $X_1, X_2, \ldots, X_n$ with finite variance $\mathrm{V}[X] > 0$,

- $\mathrm{E}\left[\hat{\mathrm{V}}[X]\right] = \mathrm{V}[X]$.
- $\hat{\mathrm{V}}[X] \xrightarrow{p} \mathrm{V}[X]$.

Proof: By linearity of expectations and Theorem 3.2.19,

$$\begin{aligned}
\mathrm{E}\left[\hat{\mathrm{V}}[X]\right] &= \mathrm{E}\left[\frac{n}{n-1}\left(\overline{X^2} - \overline{X}^2\right)\right] \\
&= \frac{n}{n-1}\mathrm{E}\left[\overline{X^2} - \overline{X}^2\right] \\
&= \frac{n}{n-1}\left(\frac{n-1}{n}\mathrm{V}[X]\right) \\
&= \mathrm{V}[X].
\end{aligned}$$

Now, by Theorem 3.2.19, $\overline{X^2} - \overline{X}^2 \xrightarrow{p} \mathrm{V}[X]$, and treating $\frac{n}{n-1}$ as a sequence of degenerate random variables, $\frac{n}{n-1} \xrightarrow{p} 1$. Thus, by the CMT,

$$\hat{\mathrm{V}}[X] = \frac{n}{n-1}\left(\overline{X^2} - \overline{X}^2\right) \xrightarrow{p} 1 \cdot \mathrm{V}[X] = \mathrm{V}[X]. \quad \square$$

As we will see, having a consistent estimator of $\mathrm{V}[X]$ will allow us to quantify the uncertainty around the estimate of $\mathrm{E}[X]$ given by the sample mean.

3.2.4 The Central Limit Theorem for Sample Means

We now present what is often considered the most profound and important theorem in statistics: the *Central Limit Theorem*. The Central Limit Theorem, loosely speaking, implies that the average of many i.i.d. random variables will follow a normal distribution. However, before we can state this theorem rigorously, we require a couple of definitions.

Definition 3.2.22. *Convergence in Distribution*
Let $(T_{(1)}, T_{(2)}, T_{(3)}, \ldots)$ be a sequence of random variables with CDFs $(F_{(1)}, F_{(2)}, F_{(3)}, \ldots)$, and let T be a random variable with CDF F. Then $T_{(n)}$ *converges in distribution* to T if, $\forall t \in \mathbb{R}$ at which F is continuous,

$$\lim_{n \to \infty} F_{(n)}(t) = F(t).$$

We write $T_{(n)} \xrightarrow{d} T$ to denote that $T_{(n)}$ converges in distribution to T.

The distribution of the random variable T to which a sequence of random variables $T_{(n)}$ converges in distribution is referred to as the *limit distribution* (or *asymptotic distribution*) of $T_{(n)}$. (This notion will be important in Section 3.2.5.) As with convergence in probability, this definition can apply to any sequence of random variables, but we use $T_{(n)}$ here because we will mainly be discussing convergence in distribution of sample statistics. We must also define the *standardized sample mean*.

Definition 3.2.23. *Standardized Sample Mean*
For i.i.d. random variables $X_1, X_2, \ldots, X_n$ with finite $\mathrm{E}[X] = \mu$ and finite $\mathrm{V}[X] = \sigma^2 > 0$, the *standardized sample mean* is

$$Z = \frac{\left(\overline{X} - \mathrm{E}\left[\overline{X}\right]\right)}{\sigma\left[\overline{X}\right]} = \frac{\sqrt{n}\left(\overline{X} - \mu\right)}{\sigma}.$$

It can be shown that $\mathrm{E}[Z] = 0$ and $\mathrm{V}[Z] = \sigma[Z] = 1$. These convenient properties are the reason why Z is called the standardized sample mean.

We can now state the Central Limit Theorem for sample means.

Theorem 3.2.24. *Central Limit Theorem*
Let $X_1, X_2, \ldots, X_n$ be i.i.d. random variables with (finite) $\mathrm{E}[X] = \mu$ and finite $\mathrm{V}[X] = \sigma^2 > 0$, and let Z be the standardized sample mean. Then

$$Z \xrightarrow{d} N(0,1),$$

or equivalently,

$$\sqrt{n}(\overline{X} - \mu) \xrightarrow{d} N(0,\sigma^2).$$

We omit the proof of this theorem.[19] The Central Limit Theorem says that, if n is large, the sampling distribution of the sample mean will tend to be approximately normal even when the population under consideration is not distributed normally. This is useful because it will allow us to rigorously quantify our uncertainty when n is large, as we will see in Section 3.4 (*Inference*).

The equivalence of the two statements of the Central Limit Theorem follows from *Slutsky's Theorem*, which will be useful in our technical derivations going forward.

[19] Full proofs of the Central Limit Theorem invariably require fairly advanced mathematics, though the proof of a special case, the De Moivre–Laplace Theorem, is relatively accessible and primarily relies on Sterling's approximation. See, e.g., Feller (1968, Sections II.9, VII.3).

Theorem 3.2.25. *Slutsky's Theorem*
Let $(S_{(1)}, S_{(2)}, S_{(3)}, \ldots)$ and $(T_{(1)}, T_{(2)}, T_{(3)}, \ldots)$ be sequences of random variables. Let T be a random variable and $c \in \mathbb{R}$. If $S_{(n)} \xrightarrow{p} c$ and $T_{(n)} \xrightarrow{d} T$, then

- $S_{(n)} + T_{(n)} \xrightarrow{d} c + T$.
- $S_{(n)} T_{(n)} \xrightarrow{d} cT$.
- $\dfrac{T_{(n)}}{S_{(n)}} \xrightarrow{d} \dfrac{T}{c}$, provided that $c \neq 0$.

We omit the proof of this theorem, but it can be derived from a variant of the Continuous Mapping Theorem (Theorem 3.2.7). We will often invoke this theorem for the special case in which $S_{(n)}$ is a degenerate random variable, either depending solely on n (for example, $\frac{n}{n-1} \xrightarrow{p} 1$) or just a constant (for example, $c \xrightarrow{p} c$). For example, the equivalence of the two statements of the Central Limit Theorem is shown as follows:

$$Z \xrightarrow{d} Z', \text{ where } Z' \sim N(0,1).$$

By Slutsky's Theorem,

$$\sigma Z \xrightarrow{d} \sigma Z',$$

and

$$\sigma Z = \sigma \frac{\sqrt{n}\left(\overline{X} - \mu\right)}{\sigma} = \sqrt{n}\left(\overline{X} - \mu\right),$$

so

$$\sqrt{n}\left(\overline{X} - \mu\right) \xrightarrow{d} \sigma Z',$$

and by Theorem 2.1.21,

$$\sigma Z' \sim N(0, \sigma^2),$$

so $\sqrt{n}(\overline{X} - \mu) \xrightarrow{d} N(0, \sigma^2)$. These steps can also be reversed, so the two statements are in fact equivalent.

Figure 3.2.2 illustrates the Central Limit Theorem in action. As the sample size increases, the distribution of the sample mean becomes both bell-shaped and increasingly tightly centered on the population mean. This holds regardless of the particular underlying distribution of X, as long as it has finite variance. However, sample means drawn from some distributions will more quickly approximate a normal distribution than others.

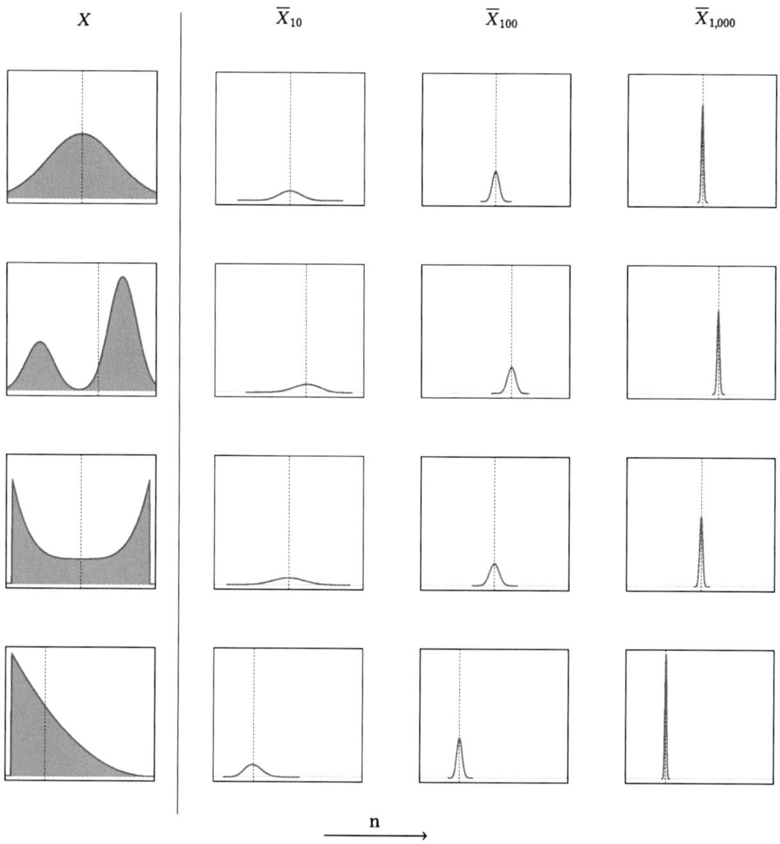

FIGURE 3.2.2. *Simulated Sampling Distributions of the Sample Mean*

3.2.5 Asymptotic Estimation Theory

We noted above that when a sample statistic $T_{(n)}$ converges in probability to a random variable T, the distribution of T is known as the limit distribution (or asymptotic distribution) of $T_{(n)}$. When we discuss the "asymptotic" properties of an estimator, we are referring to the features of its limit distribution (or some appropriate rescaling thereof).[20] We now define some such properties that may be desirable for estimators to have. We begin with a simple case: the asymptotic variant of the unbiasedness property from Section 3.2.2).

20 There is not a consensus about nomenclature here; some authors instead refer to these properties as "limit" properties or simply as features of the limit distribution.

Definition 3.2.26. *Asymptotic Unbiasedness*
An estimator $\hat{\theta}$ is *asymptotically unbiased* for θ if $\hat{\theta} \xrightarrow{d} T$, where $\mathrm{E}[T] = \theta$.

In other words, an estimator $\hat{\theta}$ is asymptotically unbiased if the expectation of its limit distribution is θ. This can introduce some small oddities. To see this, consider the following example.

Example 3.2.27. *Asymptotic Unbiasedness Does Not Imply Unbiasedness Asymptotically*
Suppose that $\forall n \in \mathbb{N}$, $\hat{\theta}_{(n)}$ has PMF

$$f_{(n)}(t) = \begin{cases} \frac{1}{n} & : \ t = \theta + n \\ \frac{n-1}{n} & : \ t = \theta. \end{cases}$$

Then, for any n,

$$\mathrm{E}\left[\hat{\theta}_{(n)}\right] = \frac{1}{n}(\theta + n) + \left(\frac{n-1}{n}\right)\theta = \frac{\theta}{n} + \frac{n}{n} + \theta\frac{n}{n} - \frac{\theta}{n} = \theta + 1.$$

So, regardless of n, $\mathrm{E}[\hat{\theta}_{(n)}] = \theta + 1$. Thus, the estimator is never unbiased; it always has a bias of 1, even as n grows arbitrarily large:

$$\lim_{n \to \infty}\left(\mathrm{E}\left[\hat{\theta}_{(n)}\right] - \theta\right) = 1.$$

Yet we can still say that $\hat{\theta}$ is asymptotically unbiased because $\hat{\theta}_{(n)} \xrightarrow{d} \theta$, and since θ is degenerate, $\mathrm{E}[\theta] = \theta$.[21] △

This gives a sense of the "weirdness" that can occur when we are talking about asymptotics. Typically, it will make sense to employ a notion of asymptotics that focuses on the limit distribution, as we can safely ignore extreme events that become infinitesimally rare as n grows large.

Another asymptotic property that will be important going forward is asymptotic normality. We define this notion for a rescaling of an estimator, as we will only be concerned with this property as it applies to consistent estimators, which—since they converge in probability to a constant—have degenerate (unscaled) limit distributions.

Definition 3.2.28. *Asymptotic Normality*
An estimator $\hat{\theta}$ is *asymptotically normal* if $\sqrt{n}(\hat{\theta} - \theta) \xrightarrow{d} N(0, \phi^2)$, for some finite $\phi > 0$.

21 Note that $\hat{\theta}$ is consistent, as $\hat{\theta}_{(n)} \xrightarrow{d} \theta$ implies $\hat{\theta}_{(n)} \xrightarrow{p} \theta$.

Asymptotic normality can thus be stated as follows: "The (rescaled) limit distribution of $\hat{\theta}$ is normal." (Note that, due to the rescaling, our definition of asymptotic normality implies consistency.) Similarly, the Central Limit Theorem can be stated as follows: "The sample mean is asymptotically normal." The notion of the limit distribution will also allow us to define an appropriate asymptotic analog to the standard error.

Definition 3.2.29. *Asymptotic Standard Error*
For an estimator $\hat{\theta}$ such that $\sqrt{n}(\hat{\theta} - \theta) \xrightarrow{d} T$, the *asymptotic standard error* of $\hat{\theta}$ is $\sqrt{\mathrm{V}[T]}$.

The asymptotic standard error is simply the standard deviation of the limit distribution. We can also define the asymptotic analog to the mean squared error. Again, we define this notion in terms of a rescaling of the estimator, since the limit distribution of any consistent estimator is the degenerate random variable θ and thus has zero MSE.[22]

Definition 3.2.30. *Asymptotic MSE*
For an estimator $\hat{\theta}$ such that $\sqrt{n}(\hat{\theta} - \theta) \xrightarrow{d} T$, the *asymptotic MSE* of $\hat{\theta}$ is $\mathrm{E}[T^2]$.

This definition of asymptotic MSE allows us to compare the asymptotic efficiency of estimators, analogously to our definition of relative efficiency.

Definition 3.2.31. *Asymptotic Relative Efficiency*
Let $\hat{\theta}_A$ and $\hat{\theta}_B$ be estimators of θ. Then $\hat{\theta}_A$ is *asymptotically more efficient* than $\hat{\theta}_B$ if it has a lower asymptotic MSE.

This definition illustrates how the notions of efficiency generalize to limit distributions. We conclude this section by discussing a concept that will be essential for quantifying the uncertainty of estimates: consistency of a sampling variance estimator and consistency of a standard error estimator.

Definition 3.2.32. *Consistency of Sampling Variance and Standard Error Estimators*
For an estimator $\hat{\theta}$ such that $\sqrt{n}(\hat{\theta} - \theta) \xrightarrow{d} T$, a sampling variance estimator $\hat{\mathrm{V}}[\hat{\theta}]$ is *consistent* if

$$n\hat{\mathrm{V}}[\theta] \xrightarrow{p} \mathrm{V}[T]$$

22 As with bias, however, consistency does not imply that $\lim_{n\to\infty} \mathrm{E}[(\hat{\theta}_{(n)} - \theta)^2] = 0$.

and a standard error estimator $\sqrt{\hat{\mathrm{V}}[\hat{\theta}]}$ is *consistent* if

$$\sqrt{n}\sqrt{\hat{\mathrm{V}}[\theta]} \xrightarrow{p} \sqrt{\mathrm{V}[T]}.^{23}$$

Note that, due to the CMT, consistency of the sampling variance estimator implies consistency of the corresponding standard error estimator, and vice versa. Consistency of these estimators, wedded to asymptotic normality, will be key to our discussion in Section 3.4 (*Inference*).

3.2.6 Estimating Standard Errors of Sample Means

So far, we have discussed the population variance $\mathrm{V}[X]$, and an estimator thereof, namely, the unbiased sample variance, $\hat{\mathrm{V}}[X]$. Additionally, in Section 3.2.1 (*Sample Means*), we showed that the sampling variance of the sample mean is $\mathrm{V}[\overline{X}] = \frac{\mathrm{V}[X]}{n}$. (Do not confuse these three quantities.) We now want to propose an estimator of the sampling variance of the sample mean, $\hat{\mathrm{V}}[\overline{X}]$. The natural choice is $\frac{\hat{\mathrm{V}}[X]}{n}$.

Theorem 3.2.33. *Estimating the Sampling Variance of the Sample Mean*
For i.i.d. random variables $X_1, X_2, \ldots, X_n$ with finite variance $\mathrm{V}[X] > 0$, let $\hat{\mathrm{V}}[\overline{X}] = \frac{\hat{\mathrm{V}}[X]}{n}$. Then

- $\mathrm{E}\left[\hat{\mathrm{V}}\left[\overline{X}\right]\right] = \mathrm{V}\left[\overline{X}\right]$.
- $n\hat{\mathrm{V}}\left[\overline{X}\right] - n\mathrm{V}\left[\overline{X}\right] = n\hat{\mathrm{V}}\left[\overline{X}\right] - \mathrm{V}[X] \xrightarrow{p} 0$.

Proof:

$$\mathrm{E}\left[\hat{\mathrm{V}}\left[\overline{X}\right]\right] = \mathrm{E}\left[\frac{\hat{\mathrm{V}}[X]}{n}\right] = \frac{\mathrm{E}\left[\hat{\mathrm{V}}[X]\right]}{n} = \frac{\mathrm{V}[X]}{n} = \mathrm{V}\left[\overline{X}\right],$$

and by Theorem 3.2.21, $\hat{\mathrm{V}}[X] \xrightarrow{p} \mathrm{V}[X]$, so since we can rearrange

$$\hat{\mathrm{V}}\left[\overline{X}\right] = \frac{\hat{\mathrm{V}}[X]}{n} \text{ and } \mathrm{V}\left[\overline{X}\right] = \frac{\mathrm{V}[X]}{n}$$

23 Note that it is equivalent to define these as $n\hat{\mathrm{V}}[\theta] - \mathrm{V}[T] \xrightarrow{p} 0$ and $\sqrt{n}\sqrt{\hat{\mathrm{V}}[\theta]} - \sqrt{\mathrm{V}[T]} \xrightarrow{p} 0$, respectively.

to get

$$n\hat{\text{V}}\left[\overline{X}\right] = \hat{\text{V}}[X] \text{ and } n\text{V}\left[\overline{X}\right] = \text{V}[X],$$

by substitution, $n\hat{\text{V}}[\overline{X}] - n\text{V}[\overline{X}] \xrightarrow{p} 0$. □

The first property states that the sampling variance of the sample mean is unbiased, and the second is equivalent to stating that it is consistent (as the limit distribution of the sample mean has variance $\text{V}[X]$). Thus, it is possible to estimate the average of a random variable (the population mean) and, furthermore, to estimate the uncertainty of that estimate. (We will formally discuss quantifying the uncertainty of an estimate in Section 3.4, *Inference*.)

As with any variance, we can take the square root of the sampling variance of the sample mean to obtain the standard error, or the standard deviation of the sampling distribution of the sample mean.

Definition 3.2.34. *Standard Error of the Sample Mean*
For i.i.d. random variables $X_1, X_2, ..., X_n$, the *standard error of the sample mean* is

$$\sigma\left[\overline{X}\right] = \sqrt{\text{V}\left[\overline{X}\right]}.$$

To estimate the standard error of the sample mean, we use $\hat{\sigma}[\overline{X}] = \sqrt{\hat{\text{V}}[\overline{X}]}$. When we see "standard error" in a paper, this is what the authors really mean: an estimate thereof. We do not know the true standard error.[24] This estimator is not unbiased,[25] but it is consistent.

Theorem 3.2.35. *Consistency of the Standard Error of the Sample Mean Estimator*

24 Since an estimator of the standard error is itself a random variable, it has its own sampling distribution and thus its own standard error, so we could, in theory, estimate the standard error of the standard error of the sample mean, thereby quantifying the uncertainty of our estimate of the uncertainty of our estimate of the population mean. However, since standard error estimators converge "quickly" to the true standard error, this is not a concern with large n.

25 This is due to Jensen's Inequality: for a random variable X and convex function g of X, $\text{E}[g(X)] \geq g(\text{E}[X])$. Corollary: for a random variable X and concave function g of X, $\text{E}[g(X)] \leq g(\text{E}[X])$. These inequalities are strict when g is strictly convex/concave and X is not degenerate. The square root function is strictly concave, so whenever $\text{V}[\hat{\text{V}}[\overline{X}]] > 0$,

$$\text{E}\left[\hat{\sigma}\left[\overline{X}\right]\right] = \text{E}\left[\sqrt{\hat{\text{V}}\left[\overline{X}\right]}\right] < \sqrt{\text{E}\left[\hat{\text{V}}\left[\overline{X}\right]\right]} = \sqrt{\text{V}\left[\overline{X}\right]} = \sigma\left[\overline{X}\right].$$

For i.i.d. random variables $X_1, X_2, ..., X_n$ with finite variance $V[X] > 0$,

$$\sqrt{n}\hat{\sigma}\left[\overline{X}\right] - \sqrt{V[X]} = \sqrt{n}\hat{\sigma}\left[\overline{X}\right] - \sqrt{n}\sigma\left[\overline{X}\right] \xrightarrow{p} 0.$$

Proof: Let $g(u) = \sqrt{u}$. By Theorem 3.2.33, $n\hat{V}[\overline{X}] - nV[\overline{X}] \xrightarrow{p} 0$. So, since g is continuous, by the CMT,

$$\sqrt{n}\hat{\sigma}\left[\overline{X}\right] = \sqrt{\hat{V}[X]} = g\left(\hat{V}[X]\right) \xrightarrow{p} g(V[X]) = \sqrt{V[X]} = \sqrt{n}\sigma\left[\overline{X}\right]. \quad \square$$

The ideas used in establishing the properties of the sample mean can take us very far. In the following section, we formalize a notion of estimation that will allow us to straightforwardly estimate well-defined population quantities with sample analogs.

3.3 THE PLUG-IN PRINCIPLE[26]

The estimation philosophy used in this chapter has been informally based on the *plug-in principle*: write down the feature of the population that we are interested in, and then use the sample analog to estimate it. For example, if we want to estimate the expected value, use the sample mean. If we want to estimate the population variance, use the sample variance. It is possible to formalize and generalize this idea, so that it encompasses a general framework for estimation. In general, the CDF of a random variable tells us everything about the behavior of the random variable. The CDF of X is

$$F(x) = \Pr[X \leq x] = E\left[I(X \leq x)\right].$$

Accordingly, there is a sample analog to the CDF, the *empirical CDF*.

Definition 3.3.1. *Empirical CDF*
For i.i.d. random variables $X_1, X_2, ..., X_n$, the *empirical CDF* $\hat{F}$ of X is

$$\hat{F}(x) = \overline{I(X \leq x)}, \forall x \in \mathbb{R}.$$[27]

Just as the CDF is a function that fully describes the population, the empirical CDF is a function that fully describes the sample. Note that the empirical CDF is always a nondecreasing step function, like the CDF of a discrete random variable. Figure 3.3.1 illustrates that this is the case even when one's

[26] This section is heavily inspired by the treatments in Wasserman (2004), Wasserman (2006), and Wasserman (2012).

[27] This definition, and everything that follows, can easily be generalized to the multivariate case. For example, in the bivariate case, for i.i.d. random vectors (X_1, Y_1), (X_2, Y_2), ..., (X_n, Y_n), the *joint* empirical CDF of (X, Y) is $\hat{F}(x,y) = \overline{I(X \leq x, Y \leq y)}$. Everything else proceeds analogously.

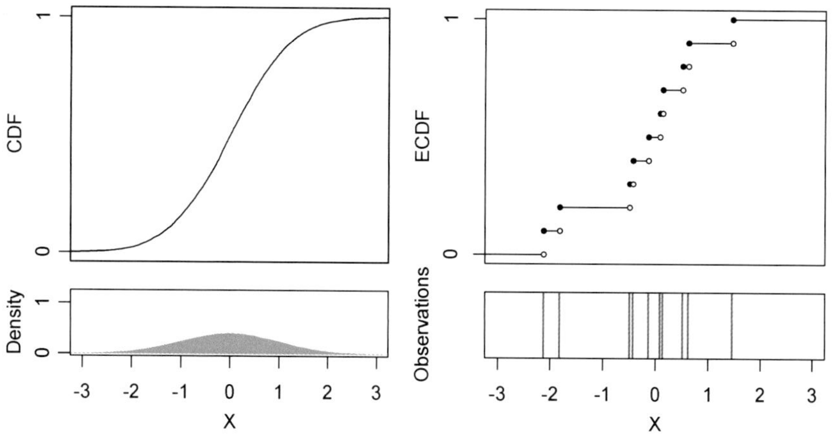

FIGURE 3.3.1. *CDF of a Continuous Random Variable, and Illustrative Empirical CDF*

sample is drawn from a continuous random variable (for which the CDF is continuous by definition, see Section 1.2.4, *Continuous Random Variables*). There are two (equivalent) ways of thinking about how $\hat{F}(x)$ is computed:

- Replace the expected value in the definition of the CDF with a sample mean.[28]
- Count the number of observations i satisfying $X_i \leq x$ and divide by n.

We know, because of the properties of the sample mean, that, $\forall x \in \mathbb{R}$, $\hat{F}(x)$ will be unbiased and consistent for $F(x)$ (see Theorem 3.2.9, *Estimating the CDF*).[29]

Before we proceed, we take a moment to establish some necessary notation. Let F be the CDF of a random variable X, and let f be the corresponding probability mass function (PMF) or probability density function (PDF). Let g be any function of X. Then let

$$\int_{-\infty}^{\infty} g(x)dF(x) = \begin{cases} \sum_x g(x)f(x) & : \ F \text{ is discrete} \\ \int_{-\infty}^{\infty} g(x)f(x)dx & : \ F \text{ is continuous.}^{30} \end{cases}$$

[28] Recall from Definition 3.2.2 (*Sample Mean*) that $\overline{\mathrm{I}(X \leq x)}$ denotes the sample mean of $\mathrm{I}(X \leq x)$.

[29] In fact, an even stronger claim holds. The Glivenko–Cantelli Theorem:

$$\sup_x \left| \hat{F}(x) - F(x) \right| \overset{a.s.}{\to} 0,$$

where the notation $\overset{a.s.}{\to}$ denotes *almost sure convergence*, which is a notion of convergence stronger than convergence in probability. (We will not discuss this type of convergence in detail.) In words, the Glivenko–Cantelli Theorem states that the biggest difference between the CDF and empirical CDF converges to zero. In fact, it converges to zero "quickly." See the Dvoretzky–Kiefer–Wolfowitz inequality.

We can now introduce the concept of a *statistical functional*. Simply put, a statistical functional is an operator on a random variable that is represented by a function of the CDF. It is simply a way to a represent a feature of a random variable.

Definition 3.3.2. *Statistical Functional*
A *statistical functional* is a function $T : \mathcal{F} \to \mathbb{R}$, where $\mathcal{F}$ is the set of all possible CDFs.

For example, for the random variable X with CDF F, we can write the expected value of X as

$$\mathrm{E}[X] = T_{\mathrm{E}}(F) = \int_{-\infty}^{\infty} x dF(x).$$

Likewise, we can write the variance of X as

$$\begin{aligned}
\mathrm{V}[X] &= T_{\mathrm{V}}(F) \\
&= \int_{-\infty}^{\infty} (x - \mathrm{E}[X])^2 dF(x) \\
&= \int_{-\infty}^{\infty} x^2 dF(x) - \mathrm{E}[X]^2 \\
&= \int_{-\infty}^{\infty} x^2 dF(x) + \left(\int_{-\infty}^{\infty} x dF(x) \right)^2 .
\end{aligned}$$

A remarkably large class of estimands can be written as $\theta = T(F)$, and the inferential targets that we will set in this book all have representations as statistical functionals. With θ as our target, we can define the *plug-in estimator* of θ as follows:

Definition 3.3.3. *Plug-In Estimator*
For i.i.d. random variables X_1, X_2, ..., X_n with common CDF F, the *plug-in estimator* of $\theta = T(F)$ is

$$\hat{\theta} = T(\hat{F}).$$

To estimate $\theta = T(F)$, apply the same functional to the *empirical CDF*. We provide two examples showing how we could derive plug-in estimators for the population mean and variances.

[30] These are special cases of Riemann–Stieltjes integration, which is a generalization of ordinary (Riemann) integration to encompass discrete, continuous, and mixed-type distributions. This in turn can be generalized further with Lebesgue integration.

Example 3.3.4. *Sample Mean as a Plug-In Estimator*
Since the expected value of X is $\text{E}[X] = T_E(F) = \int_{-\infty}^{\infty} x dF(x)$, the plug-in estimator of E[X] is

$$\begin{aligned}\hat{\text{E}}[X] &= T_E(\hat{F}) \\ &= \int_{-\infty}^{\infty} x d\hat{F}(x) \\ &= \sum_x x\hat{f}(x) \\ &= \sum_x x \frac{(\text{number of observations } i \text{ with outcome } X_i = x)}{n} \\ &= \frac{1}{n} \sum_x x(\text{number of observations } i \text{ with outcome } X_i = x) \\ &= \frac{1}{n} \sum_{i=1}^{n} x = \overline{X},\end{aligned}$$

where $\hat{f}$ is the empirical PMF. Thus, the sample mean is the plug-in estimator of the expected value. △

The analogous result for the population variance follows directly.

Example 3.3.5. *Plug-In Sample Variance as a Plug-In Estimator*
Since the variance of X is

$$\text{V}[X] = T_{\text{V}}(F) = \int_{-\infty}^{\infty} x^2 dF(x) + \left(\int_{-\infty}^{\infty} x dF(x) \right)^2,$$

the plug-in estimator of V[X] is

$$\hat{\text{V}}[X] = T_{\text{V}}(\hat{F}) = \int_{-\infty}^{\infty} x^2 d\hat{F}(x) - \left(\int_{-\infty}^{\infty} x d\hat{F}(x) \right)^2 = \overline{X^2} - \overline{X}^2.$$

Thus, the plug-in sample variance is, in fact, the plug-in estimator of the variance. △

The idea of a plug-in estimator is quite profound. We want to know a feature θ of the CDF. We express θ as a function T of the CDF. We then observe the sample analog of the CDF, namely, the empirical CDF. We know that, as n grows large, the empirical CDF tends to more and more closely approximate the CDF. We therefore estimate θ by applying the function T to the empirical CDF. Then, as n grows large, the estimate θ tends to more and more closely approximate θ. Typically, we do not need to go to the extreme of writing everything in terms of the CDF or empirical CDF, as we can derive most plug-in estimators by substituting sample quantities for population quantities (for instance, means for expectations). Nonetheless, when we talk about a plug-in estimator, we are fundamentally talking about an estimator that substitutes ("plugs in") the empirical CDF for the CDF.

3.3.1 The Usual Plug-In Regularity Conditions

Regularity conditions sufficient for plug-in estimators to have good asymptotic behavior (such as consistency and asymptotic normality) usually entail restrictions on the manner in which small changes in the empirical CDF can correspond to changes in the estimate. In particular, we assume that T is suitably *well behaved* at F; if we were to perturb the true population distribution F just a little bit, we would not expect the value that the functional takes on to change dramatically. This is perhaps intuitive: if the functional were prone to take on drastically different values for CDFs that are very close to the population distribution, we would not expect an estimator based on the empirical CDF to converge. We provide an informal statement of a key result (Wasserman 2006, Theorem 2.27), namely that mild regularity conditions are sufficient to guarantee that a plug-in estimator is asymptotically normal.

Theorem 3.3.6. *Asymptotic Normality of Plug-In Estimators*
If T is well behaved[31] at F and $\hat{\theta} = T(\hat{F})$, then $\hat{\theta}$ is asymptotically normal.

We omit the proof, which requires empirical process theory. The conditions for T to be well behaved at F are often implied by other assumptions; for instance, our assumption about finite variance was sufficient to imply that the population mean is well behaved. We will refer to these assumptions, as they apply to the functional under consideration, as the *usual plug-in regularity conditions*. The usual plug-in regularity conditions can be satisfied by assuming (and even verifying, in some cases) that the functional of interest will be well behaved in the neighborhoods of plausible population distributions.

While it can fail, the plug-in principle remains a good starting point in considering estimation strategies. In the next section, we will describe another way of estimating the distribution of a random variable, which will in turn yield natural plug-in estimators.

[31] We say T is well behaved if it is Hadamard differentiable at F with respect to the Kolmogorov distance. Formally, the Kolmogorov distance between two distributions F and G is given by the value of the largest divergence between their two CDFs, $\sup_x |F(x) - G(x)|$. Attentive readers may recall that the Glivenko–Cantelli Theorem in Footnote 29 guarantees almost sure convergence of the Kolmogorov distance between $\hat{F}$ and F to zero, providing further intuition for Theorem 3.3.6. Although we do not provide a formal definition, Wasserman (2006, Ch. 2) provides a lucid discussion of the assumption of Hadamard differentiability.

3.3.2 Kernel Estimation

The procedure illustrated above is easily applicable for discrete random variables. But what if we are dealing with a continuous random variable, and we would like to write our target in terms of the PDF? If we are willing to impose some strong assumptions about the distribution of the random variable, it becomes fairly easy to estimate its PDF (see Chapter 5). But what if we do not want to make such strong assumptions? In that case, we can still estimate the PDF using *kernel density estimation.*

The key idea behind kernel density estimation is to "smooth" the data so as to get estimates of the PDF everywhere. We can estimate the value of the PDF at a given point x by calculating the proportion of the observations that have X_i near x.

Definition 3.3.7. *Kernel Density Estimator*
Let $X_1, X_2, \ldots, X_n$ be i.i.d. continuous random variables with common PDF f. Let $K : \mathbb{R} \to \mathbb{R}$ be an even function[32] satisfying $\int_{-\infty}^{\infty} K(x)dx = 1$, and let $K_h(x) = \frac{1}{h}K(\frac{x}{h})$, $\forall x \in \mathbb{R}$ and $h > 0$. Then a *kernel density estimator* of $f(x)$ is

$$\hat{f}_K(x) = \frac{1}{n}\sum_{i=1}^{n} K_h(x - X_i), \forall x \in \mathbb{R}.$$

The function K is called the *kernel* and the scaling parameter h is called the *bandwidth*.

The kernel and bandwidth tell us how much to weight each observation X_i depending on its distance from the point of interest x. The farther an observation is from the point of interest, the less it counts. This is easiest to understand in the univariate case, though everything carries through to multiple variables as long as "distance" is defined accordingly. (Regular Euclidean distance is the usual choice.) The kernel tells us the shape of the weighting, and the bandwidth tells us how far out we should go, that is, the width or scale of the kernel. There are many common kernels (see Figure 3.3.2). Then computing estimates of the densities at every point follows directly: we add up all the observations, weighted by a metric of how much we want each one to count. The closer it is to the point of interest, the more it counts.

In order for kernel density estimates to be consistent, we will need the bandwidth h to tend to zero as n tends to infinity. Then, as long as the PDF really is continuous, kernel density estimation will be consistent.[33] This follows

32 That is, a function whose graph is symmetric about the y-axis, so that $\forall x \in \mathbb{R}, f(x) = f(-x)$.
33 We also want to make sure that $h \to 0$ at an appropriate rate, so that we are never over or undersmoothing. Silverman (1986)'s "rule of thumb" for kernel density estimation with a

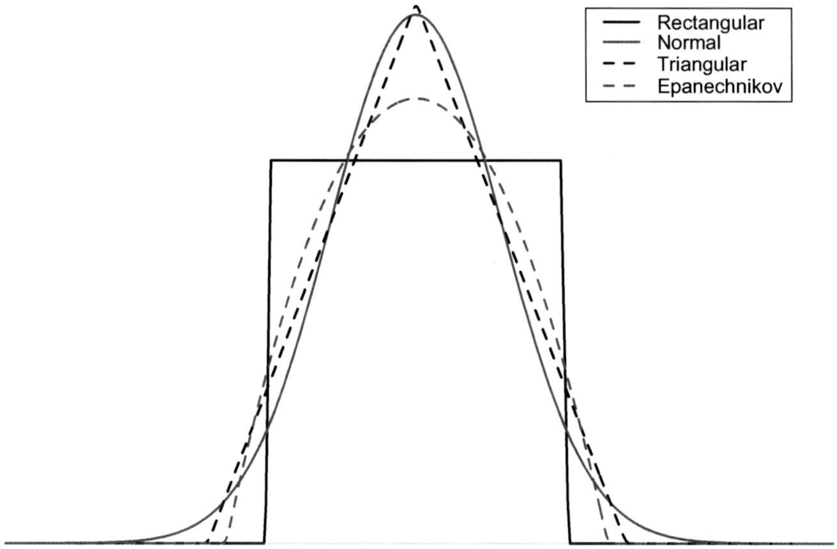

FIGURE 3.3.2. *Visualization of Different Kernels*

intuitively from the definition of the PDF:

$$f(x) = \frac{dF(x)}{dx} = \lim_{h \to 0^+} \frac{F(x+h) - F(x-h)}{2h}.$$

The following example shows how, for continuous X, the kernel density estimate (with a rectangular kernel) will be consistent for the true PDF. The proof itself leans on the plug-in principle.

Theorem 3.3.8. *Consistency of the Kernel Density Estimator (Rectangular Kernel)*
For i.i.d. continuous random variables $X_1, X_2, ..., X_n$, $\forall x \in \mathbb{R}$, if $K(x) = \frac{1}{2}\mathrm{I}(-1 \le x \le 1)$ (that is, the kernel is rectangular), and if $h \to 0$ and $nh \to \infty$ as $n \to \infty$, then $\hat{f}_K(x) \xrightarrow{p} f(x)$.

normal (Gaussian) kernel is to let

$$h = \frac{0.9 \min\left(\hat{\sigma}[X], \frac{\widehat{IQR}}{1.34}\right)}{n^{\frac{1}{5}}},$$

where $\hat{\sigma}[X] = \sqrt{\hat{\mathrm{V}}[X]}$ and $\widehat{IQR}$ is the (sample) interquartile range. Under this rule (and mild regularity conditions), the range of observations that we count toward a point's density is going to shrink at a rate on the order of $n^{-\frac{1}{5}}$. That is pretty slow, but eventually, with large enough n, we will only count observations that are very close.

Proof sketch: Our proof sketch relies on the plug-in principle. For any $h > 0$,

$$K_h(x) = \frac{1}{2h}\mathrm{I}\left(-1 \leq \frac{x}{h} \leq 1\right) = \frac{\mathrm{I}(-h \leq x \leq h)}{2h}.$$

Thus,

$$\begin{aligned}\hat{f}_K(x) &= \frac{1}{n}\sum_{i=1}^{n}\frac{\mathrm{I}(-h \leq X_i - x \leq h)}{2h} \\ &= \frac{\frac{1}{n}\sum_{i=1}^{n}\mathrm{I}(x-h \leq X_i \leq x+h)}{2h} \\ &= \frac{\hat{F}(x+h)-\hat{F}(x-h)}{2h} \\ &\xrightarrow{p} \frac{F(x+h)-F(x-h)}{2h},\end{aligned}$$

which follows from the definition of the empirical CDF and its consistency for F. Then, we know that the definition of the PDF is simply a limit of the final expression as $h \to 0$:

$$\lim_{h\to 0}\frac{F(x+h)-F(x-h)}{2h} = \frac{dF(x)}{dx} = f(x).$$

The condition that $nh \to \infty$ is sufficient to guarantee that this limit carries through in estimation. □

Now, once we have an empirical estimate of the PDF, we can compute any quantity that we want from the estimate. We can integrate our estimate of the PDF to obtain an estimate of the full CDF, and thus we can apply any statistical functional to that estimate. This provides a basis for another type of plug-in estimation: kernel plug-in estimation.

Definition 3.3.9. *Kernel Plug-In Estimator*
The *kernel plug-in estimator* of $\theta = T(F)$ is

$$\hat{\theta}_K = T(\hat{F}_K),$$

where $\hat{F}_K(x) = \int_{-\infty}^{x}\hat{f}(u)du$.

The only difference between plug-in estimation and kernel plug-in estimation is the way that we estimate the CDF. In plug-in estimation, we use the empirical CDF $\hat{F}$. In kernel plug-in estimation, we use the smooth estimate of the CDF implied by the kernel density estimator.

The main benefit of the kernel-based approach comes in the multivariate case, since by obtaining a continuous estimate of the joint PDF, we can directly obtain point predictions even when we need to condition on a continuous variable. For example, if we used kernel density estimation to estimate $f_{Y|X}(y|\mathbf{x})$ (that is, use kernel estimation to estimate $f(y,\mathbf{x})$ and $f_{\mathbf{X}}(\mathbf{x})$, and then apply Definition 1.3.14, *Conditional PDF*), then we could use our estimate $\hat{f}_{Y|\mathbf{X}}(y|\mathbf{x})$ to estimate the conditional expectation function (CEF) at any given point $\mathbf{x}$:

$$\hat{\mathrm{E}}[Y|\mathbf{X}=\mathbf{x}] = \int_{-\infty}^{\infty} y\hat{f}_{Y|\mathbf{X}}(y|\mathbf{x})dy.$$

As long as the density estimator is consistent (in an appropriately uniform sense), all of the associated plug-in estimators will be consistent. This holds for any reasonable feature of the random variable that we might be interested in (such as conditional moments).

3.4 INFERENCE

We have shown how to estimate features of a random variable or population from i.i.d. samples. But how do we know how certain we can be that these estimates closely approximate reality? Can we precisely quantify the degree of uncertainty surrounding our estimates? These questions are the subject of statistical *inference*. In this section, among other things, we shall see the importance of our discussion of the standard error and the Central Limit Theorem in Section 3.2 (*Estimation*).

3.4.1 Confidence Intervals

A *confidence interval* for θ, loosely speaking, is an estimated *interval* that covers the true value of θ with at least a given probability. For example, if we were to take an i.i.d. sample of size n of a random variable X and compute a (valid) 95% confidence interval for the population mean $\mathrm{E}[X]$, then with 95% probability, this interval will include $\mathrm{E}[X]$. We now provide a formal definition of a confidence interval.

Definition 3.4.1. *Valid Confidence Interval*
A *valid confidence interval* for θ with *coverage* $(1-\alpha)$ is a random interval $CI_{(1-\alpha)}(\theta)$,[34] such that $\Pr[\theta \in CI_{(1-\alpha)}(\theta)] \geq 1-\alpha$.

For any given $\alpha \in (0,1)$, we say that the *confidence level* is $100(1-\alpha)\%$ and that $CI_{1-\alpha}(\theta)$ is a $100(1-\alpha)\%$ confidence interval for θ. Some confidence

[34] A *random interval* is simply an interval formed by a pair of random variables. Suppose we have two random variables C_1, C_2, with $\Pr[C_1 < C_2] = 1$. Then $C = (C_1, C_2)$ is an (open) random interval.

intervals are only valid asymptotically; they only have coverage $(1-\alpha)$ with very large n. By *asymptotically valid*,[35] we mean that

$$\lim_{n\to\infty} \Pr\left[\theta \in CI_{1-\alpha}(\theta)\right] \geq 1-\alpha.$$

The types of confidence intervals we will consider in this book will only be asymptotically valid. The following theorem gives a remarkably general method for obtaining asymptotically valid confidence intervals for asymptotically normal estimators.

Theorem 3.4.2. *Normal Approximation–Based Confidence Interval*
Let $\hat{\theta}$ be an asymptotically normal estimator of θ, $\hat{\text{V}}[\hat{\theta}]$ be an consistent estimator of the sampling variance, and $\alpha \in (0,1)$. Then an asymptotically valid normal approximation–based confidence interval for θ with coverage $(1-\alpha)$ is given by

$$CI_{1-\alpha}(\theta) = \left(\hat{\theta} - z_{1-\frac{\alpha}{2}}\sqrt{\hat{\text{V}}[\hat{\theta}]}, \hat{\theta} + z_{1-\frac{\alpha}{2}}\sqrt{\hat{\text{V}}[\hat{\theta}]}\right),$$

where z_c denotes the cth quantile of the standard normal distribution; that is, $\Phi(z_c) = c$, $\forall c \in (0,1)$.

Proof: By asymptotic normality,

$$\sqrt{n}(\hat{\theta} - \theta) \xrightarrow{d} \text{N}(0, \phi^2).$$

Define the random variable

$$Z = \frac{\sqrt{n}(\hat{\theta} - \theta)}{\phi},$$

so that by Slutsky's Theorem and Theorem 2.1.21, $Z \xrightarrow{d} \text{N}(0,1)$.

Recall that by the CMT and consistency of the sampling variance estimator,

$$\sqrt{n\hat{\text{V}}[\hat{\theta}]} \xrightarrow{p} \phi.$$

Now, we plug in the *estimated* standard error. Define the random variable

$$Z' = \frac{\hat{\theta} - \theta}{\sqrt{\hat{\text{V}}[\hat{\theta}]}} = \frac{\hat{\theta} - \theta}{\sqrt{\hat{\text{V}}[\hat{\theta}]}}\frac{\sqrt{n}\phi}{\sqrt{n}\phi} = \frac{\sqrt{n}(\hat{\theta} - \theta)}{\phi}\frac{\phi}{\sqrt{n}\sqrt{\hat{\text{V}}[\hat{\theta}]}} = Z\frac{\phi}{\sqrt{n\hat{\text{V}}[\hat{\theta}]}}.$$

35 There is a technical distinction between *pointwise* and *uniform* asymptotic validity, the latter being a stronger notion. Here we consider pointwise asymptotic validity.

Then, by the CMT and consistency of the sampling variance estimator,

$$\frac{\phi}{\sqrt{n\hat{\mathbb{V}}[\hat{\theta}]}} \xrightarrow{p} 1.$$

So, by Slutsky's Theorem, $Z' \xrightarrow{d} N(0,1)$. Now, take an arbitrary $\alpha \in (0,1)$. By symmetry of the normal distribution, $z_{\frac{\alpha}{2}} = -z_{1-\frac{\alpha}{2}}$. Since $Z' \xrightarrow{d} N(0,1)$, it follows that

$$\begin{aligned}
\lim_{n\to\infty} \Pr\left[-z_{1-\frac{\alpha}{2}} \le Z' \le z_{1-\frac{\alpha}{2}}\right] &= \lim_{n\to\infty}\left(F_{Z'}\left(z_{1-\frac{\alpha}{2}}\right) - F_{Z'}\left(-z_{1-\frac{\alpha}{2}}\right)\right) \\
&= \lim_{n\to\infty}\left(F_{Z'}\left(z_{1-\frac{\alpha}{2}}\right) - F_{Z'}\left(z_{\frac{\alpha}{2}}\right)\right) \\
&= \lim_{n\to\infty} F_{Z'}\left(z_{1-\frac{\alpha}{2}}\right) - \lim_{n\to\infty} F_{Z'}\left(z_{\frac{\alpha}{2}}\right) \\
&= \Phi\left(z_{1-\frac{\alpha}{2}}\right) - \Phi\left(z_{\frac{\alpha}{2}}\right) \\
&= 1 - \frac{\alpha}{2} - \frac{\alpha}{2} = 1 - \alpha,
\end{aligned}$$

where $F_{Z'}$ denotes the CDF of Z'. Thus,

$$\begin{aligned}
\lim_{n\to\infty} \Pr\left[\theta \in CI_{1-\alpha}(\theta)\right] &= \lim_{n\to\infty} \Pr\left[\hat{\theta} - z_{1-\frac{\alpha}{2}}\sqrt{\hat{\mathbb{V}}[\hat{\theta}]} \le \theta \le \hat{\theta} + z_{1-\frac{\alpha}{2}}\sqrt{\hat{\mathbb{V}}[\hat{\theta}]}\right] \\
&= \lim_{n\to\infty} \Pr\left[-z_{1-\frac{\alpha}{2}}\sqrt{\hat{\mathbb{V}}[\hat{\theta}]} \le \theta - \hat{\theta} \le z_{1-\frac{\alpha}{2}}\sqrt{\hat{\mathbb{V}}[\hat{\theta}]}\right] \\
&= \lim_{n\to\infty} \Pr\left[-z_{1-\frac{\alpha}{2}}\sqrt{\hat{\mathbb{V}}[\hat{\theta}]} < \hat{\theta} - \theta < z_{1-\frac{\alpha}{2}}\sqrt{\hat{\mathbb{V}}[\hat{\theta}]}\right] \\
&= \lim_{n\to\infty} \Pr\left[-z_{1-\frac{\alpha}{2}} < \frac{\hat{\theta} - \theta}{\sqrt{\hat{\mathbb{V}}[\hat{\theta}]}} < z_{1-\frac{\alpha}{2}}\right]
\end{aligned}$$

$$= \lim_{n \to \infty} \Pr\left[-z_{1-\frac{\alpha}{2}} < Z' < z_{1-\frac{\alpha}{2}} \right]$$

$$= 1 - \alpha. \square$$

Specific values of $z_{1-\frac{\alpha}{2}}$ can be obtained using a Z table, graphing calculator, or statistical software, but it is useful to know the most commonly used values:

- For a 90% confidence interval, $\alpha = 0.10$ and $z_{1-\frac{\alpha}{2}} \approx 1.64$.
- For a 95% confidence interval, $\alpha = 0.05$ and $z_{1-\frac{\alpha}{2}} \approx 1.96$.
- For a 99% confidence interval, $\alpha = 0.01$ and $z_{1-\frac{\alpha}{2}} \approx 2.58$.

To ground these ideas, we provide an example of how to form a confidence interval for the population mean.

Example 3.4.3. *Confidence Interval for the Population Mean*
Suppose we had n i.i.d. draws of a random variable X. Then an approximate 95% confidence interval for the population mean $\mu = \text{E}[X]$ would be

$$CI_{.95}(\mu) = \left(\overline{X} - 1.96\sqrt{\frac{\hat{\text{V}}[X]}{n}}, \overline{X} + 1.96\sqrt{\frac{\hat{\text{V}}[X]}{n}} \right)$$

$$= \left(\overline{X} - 1.96\sqrt{\hat{\text{V}}\left[\overline{X}\right]}, \overline{X} + 1.96\sqrt{\hat{\text{V}}\left[\overline{X}\right]} \right)$$

$$= \left(\overline{X} - 1.96\hat{\sigma}\left[\overline{X}\right], \overline{X} + 1.96\hat{\sigma}\left[\overline{X}\right] \right).$$

If n is large, then, with 95% probability, $CI_{.95}(\mu)$ will encompass the true value of μ. $\triangle$

Recall, however, that these confidence intervals are only guaranteed to have proper coverage rates if n is large—this is the "asymptotically valid" qualification. This implies that, in small samples, 95% normal approximation–based confidence intervals may actually have, for example, 80% coverage. This is in part attributable to the fact that the standard error of the estimator must be estimated, and is not known—a problem that does not admit a general solution without additional assumptions.[36] This qualification will carry through to our next topic, hypothesis testing, and will be discussed more generally in Section 3.4.4 (*Micronumerosity*).

[36] Another reason for the failure in finite samples is that the sampling distribution of the estimator is only approximately normal. This approximation may be bad in finite samples. This is in part addressed in Section 3.4.3 (*The Bootstrap*), when we discuss the percentile bootstrap.

3.4.2 Hypothesis Testing

The foregoing discussion of confidence intervals naturally leads to the closely related idea of hypothesis testing. Suppose we wanted to test the *null hypothesis* that $\theta = \theta_0$. (The null hypothesis is simply the hypothesis that we are testing against.) That is, having observed our sample and computed an estimate $\hat{\theta}$, we could ask: if θ were actually equal to θ_0, what would be the probability that we would have obtained a $\hat{\theta}$ at least as far off from θ_0 as we did? This probability is called a *p-value*.

Definition 3.4.4. *p-Value*[37]
Let $\hat{\theta}$ be an estimator of θ and let $\hat{\theta}^*$ be the observed value of $\hat{\theta}$. Then

- a *lower one-tailed p-value* under the null hypothesis $\theta = \theta_0$ is

$$p = \Pr_{\theta_0}\left[\hat{\theta} \leq \hat{\theta}^*\right],$$

- an *upper one-tailed p-value* under the null hypothesis $\theta = \theta_0$ is

$$p = \Pr_{\theta_0}\left[\hat{\theta} \geq \hat{\theta}^*\right],$$

- a *two-tailed p-value* under the null hypothesis $\theta = \theta_0$ is

$$p = \Pr_{\theta_0}\left[\left|\hat{\theta} - \theta_0\right| \geq \left|\hat{\theta}^* - \theta_0\right|\right],$$

where $\Pr_{\theta_0}[\cdot]$ denotes the probability under the assumption that $\theta = \theta_0$.

Intuitively, a low p-value means "if the null hypothesis (that $\theta = \theta_0$) were true, we would infrequently encounter an result as extreme as the one that we saw. Therefore, if we *reject* the null hypothesis (that is, if we conclude that $\theta \neq \theta_0$) based solely on how extreme the result is, then that decision will be a mistake either infrequently (if $\theta = \theta_0$) or never (if $\theta \neq \theta_0$)." Thus, a low p-value offers probabilistic guarantees for those attempting to reject a null hypothesis. Note that a high p-value does not offer the same guarantees for those looking to *accept* a null hypothesis and is accordingly limited in its utility for decision making.

There is a general approach for obtaining asymptotically valid *Wald-type* p-values using the same principles as Theorem 3.4.2 (*Normal Approximation–Based Confidence Interval*). First, we will define a useful statistic, known as

[37] This is only one way of computing a p-value. It is possible to test hypotheses about θ using any variety of *test statistics*; we focus here on the case of using $\hat{\theta}$ as a test statistic.

the t-statistic. The t-statistic is a summary metric of how unusual the observed value of $\hat{\theta}$ would be under the null hypothesis that $\theta = \theta_0$.[38]

Definition 3.4.5. *t-Statistic*
Let $\hat{\theta}$ be an asymptotically normal estimator of θ, $\hat{\mathrm{V}}[\hat{\theta}]$ be a consistent estimator of the sampling variance, and $\hat{\theta}^*$ be the observed value of $\hat{\theta}$. Then the *t-statistic* is

$$t = \frac{\hat{\theta}^* - \theta_0}{\sqrt{\hat{\mathrm{V}}[\hat{\theta}]}}.$$

The utility of the t-statistic immediately becomes evident in the following theorem, which gives a general method for obtaining asymptotically valid p-values using the same principles as Theorem 3.4.2 (*Normal Approximation–Based Confidence Interval*).

Theorem 3.4.6. *Normal Approximation–Based p-Values*
Let $\hat{\theta}$ be an asymptotically normal estimator of θ, $\hat{\mathrm{V}}[\hat{\theta}]$ be a consistent estimator of the sampling variance, and $\hat{\theta}^*$ be the observed value of $\hat{\theta}$. Then

- an asymptotically valid lower one-tailed p-value under the null hypothesis that $\theta = \theta_0$ is given by

$$p = \Phi\left(\frac{\hat{\theta}^* - \theta_0}{\sqrt{\hat{\mathrm{V}}[\hat{\theta}]}}\right) = \Phi(t).$$

- an asymptotically valid upper one-tailed p-value under the null hypothesis that $\theta = \theta_0$ is given by

$$p = 1 - \Phi\left(\frac{\hat{\theta}^* - \theta_0}{\sqrt{\hat{\mathrm{V}}[\hat{\theta}]}}\right) = 1 - \Phi(t).$$

38 The t-statistic is so named because it is known to exactly follow Student's t-distribution under the null hypothesis that $\theta = \theta_0$ for certain linear estimators under a finite-sample normality assumption. We avoid discussion of the t-distribution as, all else equal, tests using the t-distribution and using a normal approximation asymptotically agree with i.i.d. data.

- an asymptotically valid two-tailed p-value under the null hypothesis that $\theta = \theta_0$ is given by

$$p = 2\left(1 - \Phi\left(\frac{|\hat{\theta}^* - \theta_0|}{\sqrt{\hat{\mathrm{V}}[\hat{\theta}]}}\right)\right) = 2\big(1 - \Phi(|t|)\big).$$

We omit the proof of this theorem, as well as a formal definition of asymptotic validity. Loosely speaking, however, asymptotic validity in the context of p-values implies that, under the null hypothesis that $\theta = \theta_0$, as $n \to \infty$, $p \xrightarrow{d} U(0,1)$. (For example, if $\theta = \theta_0$, n is large and the p-value is asymptotically valid, then across repeated samples, we would only obtain $p \leq 0.05$ in 5% of samples.) As with Section 3.4.1 (*Confidence Intervals*), asymptotically valid p-values do not have guarantees for finite samples. (See Section 3.4.4.)

One direct implication of Theorem 3.4.6 is that an asymptotically valid p-value is given by a one-to-one function of t. For example, if $|t| = 1.96$, then an asymptotically valid two-tailed p-value is given by $p = 0.05$. Traditionally, we *reject* the null hypothesis that $\theta = \theta_0$ if we obtain a p-value that is below some conventional significance threshold (usually .05) and *fail to reject* the null hypothesis otherwise.[39] (Be careful, though: many tests are likely to yield many "significant" results.) This leads to a simple rule of thumb: if the coefficient is twice the size of the standard error, we can say our result is "statistically significant at the .05 level."[40]

3.4.3 The Bootstrap

The idea of using the empirical CDF to approximate a CDF motivates our final topic for this section: the bootstrap. The bootstrap provides a procedure for estimating standard errors for many statistics of interest. The bootstrap derives its name from the phrase "pull yourself up by your bootstraps." This is an apt description, as we shall see shortly.

If we *knew* the CDF of some random variable, then we could derive the sampling distribution of any sample statistic. For example, if we knew that we had a fair coin, we would know that the sampling distribution of the sample mean would have mean $\frac{1}{2}$ and variance $\frac{1}{4n}$. In fact, we could use a computer simulation to calculate the sampling distribution of the sample mean to arbitrary

39 Similarly, by convention in empirical work, if a p-value is reported without specifying θ_0, it is assumed that the null hypothesis being tested is $\theta_0 = 0$.

40 As a result of what is best characterized as an accident of history, this criterion ($p < 0.05$) is often considered important for publication in scientific journals. While p-values can, in some contexts, be useful metrics of the strength of evidence, a sharp delineation between "significant" and "insignificant" scientific findings based on a p-value threshold (such as $p <$ 0.05) is seriously misguided—in theory and in practice.

precision by taking repeated simulated samples of size n, calculating the sample mean of each simulated sample, and observing the distribution of the resulting values. (We provide an example of such a simulation in Example 3.4.7 in the following section.)

So, characterizing the sampling variability of the sample mean (for a given n) is straightforward *if* we know the distribution that we are sampling from. The inferential problem, however, is that we do not know the distribution that we are sampling from. The bootstrap solution to this problem is quite elegant: pretend that the distribution that we are sampling from looks *exactly* like the sample that we have. That is, *plug-in* the empirical CDF for the CDF and sample from *that*. For this reason, the bootstrap is a *resampling method*.

Here, we will consider the simplest variant of the bootstrap, sometimes known as the "naive" bootstrap (for some details on alternative bootstrap procedures, see Footnote 41 and Davison and Hinkley (1997)). More specifically, to characterize the uncertainty of our estimator:

1. Take a *with replacement* sample of size *n from our sample.*[41]
2. Calculate our would-be estimate using this *bootstrap sample.*
3. Repeat steps 1 and 2 many times.
4. Using the resulting collection of *bootstrap estimates*, calculate the standard deviation of the *bootstrap distribution* of our estimator.

Given the usual plug-in regularity conditions (Section 3.3.1), this standard deviation will consistently estimate the standard error. Thus, if the asymptotic distribution of the estimator is normal, we can construct confidence intervals (and p-values) in the usual way.

This works as an inferential procedure because the bootstrap is a plug-in estimator. Under the i.i.d. sampling framework, the sampling distribution of an estimator is determined entirely by the CDF and n. Since the empirical CDF looks more and more like the CDF as n gets large, the plug-in sampling distribution yielded by the bootstrap looks more and more like the true sampling distribution. Put simply, the bootstrap works when plug-in estimation works.[42]

The bootstrap can be used to construct confidence intervals and p-values. The most straightforward way is as part of a normal approximation using Theorems 3.4.2 (*Normal Approximation–Based Confidence Interval*) and 3.4.6 (*Normal Approximation–Based p-Values*). This approach has good theoretical

41 This is the "naive" step. Refinements to the bootstrap often replace this step with alternative assumptions (for example, in one common variant of the Bayesian bootstrap, each bootstrap sample is constructed by applying weights drawn from a prespecified distribution to our sample).

42 A canonical example of an estimator for which the bootstrap fails for valid asymptotic statistical inference is the sample maximum for a bounded, continuous random variable. See, e.g., Efron and Tibshirani (1994, Ch. 7.4). We will briefly discuss a practical situation in Example 7.2.4 (*Matching Estimation*) where the bootstrap may also fail.

grounding, though there are alternative ways to construct confidence intervals (and p-values) with the bootstrap, including the percentile approach. Assuming that we have B bootstrap replicates, the percentile bootstrap estimate of a 95% confidence interval can be computed by sorting the B bootstrap estimates from smallest to largest, and forming an interval by taking the $\lfloor 0.025 \times B \rfloor^{\text{th}}$ sorted bootstrap estimate and the $\lceil 0.975 \times B \rceil^{\text{th}}$ sorted bootstrap estimate. The primary advantage of the percentile approach is that it does not at any point rely on a normal approximation, and thus often has better performance when n is small. Nevertheless, for parsimony, we will rely on the naive bootstrap under a normal approximation as we proceed.

The bootstrap is particularly useful in cases where we want to conduct inference using a weird estimator, like, say, $(\hat{\beta}_0 - \hat{\beta}_1)^3/(2 + \hat{\beta}_2^2)$. Although an analytic sampling variance estimator might be possible to derive, it might be difficult, or it might require using asymptotic approximations that yield very bad finite-sample performance. So, when we have i.i.d. sampling, the bootstrap is often a sensible way to estimate standard errors, and it saves us the hassle of having to work out an analytic sampling variance estimator in cases where it might be difficult.

3.4.4 Micronumerosity

In this section, we discuss a problem that often plagues empirical research: *micronumerosity*. As Goldberger (1991, Ch. 23.3) defined the term, micronumerosity is simply "an exotic polysyllabic name for 'small sample size.'"[43] When data are *micronumerous*, we are confronted with multiple issues.

As with Goldberger (1991), to ground ideas, we will begin with the sample mean $\overline{X}$ as an estimator of the population mean $\mathrm{E}[X]$. The primary issue is that when n is small, estimates tend to be imprecise. Theorem 3.2.34 establishes that the standard error of the sample mean is $\sigma[\overline{X}] = \sqrt{\mathrm{V}[X]/n}$. Thus, all else equal, when n is small, the standard error of $\overline{X}$ can be very large. Accordingly, when micronumerosity is present, it is difficult to estimate features of X with much precision.

[43] Goldberger (1991, Ch. 23.3) coined the term in order to satirize contemporary econometric treatments of a closely related problem in regression estimation (Chapter 4) known as *multicollinearity*. (We only briefly note multicollinearity in this book.) To provide a full context for our above definition, Goldberger notes:

> Econometrics texts devote many pages to the problem of multicollinearity in multiple regression, but they say little about the closely analogous problem of small sample size in estimating a univariate mean. Perhaps that imbalance is attributable to the lack of an exotic polysyllabic name for "small sample size." If so, we can remove that impediment by introducing the term *micronumerosity*.

We are quite fond of the term, as we believe that a memorable—and indeed sometimes exotic and polysyllabic—name can help in fixing ideas.

This carries through to how we can characterize uncertainty. As our estimates are less precise, so too are our estimates of uncertainty. Since we do not know the standard error of the sample mean, we must use an estimate thereof. Under micronumerosity, the estimated standard error has high sampling variability. This issue is exacerbated when attempting to use normal approximation–based confidence intervals and p-values, which not only rely on consistency of the standard error estimator but also asymptotic normality of the sample mean. When n is small, the sampling distribution of the sample mean may not be well approximated by a normal distribution (recall Figure 3.2.2). In such circumstances, we cannot expect that normal approximation–based confidence intervals will be valid. Definitionally, asymptotically valid inferences can only be guaranteed to be valid when data are not micronumerous.

We provide an illustrative example of the problems posed by micronumerosity. Our example will also show how computer simulations can be profitably used to investigate the small-sample behavior of statistical methods.

Example 3.4.7. *Computer Simulations of the Properties of the Sample Mean under Micronumerosity*
While our analytic results (such as consistency, asymptotic normality, and asymptotic validity of confidence intervals) have been reassuring, these results tell us little when data are micronumerous. We know that the sampling distributions of $\overline{X}$ and $\hat{\sigma}[\overline{X}]$ both depend on n. Furthermore, we know that normal approximation–based confidence intervals are only guaranteed to be valid when n is very large.

To investigate the small sample properties of the sample mean and associated measures of uncertainty, we will use computer simulations. We assume that we observe n i.i.d. draws of $X \sim U(0,1)$. To perform a simulation, we simulate $n = 10$, $n = 100$, or $n = 1{,}000$ draws from $U(0,1)$, and compute the sample mean, estimated standard error, and 90%/95%/99% normal approximation–based confidence intervals. We perform this simulation many, many times (here, we use 1 million simulations), and collect the estimates. Due to the law of large numbers, the empirical joint distribution of these quantities from our simulations approximates the true joint distribution of the estimators arbitrarily well. Our simulations are essentially plug-in estimates of the features of a random variable (an estimator) using a large number of simulated i.i.d. draws from its distribution.

In Table 3.4.1, we present summaries of the results of our simulations. We know that the sample mean is unbiased for the population mean, so we know that $\mathrm{E}[\overline{X}] = 0.5$ regardless of n, and we need not report the bias of the estimator. The first column, n, corresponds to the n associated with a given simulation. The second through fourth columns report properties of the standard error and our estimates thereof. The second column reports the true standard error (which can be exactly derived via Theorem 3.2.34). When $n = 10$, the variability of the estimate is quite high: the standard error

TABLE 3.4.1. *Implications of Micronumerosity (Standard Uniform Distribution)*

	Standard Error Properties			Coverage		
n	$\sigma[\overline{X}]$	$E[\hat{\sigma}[\overline{X}]]$	$\sigma[\hat{\sigma}[\overline{X}]]$	90% CI	95% CI	99% CI
10	0.091	0.090	0.015	86.6%	91.6%	96.5%
100	0.029	0.029	0.001	89.7%	94.7%	98.8%
1,000	0.009	0.009	0.000	90.0%	95.0%	99.0%

TABLE 3.4.2. *Implications of Micronumerosity (Bernoulli Distribution with $p = 0.5$)*

	Standard Error Properties			Coverage		
n	$\sigma[\overline{X}]$	$E[\hat{\sigma}[\overline{X}]]$	$\sigma[\hat{\sigma}[\overline{X}]]$	90% CI	95% CI	99% CI
10	0.158	0.157	0.014	89.0%	89.0%	97.8%
100	0.050	0.050	0.000	91.1%	94.3%	98.8%
1,000	0.016	0.016	0.000	89.3%	94.7%	99.0%

encompasses almost 10% of the range of possible values that X can take on. But as n increases, the standard error shrinks proportionally to $n^{-1/2}$. The third column reports the expected value of our estimate of the standard error, $\hat{\sigma}[\overline{X}]$. We see that, even in very small sample sizes, the estimator is approximately unbiased, as in all cases $\sigma[\overline{X}] \approx E[\hat{\sigma}[\overline{X}]]$. The fourth column shows the standard error of our estimate of the standard error; we see that our estimate of the standard error has high variability when $n = 10$, but that its variability quickly diminishes with n.

In the remaining columns, we show the actual coverage associated with our normal approximation–based confidence intervals. That is, across our many simulations, we count the number of times that the estimated confidence interval includes 0.5 and divide by the number of simulations. We see that, when n is small, our estimated confidence intervals are not valid. For example, when $n = 10$, the actual coverage of our 95% confidence intervals lies below the nominal level—they in fact have only 89% coverage. That is, across 89% of our simulated random draws of $n = 10$ values from the distribution X, the (nominally) 95% normal approximation–based confidence interval actually covers $E[X]$. However, as n gets larger, this problem is quickly alleviated. With $n = 100$, our confidence intervals appear to be very close to valid in this setting.

Of course, our calculations are specific to the setting of our simulation. The results above do not speak to all generative distributions. Table 3.4.2 reports the results of simulations conducted exactly as with Table 3.4.1, with only one difference: X is a Bernoulli random variable with $p = 0.5$. Our results differ substantively, particularly with respect to the coverage properties of the normal approximation–based confidence intervals. We see that, even when $n = 1{,}000$, the 90% and 95% normal-approximation confidence intervals are not exactly valid, suggesting that some distributions require larger samples in order for asymptotic approximations to be appropriate. We also see that coverage does not necessarily follow an obvious pattern in small samples; for example, due to the differing quality of the normal approximation at different points of the distribution, the 90% confidence interval coverage follows a non-monotonic trend: the coverage is higher for $n = 100$ than for $n = 1{,}000$. The small-sample behavior of statistical methods justified by asymptotic theory may be somewhat unpredictable, but we can investigate some of their properties through investigation of their behavior under different assumptions about the population distribution. △

The problems posed by micronumerosity are not limited to estimating the population mean. In fact, the problems become more pronounced when considering more complex functionals. We will face this problem shortly in Section 4.3.2 (*Overfitting*). Put simply: micronumerosity implies that we do not have enough data to estimate what we would like to estimate with enough precision. Some functionals may be easy to estimate with relatively little data, others may not. The only guaranteed solution to a problem of micronumerosity is the collection of more data as would be produced by, for instance, replication efforts.

3.5 CLUSTER SAMPLES

In this section, we consider one way in which the i.i.d. assumption might be violated. Specifically, we allow for observations to be correlated (or non-i.i.d.) within *clusters*, but i.i.d. across clusters. This accommodates a particular way in which the i.i.d. assumption might be violated, and approximates many problems that we might encounter. For example, we might believe that units within a country have correlated outcomes, but that units across countries are highly unlikely to have any statistical dependence.

To codify this idea, let us now assume that we have l i.i.d. *clusters* of observations, each consisting of m values and represented by a random vector $(X_{i1}, X_{i2}, ... X_{im})$. Throughout all our discussions of clustering in this book, we will be making the simplifying assumption that all clusters are of an identical size m. Largely, this serves to make matters notationally convenient and to resolve ambiguity about estimands (namely, how units across clusters should be weighted). Where this assumption is theoretically consequential, we make note of it in the text; otherwise, our results largely carry through as long as cluster sizes remain bounded. While observations must be independent across clusters (for example, $X_{ij} \perp\!\!\!\perp X_{i'j}$), within clusters they may be statistically dependent (that is, it is not generally the case that $X_{ij} \perp\!\!\!\perp X_{ij'}$). Let $n = lm$, so that the number of observations is the number of clusters times the number of observations per cluster. We now explore the consequences for estimation and inference of computing estimates from *cluster samples*.

3.5.1 Estimation with Clustering

In general, the random vector $(X_{i1}, X_{i2}, ... X_{im})$ is characterized by a joint CDF F. Taking l i.i.d. draws of this random vector yields an empirical joint CDF $\hat{F}$. Statistical functionals are now written as functions of the joint CDF. We can then apply the plug-in principle as we usually would for i.i.d. data, and estimate the functional of interest using the empirical joint CDF.

Let us see how this works for the sample mean. It will be useful for us to define the following random variable, the *cluster average*. The cluster average is simply the mean of the observations in that cluster.

Definition 3.5.1. *Cluster Average*
For i.i.d. random vectors[44] $(X_{11}, X_{12}, ... X_{1m})$, $(X_{21}, X_{22}, ... X_{2m})$, ..., $(X_{l1}, X_{l2}, ... X_{lm})$, the ith *cluster average* is

$$W_i = \frac{1}{m}\sum_{j=1}^{m} X_{ij}, \forall i \in \{1, 2, ..., l\}.$$

Since the random vectors are i.i.d., it follows that W_1, W_2, ..., W_l are i.i.d. With a single step, we have transformed the problem into an i.i.d. problem. As usual, we define the sample mean as the average of all the observed values.

Definition 3.5.2. *Cluster Sample Mean*
For i.i.d. random vectors $(X_{11}, X_{12}, ... X_{1m})$, $(X_{21}, X_{22}, ... X_{2m})$, ..., $(X_{l1}, X_{l2}, ... X_{lm})$, the *cluster sample mean* is

$$\overline{X} = \frac{1}{n}\sum_{i=1}^{l}\sum_{j=1}^{m} X_{ij}.$$

This step is where our simplifying assumption that all clusters are the same size really becomes operational. Since clusters are all the same size, the cluster sample mean is equivalent to the sample mean of W. If we have different cluster sizes, the following theorem will not hold.

44 Random vectors are i.i.d. if each has the same *joint* distribution and they satisfy a vector version of mutual independence.

Theorem 3.5.3. *The Cluster Sample Mean Is the Sample Mean of Cluster Averages*
Let $(X_{11}, X_{12}, \dots X_{1m})$, $(X_{21}, X_{22}, \dots X_{2m})$, ..., $(X_{l1}, X_{l2}, \dots X_{lm})$ be i.i.d. random vectors, and let W_i be the ith cluster average, $\forall i \in \{1,2,\dots,l\}$. Then

$$\overline{X} = \overline{W}.$$

Proof:

$$\overline{X} = \frac{1}{n}\sum_{i=1}^{l}\sum_{j=1}^{m} X_{ij} = \frac{1}{lm}\sum_{i=1}^{l}\sum_{j=1}^{m} X_{ij} = \frac{1}{l}\sum_{i=1}^{l}\frac{1}{m}\sum_{j=1}^{m} X_{ij} = \frac{1}{l}\sum_{i=1}^{l} W_i = \overline{W}. \quad \square$$

The sample mean is now unbiased for what we will call the *population mean cluster average*, that is, the population mean of W, $\mathrm{E}[W]$.

Theorem 3.5.4. *The Cluster Sample Mean Is Unbiased for the Population Mean Cluster Average*
Let $(X_{11}, X_{12}, \dots X_{1m})$, $(X_{21}, X_{22}, \dots X_{2m})$, ..., $(X_{l1}, X_{l2}, \dots X_{lm})$ be i.i.d. random vectors, and let W_i be the ith cluster average, $\forall i \in \{1,2,\dots,l\}$. Then

$$\mathrm{E}\left[\overline{X}\right] = \mathrm{E}[W].$$

Proof:

$$\mathrm{E}\left[\overline{X}\right] = \mathrm{E}\left[\overline{W}\right] = \mathrm{E}[W],$$

where the second equality follows from Theorem 3.2.3 (*The Expected Value of the Sample Mean is the Population Mean*). □

Characterizing the sampling variance becomes a bit more complicated, since we now need to account for the covariance between every pair of units within each cluster. However, the application of the multivariate variance rule (Theorem 2.3.2) allows for a simple representation of the sampling variance.

Theorem 3.5.5. *Sampling Variance of the Cluster Sample Mean*
Let $(X_{11}, X_{12}, \dots X_{1m})$, $(X_{21}, X_{22}, \dots X_{2m})$, ..., $(X_{l1}, X_{l2}, \dots X_{lm})$ be i.i.d. random vectors, and let W_i be the ith cluster average, $\forall i \in \{1,2,\dots,l\}$. Then the sampling variance of the cluster sample mean is

$$\mathrm{V}\left[\overline{X}\right] = \frac{1}{lm^2}\sum_{j=1}^{m}\sum_{j'=1}^{m} \mathrm{Cov}[X_{ij}, X_{ij'}].$$

Proof:

$$\begin{aligned}
\mathrm{V}\left[\overline{\mathrm{X}}\right] &= \mathrm{V}\left[\overline{W}\right] \\
&= \frac{\mathrm{V}[W]}{l} \\
&= \frac{1}{l}\mathrm{V}\left[\frac{1}{m}\sum_{j=1}^{m}\mathrm{X}_{ij}\right] \\
&= \frac{1}{lm^2}\mathrm{V}\left[\sum_{j=1}^{m}\mathrm{X}_{ij}\right] \\
&= \frac{1}{lm^2}\sum_{j=1}^{m}\sum_{j'=1}^{m}\mathrm{Cov}[\mathrm{X}_{ij},\mathrm{X}_{ij'}],
\end{aligned}$$

where the second equality follows from Theorem 3.2.4 (*Sampling Variance of the Sample Mean*) and the last follows from Theorem 2.3.2 (*Multivariate Variance Rule*). □

Alternatively, we can think about the estimator as the average of i.i.d. random variables, with mean E[X] and common variance V[W]. Accordingly, a version of the WLLN still holds, but it now says that the cluster sample mean is consistent for the population mean cluster average. This result (and the following results) will require that the number of clusters $l \to \infty$, with m not growing in n. If the number of units per cluster $m \to \infty$, no such guarantees will hold.

Theorem 3.5.6. *WLLN for Cluster Samples*
Let $(X_{11},X_{12},...X_{1m})$, $(X_{21},X_{22},...X_{2m})$, ..., $(X_{l1},X_{l2},...X_{lm})$ be i.i.d. random vectors with finite $\mathrm{E}[\mathrm{X}_{ij}]$ and finite $\mathrm{V}[\mathrm{X}_{ij}] > 0$, $\forall i \in \{1,2,...,l\}$ and $\forall j \in \{1,2,...,m\}$, and let W_i be the ith cluster average, $\forall i \in \{1,2,...,l\}$. Then

$$\overline{\mathrm{X}} \xrightarrow{p} \mathrm{E}[W].$$

Proof: As m is finite, E[W] and V[W] are finite.[45] Then, by the WLLN, $\overline{\mathrm{X}} = \overline{W} \xrightarrow{p} \mathrm{E}[W]$. □

[45] It could be the case that V[W] = 0, but then W is constant, $W = \mathrm{E}[W]$, and so it is trivially true that $\overline{\mathrm{X}} = \overline{W} \xrightarrow{p} \mathrm{E}[W]$.

Similarly, the Central Limit Theorem also still applies, though the standardized sample mean no longer reduces to $\frac{\sqrt{n}(\overline{X}-\mu)}{\sigma}$. Instead,

$$\begin{aligned}
Z &= \frac{\left(\overline{X}-\mathrm{E}\left[\overline{X}\right]\right)}{\sigma\left[\overline{X}\right]} \\
&= \frac{\left(\overline{W}-\mathrm{E}[W]\right)}{\sigma\left[\overline{W}\right]} \\
&= \frac{\left(\overline{W}-\mathrm{E}[W]\right)}{\sqrt{\mathrm{V}\left[\overline{W}\right]}} \\
&= \frac{\left(\overline{W}-\mathrm{E}[W]\right)}{\sqrt{\frac{\mathrm{V}[W]}{l}}} \\
&= \frac{\sqrt{l}\left(\overline{W}-\mathrm{E}[W]\right)}{\sigma[W]} \\
&= Z_W,
\end{aligned}$$

or the standardized sample mean of W.

Theorem 3.5.7. *Central Limit Theorem for Cluster Samples*
Let $(X_{11}, X_{12}, \ldots X_{1m})$, $(X_{21}, X_{22}, \ldots X_{2m})$, ..., $(X_{l1}, X_{l2}, \ldots X_{lm})$ be i.i.d. random vectors such that $\mathrm{E}[W]$ and $\mathrm{V}[W] > 0$ are finite, where W_i is the ith cluster average, $\forall i \in \{1,2,\ldots,l\}$. Let Z_W be the standardized sample mean. Then

$$Z_W \xrightarrow{d} \mathrm{N}(0,1),$$

or equivalently,

$$\sqrt{l}\left(\overline{X}-\mathrm{E}[W]\right) \xrightarrow{d} \mathrm{N}(0,\sigma_W^2).$$

Proof: By the Central Limit Theorem, $Z_W \xrightarrow{d} N(0,1)$, and likewise, $\sqrt{l}(\overline{X}-\mathrm{E}[W]) = \sqrt{l}(\overline{W}-\mathrm{E}[W]) \xrightarrow{d} \mathrm{N}(0,\sigma_W^2)$. □

With the Central Limit Theorem in hand, we can move on to tools for inference as usual.

3.5.2 Inference with Clustering

The tools that we have used for inference can be readily adapted to the case in which we have clustered data. The sampling variance of the cluster sample mean can be estimated using a plug-in estimator:

$$\hat{\mathrm{V}}\left[\overline{X}\right] = \hat{\mathrm{V}}\left[\overline{W}\right] = \frac{\hat{\mathrm{V}}[W]}{l},$$

where $\hat{\mathrm{V}}[W]$ is the unbiased sample variance of W. By Theorem 3.2.33 (*Estimating the Sampling Variance*) and the CMT, this estimator is consistent under analogous regularity conditions to the i.i.d. case:

$$n\hat{\mathrm{V}}\left[\overline{X}\right] = m\left(l\hat{\mathrm{V}}\left[\overline{W}\right]\right) = m\left(\hat{\mathrm{V}}[W]\right) \xrightarrow{p} m(\mathrm{V}[W]) = m\left(l\mathrm{V}\left[\overline{W}\right]\right) = n\mathrm{V}\left[\overline{X}\right].$$

Since $\overline{X}$ is asymptotically normal, normal approximation–based confidence intervals and p-values can then be obtained in the usual way, except working with W instead of X.

Example 3.5.8. *Consequences of Clustering for the Sample Mean*
How does clustering affect the sampling variance of our estimates? Let us impose a working assumption for illustrative purposes. Suppose that:

- $\forall i, j, \mathrm{V}[X_{ij}] = \sigma^2$.
- $\forall i, j, j', \rho[X_{ij}, X_{ij'}] = \rho > 0$.

In other words, the variance of each observation is identical, and every unit within a cluster shares the same correlation. Then, $\forall i, j, j', \mathrm{Cov}[X_{ij}, X_{ij'}] = \rho[X_{ij}, X_{ij'}]\sigma[X_{ij}]\sigma[X_{ij'}] = \rho\sigma^2$, so

$$\begin{aligned}
\mathrm{V}\left[\overline{X}\right] &= \frac{1}{lm^2}\sum_{j=1}^{m}\sum_{j'=1}^{m}\mathrm{Cov}[X_{ij}, X_{ij'}] \\
&= \frac{1}{lm^2}\left(m\sigma^2 + m(m-1)\rho\sigma^2\right) \\
&= \frac{\sigma^2}{lm}\big(1 + \rho(m-1)\big).
\end{aligned}$$

Let us now consider two extreme cases (still assuming that all clusters are of an identical size m). Suppose $\rho = 0$; that is, there is no *intraclass correlation*. Then

$$\mathrm{V}\left[\overline{X}\right] = \frac{\sigma^2}{lm} = \frac{\sigma^2}{n},$$

just as if we had no clustering. With no intraclass correlation, clustering induces no sampling variance inflation, so it is as though we have n i.i.d. observations.

Now suppose $\rho = 1$; that is, there is perfect intraclass correlation. Then

$$\mathrm{V}\left[\overline{X}\right] = \frac{\sigma^2}{lm}(1 + m - 1) = \frac{\sigma^2}{lm}m = \frac{\sigma^2}{l}.$$

With perfect intraclass correlation, it is as though we only have l observations. Usually, the answer lies somewhere in between. The primary consequence of clustering is that we have less information from the data, and we suffer a precision penalty accordingly. Even if n is very large, if l is small, the data may nevertheless effectively be micronumerous. △

What can we do if we want to conduct inference using an arbitrary estimator and we do not have (or do not want to derive) an analytic estimator of the sampling variance of that estimator? We again can use a variant of the bootstrap. Specifically, with clustering, one appropriate method is the *block bootstrap*, which is exactly like the bootstrap except that now we resample whole *clusters* rather than individual units. To implement the block bootstrap:

1. Take a *with replacement* sample of m clusters from our sample, keeping clusters intact.
2. Calculate our would-be estimate using this collected n observations in our block bootstrap sample.
3. Repeat steps 1 and 2 many times.
4. Using the resulting collection of block bootstrap estimates, calculate the standard deviation of the block bootstrap distribution of our estimator.

Since we drew a sample of l i.i.d. clusters to begin with, we are again replicating the sampling process, taking with-replacement samples of l clusters from our sample. The rest of the procedure is the same as before. The block bootstrap behaves well, as usual, given a large number of clusters and the usual plug-in regularity conditions.

3.6 FURTHER READINGS

Again, the readings in Chapter 1 and 2 remain relevant. Beyond these, there are a number of detailed treatments of the topics discussed in Chapter 3. For a general treatment of statistical estimation theory, we strongly recommend Wasserman (2006) and Wasserman (2012), which serve as a key inspiration for the presentation of the materials in this chapter. For the theory of survey samples, Cochran (1977) is a canonical treatment. Although we do not cover design-based inference in our book, Särndal et al. (1992) and Thompson (1997) provide excellent modern treatments of this approach to survey sampling. Lehmann (1999) and DasGupta (2008) are technical and invaluable resources for asymptotic theory. Tsybakov (2009) provides an elegant, technical treatment of nonparametric estimation theory. Newey (1990) provides an article-length overview of semiparametric efficiency theory, and remains perhaps the most readable (yet still technical and rigorous) treatment of the subject matter. Van der Laan and Rose (2011) provides a modern book-length unification of semiparametric methods and machine learning for the estimation of statistical functionals. Silverman (1986) provides an in-depth book-length treatment of kernel density estimation. Greenland et al. (2016) is a concise, important, and highly readable article about statistical testing and confidence intervals, and is strongly suggested for all readers. Lehmann and Romano (2005) also covers the theory of statistical tests, which covers much of the same material as Lehmann (1999), but at a higher level of technicality. Efron and Tibshirani (1994) and Davison and Hinkley (1997) are quite readable and comprehensive books on the bootstrap.

4

Regression

Truth is much too complicated to allow anything but approximations.

—JOHN VON NEUMANN

In Chapter 2, we considered the conditional expectation function (CEF) and best linear predictor (BLP) as ways to summarize bivariate or multivariate relationships. In this chapter, we apply the principles on estimation from Chapter 3 to the CEF and BLP in order to derive a simple and powerful tool for empirical practice: regression. In its simplest form, regression can be seen as a method for estimating the BLP using the data in our sample, much as the sample mean is an estimator for the population mean. More generally, we see that regression estimators provide a flexible way to approximate the CEF in a principled and transparent manner.

The regression estimator is central in both theoretical and applied statistics and econometrics, in part because it can be motivated by many different assumptions and statistical perspectives. For example, regression can be motivated by a restrictive parametric model known as the classical linear model, which we will discuss in Sections 5.1.1 (*The Classical Linear Model*) and 5.2.1 (*The Logic of Maximum Likelihood Estimation*). Motivations for regression abound—including motivations that even require no probability theory at all (see, e.g., Hastie, Tibshirani, and Friedman 2009, Ch. 1). Our treatment of regression focuses on our agnostic approach: although we assume i.i.d. sampling (and the usual plug-in regularity conditions), we require no assumptions about the functional form of the CEF.

4.1 REGRESSION ESTIMATION

We begin by showing how regression is a simple plug-in estimator for the BLP. We know from Section 3.3 (*The Plug-In Principle*) that plug-in estimators provide a rather general way to estimate population functionals, and the regression estimator is no exception.

4.1.1 Bivariate Case

Let us first consider the bivariate case, where we are interested in the random vector (X, Y). Recall that the BLP of Y given X is $g(X) = \alpha + \beta X$, where

$$\alpha = \mathrm{E}[Y] - \frac{\mathrm{Cov}[X, Y]}{\mathrm{V}[X]}\mathrm{E}[X],$$

$$\beta = \frac{\mathrm{Cov}[X, Y]}{\mathrm{V}[X]}.$$

Applying Theorems 2.1.13 (*Alternative Formula for Variance*) and 2.2.2 (*Alternative Formula for Covariance*), these equations can be rewritten in terms of expected values:

$$\alpha = \mathrm{E}[Y] - \frac{\mathrm{E}[XY] - \mathrm{E}[X]\mathrm{E}[Y]}{\mathrm{E}\left[X^2\right] - \mathrm{E}[X]^2}\mathrm{E}[X],$$

$$\beta = \frac{\mathrm{E}[XY] - \mathrm{E}[X]\mathrm{E}[Y]}{\mathrm{E}\left[X^2\right] - \mathrm{E}[X]^2}.$$

We can then *estimate* the BLP using plug-in estimation:

$$\hat{\alpha} = \overline{Y} - \frac{\overline{XY} - \overline{X} \cdot \overline{Y}}{\overline{X^2} - \overline{X}^2}\overline{X},$$

$$\hat{\beta} = \frac{\overline{XY} - \overline{X} \cdot \overline{Y}}{\overline{X^2} - \overline{X}^2}.$$

Thus, we can use *sample* data to estimate the population relationship: $\hat{\alpha}$ is the regression estimate of the intercept of the BLP and is consistent for α, and $\hat{\beta}$ is the regression estimate of the slope of the BLP and is consistent for β. (Consistency follows immediately from the Weak Law of Large Numbers and Continuous Mapping Theorem.)

Example 4.1.1. *Estimating the BLP*
Suppose we have a random vector (X, Y) such that

$$Y = 1 + 2X + 5U,$$

where X and U are independent and each distributed as $N(0, 1)$. We can derive the CEF of Y given X:

$$\mathrm{E}[Y|X] = \mathrm{E}[1 + 2X + 5U|X] = 1 + 2\mathrm{E}[X|X] + 5\mathrm{E}[U] = 1 + 2X.$$

In this example, the CEF is linear, so the BLP *is* the CEF, and so we have $\alpha = 1$, $\beta = 2$. Now, suppose we do not know the joint distribution of (X, Y) and we wanted to estimate the CEF of Y given X from sample data. We would observe a sample of draws from (X, Y); such a sample is shown in Table 4.1.1.

TABLE 4.1.1. *Sample of $n = 15$ Draws from (X, Y)*

Unit	Y	X
1	6.88	1.37
2	1.17	0.30
3	16.16	1.57
4	−4.84	−0.69
5	−6.17	−0.64
6	0.67	0.08
7	3.36	0.47
8	−0.69	1.33
9	8.03	−0.13
10	−3.35	0.59
11	1.87	−0.44
12	13.54	0.76
13	4.06	0.73
14	6.72	−3.54
15	7.20	−0.05

The dataset shown in the table is all that is available to the researcher. The goal is to estimate the CEF, but the CEF is hard to characterize—it could have *any* functional form.[1] From our fifteen data points, it is impossible to distinguish all the different shapes that the CEF could take. (We will provide further discussion of this point in Section 4.3.2.) Nevertheless, regression consistently estimates the minimum mean squared error (MSE) *linear* approximation of the CEF, that is, the BLP.

In Figure 4.1.2, we overlay the data points, the actual (unknown to the researcher) CEF (in black) and the regression estimate of the BLP (in red). We see that, even with an n of 15, we approximate the relationship fairly well. Naturally, if we were to add more data, we would expect that this approximation would improve accordingly. △

4.1.2 OLS Regression

Suppose now that we have K explanatory variables: $X_{[1]}, X_{[2]}, \ldots, X_{[K]}$. In this case, as we saw in Section 2.3 (*Multivariate Generalizations*), the BLP is still defined as the linear function that minimizes MSE. That is, the BLP (also known as the *population regression function*) is the linear function

[1] In this case, we know that it is in fact linear, but we are pretending we do not know that.

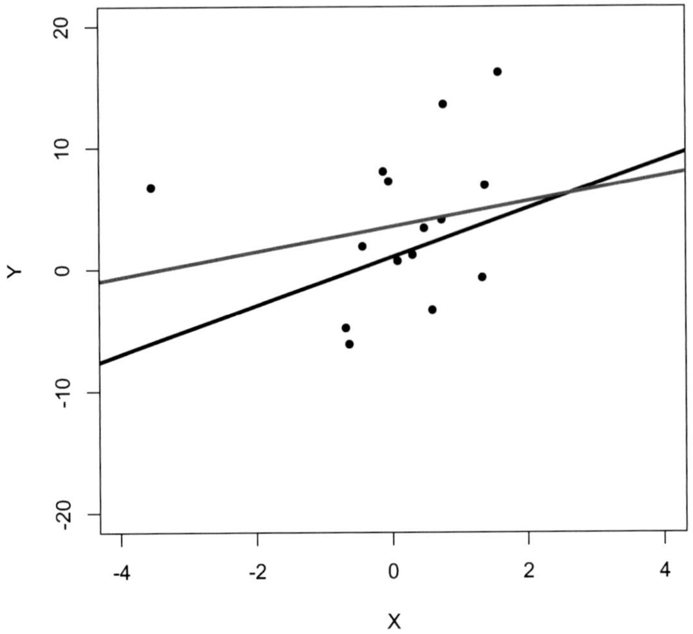

FIGURE 4.1.2. *Illustration of $n = 15$ Sample of Draws from (X, Y)*

$g(X_{[1]}, X_{[2]}, ..., X_{[K]}) = \beta_0 + \beta_1 X_{[1]} + \beta_2 X_{[2]} + ... + \beta_K X_{[K]}$ such that

$$(\beta_0, \beta_1, ..., \beta_K) = \underset{(b_0, b_1, ..., b_K) \in \mathbb{R}^{K+1}}{\arg\min} \; \mathrm{E}\left[\left(Y - (b_0 + b_1 X_{[1]} + b_2 X_{[2]} + ... b_K X_{[K]})\right)^2\right].$$

How would we estimate the BLP? Unfortunately, in the multivariate case, we no longer have the simple formulas $\alpha = \mathrm{E}[Y] - \frac{\mathrm{Cov}[X,Y]}{\mathrm{V}[X]}\mathrm{E}[X]$ and $\beta = \frac{\mathrm{Cov}[X,Y]}{\mathrm{V}[X]}$. But the plug-in principle still applies; we can still replace expectations with sample means in the definition of the BLP to obtain an estimate thereof.[2]

Definition 4.1.2. *OLS Regression Estimator*
For i.i.d. random vectors $(Y_1, \mathbf{X}_1)$, $(Y_2, \mathbf{X}_2)$, ..., $(Y_n, \mathbf{X}_n)$, the *ordinary least squares (OLS) regression estimator* is the function $\hat{g}(\mathbf{X}) = \hat{\beta}_0 + \hat{\beta}_1 X_{[1]} +$

[2] Note that the term "multivariate regression" does not refer to regression with more than one explanatory variable; rather it refers to the case where the outcome is a random vector. The multivariate generalization of regression we consider here is often referred to as "multiple regression."

$\hat{\beta}_2 X_{[2]} + ... + \hat{\beta}_K X_{[K]}$ such that

$$\begin{aligned}\hat{\boldsymbol{\beta}} &= (\hat{\beta}_0, \hat{\beta}_1, ..., \hat{\beta}_K) \\ &= \underset{(b_0,b_1,...,b_K)\in\mathbb{R}^{K+1}}{\operatorname{argmin}} \frac{1}{n}\sum_{i=1}^{n}\Big(Y_i - (b_0 + b_1 X_{[1]i} + b_2 X_{[2]i} + ... b_K X_{[K]i})\Big)^2.\end{aligned}$$

We refer to $\hat{\boldsymbol{\beta}}$ as the *OLS coefficient estimator.*

The quantity $e_i = Y_i - (\hat{\beta}_0 + \hat{\beta}_1 X_{[1]i} + \hat{\beta}_2 X_{[2]i} + ...\hat{\beta}_K X_{[K]i})$ is known as the ith *residual.* It is the difference between the observed value of Y_i and the value we would have predicted given the observed values of $X_{[1]i}$, $X_{[2]i}$, ..., $X_{[K]i}$ and our estimate of the BLP. A residual is the sample analog of a prediction *error*, which is the difference between an observed value of Y_i and the value that would have been predicted based on the observed values of $X_{[1]i}$, $X_{[2]i}$, ..., $X_{[K]i}$ and some actual population predictor (e.g, the true CEF or BLP). This estimator is called the *ordinary least squares (OLS)* regression estimator because it finds the fit that minimizes the mean of squared residuals (or, equivalently, minimizes the sum of squared residuals).[3] Thus, the regression estimator is a plug-in estimator; in order to estimate the parameters that minimize the mean squared error, we find the parameters that minimize the mean squared residual.

4.1.3 Regression with Matrix Algebra

In this section, we show how to derive a closed-form representation of the OLS regression estimator using matrix algebra. We recommend that all readers (even those who are less familiar with matrix algebra) examine the proofs in this section, as they show how matrix algebra can be profitably used to simplify linear optimization problems.

Our goal is to find the coefficient values that minimize the sum of squared residuals. To do this, we will need to represent the problem in matrix notation. In particular, we will need to define the *regressor matrix* (also known as the *design matrix* or *model matrix*).

[3] Strictly speaking, OLS is the oldest and most familiar regression method. The many others include weighted least squares and penalized regression (Section 4.3.6). In this book, "regression" refers to OLS unless otherwise noted.

Definition 4.1.3. *Regressor Matrix*
For i.i.d. random vectors $(Y_1,\mathbf{X}_1)$, $(Y_2,\mathbf{X}_2)$, ..., $(Y_n,\mathbf{X}_n)$, the *regressor matrix* for the OLS regression estimator is

$$\mathbb{X} = \begin{pmatrix} 1 & X_{[1]1} & X_{[2]1} & \cdots & X_{[K]1} \\ 1 & X_{[1]2} & X_{[2]2} & \cdots & X_{[K]2} \\ \vdots & \vdots & \vdots & \ddots & \vdots \\ 1 & X_{[1]n} & X_{[2]n} & \cdots & X_{[K]n} \end{pmatrix}.$$

(All matrices in this book shall be denoted by "blackboard bold" letters, for example, $\mathbb{X}$ and $\mathbb{W}$.)

We can now state the canonical closed-form OLS regression solution.

Theorem 4.1.4. *OLS Solution in Matrix Algebra*
Let $(\mathbf{X}_1, Y_1)$, $(\mathbf{X}_2, Y_2)$, ..., $(\mathbf{X}_n, Y_n)$ be i.i.d. random vectors. Then, if $\mathbb{X}^T\mathbb{X}$ is invertible, the OLS coefficient estimator is given by

$$\hat{\boldsymbol{\beta}} = \left(\mathbb{X}^T\mathbb{X}\right)^{-1}\mathbb{X}^T\mathbf{Y}.$$

Proof: For any $(b_0, b_1, ..., b_K) \in \mathbb{R}^{K+1}$ and for every observation i, we can define the ith residual as

$$e_i = Y_i - \left(b_0 + b_1 X_{[1]i} + b_2 X_{[2]i} + ... + b_K X_{[K]i}\right).$$

We can "stack" all n of these e_is to form a system of equations,

$$e_1 = Y_1 - \left(b_0 + b_1 X_{[1]1} + b_2 X_{[2]1} + ... b_K X_{[K]1}\right)$$

$$e_2 = Y_2 - \left(b_0 + b_1 X_{[1]2} + b_2 X_{[2]2} + ... b_K X_{[K]2}\right)$$

$$\vdots$$

$$e_n = Y_3 - \left(b_0 + b_1 X_{[1]n} + b_2 X_{[2]n} + ... b_K X_{[K]n}\right).$$

This system of equations can be rewritten in matrix form as:

$$\begin{pmatrix} e_1 \\ e_2 \\ \vdots \\ e_n \end{pmatrix} = \begin{pmatrix} Y_1 \\ Y_2 \\ \vdots \\ Y_n \end{pmatrix} - \begin{pmatrix} 1 & X_{[1]1} & X_{[2]1} & \cdots & X_{[K]1} \\ 1 & X_{[1]2} & X_{[2]2} & \cdots & X_{[K]2} \\ \vdots & \vdots & \vdots & \ddots & \vdots \\ 1 & X_{[1]n} & X_{[2]n} & \cdots & X_{[K]n} \end{pmatrix} \begin{pmatrix} b_0 \\ b_1 \\ b_2 \\ \vdots \\ b_K \end{pmatrix},$$

or equivalently, $\mathbf{e} = \mathbf{Y} - \mathbb{X}\mathbf{b}$, where $\mathbf{e} = (e_1, e_2, ..., e_n)^T$, $\mathbf{Y} = (Y_1, Y_2, ..., Y_n)^T$, $\mathbf{b} = (b_0, b_1, b_2, ..., b_K)^T$, and $\mathbb{X}$ is the regressor matrix. Thus, finding the OLS regression estimator is equivalent to the following minimization problem:

$$\hat{\boldsymbol{\beta}} = \underset{\mathbf{b}\in\mathbb{R}^{K+1}}{\arg\min} \sum_{i=1}^{n} e_i^2 = \underset{\mathbf{b}\in\mathbb{R}^{K+1}}{\arg\min} \left(\mathbf{e}^T\mathbf{e}\right) = \underset{\mathbf{b}\in\mathbb{R}^{K+1}}{\arg\min} (\mathbf{Y} - \mathbb{X}\mathbf{b})^T(\mathbf{Y} - \mathbb{X}\mathbf{b}).$$

The first-order condition (that is, setting the derivative of the sum of squared residuals with respect to the coefficients equal to zero) yields

$$-2\mathbb{X}^T(\mathbf{Y} - \mathbb{X}\hat{\boldsymbol{\beta}}) = \mathbf{0}.^4$$

Solving for $\hat{\boldsymbol{\beta}}$,

$$\begin{aligned}
-\mathbb{X}^T(\mathbf{Y} - \mathbb{X}\hat{\boldsymbol{\beta}}) &= \mathbf{0} \\
-\mathbb{X}^T\mathbf{Y} + \mathbb{X}^T\mathbb{X}\hat{\boldsymbol{\beta}} &= \mathbf{0} \\
\mathbb{X}^T\mathbb{X}\hat{\boldsymbol{\beta}} &= \mathbb{X}^T\mathbf{Y} \\
\left(\mathbb{X}^T\mathbb{X}\right)^{-1}\left(\mathbb{X}^T\mathbb{X}\right)\hat{\boldsymbol{\beta}} &= \left(\mathbb{X}^T\mathbb{X}\right)^{-1}\mathbb{X}^T\mathbf{Y} \\
\hat{\boldsymbol{\beta}} &= \left(\mathbb{X}^T\mathbb{X}\right)^{-1}\mathbb{X}^T\mathbf{Y}. \quad \square
\end{aligned}$$

Note that the condition that $\mathbb{X}^T\mathbb{X}$ must be invertible implies that all the explanatory variables cannot be written as linear combinations of one another; that is, they are not *exactly multicollinear*. Such cases arise, for instance, when the number of variables $K > n$ (an extreme case of *micronumerosity*), or when some variables have no variance. In practice, this condition suffices to make the OLS solution unique. For example, in the case of a single explanatory variable, assuming invertibility of $\mathbb{X}^T\mathbb{X}$ is equivalent to assuming that $\hat{\mathrm{V}}[X] > 0$. If this condition were not to hold, there would be infinitely many $\hat{\boldsymbol{\beta}}$ values that would all minimize the mean of squared residuals.

Some noteworthy properties of the regression estimator also follow from the matrix algebraic solution.

Theorem 4.1.5. *Properties of Residuals from the OLS Regression Estimator*

Let $(Y_1, \mathbf{X}_1)$, $(Y_2, \mathbf{X}_2)$, ..., $(Y_n, \mathbf{X}_n)$ be i.i.d. random vectors. Let $\hat{\boldsymbol{\beta}}$ be the OLS coefficient estimator, and let the ith residual $e_i = Y_i - (\hat{\beta}_0 + \hat{\beta}_1 X_{[1]i} + \hat{\beta}_2 X_{[2]i} + \ldots + \hat{\beta}_K X_{[K]i})$, $\forall i \in \{1,2,\ldots,n\}$. Then

- $\overline{e} = 0$, where $\overline{e} = \frac{1}{n}\sum_{i=1}^{n} e_i$.
- $\forall k \in \{1,2,\ldots,K\}$, $\overline{eX_{[k]}} = 0$, where $\overline{eX_{[k]}} = \frac{1}{n}\sum_{i=1}^{n} e_i X_{[k]i}$.
- $\forall k \in \{1,2,\ldots,K\}$, $\overline{eX_{[k]}} - \overline{e}\,\overline{X_{[k]}} = 0$.

4 Readers without familiarity with matrix calculus should not fret. Just take our word for it that the derivative of $(\mathbf{Y} - \mathbb{X}\hat{\boldsymbol{\beta}})^T(\mathbf{Y} - \mathbb{X}\hat{\boldsymbol{\beta}})$ with respect to $\hat{\boldsymbol{\beta}}$ is $-2\mathbb{X}^T(\mathbf{Y} - \mathbb{X}\hat{\boldsymbol{\beta}})$, noticing how this resembles the chain rule. $\mathbf{0}$ denotes the zero vector of appropriate length. We omit checking the second-order conditions.

Proof: The first-order condition $-2\mathbb{X}^T(\mathbf{Y}-\mathbb{X}\hat{\boldsymbol{\beta}}) = 0$ is equivalent to $\mathbb{X}^T\mathbf{e} = 0$, that is,

$$\begin{pmatrix} 1 & 1 & \cdots & 1 \\ X_{[1]1} & X_{[1]2} & \cdots & X_{[1]n} \\ X_{[2]1} & X_{[2]2} & \cdots & X_{[2]n} \\ \vdots & \vdots & \ddots & \vdots \\ X_{[K]1} & X_{[K]2} & \cdots & X_{[K]n} \end{pmatrix} \begin{pmatrix} e_1 \\ e_2 \\ \vdots \\ e_n \end{pmatrix} = \begin{pmatrix} 0 \\ 0 \\ \vdots \\ 0 \end{pmatrix},$$

which summarizes the system of equations

$$e_1 + e_2 + \ldots + e_n = 0,$$
$$e_1 X_{[1]1} + e_2 X_{[1]2} + \ldots + e_n X_{[1]n} = 0,$$
$$e_1 X_{[2]1} + e_2 X_{[2]2} + \ldots + e_n X_{[2]n} = 0,$$
$$\vdots$$
$$e_1 X_{[K]1} + e_2 X_{[K]2} + \ldots + e_n X_{[K]n} = 0.$$

The first equation says that the sum of the residuals is zero. If the residuals did not sum to zero, we could obtain a better fit by changing the constant term. Furthermore, dividing each equation by n,

$$\overline{e} = \frac{1}{n}\sum_{i=1}^{n} e_i = 0,$$
$$\overline{eX_{[1]}} = \frac{1}{n}\sum_{i=1}^{n} e_i X_{[1]i} = 0,$$
$$\overline{eX_{[2]}} = \frac{1}{n}\sum_{i=1}^{n} e_i X_{[2]i} = 0,$$
$$\vdots$$
$$\overline{eX_{[K]}} = \frac{1}{n}\sum_{i=1}^{n} e_i X_{[K]i} = 0,$$

which also implies that for $k = 1, 2, \ldots, K$, the sample covariance between the residuals and $X_{[k]}$ is zero: $\overline{eX_{[k]}} - \overline{e}\,\overline{X}_{[k]} = 0$. □

Naturally, these results provide sample analogs to our results on properties of deviations from the BLP as in Theorems 2.2.22 and 2.3.8. The first property, $\overline{e} = 0$, states that the residuals have mean zero, much as we know that the deviations from the BLP have expectation zero ($\mathrm{E}[\varepsilon] = 0$). Similarly, the second property, $\overline{eX_{[k]}} = 0, \forall k \in \{1, 2, \ldots, K\}$, states that the product of the residuals and the explanatory variables also has mean zero. This is analogous to noting that in the population problem, the product of the deviations from the BLP and the explanatory variables is zero: $\mathrm{E}[\varepsilon X_{[k]}] = 0, \forall k \in \{1,2,\ldots,K\}$. The final statement—that the (plug-in) sample covariance of the residuals and the explanatory variables is zero, or $\overline{eX_{[k]}} - \overline{e}\,\overline{X_{[k]}} = 0, \forall k \in \{1,2,\ldots,K\}$—is perhaps best known, and is analogous to the statement that the covariance between the deviations from the BLP and the explanatory variables is zero ($\mathrm{Cov}[\varepsilon, X_{[k]}] = 0, \forall k \in \{1,2,\ldots,K\}$).

4.2 INFERENCE

We have shown that we can estimate the BLP using plug-in estimation. Just like every other estimator we have seen, each of our coefficient estimators $\hat{\beta}_0$, $\hat{\beta}_1$, $\hat{\beta}_2$, ..., $\hat{\beta}_K$ is a random variable. Each therefore has a sampling distribution and, thus, a sampling variance. As usual, we want to *estimate* these sampling variances so that we can construct confidence intervals and perform hypothesis tests for the values of these coefficients.

4.2.1 Standard Errors and Inference

We begin our discussion of standard errors by exploring a very simple case: suppose that we had no explanatory variables. In this setting, we seek to estimate

$$\beta_0 = \underset{b_0 \in \mathbb{R}}{\arg\min}\, \mathrm{E}\left[(Y - b_0)^2\right].$$

We know from Theorem 2.1.24 (*Expected Value Minimizes MSE*) that the solution is $\beta_0 = \mathrm{E}[Y]$. The sample analog to β_0 would then be $\overline{Y}$, so using plug-in estimation, $\hat{\beta}_0 = \overline{Y}$. Thus, the regression estimate of β_0 with no explanatory variables is the sample mean.

In this simple case, inference proceeds exactly as we saw in Chapter 3: the standard error of $\hat{\beta}_0$ is

$$\sigma\left[\hat{\beta}_0\right] = \sqrt{\mathrm{V}\left[\hat{\beta}_0\right]} = \sqrt{\mathrm{V}\left[\overline{Y}\right]} = \sqrt{\frac{\mathrm{V}[Y]}{n}},$$

which we can estimate via plug-in estimation:

$$\hat{\sigma}\left[\hat{\beta}_0\right] = \sqrt{\hat{\mathrm{V}}\left[\hat{\beta}_0\right]} = \sqrt{\hat{\mathrm{V}}\left[\overline{Y}\right]} = \sqrt{\frac{\hat{\mathrm{V}}[Y]}{n}}.$$

As before, we could use the estimated sampling variance to compute a 95% confidence interval for the population mean, β_0: $CI_{.95}(\beta_0) = (\hat{\beta}_0 - 1.96\,\hat{\sigma}[\hat{\beta}_0], \hat{\beta}_0 + 1.96\,\hat{\sigma}[\hat{\beta}_0])$.

This simple case will provide some intuition going forward. Estimating standard errors becomes more complicated when we have one or more explanatory variables, but the general *principles* for estimating uncertainty, confidence intervals, and p-values translate from the sample mean to the regression estimator. For each coefficient β_k, it is possible to derive an estimate of the standard error of $\hat{\beta}_k$:

$$\hat{\sigma}\left[\hat{\beta}_k\right] = \sqrt{\hat{\mathrm{V}}\left[\hat{\beta}_k\right]}.$$

Given the usual plug-in regularity conditions, *robust standard errors* or the bootstrap provide consistent estimates of the asymptotic standard errors under i.i.d. sampling. We consider these in the following two sections.

4.2.2 Inference with Robust Standard Errors and the Bootstrap

In this section, we discuss a consistent estimator for the standard errors of the regression estimators using matrix algebra. Define the vector of errors $\boldsymbol{\varepsilon}$ as the differences between the observed values of Y and the (true) BLP of Y given the observed values of $X_{[1]}, X_{[2]}, \ldots, X_{[K]}$:

$$\boldsymbol{\varepsilon} = \mathbf{Y} - \mathbb{X}\boldsymbol{\beta}.$$

We can then decompose $\hat{\boldsymbol{\beta}}$ as

$$\begin{aligned}
\hat{\boldsymbol{\beta}} &= \left(\mathbb{X}^T\mathbb{X}\right)^{-1}\mathbb{X}^T\mathbf{Y} \\
&= \left(\mathbb{X}^T\mathbb{X}\right)^{-1}\mathbb{X}^T(\mathbb{X}\boldsymbol{\beta} + \boldsymbol{\varepsilon}) \\
&= \left(\mathbb{X}^T\mathbb{X}\right)^{-1}\mathbb{X}^T\mathbb{X}\boldsymbol{\beta} + \left(\mathbb{X}^T\mathbb{X}\right)^{-1}\mathbb{X}^T\boldsymbol{\varepsilon} \\
&= \boldsymbol{\beta} + \left(\mathbb{X}^T\mathbb{X}\right)^{-1}\mathbb{X}^T\boldsymbol{\varepsilon}.
\end{aligned}$$

This representation allows us to highlight the particular role that the deviations from the BLP play in generating the sampling variability of the regression estimator. Under the usual plug-in regularity conditions, $\sqrt{n}(\hat{\boldsymbol{\beta}} - \boldsymbol{\beta})$ converges in distribution to a multivariate normal random vector[5] with expectation zero and covariance matrix

$$\left(\mathrm{E}\left[\mathbf{X}^T\mathbf{X}\right]\right)^{-1}\mathrm{E}\left[\varepsilon^2\mathbf{X}^T\mathbf{X}\right]\left(\mathrm{E}\left[\mathbf{X}^T\mathbf{X}\right]\right)^{-1},$$

[5] A random vector is said to be *multivariate normal* if every linear combination of its components has a normal distribution.

where $\mathbf{X} = (1, X_{[1]}, X_{[2]}, ..., X_{[K]})$. We omit a derivation, but see Powell (2010), Hansen (2013, Ch. 7.2), or the informal treatment in Angrist and Pischke (2009, pp. 40–48), for constructive derivations under mild regularity conditions.

To estimate $\mathrm{V}[\hat{\boldsymbol{\beta}}]$, we need only apply the plug-in principle: plug in residuals for errors and sample means for expected values. The resulting plug-in estimator is known as the *robust sampling variance estimator* (or *sandwich estimator*).[6]

Definition 4.2.1. *Robust Sampling Variance Estimator for OLS*
Let $(Y_1, \mathbf{X}_1), (Y_2, \mathbf{X}_2), ..., (Y_n, \mathbf{X}_n)$ be i.i.d. random vectors, where $\mathbf{X} = (1, X_{[1]}, X_{[2]}, ..., X_{[K]})$. Let $\hat{\boldsymbol{\beta}}$ be the OLS coefficient estimator and $e_i = Y_i - (\hat{\beta}_0 + \hat{\beta}_1 X_{[1]i} + \hat{\beta}_2 X_{[2]i} + ... + \hat{\beta}_K X_{[K]i})$, $\forall i \in \{1, 2, ..., n\}$. Then the *robust sampling variance estimator* for $\hat{\boldsymbol{\beta}}$ is

$$\hat{\mathrm{V}}[\hat{\boldsymbol{\beta}}] = \frac{1}{n}\left(\frac{1}{n}\sum_{i=1}^{n}\mathbf{X}_i^T\mathbf{X}_i\right)^{-1}\left(\frac{1}{n}\sum_{i=1}^{n}e_i^2\mathbf{X}_i^T\mathbf{X}_i\right)\left(\frac{1}{n}\sum_{i=1}^{n}\mathbf{X}_i^T\mathbf{X}_i\right)^{-1}$$

$$= (\mathbb{X}^T\mathbb{X})^{-1}\mathbb{X}^T\mathrm{diag}(e_1^2, e_2^2, ..., e_n^2)\mathbb{X}(\mathbb{X}^T\mathbb{X})^{-1},$$

where $\mathrm{diag}(e_1^2, e_2^2, ..., e_n^2)$ is the $n \times n$ matrix whose i^{th} diagonal element is e_i^2 and whose off-diagonal elements are all zero.

(Note that $\mathrm{V}[\hat{\boldsymbol{\beta}}]$ is a covariance matrix—see Definition 2.3.1.) The estimator is known as "robust" because its validity does not require any assumptions beyond the usual plug-in regularity conditions. (The following section will consider an alternative type of variance estimation that leans on additional assumptions.) Importantly, with the robust sampling variance estimator in hand, we can derive the *robust standard error* for each OLS regression coefficient: the robust standard error estimator for $\boldsymbol{\beta}_k$ is the square root of the kth diagonal element of $\hat{\mathrm{V}}[\hat{\boldsymbol{\beta}}]$.

Recall that the robust standard error is a plug-in estimate of an asymptotic approximation of the standard error, not the true standard error. Without assumptions that would strain credulity (such as normality of errors and fixed explanatory variables), we cannot derive an unbiased estimator of—much less an exact value for—the standard error of our regression estimates given any finite n. However, under the usual plug-in regularity conditions, robust standard errors are consistent.

6 It is called the sandwich estimator because the $\mathrm{diag}(e_1^2, e_2^2, ..., e_n^2)$ term (the "meat") is sandwiched between the $(\mathbb{X}^T\mathbb{X})^{-1}$ terms (the "bread").

The bootstrap (Section 3.4.3) is again available as an alternative, and the bootstrap standard errors are also consistent under the usual plug-in regularity conditions. The bootstrap and robust standard errors agree in large samples but, as an exact resampling method, the bootstrap may have better finite sample properties. When in doubt, we recommend using the bootstrap.

Regardless of whether or not we estimate the standard error using robust standard errors or the bootstrap, we use these standard error estimates to compute normal approximation–based confidence intervals and p-values, as before (Sections 3.4.1 and 3.4.2). The following example illustrates the applicability of this approach.

Example 4.2.2. *Normal Approximation–Based Confidence Intervals for Regression*
Suppose we had a random vector $(X_{[1]}, X_{[2]}, Y)$ with the BLP

$$g(X_{[1]}, X_{[2]}) = \beta_0 + \beta_1 X_{[1]} + \beta_2 X_{[2]},$$

and suppose we obtained the following *estimates* after fitting the regression:

$$\hat{\beta}_0 = 0.60, \hat{\sigma}\left[\hat{\beta}_0\right] = 0.25,$$
$$\hat{\beta}_1 = 0.75, \hat{\sigma}\left[\hat{\beta}_1\right] = 1.25,$$
$$\hat{\beta}_2 = 3.00, \hat{\sigma}\left[\hat{\beta}_2\right] = 1.00.$$

We could then construct the following 95% confidence intervals under a normal approximation:

$$CI_{.95}(\beta_0) = (0.11, 1.09),$$
$$CI_{.95}(\beta_1) = (-1.70, 3.20),$$
$$CI_{.95}(\beta_2) = (1.04, 4.96).$$

Then, for instance, we can say approximately with 95% confidence (if n is large and the usual plug-in regularity conditions hold) that the *conditional* slope of the BLP with respect to $X_{[2]}$ lies in the interval (1.04, 4.96).[7] Likewise, normal approximation–based p-values can be computed in the manner shown in Chapter 3. So, for example, we can state that, under the null hypothesis that β_2 is zero, the probability that we would have observed a $\hat{\beta}_2$ as extreme as we did is less than 0.05. △

[7] In other words, if we repeatedly sampled n observations from $(X_{[1]}, X_{[2]}, Y)$, our interval would cover the true *conditional* slope of the BLP 95% of the time.

4.2.3 Classical Standard Errors

There is an alternative to robust standard errors and the bootstrap, known as *classical standard errors*.

Suppose we *assume* that $\mathrm{E}[\varepsilon | X_{[1]}, X_{[2]}, ..., X_{[K]}] = 0$ and $\mathrm{V}[\varepsilon | X_{[1]}, X_{[2]}, ..., X_{[K]}] = \sigma^2$ for all possible values of $X_{[1]}, X_{[2]}, ..., X_{[K]}$. The first assumption is equivalent to linearity of $\mathrm{E}[Y | X_{[1]}, X_{[2]}, ..., X_{[K]}]$, and the second assumption is known as (conditional) *homoskedasticity*. Again, let $\mathbf{X} = (1, X_{[1]}, X_{[2]}, ..., X_{[K]})$. Then, as before,

$$
\begin{aligned}
n\mathrm{V}[\hat{\boldsymbol{\beta}}] &\approx \left(\mathrm{E}[\mathbf{X}^T\mathbf{X}]\right)^{-1} \mathrm{E}[\varepsilon^2 \mathbf{X}^T\mathbf{X}] \left(\mathrm{E}[\mathbf{X}_i^T\mathbf{X}]\right)^{-1} \\
&= \left(\mathrm{E}[\mathbf{X}^T\mathbf{X}]\right)^{-1} \left(\sigma^2 \mathrm{E}[\mathbf{X}^T\mathbf{X}]\right) \left(\mathrm{E}[\mathbf{X}^T\mathbf{X}]\right)^{-1} \\
&= \sigma^2 \left(\mathrm{E}[\mathbf{X}^T\mathbf{X}]\right)^{-1},
\end{aligned}
$$

where the approximation follows from Section 4.2.2, and the first equality follows from the facts that $\mathrm{E}[\varepsilon^2 \mathbf{X}^T\mathbf{X}] = \mathrm{E}[\mathrm{E}[\varepsilon^2 \mathbf{X}^T\mathbf{X} | \mathbf{X}]]$ (by the Law of Iterated Expectations) and $\mathrm{E}[\varepsilon^2 | \mathbf{X}] = \sigma^2$ (by the linearity and homoskedasticity assumptions).

We can then derive the plug-in estimator of $\mathrm{V}[\hat{\boldsymbol{\beta}}]$, known as the *classical sampling variance estimator.*

Definition 4.2.3. *Classical Sampling Variance Estimator for OLS*
Let $(Y_1, \mathbf{X}_1), (Y_2, \mathbf{X}_2), ..., (Y_n, \mathbf{X}_n)$ be i.i.d. random vectors, where $\mathbf{X} = (1, X_{[1]}, X_{[2]}, ..., X_{[K]})$. Let $\hat{\boldsymbol{\beta}}$ be the OLS coefficient estimator and $e_i = Y_i - (\hat{\beta}_0 + \hat{\beta}_1 X_{[1]i} + \hat{\beta}_2 X_{[2]i} + ... + \hat{\beta}_K X_{[K]i})$, $\forall i \in \{1, 2, ..., n\}$. Then the *classical sampling variance estimator* for $\hat{\boldsymbol{\beta}}$ is

$$
\hat{\mathrm{V}}_{\mathrm{C}}[\hat{\boldsymbol{\beta}}] = \frac{1}{n}\hat{\sigma}^2 \left(\frac{1}{n}\sum_{i=1}^{n} \mathbf{X}_i^T \mathbf{X}_i\right)^{-1} = \hat{\sigma}^2 (\mathbb{X}^T\mathbb{X})^{-1},
$$

where $\hat{\sigma}^2 = \hat{\mathrm{V}}[Y - \mathbf{X}\hat{\boldsymbol{\beta}}]$.

This is almost the same as the sampling variance estimator for regression given in most textbooks.[8] The classical standard error estimator for β_k is then just defined as square root of the kth diagonal element of $\hat{\mathrm{V}}_{\mathrm{C}}[\hat{\boldsymbol{\beta}}]$.

Remember, however, that classical standard errors rely on a strong assumption: that the magnitude of the deviations from the BLP is *unrelated* to the

[8] The only difference is that, in most textbooks, $\hat{\sigma}^2$ uses a denominator of $n - (K+1)$ instead of $n - 1$.

values of the Xs. When this assumption and the usual plug-in regularity conditions hold, the classical sampling variance will be consistent. However, this assumption should not be invoked lightly; in real-world problems, where we have no guarantees about the process that gives rise to the data, the errors may be *heteroskedastic*. If homoskedasticity *does* hold, then in large samples, the classical and robust sampling variance estimates will agree. With large n and i.i.d. sampling, there is little reason not to use robust standard errors or the bootstrap to characterize the uncertainty of a regression fit.

4.3 ESTIMATION OF NONLINEAR CONDITIONAL EXPECTATION FUNCTIONS

In this section, we consider estimating nonlinear CEFs by changing the *specification* of the regression. By specification, we mean the manner and functional form that we use to relate explanatory variables to the outcome. We illustrate this idea by returning to an example from Chapter 2, Example 2.2.23 (*Plotting the CEF and the BLP*).

Example 4.3.1. *Best Quadratic Predictor*
Let X and Y be random variables with $X \sim U(0,1)$ and $Y = 10X^2 + W$, where $W \sim N(0,1)$ and $X \perp\!\!\!\perp W$. As shown in Example 2.2.23, the CEF of Y given X is $\mathrm{E}[Y|X] = 10X^2$, and the BLP of Y given X is $g(X) = -\frac{5}{3} + 10X$. Figure 4.3.1 plots 1,000 random draws of (X, Y) and then superimposes the graphs of the CEF (in black) and the BLP (in red), as shown in Figure 2.2.1.

Although the CEF is nonlinear, the BLP is a good first approximation of the CEF. Thus, OLS regression, which estimates the BLP, provides a principled first approximation of the CEF. The BLP is a good, but not great, approximation of the CEF. We can, however, do better while still using OLS regression.

Continuing with the above example, suppose we now create a second explanatory variable, X^2. Then we can use a new regression specification to estimate the best *quadratic* predictor:

$$\boldsymbol{\beta} = \underset{(b_0,b_1,b_2)\in\mathbb{R}^3}{\arg\min}\ \mathrm{E}\Big[\big(Y - b_0 - b_1X - b_2X^2\big)^2\Big].$$

In this example, the best linear predictor of Y given X and X^2 is the CEF:

$$\begin{aligned} g(X, X^2) &= \mathrm{E}[Y|X, X^2] \\ &= \mathrm{E}[Y|X] \\ &= \beta_0 + \beta_1 X + \beta_2 X^2 \\ &= 0 + 0X + 10X^2 \\ &= 10X^2. \end{aligned}$$

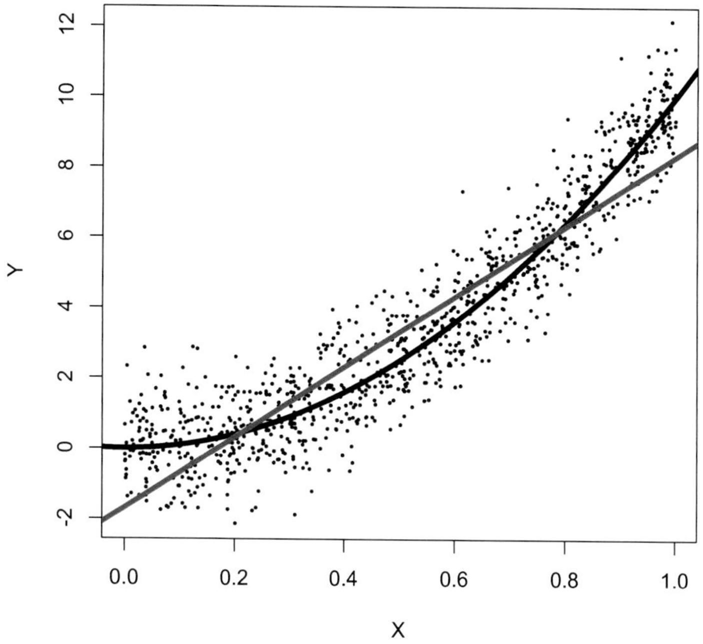

FIGURE 4.3.1. *Plotting the CEF and BLP*

More generally, if the CEF of Y is linear in X and X^2 (in other words, quadratic in X),

$$\mathrm{E}[Y|X] = \beta_0 + \beta_1 X + \beta_2 X^2,$$

then the BLP of Y given X and X^2 is the CEF, so regression of Y on X and X^2 consistently estimates the CEF. If the CEF is not linear in X and X^2, then regression of Y on X and X^2 will approximate the CEF insofar as

$$\mathrm{E}[Y|X] \approx \beta_0 + \beta_1 X + \beta_2 X^2.$$

It is important to note that, once we introduce nonlinearity, interpreting the coefficients becomes less straightforward. With bivariate regression, the estimated slope of the CEF of Y with respect to X was $\hat{\beta}_1$. Here, with a nonlinear function, we can take the derivative.

If the CEF is linear in X and X^2, then the slope is

$$\frac{\partial \mathrm{E}[Y|X]}{\partial X} = \frac{\partial \left(\beta_0 + \beta_1 X + \beta_2 X^2\right)}{\partial X} = \beta_1 + 2\beta_2 X.$$

The slope of the CEF thus depends on the value of X. So, if we estimated the βs using OLS, our estimate of the slope of the CEF at $X = x$ would be $\hat{\beta}_1 + 2\hat{\beta}_2 x$. △

In the following sections, we show that this general idea—changing how we specify the functional form of the predictor—can allow us to make even OLS regression remarkably flexible.

4.3.1 Polynomials

We can provide a more general basis for approximating the CEF using regression. The *Weierstrass Approximation Theorem* states that any continuous function defined on a closed interval can be uniformly approximated to arbitrary precision using a polynomial function.

Theorem 4.3.2. *Weierstrass Approximation Theorem*
Let $f: [a,b] \to \mathbb{R}$ be continuous. Then, $\forall \epsilon > 0$, there exists a polynomial p such that $\forall x \in [a,b]$, $|f(x) - p(x)| < \epsilon$.

We omit the proof of this theorem. We can use the Weierstrass Approximation Theorem to derive the following result.

Theorem 4.3.3. *Polynomial Approximation of the CEF*
Let X and Y be random variables, and suppose that $\mathrm{E}[Y|X = x]$ is continuous and $\mathrm{Supp}[X] = [a,b]$. Then, $\forall \epsilon > 0$, $\exists K \in \mathbb{N}$ such that, $\forall K' \geq K$,

$$\mathrm{E}\left[\left(\mathrm{E}[Y|X] - g(X, X^2, ..., X^{K'})\right)^2\right] < \epsilon,$$

where $g(X, X^2, ..., X^{K'})$ is the BLP of Y given X, X^2, ..., $X^{K'}$.

Proof: Let $\epsilon > 0$. Then $\sqrt{\epsilon} > 0$, so by the Weierstrass Approximation Theorem, there exists a polynomial p such that $\forall x \in [a,b]$,

$$\left|\mathrm{E}[Y|X = x] - p(x)\right| < \sqrt{\epsilon}.$$

Thus,

$$\mathrm{E}\left[\left(\mathrm{E}[Y|X] - p(X)\right)^2\right] < \left(\sqrt{\epsilon}\right)^2 = \epsilon.$$

Let K be the degree of p. The BLP of Y given X, X^2, ..., X^K is the minimum MSE predictor of $\mathrm{E}[Y|X]$ among polynomials of degree less than or equal to K, so by definition

$$\mathrm{E}\left[\left(\mathrm{E}[Y|X] - g(X, X^2, ..., X^K)\right)^2\right] \leq \mathrm{E}\left[\left(\mathrm{E}[Y|X] - p(X)\right)^2\right] < \epsilon,$$

where $g(X, X^2, ..., X^K)$ is the BLP of Y given X, X^2, ..., X^K. Now, let $K' \geq K$.

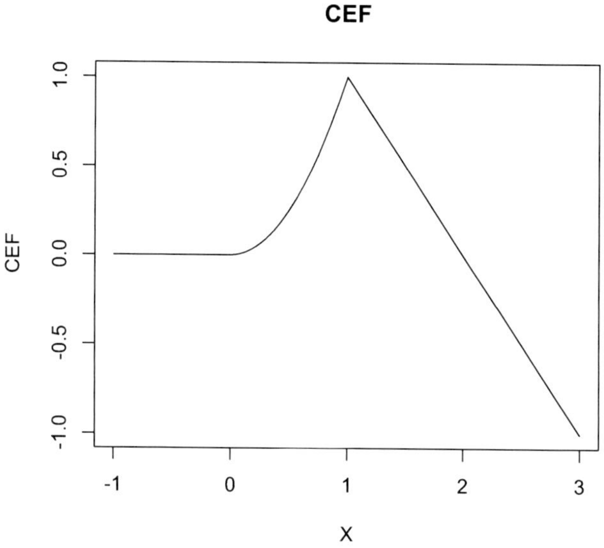

FIGURE 4.3.2. *A Nonlinear CEF*

The BLP of Y given X, X^2, ..., $X^{K'}$ is the minimum MSE predictor of $\mathrm{E}[Y|X]$ among polynomials of degree less than or equal to K', so by definition

$$\mathrm{E}\left[\left(\mathrm{E}[Y|X] - g(X, X^2, \ldots, X^{K'})\right)^2\right] \leq \mathrm{E}\left[\left(\mathrm{E}[Y|X] - g(X, X^2, \ldots, X^{K})\right)^2\right]$$
$$< \epsilon. \quad \square$$

Thus, as long as the CEF is continuous and the support of X is a closed interval, we can get MSE as small as we want with a polynomial BLP of sufficiently high degree.

Let us visualize this. Consider the following CEF, plotted in Figure 4.3.2:

$$\mathrm{E}[Y|X=x] = \begin{cases} 0 & : \quad x \in [-1,0] \\ x^2 & : \quad x \in (0,1) \\ 2-x & : \quad x \in [1,3]. \end{cases}$$

We can approximate this CEF with polynomials of X. Figure 4.3.3 shows the BLPs (assuming that $X \sim U(-1,3)$) using polynomials of degrees 1, 2, 3, 4, 5, and 10.

This is *not* to suggest that it is good practice to include a tenth-order polynomial in our regression (see Section 4.3.2). But the point stands: we can approximate the CEF to arbitrary precision using a BLP, as long as the CEF is continuous. Additionally, since regression is consistent for the BLP, this means that with large enough n, we can estimate the CEF to arbitrary precision. (More on this in Section 4.3.5, *Sieve Estimation*.)

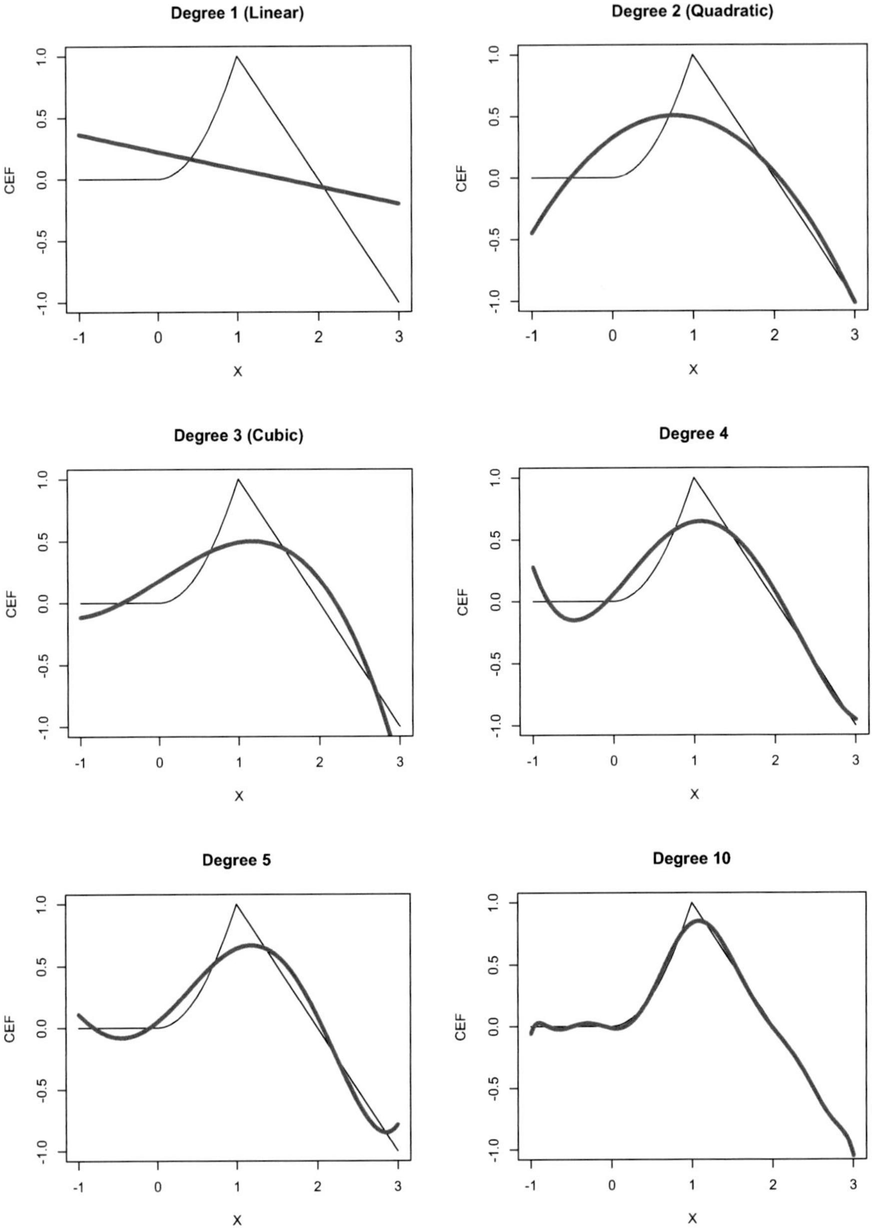

FIGURE 4.3.3. *Polynomial Approximations of a Nonlinear CEF*

The linearity assumption of regression can be relaxed in many ways; polynomials are just one way. (High-order polynomials are not a particularly good way, for reasons beyond the scope of this book—see Runge 1901; Hansen 2013, Ch. 12.6.) The remainder of this chapter describes some other methods, but before we proceed, we first discuss the key challenge encountered in doing so.

4.3.2 Overfitting

Although including many higher-order terms in a regression relaxes the assumption of linearity, it may introduce problems. In particular, using a complex specification can lead to the problem of *overfitting*. Put simply, the data suffer from micronumerosity—we do not have enough observations to fit a complex approximation well. When n is small, estimating a large number of regression coefficients may lead us to be highly sensitive to the "noise" in the data.[9] As we demonstrate in the following example, the problem of overfitting is clearest in the case where the CEF is, in fact, linear.

Example 4.3.4. *Overfitting with a Linear CEF*
Suppose we had a random vector (X, Y) such that

$$Y = X + 5 + \varepsilon,$$

where $X \sim U(-10, 10)$,[10] $\varepsilon \sim N(0, 25)$, and $X \perp\!\!\!\perp \varepsilon$. The CEF of Y given X is thus $\mathrm{E}[Y|X = x] = x + 5$.

We can compare what might happen if we tried to estimate the CEF using a linear regression versus regression with a fifth-order polynomial. First, suppose we had just ten i.i.d. observations of (X, Y). Panel (a) of Figure 4.3.4 plots ten random draws of (X, Y). In black is the true CEF (which, since it is linear, is also the true BLP). In red is the linear regression estimate given this data. Panel (b) displays the true CEF in black again, but the fifth-order polynomial regression estimate is in red.

With $n = 10$, the fifth-order polynomial does not appear to perform well as an approximation of the true CEF, since it effectively "over interprets" the random noise in the data as indicative of the underlying relationship between X and Y. This is why we call it overfitting: with small n, the more flexible

9 Overfitting can also occur when researchers fit multiple specifications to the data and report the best fitting specification; this can be shown to be equivalent to estimating additional parameters in terms of introducing overfitting. In our discussion, we assume that the inferential procedure is fixed ex ante. In practice, this assumption can be approximated through "sample splitting," which allows researchers to control overfitting by using different subsamples of the data for estimation as for inference. The logic of this procedure can be used to control overfitting more generally, as we will see when we briefly discuss a related procedure, cross-validation, in Section 4.3.6 (*Penalized Regression*).

10 In other words, X follows a *uniform distribution* with constant density on the interval $[-10, 10]$ (and zero elsewhere).

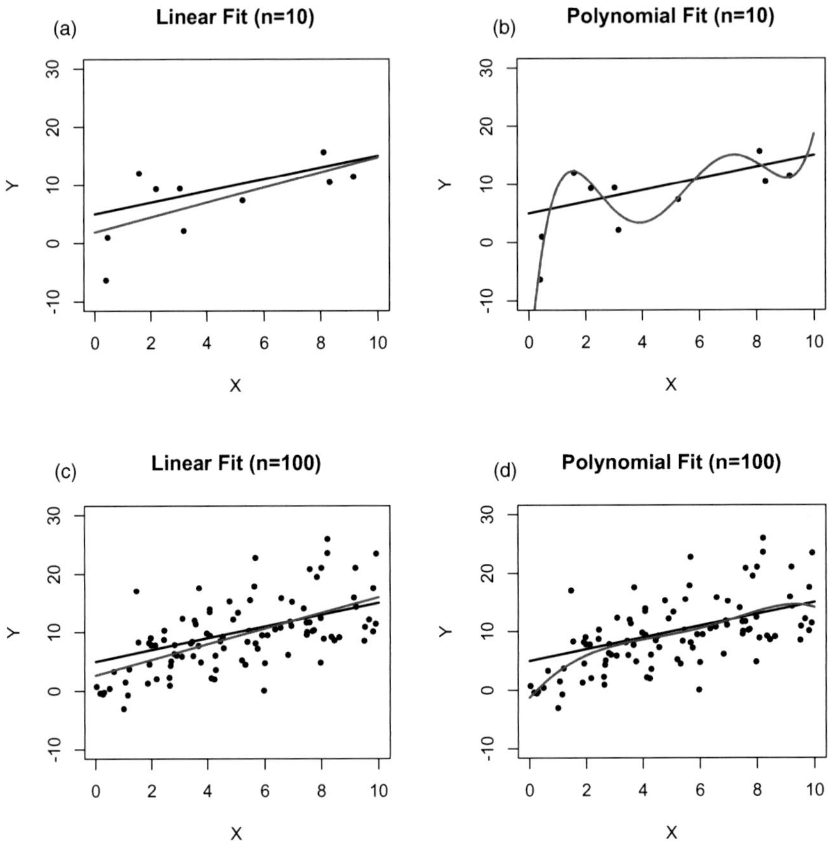

FIGURE 4.3.4. *Overfitting with a Linear CEF*

regression specification fits the estimate to the observed data *too well.* By contrast, the linear regression estimate approximates the true CEF fairly well considering the small sample size.

As overfitting is simply a case of micronumerosity (Section 3.4.4) in estimating our complicated approximation, it goes away when we have a large enough sample size. With only ten observations, trying to estimate a fifth-order polynomial (six coefficients) means we have less than two observations per coefficient to be estimated. If we went even further and estimated a ninth-order polynomial (ten coefficients), the resulting curve would pass exactly through every single observation. We would essentially be treating each observation as an $n = 1$ estimate of the CEF at that value of X. Panels (c) and (d) of Figure 4.3.4 plot 100 random draws of (X, Y) and again superimposes the true CEF (in black), as well as the linear regression fit and the fifth-order

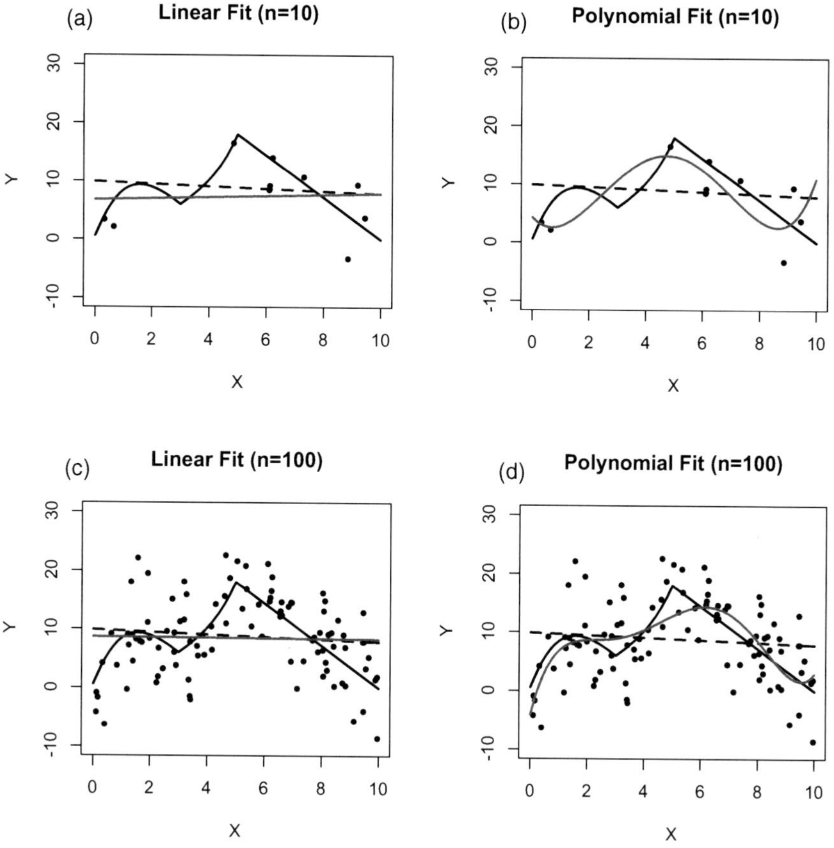

FIGURE 4.3.5. *Overfitting with a Nonlinear CEF*

polynomial regression fits (in red). With $n = 100$, both regression estimates approximate the true CEF. △

But what if the CEF actually *is* highly nonlinear? Even then, a more flexible specification is not necessarily better. The problem of overfitting remains.

Example 4.3.5. *Overfitting with a Nonlinear CEF*
Suppose we had a random vector (X, Y) such that

$$Y = g(X) + \varepsilon,$$

for some (nonlinear) function g, where $X \sim U(-10,10)$, $\varepsilon \sim N(0,25)$, and $X \perp\!\!\!\perp \varepsilon$. The CEF of Y given X is thus $\mathrm{E}[Y|X = x] = g(X)$. Let g be the function shown in black in Figure 4.3.4.

As in Figure 4.3.4, panel (a) Figure 4.3.5 plots ten random draws of (X, Y) and superimposes the true CEF (in black) and the linear regression fit (in red). Panel (b) presents the same, except with the fifth-order polynomial regression fit (in red). In both, the true BLP is illustrated with a dotted black line. As before, with $n = 10$, the fifth-order polynomial regression overfits badly. The linear regression estimate, on the other hand, is close to the BLP, and thus, by definition, nearly coincides with the best possible linear approximation of the CEF (in terms of MSE).

Once again, with more data, we can afford to be "greedier" in trying to approximate the shape of the CEF in greater detail. Panels (c) and (d) of Figure 4.3.5 plot 100 random draws of (X, Y). With $n = 100$, the fifth-order polynomial regression approximates the true CEF quite well. The linear regression, though, gives an even more precise estimate of the BLP. Even with large n and a highly nonlinear true CEF, linear regression still has the virtue of being a safe, conservative estimator that yields a good approximation of a meaningful summary feature of the joint distribution. △

4.3.3 Interactions

We have shown that, with polynomials, we can approximate any continuous CEF in one variable to arbitrary precision. This was, in a sense, a proof of concept. The same principle generalizes to the multivariate case. To see this, consider the case where we are trying to predict Y using $X_{[1]}$ and $X_{[2]}$, and the slope of the CEF with respect to $X_{[1]}$ depends on the value of $X_{[2]}$. The BLP is still the BLP, but it might fail to capture an interesting *interaction* between the variables $X_{[1]}$ and $X_{[2]}$. To formalize a bit, suppose the CEF is otherwise linear, but includes an *interaction term* $X_{[1]}X_{[2]}$:

$$\mathrm{E}\left[Y \middle| X_{[1]}, X_{[2]}\right] = \beta_0 + \beta_1 X_{[1]} + \beta_2 X_{[2]} + \beta_3 X_{[1]} X_{[2]}.$$

Much as before, we can derive the slope of the CEF with respect to $X_{[1]}$ and $X_{[2]}$ by taking partial derivatives:

$$\frac{\partial \mathrm{E}\left[Y \middle| X_{[1]}, X_{[2]}\right]}{\partial X_{[1]}} = \frac{\partial\left(\beta_0 + \beta_1 X_{[1]} + \beta_2 X_{[2]} + \beta_3 X_{[1]} X_{[2]}\right)}{\partial X_{[1]}} = \beta_1 + \beta_3 X_{[2]},$$
$$\frac{\partial \mathrm{E}\left[Y \middle| X_{[1]}, X_{[2]}\right]}{\partial X_{[2]}} = \frac{\partial\left(\beta_0 + \beta_1 X_{[1]} + \beta_2 X_{[2]} + \beta_3 X_{[1]} X_{[2]}\right)}{\partial X_{[2]}} = \beta_2 + \beta_3 X_{[1]}.$$

Thus, the *conditional* slope of the CEF with respect to $X_{[1]}$ depends on the value of $X_{[2]}$, and vice versa. In this setting (unlike in Section 4.3.1, *Polynomials*), each coefficient has a clear interpretation. If the CEF is linear in $X_{[1]}$, $X_{[2]}$, and $X_{[1]}X_{[2]}$, then

- $\beta_0 = \mathrm{E}[Y | X_{[1]} = 0, X_{[2]} = 0]$.
- β_1 is the slope of the CEF with respect to $X_{[1]}$ when $X_{[2]} = 0$.
- β_2 is the slope of the CEF with respect to $X_{[2]}$ when $X_{[1]} = 0$.

- β_3 is how each of the slopes changes when the value of the other variable is increased by one. (For example, if $X_{[1]}$ moves from 1 to 2, then the slope of the CEF with respect to $X_{[2]}$ increases by β_3; if $X_{[2]}$ moves from 7 to 4, then the slope of the CEF with respect to $X_{[1]}$ decreases by $3\beta_3$.)

Of course, if $\beta_3 = 0$, then $\mathrm{E}[Y|X_{[1]}, X_{[2]}] = \beta_0 + \beta_1 X_{[1]} + \beta_2 X_{[2]}$ and there is no interaction. All of this can be generalized for any number of X variables.

For even greater flexibility, interactions can be combined with higher-order polynomial terms.[11] For example,

$$\mathrm{E}\big[Y\big|X_{[1]}, X_{[2]}\big] = \beta_0 + \beta_1 X_{[1]} + \beta_2 X_{[2]} + \beta_3 X_{[1]} X_{[2]} + \beta_4 X_{[1]}^2 + \beta_5 X_{[2]}^2 \\ + \beta_6 X_{[1]}^2 X_{[1]} + \beta_7 X_{[1]} X_{[2]}^2 + \beta_8 X_{[1]}^2 X_{[2]}^2.$$

Once higher-order terms are included, the coefficients no longer have straightforward interpretations. Conditional slopes with respect to each X variable can still be computed by taking partial derivatives. Beyond that, it is usually easiest to compute the implied value of $\mathrm{E}[Y|X_{[1]}, X_{[2]}]$ for different values of $X_{[1]}$ and $X_{[2]}$ to see how the conditional expectation of Y changes as $X_{[1]}$ and $X_{[2]}$ change.

Again, OLS regression yields a consistent estimate of the βs for any of the above specifications. When the CEF is not linear in the variables specified, OLS consistently estimates the BLP of Y given these variables, that is, the best approximation of the CEF among all functions of the form specified by the researcher.

4.3.4 Summarizing Partial Derivatives of the CEF

The previous sections on polynomials and interactions described how we can characterize partial derivatives of the CEF, even when we are considering a nonlinear CEF. These partial derivatives of the CEF are referred to as *marginal effects* in the econometrics literature, but we refrain from using the word "effect" outside the domain of a causal model (as in Chapter 7).[12] In this section, we consider how to summarize these partial derivatives, instead of just considering them at one particular value.

[11] Theorem 4.3.3 (*Polynomial Approximation of the CEF*) can be generalized to multiple explanatory variables: if we include enough polynomial and interaction terms, we can approximate the CEF to arbitrary precision, provided the CEF is continuous and the support of $\mathbf{X}$ is a compact set.

[12] If our readers are so inclined, they may mentally replace every future instance of the term "partial derivative" in this section with "marginal effect," but they should bear in mind that these do not necessarily represent causal effects without further assumptions.

Let us assume that the CEF is differentiable with respect to a given variable $X_{[k]}$.[13] Then, the partial derivative of the CEF with respect to $X_{[k]}$ is

$$\left.\frac{\partial \mathrm{E}[Y|\mathbf{X}]}{\partial X_{[k]}}\right|_{\mathbf{X}=\mathbf{x}}.$$

Again, a plug-in estimator using the estimated CEF,

$$\left.\frac{\partial \hat{\mathrm{E}}[Y|\mathbf{X}]}{\partial X_{[k]}}\right|_{\mathbf{X}=\mathbf{x}},$$

will be consistent under proper specification and the usual plug-in regularity conditions.

Thus, it is straightforward to characterize and estimate the partial derivative of CEF of Y given $\mathbf{X}$. We now consider how to summarize the relationship between Y and a given variable $X_{[k]}$. The two most common quantities are the *average partial derivative* and the *partial derivative at the average*. We consider these in turn.

The average partial derivative represents how much a change in a particular variable $X_{[k]}$ moves the CEF, taking the expectation over the entire distribution of $(Y, \mathbf{X})$. In this sense, it is the average slope of the CEF with respect to $X_{[k]}$.

Definition 4.3.6. *Average Partial Derivative*
For a random variable Y and random vector $\mathbf{X}$, the *average partial derivative* of the CEF (of Y given $\mathbf{X}$) with respect to $X_{[k]}$ is

$$APD_{X_{[k]}} = \mathrm{E}\left[\frac{\partial \mathrm{E}[Y|\mathbf{X}]}{\partial X_{[k]}}\right].$$

A natural plug-in estimator for $APD_{X_{[k]i}}$ is obtained by replacing the expected value with a sample mean and the CEF with the estimated CEF:

$$\widehat{APD}_{X_{[k]}} = \frac{1}{n}\sum_{i=1}^{n}\left(\left.\frac{\partial \hat{\mathrm{E}}[Y|\mathbf{X}]}{\partial X_{[k]}}\right|_{\mathbf{X}=\mathbf{X}_i}\right).$$

Put simply, $\widehat{APD}_{X_{[k]}}$ entails estimating the partial derivative for every observation, and taking an average across all observations. If the regression specification coincides with the CEF, then $\widehat{APD}_{X_{[k]}}$ is a consistent estimator of $APD_{X_{[k]}}$.

[13] Beyond requiring that the CEF be differentiable at every value of $\mathbf{X}$ with positive support, this characterization only makes sense when $\mathbf{X}$ is continuous. When $\mathbf{X}$ is discrete, we would recommend computing variants of discrete analogs to partial derivatives, such as partial slopes.

The partial derivative at the average represents a conceptually different target: how much a change in a particular variable $X_{[k]}$ moves the CEF when all variables in $\mathbf{X}$ are equal to their expected value. It is the slope of the CEF with respect to $X_{[k]}$ at a single point.

Definition 4.3.7. *Partial Derivative at the Average*
For a random variable Y and random vector $\mathbf{X}$, the *partial derivative at the average* of the CEF (of Y given $\mathbf{X}$) with respect to $X_{[k]}$ is

$$PDA_{X_{[k]}} = \left.\frac{\partial \mathrm{E}[Y|\mathbf{X}]}{\partial X_{[k]}}\right|_{\mathbf{X}=\mathrm{E}[\mathbf{X}]}.$$

Again, a natural plug-in estimator is available for $PDA_{X_{[k]}}$, which replaces the expected values with sample means, and the CEF with the estimated CEF. The plug-in estimate of the partial derivative at the average with respect to $X_{[k]}$ is

$$\widehat{PDA}_{X_{[k]}} = \left.\frac{\partial \hat{\mathrm{E}}[Y|\mathbf{X}]}{\partial X_{[k]}}\right|_{\mathbf{X}=\overline{\mathbf{X}}}.$$

Note that $\widehat{PDA}_{X_{[k]}}$ is easier to compute than $\widehat{APD}_{X_{[k]}}$. $\widehat{PDA}_{X_{[k]}}$ only requires computing the partial derivative at a single point, whereas $\widehat{APD}_{X_{[k]}}$ requires computing the partial derivative at all n points in the data. As the following example shows, $APD_{X_{[k]}}$ is not generally equal to $PDA_{X_{[k]}}$.

Example 4.3.8. *Differences between the Average Partial Derivative and the Partial Derivative at the Average*
Suppose $X_{[1]} \perp\!\!\!\perp X_{[2]}$ with $X_{[1]} \sim U(0,1)$ and $X_{[2]} \sim U(0,1)$ Further suppose that the CEF is

$$\mathrm{E}\left[Y \middle| X_{[1]}, X_{[2]}\right] = \begin{cases} -X_{[1]} & : \quad X_{[2]} \leq .8 \\ 9X_{[1]} & : \quad X_{[2]} > .8. \end{cases}$$

Then, by the Law of Iterated Expectations,

$$\begin{aligned} APD_{X_{[1]}} &= \frac{\partial\left(-X_{[1]}\right)}{\partial X_{[1]}} \Pr\left[X_{[2]} \leq .8\right] + \frac{\partial\left(9X_{[1]}\right)}{\partial X_{[1]}} \Pr\left[X_{[2]i} > .8\right] \\ &= -1 \times .8 + 9 \times .2 = 1. \end{aligned}$$

But the partial derivative at the average gives a very different result:

$$PDA_{X_{[k]}} = \frac{\partial\left(-X_{[1]}\right)}{\partial X_{[1]}} = -1.$$

While the partial derivative with respect to $X_{[1]}$ is positive on average, when evaluated at the average $(X_{[1]} = X_{[2]} = 0.5)$, the partial derivative is negative. △

The average partial derivative is an intuitive way to summarize the role of a particular variable in predicting Y—it represents how much, on average, a variable influences the CEF. While the partial derivative at the average also has a well-defined meaning, it is limited to just one particular point on the probability distribution of the explanatory variables. Thus, for a researcher interested in characterizing the overall relationship between Y and $X_{[k]}$, the average partial derivative is typically preferred to the partial derivative at the average.

4.3.5 Sieve Estimation

Recalling that overfitting is a consequence of micronumerosity, we would be more willing to accept a complicated regression specification if we had considerably more data. In other words, we might be willing to accept restrictive specifications with small n, keeping in mind that if we had larger n, we would increase the complexity. This idea is formalized in the notion of *sieve estimation*. The term *sieve estimator* is something of a misnomer; a sieve estimator is not a different type of estimator, but rather an algorithm for determining what estimator we would use for any given n. We can then characterize the asymptotic behavior of the sequence of estimators defined by the algorithm.

Intrinsically, estimating something like a CEF when there is at least one continuous explanatory variable is an infinite-dimensional problem. We might need an infinite number of parameters to fully characterize the CEF—it is not as though we can just assume that it follows a given functional form. Essentially, every dataset is micronumerous if we are trying to estimate an infinitely complex function. All estimators are limited to having just so many "moving parts" given any particular n. But we want to know that if we had very large n, we would obtain an approximation with arbitrary precision.

With sieve estimation, the asymptotics of the estimator are defined to allow for increasing flexibility, such that, as n grows, the estimator becomes more and more flexible. As long as flexibility grows "slowly" enough relative to n, we can show that the estimator will be consistent. We consider here one illustrative case. Suppose we wanted to estimate the CEF of Y given X using OLS with polynomials, as in Section 4.3.1 (*Polynomials*). We can set up an estimator whose complexity depends on n.

Definition 4.3.9. *Polynomial Least Squares Sieve Estimator*
For i.i.d. random vectors (Y_1, X_1), (Y_2, X_2), ..., (Y_n, X_n), the *polynomial least squares sieve estimator* of the conditional expectation function is

$$\hat{\mathrm{E}}_n[Y|X = x] = \sum_{k=0}^{J_n} \hat{\beta}_k x^k,$$

where

$$\hat{\boldsymbol{\beta}} = \underset{\mathbf{b}\in\mathbb{R}^{J_n+1}}{\arg\min} \sum_{i=1}^{n} \left(Y_i - \sum_{k=0}^{J_n} b_k X_i^k \right),$$

where $J_n \to \infty$ and $\frac{1}{n} J_n \to 0$.

In other words, we are regressing Y on a polynomial expansion of X, but the degree of that polynomial depends on n. As $n \to \infty$, the degree of that polynomial $J_n \to \infty$, but at a slower rate. If n is very small, we estimate the best linear predictor. If n is somewhat larger, we estimate the best quadratic predictor. And so on. As long as the CEF is smooth with appropriate support across X, then $\hat{\mathrm{E}}[Y|X = x]$ will be consistent across regions of the data with nonzero probability mass (by the logic of Theorem 4.3.3, *Polynomial Approximation of the CEF*). The logic of sieve estimation provides us some reassurance that, with enough data, we can obtain good approximations of even a complex CEF.

4.3.6 Penalized Regression

In the previous sections, we discussed some natural ways to increase the complexity of the approximation that we are using: interactions and polynomials. In this section, we consider one way to effectively *reduce* the complexity of approximation: *penalization*. In the case of OLS regression, we penalize by introducing a "penalty term" that is proportional to the complexity of the model (by some definition), and minimizing the sum of the penalty term and mean squared residuals. This helps to control overfitting (see Section 4.3.2, *Overfitting*), without forcing the researcher to arbitrarily choose a simpler specification.

Perhaps the best known approach here is the *lasso* (least absolute shrinkage and selection operator, Tibshirani 1996), a form of penalized regression, which provides a way of flexibly estimating the CEF when we have either (1) a large number of variables or (2) a large number of interactions or polynomials (the two scenarios are functionally equivalent). The key for the lasso is that the penalty term is the sum of the absolute value of estimated regression coefficients (typically excluding the intercept).

Definition 4.3.10. *Lasso Estimator*
For i.i.d. random vectors $(Y_1, \mathbf{X}_1)$, $(Y_2, \mathbf{X}_2)$, ..., $(Y_n, \mathbf{X}_n)$ where $\mathbf{X} = (1, X_{[1]}, X_{[2]}, ..., X_{[K]})$, the *lasso estimator* with *penalty parameter* λ is

$$\hat{\boldsymbol{\beta}}_\lambda = \underset{\mathbf{b} \in \mathbb{R}^K}{\arg\min} \left(\frac{1}{n} \sum_{i=1}^{n} (Y_i - \mathbf{X}_i \mathbf{b})^2 + \lambda \|\mathbf{b}\|_1 \right),$$

where $\|\cdot\|_1$ is the ℓ^1 norm, that is, $\|\mathbf{b}\|_1 = \sum_{k=1}^{K} |b_k|$ (the sum of the absolute value of the coefficients).

The interpretation of lasso estimates is as we would expect: $\hat{\boldsymbol{\beta}}$ characterizes an estimate of the CEF (given the functional form of the specification being used). But note that the lasso estimator depends on what value we set λ to. If we let $\lambda = 0$, then the lasso is equivalent to regular OLS regression. If λ is large, the lasso shrinks each element of $\hat{\boldsymbol{\beta}}$ to (or toward) zero unless it substantially helps to reduce the mean of squared residuals. The lasso thus presents a way to use many explanatory variables to "automatically" obtain good predictions—including when we have more variables than observations. If we assume that, as $n \to \infty$, $\lambda \to 0$, K remains fixed, and the CEF is linear in $\mathbf{X}$ (as parameterized), then the lasso will be consistent for the CEF under the assumptions otherwise used in this chapter.

In practice, choosing λ is not easy—a great deal of machine learning literature is devoted to figuring out how to choose λ. Similar problems emerge in general for overfitting problems, much as we might struggle to decide whether or not to fit the data with or without a polynomial, or with or without an interaction. One way to address this problem is by using *leave-one-out cross-validation*. In this case, we let the leave-one-out λ, $\lambda_{loo} = \arg\min_{l \in \mathbb{R}^+} [\frac{1}{n} \sum_{i=1}^{n} (Y_i - \mathbf{X}_i \hat{\boldsymbol{\beta}}_{-i,l})^2]$, where $\hat{\boldsymbol{\beta}}_{-i,l}$ is computed from the lasso procedure with unit i excluded and $\lambda = l$. This often has good operating characteristics, though proving its asymptotic properties is outside the scope of this book. Note that there are many other penalized regression techniques, including, most notably, ridge (ℓ^2-penalized) regression or penalized regression trees. These methods operate under the same basic principles, sometimes allowing for nonlinearity in different ways. We will return to the notion of penalization in the following chapter, where it serves a similar role in reducing the complexity of our approximation.

4.4 APPLICATION: ACCESS TO CLEAN WATER AND INFANT MORTALITY

We now consider an application of regression using the *Quality of Governance* data (Teorell et al. 2016), a dataset that compiles country-level information from a variety of sources. Our goal is to assess how access to clean water predicts rates of infant mortality at the country level. Infant mortality rate is measured as the number of infants who died before reaching one year of age per 1,000 live births in a given year, and access to clean water is measured as the percentage of the population with access to a source of clean drinking

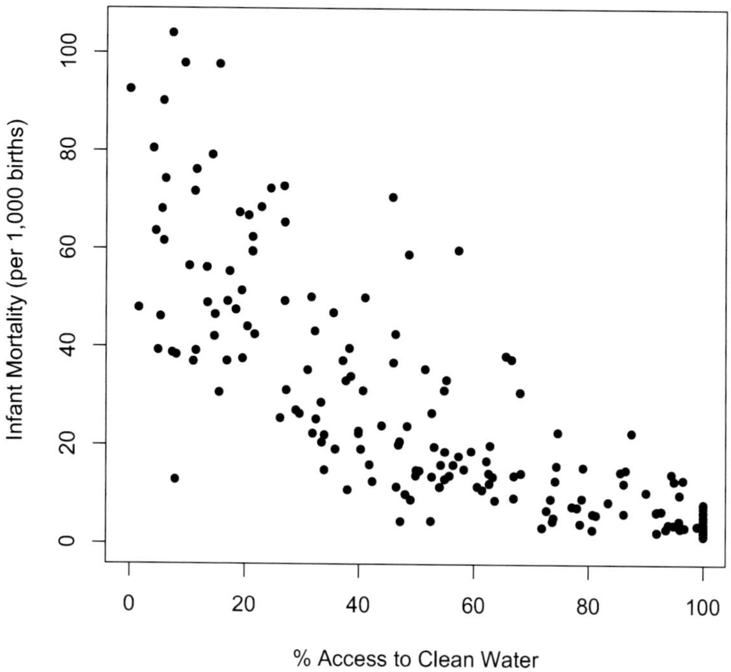

FIGURE 4.4.1. *Plotting Cross-National Infant Mortality Against Access to Clean Water*

water. We set aside the issue of measurement error here, so we should read all the results in this section as describing the relationships between the *measured* values of country-level variables. It is solely for notational convenience that we omit the qualifier "measured." The unit of observation is the country, and we have this data for 184 countries, so $n = 184$.

Figure 4.4.1 plots infant mortality against access to clean water. We assume that the data are i.i.d. draws of (Y, X), where Y denotes infant mortality and X denotes access to clean water. We can use regression to summarize the relationship between these variables. Figure 4.4.2(a) illustrates regression (1), which estimates the best predictor of the CEF of the form $\alpha + \beta X$ (in other words, the BLP). Figure 4.4.2(b) shows a second-order polynomial regression, regression (2), which estimates the best predictor of the CEF of the form $\alpha + \sum_{k=1}^{2} \beta_k X^k$. The associated estimates of the coefficients are reported in columns (1) and (2) of Table 4.4.5, with bootstrap standard error estimates in parentheses below each coefficient. The final two rows report estimates of both the average partial derivative (APD) and partial derivative at the average (PDA) with respect to water access.

As one might expect, as access to clean water increases, we see an associated decline in infant mortality. Under specification (1), we estimate that the slope

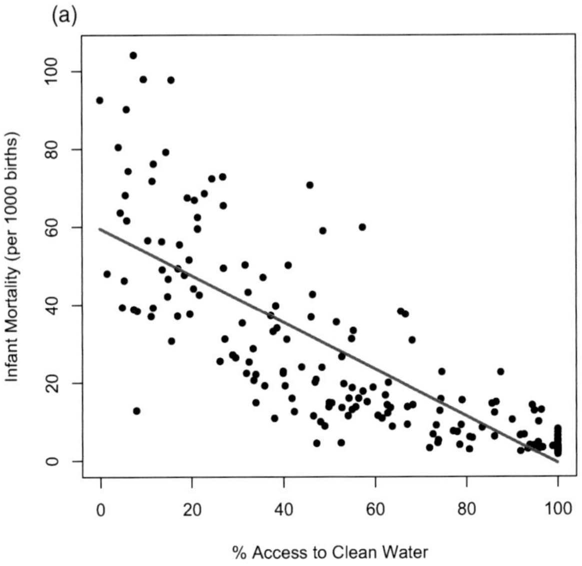

(1) OLS: $\alpha + \beta X$

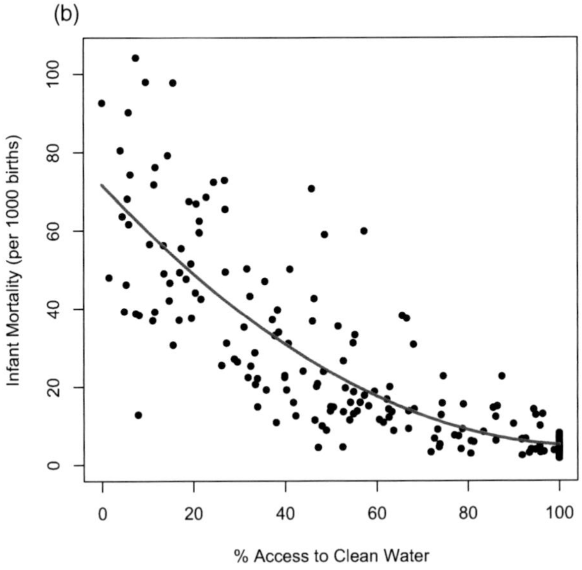

(2) OLS: $\alpha + \sum_{k=1}^{2} \beta_k X^k$

FIGURE 4.4.2. *Estimates of the CEF of Infant Mortality with Respect to Access to Clean Water*

TABLE 4.4.5. *Regression Table for Cross-National Infant Mortality*

	Infant Mortality							
	(1)	(2)	(3)	(4)	(5)	(6)	(7)	(8)
Intercept	59.583	71.751	74.186	68.113	76.686	67.385	50.900	68.631
	(2.803)	(4.714)	(3.691)	(7.559)	(6.313)	(18.739)	(27.180)	–
Water	−0.601	−1.256	−0.350	−0.706	−0.467	−0.432	1.808	−0.529
	(0.035)	(0.174)	(0.038)	(0.198)	(0.192)	(1.190)	(3.081)	–
Water^2	–	0.006	–	0.003	–	−0.006	−0.076	0.000
		(0.001)		(0.001)		(0.021)	(0.119)	–
Water^3	–	–	–	–	–	–	0.001	0.000
							(0.001)	–
Elec	–	–	-0.367	0.157	-0.398	0.137	0.990	0.062
			(0.052)	(0.274)	(0.076)	(0.855)	(1.427)	–
Elec^2	–	–	–	−0.004	–	−0.004	−0.010	−0.003
				(0.002)		(0.007)	(0.013)	–
Elec × Water	–	–	–	–	0.001	−0.003	−0.110	0.000
					(0.002)	(0.043)	(0.113)	–
Elec × Water^2	–	–	–	–	–	1.80e-4	0.003	8.95e-6
						(5.82e-4)	(0.003)	–
Elec × Water^3	–	–	–	–	–	–	-2.22e-5	8.15e-8
							(2.86e-5)	–
Elec^2 × Water	–	–	–	–	–	1.19e-5	8.20e-4	0.000
						(3.42e-4)	(9.46e-4)	–
Elec^2 × Water^2	–	–	–	–	–	−9.53e-7	−2.39e-5	0.000
						(4.10e-6)	(2.26e-5)	–
Elec^2 × Water^3	–	–	–	–	–	–	1.66e-7	0.000
							(1.78e-7)	–
$\widehat{APD}_{\text{Water}}$	−0.601	−0.603	−0.350	−0.363	−0.367	−0.350	−0.362	−0.345
	(0.036)	(0.043)	(0.037)	(0.050)	(0.052)	(0.076)	(0.124)	(0.075)
$\widehat{PDA}_{\text{Water}}$	-0.601	−0.603	−0.350	−0.363	−0.367	−0.344	−0.092	−0.394
	(0.034)	(0.045)	(0.038)	(0.049)	(0.053)	(0.140)	(0.212)	(0.087)

Regressions (1)–(7) report OLS coefficients and regression (8) reports lasso coefficients. $n = 184$ for all regressions. The final two rows report the estimated average partial derivatives and partial derivatives at the average with respect to access to clean water. Bootstrap standard error estimates are reported in parentheses under each estimate.

of the BLP is approximately −0.601, so for every additional percentage point increase in population with access to clean water, we would predict approximately six fewer deaths before one year of age per 10,000 live births. (Note, however, that there is nothing necessarily causal about this relationship.) The relationship is also nonlinear: the coefficient on the quadratic term in regression (2) is highly statistically significant ($p < 0.001$). But while the CEF is better approximated by the polynomial specification, the key insight is conveyed by the BLP. To see this, we can note that the APD and PDA estimates are nearly identical across both specifications.

What if we want to consider an additional explanatory variable? We might seek to characterize the relationship between infant mortality and access to clean water, *conditional* on another explanatory variable. We now assume that the data are i.i.d. draws of (Y, X, Z), where Z is the percentage of the population with access to electricity. Figure 4.4.3 plots infant mortality against access to clean water and electricity.

With two explanatory variables, the estimated approximation of the CEF is no longer a line or curve, but rather a surface. Figure 4.4.4 plots the estimates for six regression specifications. The estimate of the CEF in regression (3) predicts the CEF as a plane. With no higher-order terms or interactions, the coefficients can easily be interpreted as conditional slopes. For example, holding access to electricity constant, for every additional percentage point increase in population with access to clean water, we would predict approximately 3.5 fewer deaths before one year of age per 10,000 live births. Notice that this conditional relationship is smaller than in regression (1). Since we have no interactions, our estimate of the slope of the CEF with respect to X does not depend on the value of Z.

The estimate of the CEF in regression (4) includes quadratic terms for both X and Z, so its graph is a curved surface. Regression (5) includes an interaction term, allowing the conditional slope of the estimated CEF with respect to X to vary depending on the value of Z, and vice versa. However, the coefficient on the interaction turns out to be quite small (and not statistically significant), so the regression (5) estimate is very similar to the regression (3) estimate: the conditional slope with respect to clean water access only slightly increases (that is, becomes less steep) as access to electricity increases.

Regression (6) includes higher-order interaction terms: in addition to an interaction term for X and Z, the specification accounts for the interaction of X and Z^2, Z and X^2, and X^2 and Z^2. Regression (7) includes even more higher-order interaction terms. Finally, regression (8) estimates the CEF using the lasso with λ chosen via leave-one-out cross-validation, with interactions on electricity up to the second order and water up to the third order. When we include higher-order terms—as in regression (4) as well as (6), (7), and (8)—the conditional relationship between clean water access and infant mortality becomes more difficult to characterize from the coefficients alone.

The coefficient estimates for each of these regressions are reported in columns (3) through (8) of Table 4.4.5, with bootstrap standard error estimates in parentheses below each coefficient.[14]

14 Note that the lasso has a "sparsity" property that is manifest here—most coefficients are set to exactly zero. This sparsity property implies that standard errors cannot generally be computed for the lasso coefficients without very strong assumptions, though this is a topic of ongoing inquiry. See Leeb and Pötscher (2006).

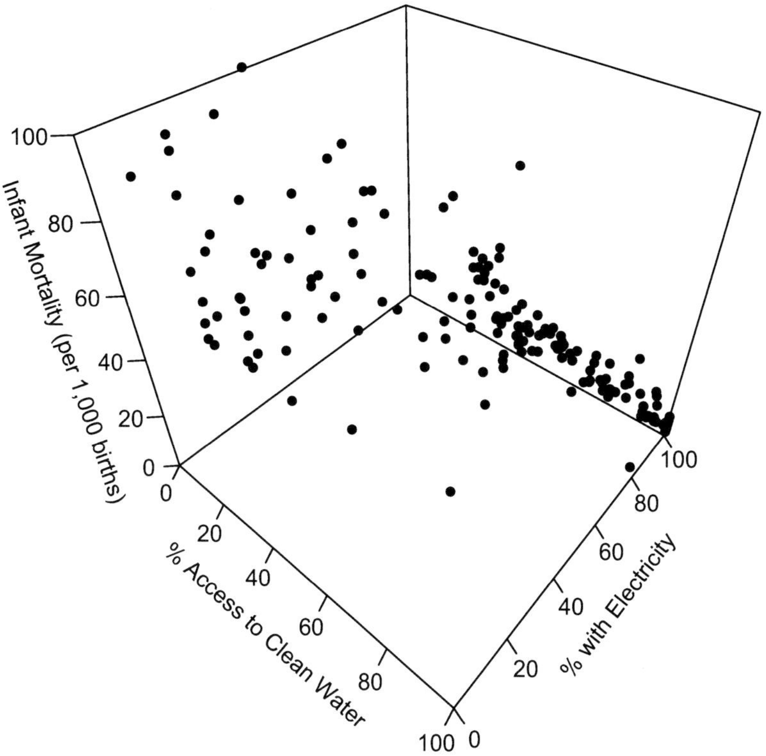

FIGURE 4.4.3. *Plotting Cross-National Infant Mortality Against Access to Clean Water and Electricity*

More generally, we can see how the APD and PDA allow us to draw comparisons across specifications. Once we start conditioning on access to electricity in column (3), we see that our estimates of the APD are nearly halved. Importantly, we see that in columns (3) through (8), our estimate of the APD is largely unchanged by introducing nonlinear specifications, suggesting that the linear approximation may be sufficient for estimating the APD. However, as we increase the complexity of the specification, the standard errors grow quickly for both the estimated APD and PDA, suggesting overfitting. We see that the PDA can be more sensitive to model overfitting—the standard errors are typically larger, and the behavior of the estimator can be sensitive to specification. This is because the PDA is evaluated at a single point, and thus can be very sensitive to nonlinearity, whereas the APD averages across all values. The APD is typically a more sensible way to summarize the conditional relationship between access to water and infant mortality.

(3) OLS: $\alpha + \beta X + \gamma Z$

(4) OLS: $\alpha + \sum_{\kappa=1}^{2} \beta_{\kappa} X^{\kappa} + \sum_{\kappa=1}^{2} \gamma \kappa Z^{\kappa}$

(5) OLS: $\alpha + \beta X + \gamma Z + \omega XZ$

(6) OLS: $\alpha + \beta X + \gamma Z + \sum_{\kappa=1}^{2} \sum_{l=1}^{2} \omega_{\kappa l} X^{\kappa} Z^{l}$

(7) OLS: $\alpha + \beta X + \gamma Z + \sum_{\kappa=1}^{3} \sum_{l=1}^{2} \omega_{\kappa l} X^{\kappa} Z^{l}$

(8) Lasso: $\alpha + \beta X + \gamma Z + \sum_{\kappa=1}^{3} \sum_{l=1}^{2} \omega_{\kappa l} X^{\kappa} Z^{l}$

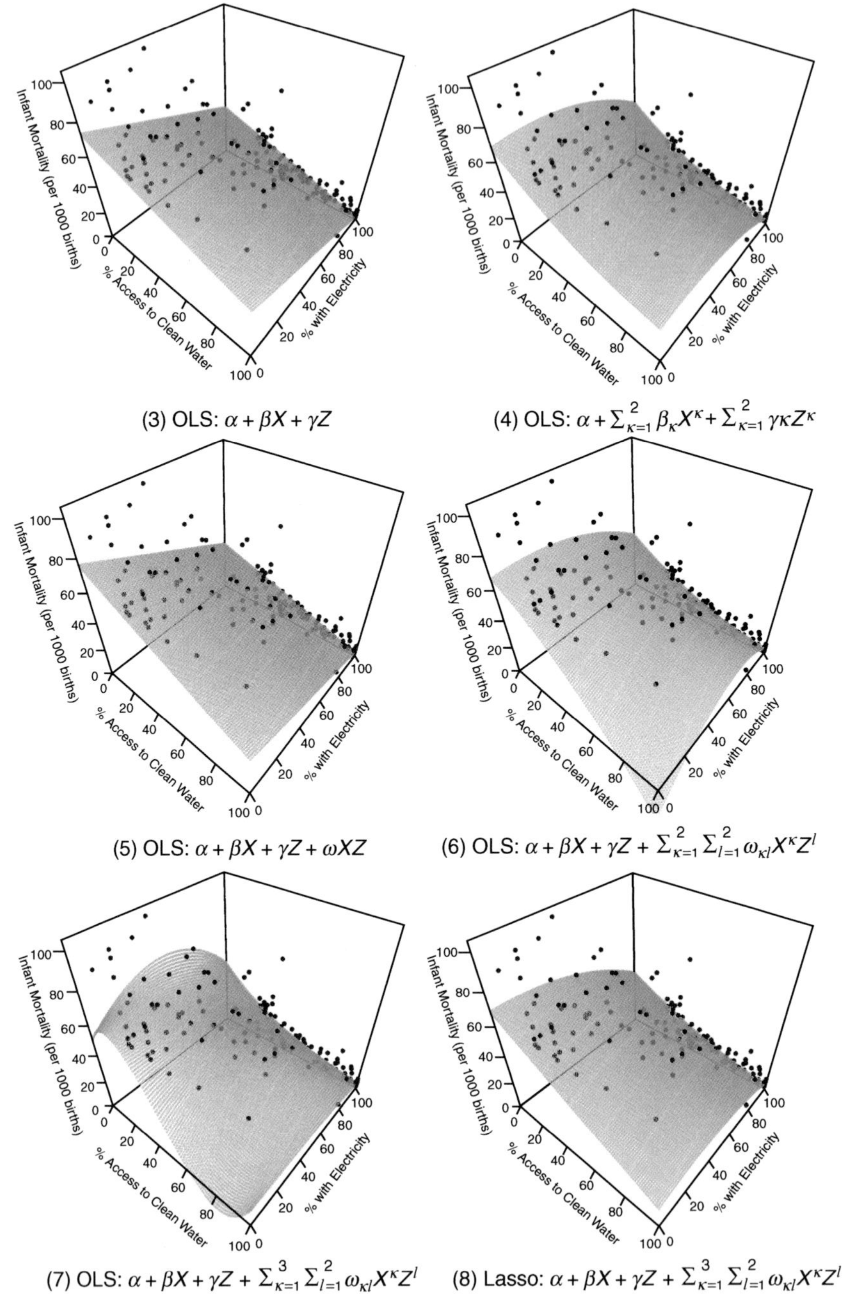

FIGURE 4.4.4. *Estimates of the CEF of Infant Mortality with Respect to Access to Clean Water and Electricity*

4.5 FURTHER READINGS

Textbook discussions of regression are extremely common: see, e.g., Greene (2012) and Davidson and MacKinnon (2004) for traditional approaches under a more structural paradigm. Freedman (2009) provides a skeptical treatment of a structural approach to regression. Here, we discuss the articles and books that most closely relate to the agnostic paradigm. The readings from Chapter 2 remain highly relevant, particularly Hansen (2013), Goldberger (1991), and Angrist and Pischke (2009), all of which link closely to the presentation of materials here. Buja et al. (mimeo.) provides an in-depth article-length treatment of the properties of regression and associated standard errors when the CEF is not linear in the explanatory variables. Chen (2007) provides an elegant derivation of the asymptotic properties of a broad family of sieve estimators. Our book only considers the asymptotic properties of standard error estimators; Imbens and Kolesar (in press) provides practical recommendations for estimating standard errors with small samples. Cameron and Miller (2015) is a similarly practical article, considering robust standard error estimation under clustering. The idea of kernel estimation (Definition 3.3.7) can be wedded to regression to yield kernel regression (for example, the canonical Nadaraya–Watson estimator) and generalizations (such as LOESS). These can be thought of as locally weighted regression fits of observations near a given set of values for the explanatory variables, with larger weights assigned to observations closer to the point of prediction; 2006 provides a clear treatment. We strongly recommend James et al. (2014) and its more technical analog Hastie, Tibshirani, and Friedman (2009) for in-depth, book-length treatments of statistical prediction, including (penalized) regression and its generalizations. For article-length overviews of prediction methods with high-dimensional data, we recommend Varian (2014) and Belloni, Chernozhukov, and Hansen (2014).

5

Parametric Models

All models are wrong, but some are useful.

—George Box

We have thus far focused on making credible inferences based on an agnostic view of the world. That is, our inferences have not depended on having full (or nearly full) knowledge of how our data were generated. This approach has not been the historical norm in statistics or econometrics. Instead, these disciplines have primarily been developed around the idea of constructing statistical models to explain observed phenomena, and then imposing distributional assumptions to justify inferences within the framework of the model.

In this chapter, we show how these stronger distributional assumptions can be used profitably to assist in statistical inference, even when these assumptions do not exactly hold. Much as regression provides a method for estimating a best linear approximation of a potentially infinite-dimensional conditional expectation function, we will see that maximum likelihood estimation provides a method for estimating a "best" *parametric* approximation of a potentially infinite-dimensional cumulative distribution function. We begin by defining parametric models, and discussing some canonical examples.

5.1 MODELS AND PARAMETERS

A *parametric model* is a model that assumes that the distribution of some outcome variable Y, conditional on a set of explanatory variables $\mathbf{X}$, can be fully characterized by a finite number of *parameters*. We formalize this as follows:

Definition 5.1.1. *Parametric Model*
For a random variable Y and random vector $\mathbf{X}$ of length K, a *parametric model* is a set of functions $g : \mathbb{R}^{K+1} \to \mathbb{R}$ indexed by a real-valued

parameter vector $\boldsymbol{\theta}$ of length τ:

$$\{g(y, \mathbf{x}; \boldsymbol{\theta}) : \boldsymbol{\theta} \in \boldsymbol{\Theta}\},[1]$$

where $\boldsymbol{\Theta} \subseteq \mathbb{R}^{\tau}$. The set $\boldsymbol{\Theta}$ is called the *parameter space*. The model is said to be *true* if $\exists \boldsymbol{\theta} \in \boldsymbol{\Theta}$ such that

$$f_{Y|\mathbf{X}}(y|\mathbf{x}) = g(y, \mathbf{x}; \boldsymbol{\theta}).$$

A model is simply a set of distributions. We label each distribution distinctly with $\boldsymbol{\theta}$, which is the *parameter vector* that describes that distribution. For a parametric model, $\boldsymbol{\theta}$ is assumed to have a finite number of real-valued elements. This parametric approach contrasts with our approach in earlier chapters: for all our key results, we did not require restrictive distributional assumptions on any of the variables—g was allowed to be unknown and perhaps characterized by an infinite-dimensional $\boldsymbol{\theta}$.

To illustrate how parametric models work, we will start with an extremely simple example: the (potentially) biased coin that we considered in Example 1.2.7 (*A Biased Coin Flip*).

Example 5.1.2. *A Biased Coin Flip*
Let $Y = 0$ if the coin comes up heads and $Y = 1$ if the coin comes up tails. The only unknown quantity is the probability p that the coin turns up tails. Thus, Y is a Bernoulli random variable with probability p. Since there are no explanatory variables, we need only consider the (unconditional) PMF $f_Y(y)$. Let

$$f_Y(y) = g(y; p) = \begin{cases} 1-p & : \ y = 0 \\ p & : \ y = 1 \\ 0 & : \ \text{otherwise.} \end{cases}$$

Then $\boldsymbol{\theta} = p$, since p completely determines the distribution of the random variable Y. The parameter space is $\boldsymbol{\Theta} = [0, 1]$, which is the unit interval. This is, technically, a parametric model for Y. If we knew just one number, p, then we would know everything there is to know about the distribution of Y. △

In this setting, assuming a parametric model is unobjectionable, as the problem itself naturally only admits so much complexity. Similarly, consider a roll of a (potentially) loaded six-sided die.

1 Two notes on notation: (1) We separate $\boldsymbol{\theta}$ from the arguments of g with a semicolon. (2) When we have no explanatory variables, we will use as shorthand $f_Y(y) = g(y; \boldsymbol{\theta})$.

Example 5.1.3. *A Loaded Die Roll*
Let Y take on the value of the side of the die that comes up. Our model is

$$f_Y(y) = g(y;\mathbf{p}) = \begin{cases} p_1 & : \ y=1 \\ p_2 & : \ y=2 \\ p_3 & : \ y=3 \\ p_4 & : \ y=4 \\ p_5 & : \ y=5 \\ p_6 & : \ y=6 \\ 0 & : \ \text{otherwise,} \end{cases}$$

where $\mathbf{p} = (p_1,p_2,p_3,p_4,p_5,p_6)$. Then $\boldsymbol{\theta} = \mathbf{p}$, since those six values completely determine the distribution of Y. The parameter space is

$$\Theta = \left\{ \mathbf{p} \in \mathbb{R}^6 : \forall i, 0 \leq p_i \leq 1, \text{ and } \sum_{i=1}^{6} p_i = 1 \right\},$$

that is, the components of $\mathbf{p}$ must each be between zero and one, and must all sum to one. This is, again, a parametric model for Y. Formally, Y follows a *categorical distribution* (also known as a *generalized Bernoulli distribution*) with event probabilities p_1, p_2, p_3, p_4, p_5, and p_6. △

Examples 5.1.2 and 5.1.3 represent the simplest types of statistical models. These models describe the (unconditional) distribution of a random variable Y in terms of a finite number of parameters. However, as Definition 5.1.1 suggests, some of the most important and widely used models characterize the *conditional* distribution of an outcome variable Y given a set of explanatory variables $\mathbf{X}$. We can now consider some of these more complicated models.

5.1.1 The Classical Linear Model

The *classical linear model* is the workhorse of conventional applied econometrics and statistics, and is typically afforded a great deal of attention in conventional textbooks. This model can be defined in accordance with our general definition of a parametric model as follows:

Definition 5.1.4. *Classical Linear Model*
For a random variable Y and random vector $\mathbf{X} = (1, X_{[1]}, X_{[2]}, ..., X_{[K]})$, the *classical linear model* is a parametric model with

$$g\big(y,\mathbf{x};(\boldsymbol{\beta},\sigma)\big) = \phi\big(y;(\mathbf{x}\boldsymbol{\beta},\sigma^2)\big),$$

where $\boldsymbol{\beta} = (\beta_0, \beta_1, ..., \beta_K)^T$, $\phi(y; (\mu, \sigma^2))$ denotes the PDF of the normal distribution with mean μ and variance σ^2, and the parameter space is $\boldsymbol{\Theta} = \{(\boldsymbol{\beta}, \sigma) \in \mathbb{R}^{K+2} : \sigma \geq 0\}$.

Equivalently, the classical linear model can also be written in the following (much more common) form:

$$Y = \mathbf{X}\boldsymbol{\beta} + \varepsilon,$$

where $\boldsymbol{\beta} = (\beta_0, \beta_1, ..., \beta_K)^T$ and $\varepsilon \sim N(0, \sigma^2)$. This representation illustrates the two key elements of the classical linear model: the response is linear in the explanatory variables, and errors are i.i.d. normal with expectation zero. The fact that the deviations from the linear component are mean zero and independent of $\mathbf{X}$ should be somewhat familiar; these are the properties of the deviations from the CEF (Theorem 2.2.19). The following theorem codifies this connection between the classical linear model and the CEF.

Theorem 5.1.5. *CEF of the Classical Linear Model*
For a random variable Y and random vector $\mathbf{X} = (1, X_{[1]}, X_{[2]}, ..., X_{[K]})$, if the classical linear model is true, then the CEF of Y given $\mathbf{X}$ is

$$\mathrm{E}[Y|\mathbf{X} = \mathbf{x}] = \mathbf{x}\boldsymbol{\beta}, \forall \mathbf{x} \in \mathrm{Supp}[\mathbf{X}].$$

Proof: If the classical linear model is true, then $f_{Y|\mathbf{X}} = \phi(y; (\mathbf{x}\boldsymbol{\beta}, \sigma^2))$. So, by Definition 2.2.10 (*Conditional Expectation*), $\forall \mathbf{x} \in \mathrm{Supp}[\mathbf{X}]$,

$$\mathrm{E}[Y|\mathbf{X} = \mathbf{x}] = \int_{-\infty}^{\infty} y\phi\big(y; (\mathbf{x}\boldsymbol{\beta}, \sigma^2)\big)dy = \mathbf{x}\boldsymbol{\beta},$$

since the second expression is just the expectation of a random variable with distribution $N(\mathbf{x}\boldsymbol{\beta}, \sigma^2)$. □

Note that, as in Section 2.2.4, since the CEF is linear, the BLP is also the CEF here. Let us consider an example of the classical linear model in practice.

Example 5.1.6. *Modeling SAT Scores*
Suppose that we are trying to model SAT scores for high school students. We have the following information about each student i:

- $Income_i$: student i's family income in the previous calendar year,
- $Tutoring_i$: an indicator for whether or not student i received tutoring,
- GPA_i: student i's high school GPA, and
- Y_i: student i's SAT score.

Let $\mathbf{X}_i = (1, Income_i, Tutoring_i, GPA_i)$. Then we might impose the following linear model:

$$\begin{aligned} Y_i &= \mathbf{X}_i\boldsymbol{\beta} + \varepsilon_i \\ &= \beta_0 + \beta_1 \cdot Income_i + \beta_2 \cdot Tutoring_i + \beta_3 \cdot GPA_i + \varepsilon_i, \end{aligned}$$

where $\varepsilon_i \sim N(0,\sigma^2)$. The final term ε_i represents the "disturbance," that is, all variation in SAT scores that is not explained by income, tutoring, GPA, and the constant.

In this example, the linear model implies that, if we knew just five numbers, we would know *everything* about the distribution of SAT scores conditional on income, tutoring, and GPA. It is a parametric model with parameter vector $\boldsymbol{\theta} = (\beta_0, \beta_1, \beta_2, \beta_3, \sigma)$. The conditional PDF of Y_i given $\mathbf{X}_i$ is assumed to be of the form

$$f_{Y_i|\mathbf{X}_i}(y_i|\mathbf{x}_i) = \phi\big(y_i; (\beta_0 + \beta_1 \cdot Income_i + \beta_2 \cdot Tutoring_i + \beta_3 \cdot GPA_i, \sigma^2)\big). \ \triangle$$

Defenders of the classical linear model would argue that "all the things that we do not measure probably add up to a normal distribution" and that the assumption that $\varepsilon_i \sim N(0,\sigma^2)$ is a harmless technical convenience. It is true that assuming a normally distributed disturbance is not entirely unreasonable, since the Central Limit Theorem implies that the sum of many small, independent, random perturbations will tend to be normally distributed. But, at the same time, we would be hard-pressed to accept this assumption literally, much as we would be unlikely to accept an assumption of linearity literally in most settings.

5.1.2 Binary Choice Models

Let us consider another class of commonly used statistical models: *binary choice models*. Binary choice models allow for the prediction of outcomes that are governed by a Bernoulli distribution (Example 1.2.7). In short, a binary choice model assumes that the conditional probability associated with the Bernoulli distribution is governed by a known function of the explanatory variables. We provide a formal definition below.

Definition 5.1.7. *Binary Choice Model*[2]

For a binary random variable Y and random vector $\mathbf{X} = (1, X_{[1]}, X_{[2]}, ..., X_{[K]})$, a *binary choice model* is a parametric model with

$$g(y, \mathbf{X}; \boldsymbol{\beta}) = \begin{cases} 1 - h(\mathbf{X}\boldsymbol{\beta}) & : \ y = 0 \\ h(\mathbf{X}\boldsymbol{\beta}) & : \ y = 1 \\ 0 & : \ \text{otherwise}, \end{cases}$$

where $\boldsymbol{\beta} = (\beta_0, \beta_1, \ldots, \beta_K)^T$, the *mean function* $h : \mathbb{R} \to [0,1]$ is known, and the parameter space is $\boldsymbol{\Theta} = \mathbb{R}^{K+1}$.

The function h is called the *mean function*[3] because it governs the shape of the CEF. This is codified in the following theorem.

Theorem 5.1.8. *CEF of a Binary Choice Model*
For a binary random variable Y and random vector $\mathbf{X} = (1, X_{[1]}, X_{[2]}, \ldots, X_{[K]})$, if the binary choice model with mean function h is true, the CEF of Y given $\mathbf{X}$ is

$$\mathrm{E}[Y|\mathbf{X} = \mathbf{x}] = h(\mathbf{X}\boldsymbol{\beta}), \forall \mathbf{x} \in \mathrm{Supp}[\mathbf{X}].$$

A proof follows from Example 2.1.3. Importantly, one consequence of a binary choice model is that all predictions of the CEF must be bounded in $[0,1]$, since the mean function has codomain $[0,1]$. Note that, importantly, the CEF may be nonlinear in $\mathbf{X}$. Linear approximations of the CEF (such as the BLP) need not respect the bounds of the interval $[0,1]$; predictions of conditional expectations from such approaches might yield negative predictions or predictions greater than one. Such predictions would be nonsensical, and in fact are incompatible with the Kolmogorov axioms (Definition 1.1.2). In settings where respecting the bounds of predictions is important (we will have such a case in Section 7.2.3), we will generally prefer to use a binary choice model rather than an approach (like regression) that might yield nonsensical predictions.

The two most commonly used binary choice models are *logit* and *probit*, which differ only in the shape of their mean function. We define both models below.

Definition 5.1.9. *Logit Model*
For a binary random variable Y and random vector $\mathbf{X} = (1, X_{[1]}, X_{[2]}, \ldots, X_{[K]})$, a *logit model* is a binary choice model where the mean function is the logistic function:

$$h(\mathbf{X}\boldsymbol{\beta}) = \frac{e^{\mathbf{X}\boldsymbol{\beta}}}{1 + e^{\mathbf{X}\boldsymbol{\beta}}}.$$

2 Technically, we are restricting our attention to a special type of binary choice model: *index models*. Index models assume that the explanatory variables enter into the parametric model only through the linear *index* $\mathbf{X}\boldsymbol{\beta}$. In practice, this can be relaxed in many ways, including the polynomials and interactions that we considered in Section 4.3 (*Estimation of Nonlinear Conditional Expectation Functions*).

3 The *link function*, or the inverse of the mean function, is conventionally how such models are parameterized.

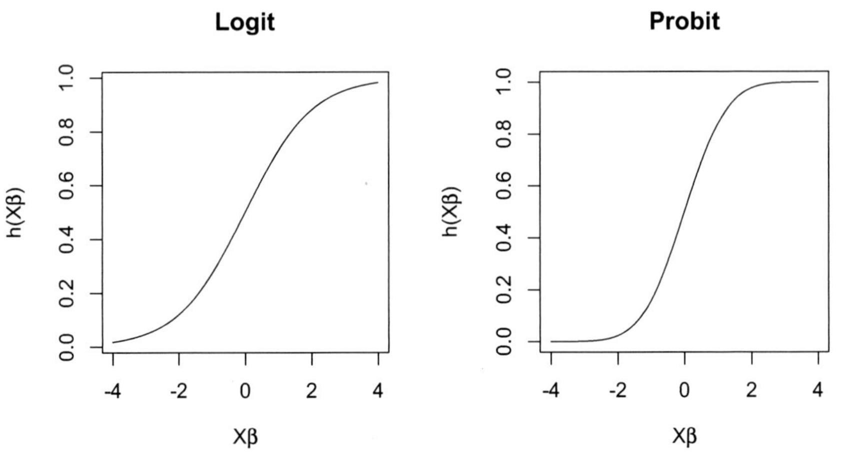

FIGURE 5.1.1. *Logit and Probit Functions*

Definition 5.1.10. *Probit Model*
For a binary random variable Y and random vector $\mathbf{X} = (1, X_{[1]}, X_{[2]}, ..., X_{[K]})$, a *probit model* is a binary choice model where the mean function is the CDF of the standard normal distribution:

$$h(\mathbf{X}\boldsymbol{\beta}) = \Phi(\mathbf{X}\boldsymbol{\beta}).$$

Figure 5.1.1 displays the graphs of these functions.

Note that the mean functions for logit and probit have very similar shapes, differing primarily in scale.[4] In both models, large changes in $\mathbf{X}\boldsymbol{\beta}$ at extreme values correspond to relatively small changes in the conditional probability of $Y = 1$.

We conclude this section with an example of how binary choice models work in practice.

Example 5.1.11. *Modeling the Decision to Buy a Car*
Suppose that we are trying to model the probability that an individual will buy a car. We have the following information about each individual i:

- $Income_i$: individual i's income in the previous calendar year.
- $Distance_i$: individual i's distance from their workplace.
- $PublicTransit_i$: an indicator for whether or not individual i has access to public transportation.
- Y_i: an indicator for whether or not individual i bought a car.

4 As a result, for most reasonable data generating processes, conclusions drawn using logit and probit models should not differ much.

Let $\mathbf{X}_i = (1, Income_i, Distance_i, PublicTransit_i)$. Then we might assume that

$$\begin{aligned}\Pr[Y_i = 1 \mid \mathbf{X}_i] &= h(\mathbf{X}_i\boldsymbol{\beta}) \\ &= h(\beta_0 + \beta_1 \cdot Income_i + \beta_2 \cdot Distance_i + \beta_3 \cdot PublicTransit_i).\end{aligned}$$

Once we assume the form of h, this is a parametric model: assuming the model is true, knowledge of $\boldsymbol{\beta}$ tells us everything about the conditional distribution of Y_i given $\mathbf{X}_i$. For example, if h is the standard normal CDF, then we have a probit model with

$$\begin{aligned}\Pr[Y_i = 1 \mid \mathbf{X}_i] &= \Phi(\mathbf{X}_i\boldsymbol{\beta}) \\ &= \Phi(\beta_0 + \beta_1 \cdot Income_i + \beta_2 \cdot Distance_i + \beta_3 \cdot PublicTransit_i).\end{aligned}$$

If β_0, β_1, β_2, and β_3 are known, this equation fully describes the conditional distribution of Y_i given $\mathbf{X}_i$. $\triangle$

5.2 MAXIMUM LIKELIHOOD ESTIMATION

Once we have chosen a parametric model to describe an observed phenomenon, how can we estimate its parameters from the data? As usual, we will assume that we have independent and identically distributed (i.i.d.) observations. It can then be shown that, if we assume that the parametric model is true, then a procedure known as *maximum likelihood (ML) estimation* yields consistent, asymptotically efficient, and asymptotically normal estimates of the parameters. Indeed, under this assumption, there exists no "regular" estimator that has better asymptotic efficiency. However, even when the parametric model is not true, we will show that ML estimation nevertheless yields an approximation that is sensible and can be used profitably for plug-in estimation.

5.2.1 The Logic of Maximum Likelihood Estimation

Suppose that we have n i.i.d. observations of a discrete random vector $(Y, \mathbf{X})$, and suppose that we assume the model

$$f_{Y|\mathbf{X}}(y \mid \mathbf{x}) = g(y, \mathbf{x}; \boldsymbol{\theta}),$$

so that the conditional PMF of Y given $\mathbf{X}$ is entirely characterized by some known function g and the parameter vector $\boldsymbol{\theta}$. The idea behind ML estimation is that we want to find the parameters $\boldsymbol{\theta}$ that would have maximized the probability of obtaining the data that we actually observed. In other words, since we do not know the parameters but we *do* know the outcome—or rather, n i.i.d. outcomes—our best guess for the parameters is the values that would have made that particular set of outcomes as likely as possible.

To formally describe ML estimation, we must first define the *likelihood function.*

Definition 5.2.1. *Likelihood Function*
Let Y be a random variable and $\mathbf{X}$ be a random vector, and assume the parametric model $f_{Y|\mathbf{X}}(y|\mathbf{x}) = g(y,\mathbf{x};\boldsymbol{\theta})$. Then the *likelihood function* is

$$\mathcal{L}(\mathbf{t}\,|\,Y,\mathbf{X}) = g(Y,\mathbf{X};\mathbf{t}).$$

Thus, if the model is true, the likelihood function maps each candidate parameter value $\mathbf{t}$ to the conditional probability/density of the observed values of Y given the observed values of $\mathbf{X}$, assuming $\mathbf{t}$ is the true parameter value.[5]

We can generalize this to the case where we have i.i.d. observations. Let $(Y_1,\mathbf{X}_1)$, $(Y_2,\mathbf{X}_2)$, ..., $(Y_n,\mathbf{X}_n)$ be i.i.d. observations of $(Y,\mathbf{X})$, and let

$$\mathbf{Y} = \begin{pmatrix} Y_1 \\ Y_2 \\ \vdots \\ Y_n \end{pmatrix} \text{ and } \mathbb{X} = \begin{pmatrix} X_{[1]1} & X_{[2]1} & \cdots & X_{[K]1} \\ X_{[1]2} & X_{[2]2} & \cdots & X_{[K]2} \\ \vdots & \vdots & \ddots & \vdots \\ X_{[1]n} & X_{[2]n} & \cdots & X_{[K]n} \end{pmatrix}.$$

Then

$$\mathcal{L}(\mathbf{t}\,|\,\mathbf{Y},\mathbb{X}) = \prod_{i=1}^{n} \mathcal{L}(\mathbf{t}\,|\,Y_i,\mathbf{X}_i).$$

We can now formally define the maximum likelihood estimator.

Definition 5.2.2. *Maximum Likelihood Estimator*
Let Y be a random variable and $\mathbf{X}$ be a random vector. Let $(Y_1,\mathbf{X}_1)$, $(Y_2,\mathbf{X}_2)$, ..., $(Y_n,\mathbf{X}_n)$ be i.i.d. observations of $(Y,\mathbf{X})$, and let

$$\mathbf{Y} = \begin{pmatrix} Y_1 \\ Y_2 \\ \vdots \\ Y_n \end{pmatrix} \text{ and } \mathbb{X} = \begin{pmatrix} X_{[1]1} & X_{[2]1} & \cdots & X_{[K]1} \\ X_{[1]2} & X_{[2]2} & \cdots & X_{[K]2} \\ \vdots & \vdots & \ddots & \vdots \\ X_{[1]n} & X_{[2]n} & \cdots & X_{[K]n} \end{pmatrix}.$$

[5] Formally, we would say that the likelihood function is itself a random function, $\mathcal{L} : \Omega \to \mathscr{L}$, where $\mathscr{L}$ is the space of functions $L : \mathbb{R} \to [0,1]$.

Then, for the parametric model $f_{Y|\mathbf{X}}(y|\mathbf{x}) = g(y,\mathbf{x};\boldsymbol{\theta})$ with $\boldsymbol{\theta} \in \boldsymbol{\Theta}$, the *maximum likelihood estimator* of $\boldsymbol{\theta}$ is

$$\hat{\boldsymbol{\theta}}_{ML} = \underset{\mathbf{t}\in\boldsymbol{\Theta}}{\arg\max}\, \mathcal{L}(\mathbf{t}\,|\,\mathbf{Y},\mathbb{X}) = \underset{\mathbf{t}\in\boldsymbol{\Theta}}{\arg\max} \prod_{i=1}^{n} \mathcal{L}(\mathbf{t}\,|\,Y_i,\mathbf{X}_i),$$

or, equivalently,

$$\hat{\boldsymbol{\theta}}_{ML} = \underset{\mathbf{t}\in\boldsymbol{\Theta}}{\arg\max}\big[\log \mathcal{L}(\mathbf{t}\,|\,\mathbf{Y},\mathbb{X})\big] = \underset{\mathbf{t}\in\boldsymbol{\Theta}}{\arg\max} \sum_{i=1}^{n} \log \mathcal{L}(\mathbf{t}\,|\,Y_i,\mathbf{X}_i),$$ [6]

where $\log \mathcal{L}(\mathbf{t}\,|\,\mathbf{Y},\mathbb{X})$ is known as the *log-likelihood*.

The equivalence of the two formulations of the ML estimator arises because the natural logarithm—which we write as log—is a strictly increasing function; therefore, the maximum log-likelihood must be attained at the same point as the maximum likelihood. Depending on the type of problem we are considering, we might prefer one formulation over another, though typically the log-likelihood is preferred as sums tend to be more analytically tractable than products.

Readers may note a certain similarity of the ML estimator to the form of the OLS regression estimator (Definition 4.1.2): both estimators can be written as optimization problems. The OLS estimator minimizes the sum of squared residuals, and the ML solution maximizes the sum over every unit's log-likelihood function.[7]

To ground these ideas, we will consider two simple examples. We begin with our usual coin flip example.

Example 5.2.3. *Maximum Likelihood Estimation for a Biased Coin Flip*
As usual, let $Y = 0$ if the coin comes up heads and $Y = 1$ if the coin comes up tails. Our model is

$$f_Y(y) = g(y;p) = \begin{cases} 1-p & : \ y = 0 \\ p & : \ y = 1 \\ 0 & : \ \text{otherwise,} \end{cases}$$

with $\boldsymbol{\Theta} = [0,1]$. The one thing we do not know is the parameter p, the probability that the coin turns up tails. Suppose that we observed n i.i.d. coin flips: $\mathbf{Y} = (Y_1, Y_2, ..., Y_n)^T$. How do we compute the ML estimate of p? We will consider three cases separately.

6 Recall that $\log(\prod_{i=1}^{n} \mathcal{L}(\mathbf{t}\,|\,Y_i,\mathbf{X}_i)) = \sum_{i=1}^{n} \log \mathcal{L}(\mathbf{t}\,|\,Y_i,\mathbf{X}_i)$.

7 It is for this reason that both estimators are special cases of *M-estimators*; see, e.g., Stefanski and Boos (2002).

First, suppose that $\mathbf{Y} = (0,0,\ldots,0)^T$. Then, $\forall i \in \{1,2,\ldots,n\}$, $\mathcal{L}(\hat{p}\,|\,Y_i) = g(Y_i\,|\,\hat{p}) = 1-\hat{p}$, so

$$\mathcal{L}(\hat{p}\,|\,\mathbf{Y}) = \prod_{i=1}^{n}(1-\hat{p}) = (1-\hat{p})^n,$$

which, among all $\hat{p} \in [0,1]$, is clearly maximized at $\hat{p} = 0 = \overline{Y}$.

Now, suppose that $\mathbf{Y} = (1,1,\ldots,1)^T$. Then, $\forall i \in \{1,2,\ldots,n\}$, $\mathcal{L}(\hat{p}\,|\,Y_i) = g(Y_i\,|\,\hat{p}) = \hat{p}$, so

$$\mathcal{L}(\hat{p}\,|\,\mathbf{Y}) = \prod_{i=1}^{n}\hat{p} = \hat{p}^n,$$

which, among all $\hat{p} \in [0,1]$, is clearly maximized at $\hat{p} = 1 = \overline{Y}$.

Finally, suppose that $\exists i \in \{1,2,\ldots,n\}$ such that $Y_i = 0$ and $\exists i' \in \{1,2,\ldots,n\}$ such that $Y_{i'} = 1$. Let $I_0 = \{i : Y_i = 0\}$ and $I_1 = \{i : Y_i = 1\}$. (By assumption, $I_0 \neq \emptyset$ and $I_1 \neq \emptyset$.) Then

$$\mathcal{L}(\hat{p}\,|\,\mathbf{Y}) = \prod_{i=1}^{n}\mathcal{L}(\hat{p}\,|\,Y_i) = \prod_{i\in I_0}(1-\hat{p})\prod_{i\in I_1}\hat{p} = (1-\hat{p})^{N_0}\hat{p}^{N_1},$$

where $N_0 = |I_0|$ (the observed number of heads) and $N_1 = |I_1|$ (the observed number of tails).[8]

Notice that $\hat{p} = 0$ or $\hat{p} = 1$ yields $\mathcal{L}(\hat{p}\,|\,\mathbf{Y}) = 0$, whereas any $\hat{p} \in (0,1)$ yields $\mathcal{L}(\hat{p}\,|\,\mathbf{Y}) = (1-\hat{p})^{N_0}\hat{p}^{N_1} > 0$, so $\mathcal{L}(\hat{p}\,|\,\mathbf{Y})$ is not maximized at $\hat{p} = 0$ or $\hat{p} = 1$. So, since we know the solution is some $\hat{p}$ such that $\mathcal{L}(\hat{p}\,|\,\mathbf{Y}) > 0$, we can take the log-likelihood:

$$\log\mathcal{L}(\hat{p}\,|\,\mathbf{Y}) = \log\left((1-\hat{p})^{N_0}\hat{p}^{N_1}\right) = N_0\log(1-\hat{p}) + N_1\log(\hat{p}).$$

The first-order condition is

$$\frac{\partial \log\mathcal{L}(\hat{p}\,|\,\mathbf{Y})}{\partial \hat{p}} = 0.$$

This yields

$$-\frac{N_0}{1-\hat{p}} + \frac{N_1}{\hat{p}} = 0.$$

[8] We use uppercase letters here since N_0 and N_1 are random variables. Note that, by assumption, $N_0 > 0$ and $N_1 > 0$.

Solving for $\hat{p}$,[9]

$$\begin{aligned}
\frac{N_1}{\hat{p}} &= \frac{N_0}{1-\hat{p}} \\
\frac{1-\hat{p}}{\hat{p}} &= \frac{N_0}{N_1} \\
\frac{1}{\hat{p}} - 1 &= \frac{N_0}{N_1} \\
\frac{1}{\hat{p}} &= \frac{N_0}{N_1} + 1 \\
\frac{1}{\hat{p}} &= \frac{N_0 + N_1}{N_1} \\
\frac{1}{\hat{p}} &= \frac{n}{N_1} \\
\hat{p} &= \frac{N_1}{n} \\
\hat{p} &= \frac{1}{n}\sum_{i=1}^{n} Y_i \\
\hat{p} &= \overline{Y}.
\end{aligned}$$

Thus, the ML estimate of the probability of the coin coming up tails is the proportion of flips that came up tails—in other words, the sample mean. That is just the usual plug-in estimate, which corresponds to the sample mean (and, therefore, the regression estimate with no predictors). We know from the Weak Law of Large Numbers (WLLN) that the sample mean is a consistent estimator for p.

To illustrate this more concretely, suppose that we tossed the coin $n = 3$ times and observed $\mathbf{Y} = (1, 0, 1)$. What would be the ML estimate for p? Figure 5.2.1 shows the likelihood as a function of p given this data. The ML estimate for p corresponds to the maximum in the figure: $\hat{p}_{ML} = \frac{2}{3}$, which is again the plug-in estimate, the proportion of flips that came up tails. △

We now turn to the ML estimate of the classical linear model, where a rather remarkable equivalence will be established. This will be a setting where taking the log-likelihood eases the analytic calculations greatly.

9 The second-order condition is

$$\begin{aligned}
\frac{\partial^2 \log \mathcal{L}(\hat{p}\,|\,\mathbf{Y})}{\partial \hat{p}^2} &= \frac{\partial}{\partial \hat{p}}\left(-\frac{N_0}{1-\hat{p}} + \frac{N_1}{\hat{p}}\right) = -(-1)\frac{N_0}{(1-\hat{p})^2}(-1) + (-1)\frac{N_1}{\hat{p}^2} \\
&= -\left(\frac{N_0}{(1-\hat{p})^2} + \frac{N_1}{\hat{p}^2}\right) < 0,
\end{aligned}$$

and we already checked the edge cases, so a unique solution will be an absolute maximum.

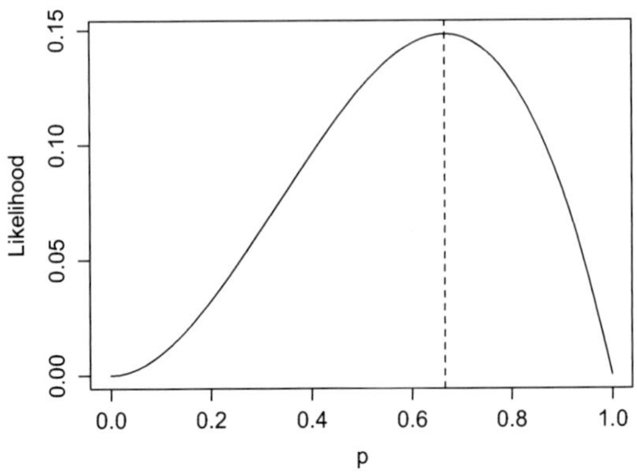

FIGURE 5.2.1. *A Likelihood Function for Three Coin Tosses*

Example 5.2.4. *Maximum Likelihood Estimation of the Classical Linear Model*
Let Y be a random variable and $\mathbf{X} = (1, X_{[1]}, X_{[2]}, ..., X_{[K]})$ be a random vector. Suppose that

$$Y = \mathbf{X}\boldsymbol{\beta} + \varepsilon,$$

where $\boldsymbol{\beta} = (\beta_0, \beta_1, ..., \beta_K)^T$ and $\varepsilon \sim N(0, \sigma^2)$ conditional on $\mathbf{X}$. Let $(Y_1, \mathbf{X}_1)$, $(Y_2, \mathbf{X}_2)$, ..., $(Y_n, \mathbf{X}_n)$ be i.i.d. observations of $(Y, \mathbf{X})$, and let

$$\mathbf{Y} = \begin{pmatrix} Y_1 \\ Y_2 \\ \vdots \\ Y_n \end{pmatrix}, \quad \mathbb{X} = \begin{pmatrix} 1 & X_{[1]1} & X_{[2]1} & \cdots & X_{[K]1} \\ 1 & X_{[1]2} & X_{[2]2} & \cdots & X_{[K]2} \\ \vdots & \vdots & \vdots & \ddots & \vdots \\ 1 & X_{[1]n} & X_{[2]n} & \cdots & X_{[K]n} \end{pmatrix}, \text{ and } \mathbf{b} = \begin{pmatrix} b_0 \\ b_1 \\ b_2 \\ \vdots \\ b_K \end{pmatrix}.$$

Then

$$\begin{aligned} \mathcal{L}\big((\mathbf{b}, s) \,\big|\, \mathbf{Y}, \mathbb{X}\big) &= \prod_{i=1}^{n} \phi\big(Y_i, (\mathbf{X}_i\mathbf{b}, s^2)\big) \\ &= \prod_{i=1}^{n} \frac{1}{s\sqrt{2\pi}} e^{\frac{-(Y_i - \mathbf{X}_i\mathbf{b})^2}{2s^2}}. \end{aligned}$$

So the log-likelihood is

$$\log \mathcal{L}\big((\mathbf{b}, s) \,\big|\, \mathbf{Y}, \mathbb{X}\big) = \log\left(\prod_{i=1}^{n} \frac{1}{s\sqrt{2\pi}} e^{\frac{-(Y_i - \mathbf{X}_i\mathbf{b})^2}{2s^2}} \right)$$

$$= \sum_{i=1}^{n} \log \left(\frac{1}{s\sqrt{2\pi}} e^{\frac{-(Y_i - \mathbf{X}_i \mathbf{b})^2}{2s^2}} \right)$$

$$= \sum_{i=1}^{n} \left(\log \left(\frac{1}{s\sqrt{2\pi}} \right) + \frac{-(Y_i - \mathbf{X}_i \mathbf{b})^2}{2s^2} \right).$$

We want to find the **b** that maximizes $\log \mathcal{L}((\mathbf{b}, s) \mid \mathbf{Y}, \mathbb{X})$:[10]

$$\hat{\boldsymbol{\beta}}_{ML} = \underset{\mathbf{b} \in \mathbb{R}^K}{\arg\max} \big(\log \mathcal{L}(\mathbf{b} \mid \mathbf{Y}, \mathbb{X}) \big)$$

$$= \underset{\mathbf{b} \in \mathbb{R}^K}{\arg\max} \sum_{i=1}^{n} \left(\log \left(\frac{1}{s\sqrt{2\pi}} \right) + \frac{-(Y_i - \mathbf{X}_i \mathbf{b})^2}{2s^2} \right)$$

$$= \underset{\mathbf{b} \in \mathbb{R}^K}{\arg\max} \sum_{i=1}^{n} \big(-(Y_i - \mathbf{X}_i \mathbf{b})^2 \big)$$

$$= \underset{\mathbf{b} \in \mathbb{R}^K}{\arg\min} \sum_{i=1}^{n} (Y_i - \mathbf{X}_i \mathbf{b})^2.$$

So the ML estimator for $\boldsymbol{\beta}$ is the $\hat{\boldsymbol{\beta}}$ that minimizes the sum of squared residuals. This establishes the formal tie between ML estimation and regression. The ML estimator for $\boldsymbol{\beta}$ is the regression estimator when it is assumed that:

- the linear model is true, and
- the errors are $\varepsilon \sim N(0, \sigma^2)$ conditional on **X**.

Many textbooks justify OLS under these strong distributional assumptions, but these assumptions are not necessary. Contrast this with our nonparametric results, which require no such distributional assumptions. Under i.i.d. sampling, OLS consistently estimates the best linear predictor (BLP) of the outcome—and of the conditional expectation function (CEF). △

It is an unusual feature of these simple cases that there exist closed-form solutions for our ML estimates. (The cases in which they coincide with conventional methods are, naturally, the most amenable to closed-form solutions.) However, in practice, ML estimators rarely have closed-form solutions. Instead, one usually has to calculate the solution numerically using a computer.[11] This is the case, for example, for logit and probit. We conclude

[10] We do not need to estimate σ here, but simple algebraic manipulations show that its ML estimator will equal $\frac{1}{n}\sum_{i=1}^{n}(Y_i - \mathbf{X}_i \hat{\boldsymbol{\beta}})^2$, or the plug-in sample variance of the residuals.)

[11] There are many algorithms that can be implemented to find the minimum of a function, generally involving some type of iterated search. For example, the *Newton–Raphson method*

this section by discussing maximum likelihood estimation of the probit model.

Example 5.2.5. *Maximum Likelihood Estimation of the Probit Model*
Let Y be a binary random variable and $\mathbf{X} = (1, X_{[1]}, X_{[2]}, ..., X_{[K]})$ be a random vector. Suppose that

$$\Pr[Y = 1 \mid \mathbf{X}] = \Phi(\mathbf{X}\boldsymbol{\beta}),$$

where $\boldsymbol{\beta} = (\beta_0, \beta_1, ..., \beta_K)^T$. This implies that

$$f_{Y|\mathbf{X}}(Y|\mathbf{X}) = g(Y, X; \boldsymbol{\beta}) = \Phi(\mathbf{X}\boldsymbol{\beta})^Y \big(1 - \Phi(\mathbf{X}\boldsymbol{\beta})\big)^{1-Y}.$$

Let $(Y_1, \mathbf{X}_1)$, $(Y_2, \mathbf{X}_2)$, ..., $(Y_n, \mathbf{X}_n)$ be i.i.d. observations of $(Y, \mathbf{X})$, and let

$$\mathbf{Y} = \begin{pmatrix} Y_1 \\ Y_2 \\ \vdots \\ Y_n \end{pmatrix}, \; \mathbb{X} = \begin{pmatrix} 1 & X_{[1]1} & X_{[2]1} & \cdots & X_{[K]1} \\ 1 & X_{[1]2} & X_{[2]2} & \cdots & X_{[K]2} \\ \vdots & \vdots & \vdots & \ddots & \vdots \\ 1 & X_{[1]n} & X_{[2]n} & \cdots & X_{[K]n} \end{pmatrix}, \text{ and } \mathbf{b} = \begin{pmatrix} b_0 \\ b_1 \\ b_2 \\ \vdots \\ b_K \end{pmatrix}.$$

Then

$$\mathcal{L}(\mathbf{b} \mid \mathbf{Y}, \mathbb{X}) = \prod_{i=1}^{n} \Phi(\mathbf{X}_i\mathbf{b})^{Y_i} \big(1 - \Phi(\mathbf{X}_i\mathbf{b})\big)^{1-Y_i}.$$

Thus, the log-likelihood is

$$\begin{aligned} \log \mathcal{L}(\mathbf{b}|\mathbf{Y}, \mathbb{X}) &= \log\left(\prod_{i=1}^{n} \Phi(\mathbf{X}_i\mathbf{b})^{Y_i}\big(1 - \Phi(\mathbf{X}_i\mathbf{b})\big)^{1-Y_i}\right) \\ &= \sum_{i=1}^{n} \log\Big(\Phi(\mathbf{X}_i\mathbf{b})^{Y_i}\big(1 - \Phi(\mathbf{X}_i\mathbf{b})\big)^{1-Y_i}\Big) \\ &= \sum_{i=1}^{n} \Big(Y_i \log \Phi(\mathbf{X}_i\mathbf{b}) + (1 - Y_i) \log\big(1 - \Phi(\mathbf{X}_i\mathbf{b})\big)\Big). \end{aligned}$$

works by taking the second-order polynomial approximation (that is, the Taylor expansion) of the function at a given point by taking numerical derivatives. The first point must be specified as a starting (or "seed") value. Then it updates to guess the point that maximizes the polynomial approximation. Then it repeats the procedure until it finds a fixed point—a point where the estimate of the maximum does not change by more than a specified tolerance when the procedure is repeated again. Note: depending on the seed value, this method, and many others like it, may not necessarily converge to the global maximum if the function is not strictly concave.

So, given the outcomes for $\mathbf{Y}$ and $\mathbb{X}$, we would obtain the ML estimate by using a computer to calculate

$$\hat{\boldsymbol{\beta}}_{ML} = \underset{\mathbf{b} \in \mathbb{R}^{K+1}}{\arg\max} \sum_{i=1}^{n} \Big(Y_i \log \Phi(\mathbf{X}_i \mathbf{b}) + (1 - Y_i) \log\big(1 - \Phi(\mathbf{X}_i \mathbf{b})\big) \Big). \quad \triangle$$

5.2.2 Maximum Likelihood Estimation when the Parametric Model Is True

Although we do not necessarily believe that the parametric model is true, it will be useful to establish the consistency of the ML estimator when the model is, in fact, true. We provide a slightly informal statement, along with a proof sketch (based on the plug-in principle) for the consistency of the ML estimator.

Theorem 5.2.6. *Consistency of the Maximum Likelihood Estimator*
Let Y be a random variable and $\mathbf{X}$ be a random vector. Let $(Y_1, \mathbf{X}_1)$, $(Y_2, \mathbf{X}_2)$, ..., $(Y_n, \mathbf{X}_n)$ be i.i.d. observations of $(Y, \mathbf{X})$. If the parametric model $f_{Y|\mathbf{X}}(y|\mathbf{x}) = g(y, \mathbf{x}; \boldsymbol{\theta})$ is true and some requisite regularity conditions (such as having a continuous likelihood function, a compact parameter space, and a unique maximum) are satisfied, then $\hat{\boldsymbol{\theta}}_{ML} \xrightarrow{p} \boldsymbol{\theta}$.

Proof sketch: For a more complete derivation, see Wasserman (2004). Let $(Y_1, \mathbf{X}_1)$, $(Y_2, \mathbf{X}_2)$, ..., $(Y_n, \mathbf{X}_n)$ be i.i.d. observations of $(Y, \mathbf{X})$, and let

$$\mathbf{Y} = \begin{pmatrix} Y_1 \\ Y_2 \\ \vdots \\ Y_n \end{pmatrix} \quad \text{and} \quad \mathbb{X} = \begin{pmatrix} X_{[1]1} & X_{[2]1} & \cdots & X_{[K]1} \\ X_{[1]2} & X_{[2]2} & \cdots & X_{[K]2} \\ \vdots & \vdots & \ddots & \vdots \\ X_{[1]n} & X_{[2]n} & \cdots & X_{[K]n} \end{pmatrix}.$$

Let

$$L_n(\mathbf{t}) = \frac{1}{n} \log \mathcal{L}(\mathbf{t} | \mathbf{Y}, \mathbb{X}).$$

By definition (and the assumption of a unique maximum), $\mathbf{t} = \hat{\boldsymbol{\theta}}_{ML}$ uniquely maximizes $\log \mathcal{L}(\mathbf{t}|\mathbf{Y}, \mathbb{X})$ and therefore uniquely maximizes $L_n(\mathbf{t})$. Now, note that

$$\frac{1}{n} \log \mathcal{L}(\mathbf{t} | \mathbf{Y}, \mathbb{X}) = \frac{1}{n} \log \left(\prod_{i=1}^{n} g(Y_i, \mathbf{X}_i; \mathbf{t}) \right) = \frac{1}{n} \sum_{i=1}^{n} \log g(Y_i, \mathbf{X}_i; \mathbf{t}).$$

This is a sample mean, so by the WLLN,

$$\frac{1}{n} \sum_{i=1}^{n} \log g(Y_i, \mathbf{X}_i; \mathbf{t}) \xrightarrow{p} \mathrm{E}\big[\log g(Y, \mathbf{X}; \mathbf{t})\big].$$

Let $L(\mathbf{t}) = \mathrm{E}[\log g(Y, \mathbf{X}; \mathbf{t})] = \mathrm{E}[\log \mathcal{L}(\mathbf{t} | Y, \mathbf{X})]$, so that we can write the above statement as

$$L_n(\mathbf{t}) \xrightarrow{p} L(\mathbf{t}),$$

that is, the sample mean of the likelihood of each observation given parameter values $\mathbf{t}$ converges to the expected likelihood of a single observation given parameter values $\mathbf{t}$.

We now require the following lemma: $\forall \mathbf{t} \in \mathbf{\Theta}$,

$$L(\mathbf{t}) \leq L(\boldsymbol{\theta}),$$

with

$$L(\mathbf{t}) = L(\boldsymbol{\theta}) \iff \Pr\big[g(Y, \mathbf{X}; \mathbf{t}) = g(Y, \mathbf{X}; \boldsymbol{\theta})\big] = 1.$$

That is, the expected value of the log-likelihood function is uniquely maximized when $\mathbf{t} = \boldsymbol{\theta}$. We omit the proof of this lemma, but essentially, for any $\mathbf{t} \neq \boldsymbol{\theta}$, we know that the distribution associated with $\boldsymbol{\theta}$ would have to fit the true distribution exactly, and any other distribution does not.

So, to complete our sketch, we have shown that

- $\hat{\boldsymbol{\theta}}_{ML}$ uniquely maximizes $L_n(\mathbf{t})$,
- $L_n(\mathbf{t}) \xrightarrow{p} L(\mathbf{t})$, and
- $\boldsymbol{\theta}$ uniquely maximizes $L(\mathbf{t})$.

Given suitable regularity conditions, the ML estimate $\hat{\boldsymbol{\theta}}_{ML} \xrightarrow{p} \boldsymbol{\theta}$, so $\hat{\boldsymbol{\theta}}_{ML}$ is consistent. □

What this proof sketch illustrates is that the ML estimator is itself a type of plug-in estimator. The inferential target, $\boldsymbol{\theta}$, is a feature of the population distribution: the parameter values that maximize the expected value of the log-likelihood function. To estimate this population quantity, we use the sample analog: the parameter values that maximize the sample mean of the likelihood function. Since the sample will more and more closely approximate the population distribution as n grows large, the ML estimate will get closer and closer to the true parameter values.

5.2.3 Maximum Likelihood Estimation when the Parametric Model Is Not True

What happens if the parametric model is wrong (that is, not true)? In such settings, we call the model *misspecified*. What, then, does ML estimation give us, asymptotically under misspecification? The somewhat technical answer is that ML estimation will consistently estimate the parameters that minimize the *Kullback–Leibler (KL) divergence* of the hypothesized distribution from the true distribution.[12]

Definition 5.2.7. *Kullback–Leibler Divergence for Continuous Distributions*
For probability density functions $p(\cdot)$ and $q(\cdot)$, the *Kullback–Leibler divergence* is

$$\mathrm{KL}\big[p(\cdot)\,\|\,q(\cdot)\big] = \int_{-\infty}^{\infty} p(t)\log\left(\frac{p(t)}{q(t)}\right)dt.$$

The KL divergence is defined analogously for discrete random variables, with a sum replacing the integral and PMFs replacing PDFs. The Kullback–Leibler divergence is an important idea in multiple fields, including information theory, as it characterizes how well one distribution approximates another distribution.[13] We can intuitively see this by looking at an extreme case: the KL divergence between any distributions $p(\cdot)$ and $q(\cdot)$ is zero whenever P and Q have identical distributions, as $\frac{p(t)}{q(t)} = 1$ at every point t. For any distributions $p(\cdot)$ and $q(\cdot)$ that differ, the KL divergence will be nonzero and positive.

Theorem 5.2.8. *The ML Estimator Is Consistent for the Minimum KL Divergence Predictor*
Let Y be a random variable and $\mathbf{X}$ be a random vector. Let $(Y_1,\mathbf{X}_1)$, $(Y_2,\mathbf{X}_2)$, ..., $(Y_n,\mathbf{X}_n)$ be i.i.d. observations of $(Y,\mathbf{X})$. Then the ML estimate of $f_{Y|\mathbf{X}}(y|\mathbf{x})$, $g(y,\mathbf{x};\hat{\boldsymbol{\theta}}_{ML})$ consistently estimates the minimum Kullback–Leibler divergence approximation of $f_{Y|\mathbf{X}}(y|\mathbf{x})$ among all probability distributions of the form $g(y,\mathbf{x};\mathbf{t})$. That is, assuming that there exists a unique

$$\tilde{\boldsymbol{\theta}} = \underset{\mathbf{t}\in\boldsymbol{\Theta}}{\arg\min}\,\mathrm{KL}\big[f_{Y|\mathbf{X}}(\cdot\,|\mathbf{x})\,\|\,g(\cdot\,,\mathbf{x};\mathbf{t})\big],$$

then

$$\hat{\boldsymbol{\theta}}_{ML} \xrightarrow{p} \tilde{\boldsymbol{\theta}}.$$

We omit the proof of this theorem. What is important here is to note that this fact resembles a result we derived for OLS, only with a different metric for the "distance" between distributions (KL divergence rather than MSE).

12 The parameters that minimize KL divergence are sometimes referred to as the *quasi-ML* parameters.
13 The attentive reader may notice that the KL divergence is not symmetric; there exist probability density functions $p(\cdot)$ and $q(\cdot)$ such that $\mathrm{KL}[p(\cdot)\|q(\cdot)] \neq \mathrm{KL}[q(\cdot)\|p(\cdot)]$.

Among all linear predictors, OLS consistently estimates the one "closest" (in terms of MSE) to the CEF. Likewise, among all conditional distributions of the form given by the hypothesized model, ML estimation consistently estimates the one "closest" (in terms of KL divergence) to the true conditional distribution. In short, there exists a sensible definition of "best" under which ML estimation consistently estimates the best-fitting distribution among all distributions in the assumed parametric family.

The idea behind the proof of Theorem 5.2.8 is again related to the plug-in principle. There is a population quantity of interest, $\tilde{\boldsymbol{\theta}}$: the parameter values that minimize the KL divergence of the hypothesized distribution from the true population distribution. It can be shown that the ML estimate is equal to the sample analog: the parameter values that minimize the KL divergence of the hypothesized distribution from the observed data. So, since the distribution of the observed data converges to the population distribution as n grows large, the ML estimate converges to the value that minimizes the KL divergence of the hypothesized distribution from the true population distribution.

If in fact $f_{Y|\mathbf{X}}(y|\mathbf{x}) = g(y,\mathbf{x};\boldsymbol{\theta})$, then $\mathrm{KL}[f_{Y|\mathbf{X}}(\cdot|\mathbf{x})\,\|\,g(\cdot,\mathbf{x};\boldsymbol{\theta})] = 0$. Thus, if the model is true, the minimum KL divergence approximation is the true distribution, so $\tilde{\boldsymbol{\theta}} = \boldsymbol{\theta}$, and thus ML estimation consistently estimates the true parameter values, as before. When the parametric model is true, ML asymptotically gets the distribution exactly right. When the parametric model is not true, ML asymptotically gets it "as right as possible." The following example considers a visualization.

Example 5.2.9. *Maximum Likelihood Estimation of an Unusual Distribution*

Suppose that the true distribution of Y were given by the histogram on the lefthand side of Figure 5.2.2. Suppose that we erroneously assumed that Y was normally distributed:

$$g\big(y;(\mu,\sigma)\big) = \frac{1}{\sigma\sqrt{2\pi}}e^{-\frac{(y-\mu)^2}{2\sigma^2}}.$$

Then the asymptotic ML estimate of the distribution would be as shown in red on the righthand side of the figure. △

A simpler example is the coin flip from Example 5.1.2 (*A Biased Coin Flip*). When we observe $\mathbf{y} = (1,0,1)$, we can match that empirical distribution exactly by setting $p = \frac{2}{3}$. With i.i.d. observations, the empirical distribution will converge to the true distribution as n grows large. Thus, asymptotically, the ML estimate will exactly characterize the probability distribution of Y.

Cases like the coin flip, where the model $f_{Y|\mathbf{X}}(y|\mathbf{x})$ can be virtually ensured to be true, may be rare in practice, however. In general, ML estimation is best thought of as an explicit means for approximating $f_{Y|\mathbf{X}}(y|\mathbf{x})$.

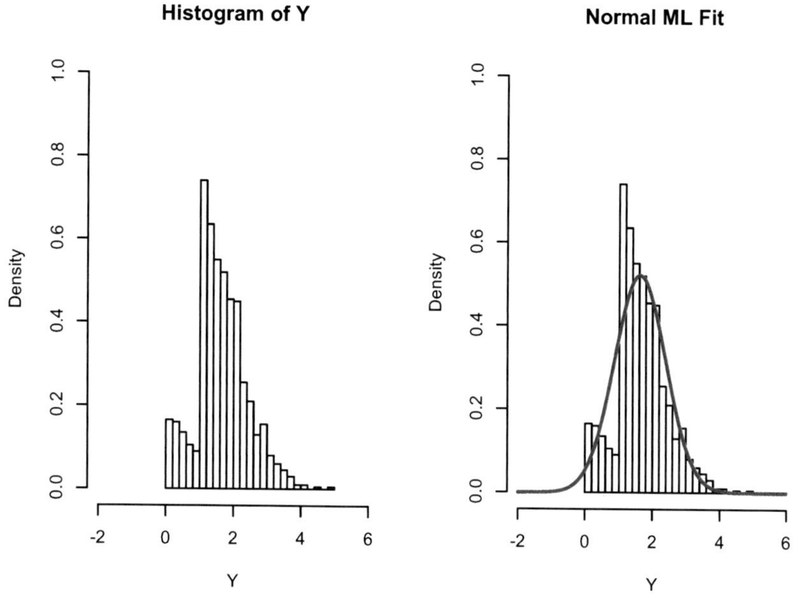

FIGURE 5.2.2. *Minimum KL Divergence Approximation of an Unusual Distribution*

5.2.4 Maximum Likelihood Plug-In Estimation

Once we conceive of maximum likelihood as an approximation tool, we begin to see its real benefits. Suppose that what we are interested in is not the parameters of the model per se, but instead some other feature of the distribution of $(Y, \mathbf{X})$. We know from Chapter 3 that the joint CDF of Y and $\mathbf{X}$ can be estimated to arbitrary precision. But we can use ML estimation to potentially improve the precision of our estimates by imposing a parametric model that seems likely to approximate the shape of the true CEF reasonably well. As before (Definitions 3.3.3 or 3.3.9), we can formally define a plug-in estimator.

Definition 5.2.10. *Maximum Likelihood Plug-In Estimator*
For i.i.d. random vectors $(Y_1, \mathbf{X}_1)$, $(Y_2, \mathbf{X}_2)$, ..., $(Y_n, \mathbf{X}_n)$ with common CDF F, the *ML plug-in estimator* of $\psi = T(F)$ is

$$\hat{\psi}_{ML} = T(\hat{F}_{ML}),$$

where

$$\hat{F}_{ML}(y, \mathbf{x}) = \frac{1}{n}\sum_{i=1}^{n}\left(\mathrm{I}(X_{[1]i} \leq x_{[1]i}, X_{[2]} \leq x_{[2]i}, \dots, X_{[K]i} \leq x_{[x]}) \sum_{v \leq y} g(v, \mathbf{X}_i; \hat{\boldsymbol{\theta}}_{ML}) \right)$$

if $f_{Y|X}(y|\mathbf{x})$ is a PMF, and

$$\hat{F}_{ML}(y,\mathbf{x}) = \frac{1}{n}\sum_{i=1}^{n}\left(\mathrm{I}(X_{[1]i} \le x_{[1]i}, X_{[2]} \le x_{[2]i}, \ldots, X_{[K]i} \le x_{[x]})\int_{-\infty}^{y} g(v,\mathbf{X}_i;\hat{\boldsymbol{\theta}}_{ML})dv\right)$$

if $f_{Y|X}(y|\mathbf{x})$ is a PDF.

The definition follows from invoking the Law of Iterated Expectations and substituting sample quantities for population analogs. To see the ML plug-in estimator in action, let us consider the CEF of Y given $\mathbf{X}=\mathbf{x}$. Given the definition of a conditional expectation (Definition 2.2.10),

$$\mathrm{E}[Y|\mathbf{X}=\mathbf{x}] = \int_{-\infty}^{\infty} yg(y,\mathbf{x};\boldsymbol{\theta})dy.$$

The ML plug-in estimator is then obtained by substituting the ML estimate, $\hat{\boldsymbol{\theta}}_{ML}$, for the true values of $\boldsymbol{\theta}$:

$$\hat{\mathrm{E}}[Y|\mathbf{X}=\mathbf{x}] = \int_{-\infty}^{\infty} yg(y,\mathbf{x};\hat{\boldsymbol{\theta}}_{ML})dy.$$

As usual, in practice, we do not always have to go this far. For example, in the case of the CEF of the classical linear model (Theorem 5.1.5), we need only use $\hat{\mathrm{E}}[Y|\mathbf{X}=\mathbf{x}] = \mathbf{x}\hat{\boldsymbol{\beta}}_{ML}$; and in the case of the CEF of a binary choice model (Theorem 5.1.8), we need only use $\hat{\mathrm{E}}[Y|\mathbf{X}=\mathbf{x}] = h(\mathbf{x}\hat{\boldsymbol{\beta}}_{ML})$.

If the parametric model is true, then under the usual plug-in regularity conditions, $\hat{\mathrm{E}}[Y|\mathbf{X}=\mathbf{x}]$ will be consistent for the CEF evaluated at $\mathbf{X}=\mathbf{x}$. If the parametric model is not true, then our estimator of the CEF will have no guarantees of consistency. However, insofar as the parametric model is a good approximation, the ML plug-in estimator can be expected to behave well.

5.2.5 Mixture Models

We can use an extension of ML estimation, where we will allow for the possibility that *multiple* distributions give rise to the data. This approach is known as *mixture modeling*. While one model may fail in approximating Y well, many may succeed.

Suppose that the distribution of Y conditional on $\mathbf{X}$ can be represented as a weighted average of M different parametric models,

$$\begin{aligned} f_{Y|X}(y|\mathbf{x}) &= g(y,\mathbf{x};\boldsymbol{\theta}) \\ &= p_1 g_1(y,\mathbf{x};\boldsymbol{\theta}_1) + p_2 g_2(y,\mathbf{x};\boldsymbol{\theta}_2) + \ldots + \left(1-\sum_{m=1}^{M-1} p_m\right) g_M(y,\mathbf{x};\boldsymbol{\theta}_M), \end{aligned}$$

where $\boldsymbol{\theta} = (p_1, \boldsymbol{\theta}_1, p_2, \boldsymbol{\theta}_2, ..., p_{M-1}, \boldsymbol{\theta}_{M-1}, \boldsymbol{\theta}_M)$. Then, as before, $\prod_{i=1}^{n} g(Y_i, \mathbf{X}_i; \boldsymbol{\theta})$ can be maximized to find the ML estimate of $\boldsymbol{\theta}$. (This can sometimes be computationally tricky.)

If any subset of the models in $(g_1(y, \mathbf{x}; \boldsymbol{\theta}_1), ..., g_M(y, \mathbf{x}; \boldsymbol{\theta}_M))$ jointly characterize the conditional distribution of Y, then this estimator is consistent and asymptotically efficient. When the models are not valid (even jointly), our estimates should be interpreted explicitly as an approximation.

Example 5.2.11. *Mixture Model Approximation*
Consider again the unusual distribution discussed in Example 5.2.9 (*Maximum Likelihood Estimation of an Unusual Distribution*), visualized in Figure 5.2.3.

In Example 5.2.9, we showed the consequences of modeling this distribution as normal:

$$g_N\big(y; (\mu_N, \sigma_N)\big) = \frac{1}{\sigma_N \sqrt{2\pi}} e^{-\frac{(y-\mu_N)^2}{2\sigma_N^2}}.$$

This model was not true, but nevertheless a useful first-order approximation. But let us consider some other models to approximate this distribution. For

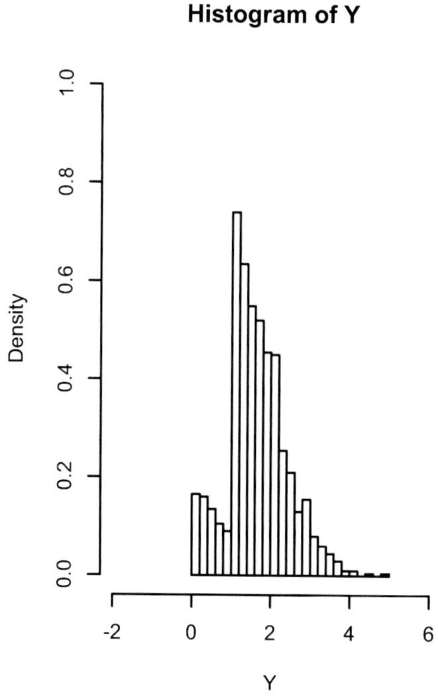

FIGURE 5.2.3. *Unusual Distribution*

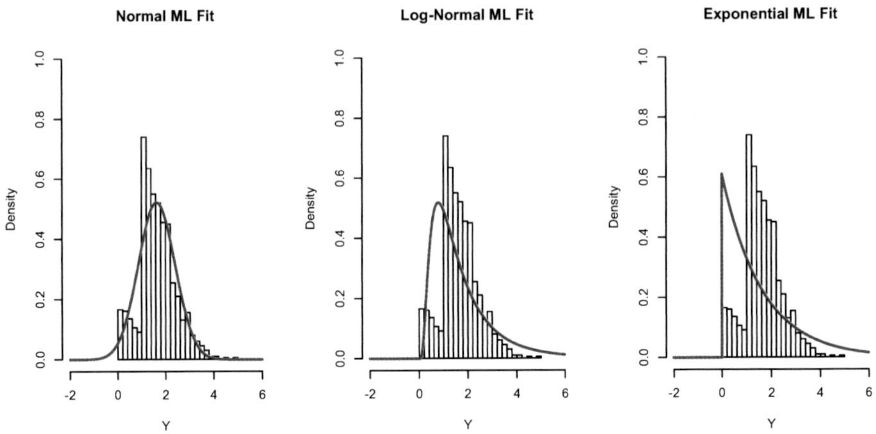

FIGURE 5.2.4. *Normal, Log-Normal, and Exponential Maximum Likelihood Approximations*

example, we could model the distribution as *log-normal*:

$$g_{LN}\big(y;(\mu_{LN},\sigma_{LN})\big)=\frac{1}{y\sigma_{LN}\sqrt{2\pi}}e^{-\frac{(\log y-\mu_{LN})^2}{2\sigma_{LN}^2}},$$

or we could model the distribution as *exponential*:

$$g_E(y;\lambda_E)=\lambda_E e^{-\lambda_E y}.$$

The ML estimates from each of these models are visualized in Figure 5.2.4.

As we can see, all these estimates perform relatively poorly in characterizing the true distribution. But what happens when we combine them, and allow for the distribution of Y to be an optimal combination of the three distributions?

Consider a mixture model that incorporates all three models:

$$\begin{aligned}g(y;\boldsymbol{\theta}) &= p_N g_N\big(y;(\mu_N,\sigma_N)\big)+p_{LN}g_{LN}\big(y;(\mu_{LN},\sigma_{LN})\big)\\&\quad+(1-p_N-p_{LN})g_E(y;\lambda_E)\\&= p_N\frac{1}{\sigma_N\sqrt{2\pi}}e^{-\frac{(y-\mu_N)^2}{2\sigma_N^2}}+p_{LN}\frac{1}{y\sigma_{LN}\sqrt{2\pi}}e^{-\frac{(\log y-\mu_{LN})^2}{2\sigma_{LN}^2}}\\&\quad+(1-p_N-p_{LN})\lambda_E e^{-\lambda_E y},\end{aligned}$$

where $\boldsymbol{\theta}=(p_N,p_{LN},\mu_N,\sigma_N,\mu_{LN},\sigma_{LN},\lambda_E)$. Figure 5.2.5 visualizes the ML estimate of this mixture model, which provides a markedly better approximation. △

Technically, mixture models are parametric, as the implied distribution of Y given $\mathbf{X}$ is fully governed by a finite number of parameters. But ML estimates of mixture models often have the operating characteristics of nonparametric

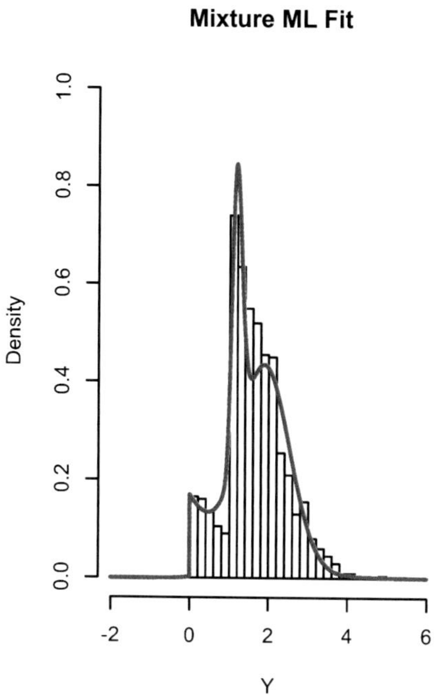

FIGURE 5.2.5. *Mixture Model Maximum Likelihood Approximation*

estimators, and may often outperform explicitly nonparametric methods, including kernel methods. There is, of course, a cost: using a mixture model in this way increases the complexity of the model relative to simpler ML specifications. Accordingly, when using mixture models with small n, we may suffer from overfitting (Section 4.3.2) from trying to be too flexible in approximating the data.

Depending on how we conceptualize their asymptotics, ML estimates of mixture models can be thought of as nonparametric estimators. If we imagined a sieve estimator where we added more and more models in a systematic way as n grew large in a sufficiently general way, then this would result in an infinite-dimensional model that could approximate any arbitrary distribution. Of course, once we have our ML estimate of the density function $f_{Y|\mathbf{X}}(y|\mathbf{x})$, we again can do whatever we want with it, including characterizing the CEF, partial derivatives, or any other distributional feature.

5.2.6 Penalized Maximum Likelihood Regression

As with linear regression, it is possible to generalize ML estimation to allow for penalization for model complexity. Analogously to our discussion of penalized regression in Section 4.3.6, this can be formalized by introducing a penalty term and minimizing the sum of the penalty and the negative log-likelihood. Penalized ML estimation is important in controlling model overfitting, even of the type introduced by mixture models.

Here we discuss one such approach: ℓ^1-penalized ML estimation, or the analog of the lasso in the domain of ML estimation. Mirroring the language of Section 4.3.6, it is a way of flexibility estimating the conditional density function when we have a very large number of parameters to estimate. The ℓ^1-penalized ML estimate,

$$\hat{\boldsymbol{\theta}} = \underset{\boldsymbol{\theta} \in \boldsymbol{\Theta}}{\arg\min}\left(-\log \mathcal{L}(\boldsymbol{\theta} \mid \mathbf{Y}, \mathbb{X}) + \lambda \left\|\boldsymbol{\theta}^P\right\|_1\right),$$

where $\boldsymbol{\theta}^P$ represents a subvector of $\boldsymbol{\theta}$ corresponding to model parameters subject to penalty; $\|\cdot\|_1$ is again the ℓ^1 norm,

$$\left\|\boldsymbol{\theta}^P\right\|_1 = \sum_{k=1}^{\left|\boldsymbol{\theta}^P\right|} \left|\boldsymbol{\theta}_k^P\right|,$$

which is the sum of the absolute value of the model parameters subject to penalty; and λ is again a penalty parameter. Typically, $\boldsymbol{\theta}^P$ contains parameters whose scale directly corresponds to model complexity (for example, elements of $\boldsymbol{\beta}$ in the classical linear model), but not parameters whose scale does not correspond to model complexity (for example, σ^2 in the classical linear model).

We want to keep the model parameters close to zero, unless they really help to maximize the log-likelihood. Subject to the constraints of the parametric model being used, penalization presents a way to use many explanatory variables to "automatically" get good estimates of the conditional outcome distribution—including when we have more variables than observations. The interpretation of penalized ML estimates proceeds exactly as with ML estimates, and plug-in estimates of, for instance, average partial derivatives can be straightforwardly obtained.

As with the case of penalized regression, choosing λ is not easy, and there is no general best way to estimate it. As with the lasso, cross-validation (see Section 4.3.6 for details) often has good operating characteristics. As long as we assume that, as $n \to \infty$, λ does not grow too quickly, then the ℓ^1-penalized estimator will usually be consistent for the minimum MKLD Predictor (see Section 5.2.3). Other penalization methods exist—ridge-type (ℓ^2-penalized) ML estimates and penalized mixture models—and all operate under the same principles.

5.2.7 Inference

A remaining question is how to characterize uncertainty for our ML estimates. There is debate over whether or not robust standard errors and/or the bootstrap are appropriate for parametric models. It is possible to estimate standard errors that exploit all the parametric assumptions that we have used to generate the model. If we have estimates of the full distribution of Y conditional on X, we can use that information to construct a standard error estimate. If the model is true, then we can directly use the model to estimate the standard errors. This approach, like classical standard errors for regression (Section 4.2.3), is valid if strong assumptions hold. Here, model-based standard errors depend on model validity. That is, if the parametric model is not true, model-based standard errors are not generally consistent.

Fortunately, the bootstrap and robust standard errors (the form of which we do not detail here) are available. In large samples, under the usual plug-in regularity conditions, they accurately characterize the sampling variability of our estimates, even when the model is not true. While parametric models are almost certainly wrong, the estimates produced by ML estimation may still be meaningful as approximations. In Section 4.2.3, we considered "classical sampling variance estimation" for the OLS estimator—an estimator that is logically equivalent to the classical standard error for the ML estimate of the classical linear model. The estimates associated with OLS and other maximum likelihood solutions may have value as approximations even when the parametric model is not true. We should not needlessly run the risk of misstating the sampling variability of these estimates. Given the possibility that any given parametric model is not true, for the types of problems that applied researchers face, robust standard errors or the bootstrap are typically preferable.

As long as we do not take the parametric model too seriously, ML estimation can be construed as a principled way of approximating a probability distribution. When we are interested in the features of the probability distribution, then the ML estimates are best construed as approximations to these features. Robust standard errors and the bootstrap guarantee, in large samples, that we are accurately quantifying the sampling variability of these approximations. Model-based standard errors offer no such guarantee.

5.3 A NOTE ON MODELS AS APPROXIMATIONS

We began this chapter with a famous quote by the statistician George Box. Many texts in statistics and econometrics include this quotation. In most cases, however, it is essentially taken to justify a more or less cavalier approach to statistical models, one that casually treats them as though they were true.

In this chapter, we have adhered to a more conservative interpretation of Box's aphorism. All models are wrong; they are, at best, approximations of reality. But, even without assuming that they are exactly true, when employed and interpreted correctly, they can nonetheless be useful for obtaining estimates of features of probability distributions.

5.4 FURTHER READINGS

Cameron and Trivedi (2005) contains an excellent treatment of the properties of ML and other estimators when the motivating model is wrong. Similarly, Stefanski and Boos (2002) is a very clear, somewhat technical, article-length exposition of this topic. For more traditional approaches under a structural paradigm, we recommend the following textbooks, all of which are comprehensive, clear and highly readable: Hayashi (2001), Wooldridge (2010), and Greene (2012). For a more skeptical treatment of many of the same materials, we strongly recommend the elegant, clear, and canonical Freedman (2009).

PART III

IDENTIFICATION

6

Missing Data

Don't play what's there; play what's not there.

—MILES DAVIS

In Part II, we showed that, if we observe a sufficient number of independent and identically distributed (i.i.d.) draws of a random vector, we can estimate any feature of its distribution to arbitrary precision. Given any finite number of such observations, we can both estimate these features and, furthermore, estimate our degree of uncertainty about these estimates. Thus, if we could always observe i.i.d. draws of any random vector whose distribution we might be interested in, this book could have concluded with Chapter 5.

Unfortunately, we often want to learn about the distributions of random vectors that are *not* directly observable. What can we learn about the distribution of an *unobservable* random vector, given full knowledge of the distribution of a related *observable* random vector? This question is the core of nonparametric statistical *identification*, an idea that we will explore in Part III. The answer will invariably depend on what assumptions we are willing to make about the relationship between the observable and unobservable distributions. This notion can be formalized in the following definition of identification:

Definition 6.0.1. *Point Identification*
Suppose we have complete knowledge of the joint CDF, F, of some observable random vector. Then a statistical functional of some unobservable random vector with joint CDF F_u, $T(F_u)$, is *point identified* by a set of assumptions A_u if there exists one and only one value of $T(F_u)$ that is logically compatible with F given A_u.[1]

1 The notation F_u and A_u will not be used again.

In this chapter, we illustrate the basic concepts of identification by considering a simple but common problem: missing data. Readers will notice that sections in this chapter bear a remarkable resemblance to those in Chapter 7, *Causal Inference*. This is not a mistake. Rather, we will show that causal inference can viewed as a missing data problem (see further discussion in Section 7.1.2). Consequently, the tools we use for identification and estimation with missing data are the same tools we will use with missing potential outcomes. To highlight these parallels, section numbers in brackets will reference the analogous section in Chapter 7. However, given the central role that causal claims play in much of empirical social scientific inquiry, Chapter 7 will go into greater detail than the relatively abbreviated, but foundational, treatment of missing data in this chapter.

6.1 IDENTIFICATION WITH MISSING DATA [7.1]

What can we learn about the distribution of a random variable of interest from a random sample when some values in the sample are missing? For example, if we ran a survey asking people whom they voted for, some people might not respond to the vote choice question. We want to know the population distribution of outcomes for this question, but we do not observe the outcomes for some people.

Suppose that we are interested in estimating the expected value (or the full distribution) of some random variable Y_i.[2] However, we do not observe Y_i for any unit in our sample that does not respond. Formally, let R_i be an indicator for whether or not the outcome Y_i for unit i is observed (that is, $R_i = 1$ if unit i responded and $R_i = 0$ otherwise), and let Y_i^* denote the censored version of Y_i. Then we can define the following model of missing data:

Definition 6.1.1. *Stable Outcomes Model*
For an outcome variable Y_i, the *stable outcomes model* is

$$Y_i^* = \begin{cases} -99 & : R_i = 0 \\ Y_i & : R_i = 1 \end{cases}$$
$$= Y_i R_i + (-99)(1 - R_i),$$

[2] Since we are assuming i.i.d. sampling, our inferences do not depend on the unit subscript i. That is, learning about the random variable Y is equivalent to learning about the population distribution of Y_i values. However, whereas in Part II we largely treated i.i.d. random variables simply as abstract mathematical objects, in Part III i.i.d. random variables represent individual units in a random sample from some actual population. We therefore use the subscript i to emphasize that we are modeling the (observed and unobserved) features of sampled units from a population as i.i.d. random variables.

where Y_i^* is the censored version of Y_i and R_i is an indicator for whether Y_i is observed for unit i.[3]

We refer to this as the *stable outcomes* framework because the underlying Y_i for unit i is stable in that it does not depend on how the question was asked, who was asked, or who responded.

Suppose that our inferential target is the expected value of Y_i, $\mathrm{E}[Y_i]$. We do *not* directly observe i.i.d. draws of Y_i; we only observe i.i.d. draws of the random vector (Y_i^*, R_i). Thus, without making further assumptions about the joint distribution of Y_i and R_i, we cannot directly estimate $\mathrm{E}[Y_i]$. So the question is: given full knowledge of the joint distribution of (Y_i^*, R_i), what assumptions yield what information about $\mathrm{E}[Y_i]$?

6.1.1 Bounds [7.1.3]

Let us start with a minimal assumption. Suppose that Y_i is *bounded*: $\mathrm{Supp}[Y_i] \subseteq [a,b]$, for some $a \leq b$. Under this assumption, we can derive *sharp bounds*—that is, bounds that cannot be improved upon without further assumptions—on $\mathrm{E}[Y_i]$.[4]

We can compute sharp bounds by imputing the "worst-case scenario" for all missing data. To compute a lower bound, assume that all missing values of Y_i equal the lowest possible value, a. For an upper bound, assume that all missing values of Y_i equal the highest possible value, b.

Example 6.1.2. *Bounding the Expected Value*
Suppose that Y_i is binary: $\mathrm{Supp}[Y_i] \subseteq \{0,1\} \subseteq [0,1]$. We might observe the following data:

Unit	Y_i^*	R_i
1	1	1
2	−99	0
3	1	1
4	0	1
5	1	1
6	−99	0

3 The value −99 is commonly used in datasets to denote missing data, but the specific number used is irrelevant.

4 These bounds are often referred to as *Manski bounds* due to his seminal work on the topic. See, e.g., Manski (2003).

Given the assumption of stable outcomes, this implies

Unit	Y_i	R_i
1	1	1
2	?	0
3	1	1
4	0	1
5	1	1
6	?	0

For units 2 and 6, we only know that $Y_i \in \{0, 1\}$. To estimate a lower bound, we replace these missing values with the lowest possible value:

Unit	Y_i	R_i
1	1	1
2	0	0
3	1	1
4	0	1
5	1	1
6	0	0

Then, using the sample mean as a plug-in estimator for the expected value, our estimated lower bound for $\text{E}[Y_i]$ is $\frac{1}{2}$. Likewise, to estimate an upper bound, we replace these missing values with the lowest possible values:

Unit	Y_i	R_i
1	1	1
2	1	0
3	1	1
4	0	1
5	1	1
6	1	0

Thus, our estimated upper bound for $\text{E}[Y_i]$ is $\frac{5}{6}$. $\triangle$

More generally, we can write down exact sharp bounds for $\text{E}[Y_i]$ in terms of the joint distribution of (Y_i^*, R_i), which can, in theory, be estimated to arbitrary precision.

Theorem 6.1.3. *Sharp Bounds for the Expected Value*
Let Y_i and R_i be random variables with $\text{Supp}[Y_i] \subseteq [a, b]$ and $\text{Supp}[R_i] = \{0, 1\}$, and let $Y_i^* = Y_i R_i + (-99)(1 - R_i)$. Then

$$\text{E}[Y_i] \in \Big[\text{E}[Y_i^* \mid R_i = 1]\Pr[R_i = 1] + a\Pr[R_i = 0],\\ \text{E}[Y_i^* \mid R_i = 1]\Pr[R_i = 1] + b\Pr[R_i = 0]\Big].$$

Proof: By the Law of Iterated Expectations,

$$\mathrm{E}[Y_i] = \mathrm{E}[Y_i \mid R_i = 1]\Pr[R_i = 1] + \mathrm{E}[Y_i \mid R_i = 0]\Pr[R_i = 0].$$

Then, since $Y_i^* = Y_i R_i + (-99)(1 - R_i)$,

$$\begin{aligned}\mathrm{E}[Y_i^* \mid R_i = 1] &= \mathrm{E}[Y_i R_i + (-99)(1 - R_i) \mid R_i = 1] \\ &= \mathrm{E}[Y_i \cdot 1 + (-99) \cdot 0 \mid R_i = 1] \\ &= \mathrm{E}[Y_i \mid R_i = 1].\end{aligned}$$

Thus,

$$\mathrm{E}[Y_i] = \mathrm{E}[Y_i^* \mid R_i = 1]\Pr[R_i = 1] + \mathrm{E}[Y_i \mid R_i = 0]\Pr[R_i = 0].$$

Since $\mathrm{Supp}[Y_i] \subseteq [a, b]$, $\mathrm{E}[Y_i \mid R_i = 0] \geq a$, and therefore

$$\begin{aligned}\mathrm{E}[Y_i] &= \mathrm{E}[Y_i^* \mid R_i = 1]\Pr[R_i = 1] + \mathrm{E}[Y_i \mid R_i = 0]\Pr[R_i = 0] \\ &\geq \mathrm{E}[Y_i^* \mid R_i = 1]\Pr[R_i = 1] + a\Pr[R_i = 0].\end{aligned}$$

Likewise, since $\mathrm{Supp}[Y_i] \subseteq [a, b]$, $\mathrm{E}[Y_i \mid R_i = 0] \leq b$, and therefore

$$\begin{aligned}\mathrm{E}[Y_i] &= \mathrm{E}[Y_i^* \mid R_i = 1]\Pr[R_i = 1] + \mathrm{E}[Y_i \mid R_i = 0]\Pr[R_i = 0] \\ &\leq \mathrm{E}[Y_i^* \mid R_i = 1]\Pr[R_i = 1] + b\Pr[R_i = 0].\end{aligned}$$

Thus,

$$\begin{aligned}\mathrm{E}[Y_i] \in \big[&\mathrm{E}[Y_i^* \mid R_i = 1]\Pr[R_i = 1] + a\Pr[R_i = 0], \\ &\mathrm{E}[Y_i^* \mid R_i = 1]\Pr[R_i = 1] + b\Pr[R_i = 0]\big]. \quad \square\end{aligned}$$

One feature of these bounds is that their width is proportional to the amount of missing data; fundamental uncertainty grows as we observe less of the distribution of Y_i.

Estimation of these bounds follows from the plug-in principle (Section 3.3): substituting sample means for expected values. The following theorem establishes that the plug-in estimator of the bounds is unbiased and consistent.

Theorem 6.1.4. *Estimating Sharp Bounds for the Expected Value*
Let Y_i and R_i be random variables with $\mathrm{Supp}[Y_i] \subseteq [a, b]$ and $\mathrm{Supp}[R_i] = \{0, 1\}$, and let $Y_i^* = Y_i R_i + (-99)(1 - R_i)$. Then, given n i.i.d. observations of (Y_i^*, R_i), the plug-in estimator

$$\frac{1}{n}\sum_{i=1}^{n}\big(Y_i^* R_i + a(1 - R_i)\big)$$

is unbiased and consistent for the lower bound for $\mathrm{E}[Y_i]$. Likewise, the plug-in estimator

$$\frac{1}{n}\sum_{i=1}^{n}\left(Y_i^* R_i + b(1 - R_i)\right)$$

is unbiased and consistent for the upper bound for $\mathrm{E}[Y_i]$.

Proof: Let $Y_i^L = Y_i^* R_i + a(1 - R_i)$, so that

$$\overline{Y_i^L} = \frac{1}{n}\sum_{i=1}^{n}\left(Y_i^* R_i + a(1 - R_i)\right).$$

By Theorem 3.2.3 (*The Expected Value of the Sample Mean is the Population Mean*) and the Weak Law of Large Numbers (WLLN), $\overline{Y_i^L}$ is unbiased and consistent for $\mathrm{E}[Y_i^L]$, and by the Law of Iterated Expectations,

$$\begin{aligned}
\mathrm{E}\big[Y_i^L\big] &= \mathrm{E}\big[Y_i^L \,\big|\, R_i = 1\big]\Pr[R_i = 1] + \mathrm{E}\big[Y_i^L \,\big|\, R_i = 0\big]\Pr[R_i = 0] \\
&= \mathrm{E}\big[Y_i^* R_i + a(1 - R_i) \,\big|\, R_i = 1\big]\Pr[R_i = 1] \\
&\quad + \mathrm{E}\big[Y_i^* R_i + a(1 - R_i) \,\big|\, R_i = 0\big]\Pr[R_i = 0] \\
&= \mathrm{E}\big[Y_i^* \cdot 1 + a \cdot 0 | R_i = 1\big]\Pr\big[R_i = 1\big] \\
&\quad + \mathrm{E}\big[Y_i^* \cdot 0 + a \cdot 1 | R_i = 0\big]\Pr\big[R_i = 0\big] \\
&= \mathrm{E}\big[Y_i^* | R_i = 1\big]\Pr\big[R_i = 1\big] + a\Pr\big[R_i = 0\big].
\end{aligned}$$

Thus, $\overline{Y_i^L}$ is unbiased and consistent for $\mathrm{E}[Y_i^* | R_i = 1]\Pr[R_i = 1] + a\Pr[R_i = 0]$.

Similarly, let $Y_i^U = Y_i^* R_i + b(1 - R_i)$, so that

$$\overline{Y_i^U} = \frac{1}{n}\sum_{i=1}^{n}\left(Y_i^* R_i + b(1 - R_i)\right).$$

Then, by the same logic, it follows that $\overline{Y_i^U}$ is unbiased and consistent for $\mathrm{E}[Y_i^* | R_i = 1]\Pr[R_i = 1] + b\Pr[R_i = 0]$. □

Note that these plug-in estimators will reproduce our bounds estimate of $[\frac{1}{2}, \frac{5}{6}]$ from Example 6.1.2 (*Missing Data with Binary Outcomes*). Under the usual plug-in regularity conditions, asymptotically valid confidence intervals for each bound can be computed using the bootstrap.

Without further assumptions, these bounds are the absolute best we can do. Thus, under these minimal assumptions, $\mathrm{E}[Y_i]$ is *partially identified* (or *set identified*) as opposed to *point identified*. That is, even with full knowledge of the joint distribution of (Y_i^*, R_i), we can do no better than the above bounds. We are left with an interval of plausible values, none of which can be logically ruled out given the assumptions that we have imposed. We cannot identify the exact value of $\mathrm{E}[Y_i]$. Adding more assumptions inherently reduces the credibility of our estimate. With stronger assumptions, we might be able to narrow the interval, perhaps even to a point. But the cost is that our estimate becomes less believable. Manski (2003) refers to this as the "Law of Decreasing Credibility."

Sometimes, we should not feel comfortable strengthening our assumptions. Bounded support of outcomes may be the only assumption that we are willing to impose given what we know—or, more to the point, what we do not know—about how our data were generated. If the bounds are not good enough, we need further information about the generative process—in this case, the determinants of non-response—to justify the stronger (that is, more restrictive) assumptions required to obtain a more precise estimate.

6.1.2 Missing Completely at Random [7.1.4]

We can consider one of these stronger assumptions. Suppose that the data are *missing completely at random*. This is generally considered to be one of the strongest of all the nonparametric assumptions that we could impose.

Definition 6.1.5. *Missing Completely at Random (MCAR)*
Let Y_i and R_i be random variables with $\mathrm{Supp}[R_i] = \{0,1\}$, and let $Y_i^* = Y_iR_i + (-99)(1 - R_i)$. Then Y_i is *missing completely at random* if the following conditions hold:

- $Y_i \perp\!\!\!\perp R_i$ (independence of outcome and response).
- $\Pr[R_i = 1] > 0$ (nonzero probability of response).

In other words, the distribution of outcomes for the population of people who respond is the same as the distribution of outcomes for the population of people who do not respond. The MCAR assumption is sufficient to point identify $\mathrm{E}[Y_i]$, as we can then write down an exact, unique expression for $\mathrm{E}[Y_i]$ in terms of the joint distribution of observables, (Y_i^*, R_i).

Theorem 6.1.6. *Expected Value under MCAR*
Let Y_i and R_i be random variables with $\mathrm{Supp}[R_i] = \{0,1\}$, and let $Y_i^* = Y_iR_i + (-99)(1 - R_i)$. Then, if Y_i is missing completely at random,

$$\mathrm{E}[Y_i] = \mathrm{E}[Y_i^* \mid R_i = 1].$$

Proof: By independence (see Theorem 2.2.25, *Implications of Independence, Part III*),

$$\mathrm{E}[Y_i] = \mathrm{E}[Y_i \mid R_i = 1],$$

and by stable outcomes,

$$\mathrm{E}[Y_i \mid R_i = 1] = \mathrm{E}[Y_i^* \mid R_i = 1].$$

Thus,

$$\mathrm{E}[Y_i] = \mathrm{E}[Y_i^* | R_i = 1]. \quad \square$$

Assuming MCAR thus makes it extremely easy to estimate the population mean when we have missing data. The plug-in estimator is just the sample mean of the non-missing values:

$$\hat{\mathrm{E}}[Y_i] = \hat{\mathrm{E}}[Y_i^* | R_i = 1] = \frac{\sum_{i=1}^{n} Y_i^* R_i}{\sum_{i=1}^{n} R_i}.$$

For instance, in Example 6.1.2 (*Missing Data with Binary Outcomes*), our estimate of $\mathrm{E}[Y_i]$ assuming MCAR would be $\frac{3}{4}$. Our ability to draw inferences with missing data thus entirely depends on the strength of the assumptions that we are willing to impose.

One way to think about MCAR is as follows: given a large enough n, we can impute the outcomes for non-responders using the sample mean for responders.

Example 6.1.7. *Imputation under MCAR*
Again, consider Example 6.1.2. We have

Unit	Y_i	R_i
1	1	1
2	?	0
3	1	1
4	0	1
5	1	1
6	?	0

Assuming MCAR, $\mathrm{E}[Y_i | R_i = 0] = \mathrm{E}[Y_i]$, which we can estimate using the above plug-in estimator. Thus, we can impute the missing values as follows:

Unit	Y_i	R_i
1	1	1
2	$\hat{\mathrm{E}}[Y_i] = \frac{3}{4}$	0
3	1	1
4	0	1
5	1	1
6	$\hat{\mathrm{E}}[Y_i] = \frac{3}{4}$	0

Then the sample mean with the missing values imputed is $\frac{3}{4}$.[5] $\triangle$

[5] Recall that, with only six observations, the data are too micronumerous to guarantee that our plug-in estimate would be anywhere near the true value of $\mathrm{E}[Y_i]$. This example is merely illustrative.

Under the MCAR assumption, imputation is essentially a pointless extra step, since we are using $\hat{\mathrm{E}}[Y_i]$ to impute the missing values in order to get $\hat{\mathrm{E}}[Y_i]$ again. But the utility of this way of thinking about estimating expectations with missing data will become clear in Section 6.2 (*Estimation with Missing Data*).

With the exception of missingness resulting from randomized sampling, the MCAR assumption is unlikely to hold in practice. In the following section, we consider an assumption that incorporates the use of covariates, and is perhaps more palatable in many settings.

6.1.3 Missing at Random [7.1.5]

If we have additional information on each unit, we can impose an alternative, and in many ways weaker, version of the MCAR assumption. This assumption is known as *missing at random (MAR)* or *ignorability*. (We will use the term "MAR" in this chapter; the term "ignorability" will be used for its analog, "strong ignorability," in Section 7.1.5.) MAR is just like MCAR except *conditional on covariates*. (So it is not missing *completely* at random, just missing at random once we condition on covariates.)

Formally, suppose that for each unit i, we observe a vector of covariates $\mathbf{X}_i$. Importantly, we observe $\mathbf{X}_i$ even when $R_i = 0$. That is, we know the covariate values for all units; we only have missing data on the outcome variable Y_i. Now, the random vector of observables is $(Y_i^*, R_i, \mathbf{X}_i)$. Then the MAR assumption looks just like MCAR, except that everything is conditional on $\mathbf{X}_i$.

Definition 6.1.8. *Missing at Random (MAR)*
Let Y_i and R_i be random variables with $\mathrm{Supp}[R_i] = \{0,1\}$, let $Y_i^* = Y_iR_i + (-99)(1-R_i)$, and let $\mathbf{X}_i$ be a random vector. Then Y_i is *missing at random* conditional on $\mathbf{X}_i$ if the following conditions hold:

- $Y_i \perp\!\!\!\perp R_i | \mathbf{X}_i$ (independence of outcome and response conditional on $\mathbf{X}_i$).[6]
- $\exists \epsilon > 0$ such that $\Pr[R_i = 1 | \mathbf{X}_i] > \epsilon$ (nonzero probability of response conditional on $\mathbf{X}_i$).[7]

6 Formally, *conditional independence* is defined as follows: for random variables X, Y, and Z with joint probability mass function/probability density function (PMF/PDF) $f(x,y,z)$, $Y \perp\!\!\!\perp Z | X$ if, $\forall y,z \in \mathbb{R}$ and $\forall x \in \mathrm{Supp}[X]$,

$$f_{(Y,Z)|X}\big((y,z)\,\big|\,x\big) = f_{Y|X}(y|x) f_{Z|X}(z|x).$$

If $Y \perp\!\!\!\perp Z | X$, all the implications of independence derived in Chapters 1 and 2 hold conditional on X; for example, $\mathrm{E}[Y|X] = \mathrm{E}[Y|Z,X]$.

7 The notation $\Pr[\cdot|X]$ is defined analogously to $\mathrm{E}[\cdot|X]$ and $\mathrm{V}[\cdot|X]$. For example, if we define the function $P_{\{Y=y\}}(x) = \Pr[Y = y | X = x]$, then $\Pr[Y = y | X]$ denotes the random variable

The first of these conditions is known as a *conditional independence assumption*. Stated in words, the conditional independence assumption says that, among units with the same measured background characteristics, the types that respond and the types that do not respond are exactly the same in terms of their distribution of Y_i values. This assumption is not to be taken lightly, and cannot generally be expected to hold in practice.

Almost every common method of dealing with missing data in applied practice (multiple imputation, reweighting, etc.) depends on some variant of the MAR assumption. The MAR assumption is sufficiently strong to allow us to point identify $\mathrm{E}[Y_i]$.

Theorem 6.1.9. *Expected Value under MAR*
Let Y_i and R_i be random variables with $\mathrm{Supp}[R_i] = \{0,1\}$, let $Y_i^* = Y_iR_i + (-99)(1-R_i)$, and let $\mathbf{X}_i$ be a discrete random vector.[8] Then, if Y_i is MAR conditional on $\mathbf{X}_i$,

$$\mathrm{E}[Y_i] = \sum_{\mathbf{x}} \mathrm{E}[Y_i^* | R_i = 1, \mathbf{X}_i = \mathbf{x}] \Pr[\mathbf{X}_i = \mathbf{x}].$$

Proof: By the Law of Iterated Expectations,

$$\mathrm{E}[Y_i] = \mathrm{E}\big[\mathrm{E}[Y_i | \mathbf{X}_i]\big] = \sum_{\mathbf{x}} \mathrm{E}[Y_i | \mathbf{X}_i = \mathbf{x}] \Pr[\mathbf{X}_i = \mathbf{x}].$$

By MAR (and stable outcomes),

$$\mathrm{E}[Y_i | \mathbf{X}_i] = \mathrm{E}[Y_i | R_i = 1, \mathbf{X}_i] = \mathrm{E}[Y_i^* | R_i = 1, \mathbf{X}_i].$$

Thus,

$$\mathrm{E}[Y_i] = \sum_{\mathbf{x}} \mathrm{E}[Y_i^* | R_i = 1, \mathbf{X}_i = \mathbf{x}] \Pr[\mathbf{X}_i = \mathbf{x}]. \quad \square$$

Since we can observe the random vector $(Y_i^*, R_i, \mathbf{X}_i)$, we can point identify $\mathrm{E}[Y_i^* | R_i = 1, \mathbf{X}_i = \mathbf{x}]$ and $\Pr[\mathbf{X}_i = \mathbf{x}]$. Thus, under MAR, $\mathrm{E}[Y_i]$ is point identified. Furthermore, note what the second line of the above proof implies that the conditional expectation function (CEF) of Y_i given $\mathbf{X}_i$ is point identified under MAR.

$P_{\{Y=y\}}(X)$. Hence, the statement that $\Pr[R_i = 1 | \mathbf{X}_i] > \epsilon$ is equivalent to $\forall \mathbf{x} \in \mathrm{Supp}[\mathbf{X}_i], \Pr[R_i = 1 | \mathbf{X}_i = \mathbf{x}] > \epsilon$.

8 We assume here that $\mathbf{X}_i$ is discrete for ease of exposition. This assumption is not necessary, but it lets us work with PMFs instead of PDFs. The continuous case is analogous. Recall that we are writing $\sum_{\mathbf{x}}$ as a shorthand for $\sum_{\mathbf{x} \in \mathrm{Supp}[\mathbf{X}_i]}$.

Theorem 6.1.10. *CEF under MAR*
Let Y_i and R_i be random variables with $\text{Supp}[R_i] = \{0,1\}$, let $Y_i^* = Y_iR_i + (-99)(1-R_i)$, and let $\mathbf{X}_i$ be a random vector. Then, if Y_i is MAR conditional on X_i,

$$\text{E}[Y_i|\mathbf{X}_i] = \text{E}[Y_i^*|R_i = 1, \mathbf{X}_i].$$

A proof directly follows from the second line of the proof of Theorem 6.1.9. Thus, under MAR, the CEF of observable outcomes is identical to the CEF of all outcomes. This result provides some optimism about our ability to approximate and estimate the CEF using only observable quantities. As we will see shortly, the tools developed in Chapter 4 are readily applicable here.

6.1.4 The Role of the Propensity Score for Missing Data [7.1.6]

Before we discuss some other methods of estimating the expected value with missing data, we must first establish a fundamental result. If strong ignorability holds, we need not condition on all the covariates; instead, we can condition on a summary measure of response and the covariates. This summary measure is the *propensity score*, which corresponds to the value of the *response propensity function* evaluated at a unit's covariate values.

Definition 6.1.11. *Response Propensity Function*
Suppose we observe $(R_i, \mathbf{X}_i)$, where $\text{Supp}[R_i] = \{0,1\}$. Then the *response propensity function* is

$$p_R(\mathbf{x}) = \Pr[R_i = 1|\mathbf{X}_i = \mathbf{x}], \forall \mathbf{x} \in \text{Supp}[\mathbf{X}_i].$$

The random variable $p_R(\mathbf{X}_i)$ is known as the propensity score for unit i.[9] The propensity score is the conditional probability of response given the covariates; equivalently, it is the CEF of R_i with respect to $\mathbf{X}_i$ evaluated at $\mathbf{x}$. The propensity score for any given covariate profile is a function of the covariates: if we know that $\mathbf{X}_i = \mathbf{x}$ and we know the full joint distribution of $(R_i, \mathbf{X}_i)$, then we know $\Pr[R_i = 1|\mathbf{X}_i = \mathbf{x}]$.

The following theorem states the key properties of the propensity score under MAR.

Theorem 6.1.12. *MAR and the Propensity Score*
Let Y_i and R_i be random variables with $\text{Supp}[R_i] = \{0,1\}$, let $Y_i^* =$

[9] The term "propensity score" is more commonly used in the context of causal inference. We will discuss this in Chapter 7.

$Y_i R_i + (-99)(1 - R_i)$, and let $\mathbf{X}_i$ be a random vector. Then, if Y_i is MAR conditional on $\mathbf{X}_i$,

- $R_i \perp\!\!\!\perp \mathbf{X}_i | p_R(\mathbf{X}_i)$. (Balance conditional on $p_R(\mathbf{X}_i)$)
- $Y_i \perp\!\!\!\perp R_i | p_R(\mathbf{X}_i)$. (Independence of outcome and response conditional on $p_R(\mathbf{X}_i)$)
- $\exists \epsilon > 0$ such that $\Pr[R_i = 1 | p_R(\mathbf{X}_i)] > \epsilon$. (Nonzero probability of response conditional on $p_R(\mathbf{X}_i)$)

Proof: We will prove the first two properties and omit a proof of the third.

Balance: Since R_i is binary, its distribution is fully governed by its expected value (Example 5.1.2), so

$$R_i \perp\!\!\!\perp \mathbf{X}_i \,|\, p_R(\mathbf{X}_i) \iff \mathrm{E}\big[R_i \,|\, \mathbf{X}_i, p_R(\mathbf{X}_i)\big] = \mathrm{E}\big[R_i \,|\, p_R(\mathbf{X}_i)\big].$$

Since conditioning on a function of $\mathbf{X}_i$ provides no additional information when we have already conditioned on $\mathbf{X}_i$,

$$\mathrm{E}\big[R_i \,|\, \mathbf{X}_i, p_R(\mathbf{X}_i)\big] = \mathrm{E}[R_i | \mathbf{X}_i] = p_R(\mathbf{X}_i),$$

and by the Law of Iterated Expectations,

$$\mathrm{E}\big[R_i \,|\, p_R(\mathbf{X}_i)\big] = \mathrm{E}\big[\mathrm{E}[R_i | \mathbf{X}_i] \,|\, p_R(\mathbf{X}_i)\big] = \mathrm{E}\big[p_R(\mathbf{X}_i) \,|\, p_R(\mathbf{X}_i)\big] = p_R(\mathbf{X}_i).$$

Therefore,

$$\mathrm{E}\big[R_i \,|\, \mathbf{X}_i, p_R(\mathbf{X}_i)\big] = p_R(\mathbf{X}_i) = \mathrm{E}\big[R_i \,|\, p_R(\mathbf{X}_i)\big],$$

and thus $R_i \perp\!\!\!\perp \mathbf{X}_i | p_R(\mathbf{X}_i)$.

Independence of outcome and response: Since R_i is binary,

$$R_i \perp\!\!\!\perp Y_i \,|\, p_R(\mathbf{X}_i) \iff \mathrm{E}\big[R_i \,|\, Y_i, p_R(\mathbf{X}_i)\big] = \mathrm{E}\big[R_i \,|\, p_R(\mathbf{X}_i)\big].$$

By the Law of Iterated Expectations,

$$\mathrm{E}\big[R_i \,|\, Y_i, p_R(\mathbf{X}_i)\big] = \mathrm{E}\big[\mathrm{E}[R_i | Y_i, \mathbf{X}_i] \,|\, Y_i, p_R(\mathbf{X}_i)\big],$$

and by MAR,

$$\mathrm{E}[R_i | Y_i, \mathbf{X}_i] = \mathrm{E}[R_i | \mathbf{X}_i] = p_R(\mathbf{X}_i).$$

So, by substitution,

$$\mathrm{E}\big[R_i \,|\, Y_i, p_R(\mathbf{X}_i)\big] = \mathrm{E}\big[p_R(\mathbf{X}_i) \,|\, Y_i, p_R(\mathbf{X}_i)\big] = p_R(\mathbf{X}_i) = \mathrm{E}\big[R_i \,|\, p_R(\mathbf{X}_i)\big],$$

and thus $R_i \perp\!\!\!\perp Y_i | p_R(\mathbf{X}_i)$. □

In short, Theorem 6.1.12 says that conditioning on the propensity score is equivalent to conditioning on all the covariates. This implies that if Y_i is MAR conditional on $\mathbf{X}_i$, then Y_i is also MAR conditional on just the propensity score $p_R(\mathbf{X}_i)$.

We have shown that, in order to identify the population mean, we do not need to condition on all the covariates as long as we condition on the propensity score. This result is thought to be useful, since estimation is complicated when we attempt to nonparametrically condition on a large number of variables (unless we use a simple approximation like OLS). But there is a problem here: with real data, propensity scores must also be estimated using the same number of variables. If the form of the response propensity function is unknown, then this poses a similar nonparametric problem. We consider this in Section 6.2.4, as the some of the plug-in estimators developed in the next section rely on having estimates that well approximate the true propensity score.

6.2 ESTIMATION WITH MISSING DATA UNDER MAR [7.2]

We have shown that, under the MCAR assumption, a plug-in estimator of $\mathrm{E}[Y_i]$ is simply the sample mean of the observed outcomes. Under MAR, the intuition is much the same, but estimation becomes more complicated. In this section, we discuss several estimators that implement the MAR assumption.

6.2.1 Plug-In Estimation [7.2.1]

If we have discrete covariates, then under the MAR assumption, we can estimate $\mathrm{E}[Y_i]$ with a simple plug-in estimator. Recall from Theorem 6.1.9 that, if $\mathbf{X}_i$ is discrete,

$$\mathrm{E}[Y_i] = \sum_{\mathbf{x}} \mathrm{E}[Y_i^* \mid R_i = 1, \mathbf{X}_i = \mathbf{x}] \Pr[\mathbf{X}_i = \mathbf{x}].$$

So the plug-in estimator is

$$\begin{aligned}\hat{\mathrm{E}}[Y_i] &= \sum_{\mathbf{x} \in \widehat{\mathrm{Supp}}[\mathbf{X}_i]} \hat{\mathrm{E}}[Y_i^* | R_i = 1, \mathbf{X}_i = \mathbf{x}] \widehat{\Pr}[\mathbf{X}_i = \mathbf{x}] \\ &= \sum_{\mathbf{x} \in \widehat{\mathrm{Supp}}[\mathbf{X}_i]} \frac{\sum_{i=1}^n Y_i^* R_i \cdot \mathrm{I}(\mathbf{X}_i = \mathbf{x})}{\sum_{i=1}^n R_i \cdot \mathrm{I}(\mathbf{X}_i = \mathbf{x})} \cdot \frac{\sum_{i=1}^n \mathrm{I}(\mathbf{X}_i = \mathbf{x})}{n},\end{aligned}$$

where $\mathrm{I}(\cdot)$ is the indicator function and $\widehat{\mathrm{Supp}}[\mathbf{X}_i]$ is the set of all observed values of $\mathbf{X}_i$ (that is, the plug-in estimator for the support of $\mathbf{X}_i$).[10]

This estimator is sometimes known as the *post-stratification* estimator for missing data—the first ratio is the average observed value of Y_i within a given

[10] This requires that we have at least one unit who responded with $\mathbf{X}_i = \mathbf{x}$ for every covariate profile $\mathbf{x} \in \widehat{\mathrm{Supp}}[\mathbf{X}_i]$, otherwise we will have a zero in the denominator. See Footnote 15.

stratum (the subset of observations in which $\mathbf{X}_i = \mathbf{x}$), and the second ratio is the stratum's share of the overall sample. This is essentially the sample analog to the Law of Iterated Expectations.

Example 6.2.1. *Plug-In Estimation of the Expected Value*
Consider again Example 6.1.2 (*Missing Data with Binary Outcomes*), but now assume that we also observe a binary covariate X_i for every unit.

Unit	Y_i	R_i	X_i
1	1	1	0
2	?	0	0
3	1	1	0
4	0	1	0
5	1	1	1
6	?	0	1

Assuming MAR, the above plug-in estimator yields the estimate

$$\hat{\mathrm{E}}[Y_i] = \hat{\mathrm{E}}[Y_i^* | R_i = 1, X_i = 0]\widehat{\Pr}[X_i = 0] + \hat{\mathrm{E}}[Y_i^* | R_i = 1, X_i = 1]\widehat{\Pr}[X_i = 1]$$
$$= \frac{2}{3} \cdot \frac{4}{6} + 1 \cdot \frac{2}{6} = \frac{7}{9}.$$

Note that this estimate differs from the MCAR-based estimate of $\frac{3}{4}$. We can think of the MAR assumption as allowing us to impute the outcomes for non-responders, only now we impute each missing outcome using the sample mean of respondents with the same covariate values, since under MAR, $\forall \mathbf{x} \in \mathrm{Supp}[\mathbf{X}_i], \mathrm{E}[Y_i | R_i = 0, \mathbf{X}_i = \mathbf{x}] = \mathrm{E}[Y_i | \mathbf{X}_i = \mathbf{x}]$. In Example 6.1.2, this yields

Unit	Y_i	R_i	X_i
1	1	1	0
2	$\hat{\mathrm{E}}[Y_i \vert X_i = 0] = \frac{2}{3}$	0	0
3	1	1	0
4	0	1	0
5	1	1	1
6	$\hat{\mathrm{E}}[Y_i \vert X_i = 1] = 1$	0	1

Then the sample mean with the missing values imputed is $\frac{7}{9}$, which is just the plug-in estimate. △

Similar methods exist for filling in *joint* distributions when we also have missing values for $\mathbf{X}_i$ as well as outcomes. We then need to invoke MAR with respect to all the non-missing variables.

The logic behind this plug-in estimator is also the basis for survey reweighting. Suppose that we have undersampled a certain group characterized by

$\mathbf{X}_i = \mathbf{x}$, and suppose that we know the population distribution of $\mathbf{X}_i$. If we assume MAR, we can obtain a consistent estimate using the above plug-in estimator.

Example 6.2.2. *Survey Reweighting*

Suppose that we conducted an Internet survey asking a large number of adult U.S. citizens (1) their height (in inches) and (2) their gender. Assume that no one lies or otherwise misreports.[11] Our goal is to estimate the average height of adult Americans. The problem is: people who answer Internet surveys may be unusual, both in ways we can measure and ways we cannot.

Suppose that we obtained results characterized by the following summary statistics:

$$\hat{\mathrm{E}}[Y_i^* \mid R_i = 1, X_i = 0] = 64, \quad \widehat{\Pr}[X_i = 0 \mid R_i = 1] = \tfrac{3}{10},$$
$$\hat{\mathrm{E}}[Y_i^* \mid R_i = 1, X_i = 1] = 70, \quad \widehat{\Pr}[X_i = 1 \mid R_i = 1] = \tfrac{7}{10},$$

where X_i is an indicator variable for gender.[12] The unadjusted estimate of the national average height is

$$\begin{aligned}\hat{\mathrm{E}}[Y_i] &= \hat{\mathrm{E}}[Y_i^* \mid R_i = 1, X_i = 0]\widehat{\Pr}[X_i = 0 \mid R_i = 1] \\ &\quad + \hat{\mathrm{E}}[Y_i^* \mid R_i = 1, X_i = 1]\widehat{\Pr}[X_i = 1 \mid R_i = 1] \\ &= 64 \cdot \frac{3}{10} + 70 \cdot \frac{7}{10} \\ &= 68.2 \text{ inches.}\end{aligned}$$

This is the estimate we would obtain if we used a plug-in estimator after assuming MCAR, that is, if we used the sample mean as our estimate. But we can do better. Assume that the adult U.S. population is 50% women, so we know that $\Pr[X_i = 0] = \Pr[X_i = 1] = \frac{1}{2}$. Then, under MAR with respect to X_i,

$$\begin{aligned}\mathrm{E}[Y_i] &= \sum_x \mathrm{E}[Y_i \mid X_i = x]\Pr[X_i = x] \\ &= \sum_x \mathrm{E}[Y_i^* \mid R_i = 1, X_i = x]\Pr[X_i = x] \\ &= \mathrm{E}[Y_i^* \mid R_i = 1, X_i = 0] \cdot \frac{1}{2} + \mathrm{E}[Y_i^* \mid R_i = 1, X_i = 1] \cdot \frac{1}{2}.\end{aligned}$$

Thus, the *adjusted* plug-in estimate of $\mathrm{E}[Y_i]$ is

$$\begin{aligned}\hat{\mathrm{E}}[Y_i] &= \hat{\mathrm{E}}[Y_i^* \mid R_i = 1, X_i = 0] \cdot \frac{1}{2} + \hat{\mathrm{E}}[Y_i^* \mid R_i = 1, X_i = 1] \cdot \frac{1}{2} = 64 \cdot \frac{1}{2} + 70 \cdot \frac{1}{2} \\ &= 67 \text{ inches. } \triangle\end{aligned}$$

[11] We would recommend that readers not do so outside of this example.

[12] By convention, "men are odd": $X_i = 0$ for women and $X_i = 1$ for men. For simplicity in exposition, we assume that non-binary genders were not recorded in this survey.

It should be clear that the adjusted estimate is more reasonable than the unadjusted estimate. We know that the U.S. population is about 50% women. Additionally, we know (and our data confirm) that gender is associated with height—men are taller on average. So clearly, the distribution of heights in a sample that is 70% men is likely to be unrepresentative of the distribution of heights in the general population. The adjusted estimate allows us to correct for this sampling bias.

However, if MAR conditional on gender does not hold, this adjusted plug-in estimator may still be inconsistent. There might be unobserved (or perhaps even unobservable) determinants of response that are related to height. Is there any reason why Internet survey respondents might tend to be shorter or taller on average than the general population, even conditional on gender?

Thus far, we have dealt with estimation under MAR only in the special case where we have a single discrete covariate that can take on just a small number of values. Once we introduce continuous (or perhaps many) covariates, we cannot use this estimator anymore. The remainder of this chapter considers the many ways in which we might construct estimators when we believe that MAR holds.

6.2.2 Regression Estimation [7.2.2]

Given that we know that the CEF of observable data is equivalent to the CEF of all (not fully observable) data under MAR, this suggests that we might be able to use OLS regression to approximate the CEF of the full data. This approximation can then be used to predict $\text{E}[Y_i]$ using a plug-in estimator. The following example illustrates this idea.

Example 6.2.3. *Addressing Missing Data with OLS Regression*
Once again, consider Example 6.1.2 (*Missing Data with Binary Outcomes*), but now assume that we observe two covariates for every unit:

Unit	Y_i	R_i	$X_{[1]i}$	$X_{[2]i}$
1	1	1	0	3
2	?	0	0	7
3	1	1	0	9
4	0	1	0	5
5	1	1	1	4
6	?	0	1	3

Under MAR, $\forall \mathbf{x} \in \text{Supp}[\mathbf{X}_i], \text{E}[Y_i|R_i = 0, \mathbf{X}_i = \mathbf{x}] = \text{E}[Y_i|\mathbf{X}_i = \mathbf{x}]$, so we want to fill in all the missing values of Y_i with $\hat{\text{E}}[Y_i|X_{[1]i} = x_{[1]}, X_{[2]i} = x_{[2]}]$.

Let us see how we could do this using regression. Suppose we assumed that, at least to a first approximation,

$$\text{E}\big[Y_i \,\big|\, X_{[1]i}, X_{[2]i}\big] = \text{E}\big[Y_i^* \,\big|\, R_i = 1, X_{[1]i}, X_{[2]i}\big] = \beta_0 + \beta_1 X_{[1]i} + \beta_2 X_{[2]i}.$$

(The first equality is implied by MAR; the second is a functional form assumption.) Then we could estimate the coefficients with ordinary least squares (OLS) and use the resulting equation to impute the missing values:

Unit	Y_i	R_i	$X_{[1]i}$	$X_{[2]i}$
1	1	1	0	3
2	$\hat{\beta}_0+\hat{\beta}_1\cdot 0+\hat{\beta}_2\cdot 7$	0	0	7
3	1	1	0	9
4	0	1	0	5
5	1	1	1	4
6	$\hat{\beta}_0+\hat{\beta}_1\cdot 1+\hat{\beta}_2\cdot 3$	0	1	3

(Remember: these are just expectations for units with the same covariate values; we cannot *actually* fill in the missing outcomes.) Equivalently, we could instead impute *all* of the Y_i values, which will yield the same estimate for $\mathrm{E}[Y_i]$ and is more straightforward to implement:

Unit	Y_i	R_i	$X_{[1]i}$	$X_{[2]i}$
1	$\hat{\beta}_0+\hat{\beta}_1\cdot 0+\hat{\beta}_2\cdot 3$	1	0	3
2	$\hat{\beta}_0+\hat{\beta}_1\cdot 0+\hat{\beta}_2\cdot 7$	0	0	7
3	$\hat{\beta}_0+\hat{\beta}_1\cdot 0+\hat{\beta}_2\cdot 9$	1	0	9
4	$\hat{\beta}_0+\hat{\beta}_1\cdot 0+\hat{\beta}_2\cdot 5$	1	0	5
5	$\hat{\beta}_0+\hat{\beta}_1\cdot 1+\hat{\beta}_2\cdot 4$	1	1	4
6	$\hat{\beta}_0+\hat{\beta}_1\cdot 1+\hat{\beta}_2\cdot 3$	0	1	3

In either case, the estimate of $\mathrm{E}[Y_i]$ is then the sample mean with imputed values for potential outcomes. This estimator would be consistent if MAR held and if the functional form of the CEF were in fact $\mathrm{E}[Y_i^*|R_i=1,X_{[1]i},X_{[2]i}]=\beta_0+\beta_1 X_{[1]i}+\beta_2 X_{[2]i}$. △

The above example described the case of estimating a linear approximation to the CEF. We could have considered nonlinear (Section 4.3) specifications, including interactions or polynomials. Once we have an estimate of the CEF, we can define the following plug-in estimator for $\mathrm{E}[Y_i]$.

Definition 6.2.4. *Regression Estimator for Missing Data*
Let Y_i and R_i be random variables with $\mathrm{Supp}[R_i]=\{0,1\}$. Let $Y_i^*=Y_iR_i+(-99)(1-R_i)$ and let $\mathbf{X}_i$ be a random vector. Then, given n i.i.d. observations of $(Y_i^*,R_i,\mathbf{X}_i)$, the *regression estimator* for $\mathrm{E}[Y_i]$ is

$$\hat{\mathrm{E}}_R[Y_i]=\frac{1}{n}\sum_{i=1}^{n}\hat{\mathrm{E}}[Y_i^*|R_i=1,\mathbf{X}_i],$$

where $\hat{\mathrm{E}}[Y_i^*|R_i=1,\mathbf{X}_i=\mathbf{x}]$ is an estimator of the CEF.

As the regression estimator is a plug-in estimator, we have a good sense of its theoretical properties: the estimator will behave well when the CEF is well characterized by the specification of the regression and the usual plug-in regularity conditions hold.

6.2.3 Hot Deck Imputation [7.2.4]

Another method of imputing missing outcomes is *hot deck imputation*, using nearest-neighbor matching with the propensity score (which, for the moment, we assume is known). We begin by discussing hot deck imputation because it is one of the simplest approaches, and because it will convey broader intuitions about imputation estimators. The following example illustrates hot deck imputation.

Example 6.2.5. *Imputation with the Propensity Score*
Suppose that we had the following data:

Unit	Y_i	R_i	$X_{[1]i}$	$X_{[2]i}$	$p_R(\mathbf{X}_i)$
1	2	1	0	3	0.33
2	?	0	0	7	0.14
3	3	1	0	9	0.73
4	10	1	0	5	0.35
5	12	1	1	4	0.78
6	?	0	1	3	0.70

Assume that MAR holds and that our goal is to estimate $\text{E}[Y_i]$. By Theorem 6.1.12 (*MAR and the Propensity Score*), the MAR assumption implies that $\text{E}[Y_i|R_i = 0, p_R(\mathbf{X}_i)] = \text{E}[Y_i|p_R(\mathbf{X}_i)]$, so we can impute the missing outcomes with estimates of $\text{E}[Y_i|p_R(\mathbf{X}_i)]$:

Unit	Y_i	R_i	$X_{[1]i}$	$X_{[2]i}$	$p_R(\mathbf{X}_i)$
1	2	1	0	3	0.33
2	$\hat{\text{E}}[Y_i|p_R(\mathbf{X}_i) = 0.14]$	0	0	7	0.14
3	3	1	0	9	0.73
4	10	1	0	5	0.35
5	12	1	1	4	0.78
6	$\hat{\text{E}}[Y_i|p_R(\mathbf{X}_i) = 0.70]$	0	1	3	0.70

Then, if our estimator of $\text{E}[Y_i|p_R(\mathbf{X}_i) = p_R(\mathbf{x})]$ is consistent, the sample mean with the missing values imputed will be a consistent estimator of the population mean.

Hot deck imputation is perhaps one of the simplest imputation estimators: for each missing unit, find the observed unit that is closest on $p_R(\mathbf{X}_i)$ and use that unit's outcome to fill in the missing outcome.[13] In this example, we have two unobserved outcomes to impute. Unit 2 has the propensity score $p_R(\mathbf{X}_2) = 0.14$. The observed unit with the closest propensity score is unit 1 with $p_R(\mathbf{X}_1) = 0.33$, so we use $Y_1 = 2$ to impute Y_2. Likewise, unit 6 has the propensity score $p_R(\mathbf{X}_6) = 0.70$, and the observed units with closest propensity score is unit 3 with $p_R(\mathbf{X}_3) = 0.73$, so we use $Y_3 = 3$ to impute Y_6. This yields

Unit	Y_i	R_i	$X_{[1]i}$	$X_{[2]i}$	$p_R(\mathbf{X}_i)$
1	2	1	0	3	0.33
2	2	0	0	7	0.14
3	3	1	0	9	0.73
4	10	1	0	5	0.35
5	12	1	1	4	0.78
6	3	0	1	3	0.70

So the hot deck imputation estimate of $\text{E}[Y_i]$ is $\frac{32}{6} = \frac{16}{3} \approx 5.33$. △

We would hesitate to recommend the use of hot deck imputation in practice. Intuitively, hot deck imputation discards a great deal of information about the data. In the above example, we used $Y_1 = 2$ to impute Y_2 because $p_R(\mathbf{X}_1) = 0.33$ is closest to $p_R(\mathbf{X}_2) = 0.14$. But $p_R(\mathbf{X}_4) = 0.35$ is almost as close to $p_R(\mathbf{X}_1)$, so $Y_4 = 10$ probably also gives us some information about $\text{E}[Y_i | p_R(\mathbf{X}_i) = 0.14]$. So why would we ignore Y_4 entirely and just use Y_1 as our guess for Y_2? This seems hard to justify.

Furthermore, in order to use hot deck imputation based on the propensity score, we need to have estimates of the propensity scores to work with. We take up this issue in the following section.

6.2.4 Maximum Likelihood Plug-In Estimation of Propensity Scores [7.2.5]

We can also use ML to estimate unknown propensity scores, which can in turn be used in estimators like hot deck imputation (with the caveats listed above) and the weighting estimators that we will consider shortly. Recall from Definition 6.1.11 that the propensity score $p_R(\mathbf{x}) = \Pr[R_i = 1 | \mathbf{X}_i = \mathbf{x}]$, and, from Example 2.1.3, that $\Pr[R_i = 1 | \mathbf{X}_i = \mathbf{x}] = \text{E}[R_i | \mathbf{X}_i = \mathbf{x}]$. Therefore, estimating the response propensity function is equivalent to estimating the CEF of R_i with respect to $\mathbf{X}_i$. However, this is a case where OLS would not be suitable for estimating an unknown CEF. We know that $\text{Supp}[\text{E}[R_i | \mathbf{X}_i]] \in [0, 1]$, and thus we might be concerned that a linear approximation would yield impossible propensity score estimates (predictions greater than zero or less than one).

[13] The name "hot deck imputation" derives from the era when data were stored on punch cards. To impute missing outcomes, one would use an observed value from the same dataset—a stack of cards—which was still hot from being processed.

We know, however, that if we assume a binary choice model, it will respect the constraints on the distribution of R_i.

Suppose now that we have a binary choice model for response with mean function h. If this model is true, then following Section 5.2.4, we have can use a ML estimator to obtain propensity score estimates: $\hat{p}_R(\mathbf{X}_i) = h(\mathbf{X}_i\hat{\boldsymbol{\beta}}_{ML})$. If the binary choice model is true, then, under the usual plug-in regularity conditions, $\hat{p}_R(\mathbf{x})$ will be consistent for $p_R(\mathbf{x})$. If the model is not true, then our estimates of the propensity score will only be as good as our approximation permits. Of course, if data permit, we could fit a more complex approximation, perhaps altering how $\mathbf{X}_i$ is specified (to include, say, polynomials or interactions) or using a mixture model (Section 5.2.5). Regardless of the exact specification, we will assume as we proceed that we are using an ML plug-in estimate from a binary choice model, $\hat{p}_R(\mathbf{x})$, for our plug-in estimates, though our results do not depend on this.

6.2.5 Weighting Estimators [7.2.6]

We are not limited to hot deck imputation in order to use the propensity score to estimate $\mathrm{E}[Y_i]$. An alternative is provided by *inverse probability–weighted (IPW) estimators*. Before we can describe these estimators, we first establish an important population result. Transforming the observed outcomes by weighting by $\frac{1}{p_R(\mathbf{X}_i)}$ allows us to express the expected value of the (not fully observable) data as an expected value of the (reweighted) observable data.

Theorem 6.2.6. *Reweighting under MAR*
Let Y_i and R_i be random variables with $\mathrm{Supp}[R_i] = \{0,1\}$. Let $Y_i^* = Y_iR_i + (-99)(1 - R_i)$ and let $\mathbf{X}_i$ be a random vector. Then, if R_i is MAR conditional on $\mathbf{X}_i$,

$$\mathrm{E}[Y_i] = \mathrm{E}\left[\frac{Y_i^* R_i}{p_R(\mathbf{X}_i)}\right].$$

Proof: By definition,

$$\mathrm{E}\left[\frac{Y_i^* R_i}{p_R(\mathbf{X}_i)}\middle|\mathbf{X}_i\right] = \mathrm{E}\left[Y_i^* \cdot \frac{R_i}{\Pr[R_i = 1|\mathbf{X}_i]}\middle|\mathbf{X}_i\right],$$

and by stable outcomes,

$$\mathrm{E}\left[Y_i^* \cdot \frac{R_i}{\Pr[R_i = 1|\mathbf{X}_i]}\middle|\mathbf{X}_i\right] = \mathrm{E}\left[Y_i \cdot \frac{R_i}{\Pr[R_i = 1|\mathbf{X}_i]}\middle|\mathbf{X}_i\right].$$

Then, since MAR holds, $Y_i \perp\!\!\!\perp R_i | \mathbf{X}_i$, so

$$\begin{aligned}
\mathrm{E}\left[Y_i \cdot \frac{R_i}{\Pr[R_i = 1 | \mathbf{X}_i]} \middle| \mathbf{X}_i\right] &= \mathrm{E}[Y_i | \mathbf{X}_i] \cdot \mathrm{E}\left[\frac{R_i}{\Pr[R_i = 1 | \mathbf{X}_i]} \middle| \mathbf{X}_i\right] \\
&= \mathrm{E}[Y_i | \mathbf{X}_i] \cdot \frac{\mathrm{E}[R_i | \mathbf{X}_i]}{\Pr[R_i = 1 | \mathbf{X}_i]} \\
&= \mathrm{E}[Y_i | \mathbf{X}_i] \cdot \frac{\Pr[R_i = 1 | \mathbf{X}_i]}{\Pr[R_i = 1 | \mathbf{X}_i]} \\
&= \mathrm{E}[Y_i | \mathbf{X}_i].
\end{aligned}$$

Thus,

$$\mathrm{E}\left[\frac{Y_i^* R_i}{p_R(\mathbf{X}_i)} \middle| \mathbf{X}_i\right] = \mathrm{E}[Y_i | \mathbf{X}_i].$$

So, by the Law of Iterated Expectations,

$$\begin{aligned}
\mathrm{E}[Y_i] &= \mathrm{E}\big[\mathrm{E}[Y_i | \mathbf{X}_i]\big] \\
&= \mathrm{E}\left[\mathrm{E}\left[\frac{Y_i^* R_i}{p_R(\mathbf{X}_i)} \middle| \mathbf{X}_i\right]\right] \\
&= \mathrm{E}\left[\mathrm{E}\left[\frac{Y_i R_i}{p_R(\mathbf{X}_i)} \middle| \mathbf{X}_i\right]\right] \\
&= \mathrm{E}\left[\frac{Y_i R_i}{p_R(\mathbf{X}_i)}\right]. \quad \square
\end{aligned}$$

The IPW estimator is again a plug-in estimator: we replace $p_R(\mathbf{X}_i)$ with an estimate thereof, $\hat{p}_R(\mathbf{X}_i)$ (as in the previous section), and substitute a sample mean for an expected value.

Definition 6.2.7. *Inverse Probability–Weighted (IPW) Estimator for Missing Data*
Let Y_i and R_i be random variables with $\mathrm{Supp}[R_i] = \{0,1\}$. Let $Y_i^* = Y_i R_i + (-99)(1 - R_i)$ and let $\mathbf{X}_i$ be a random vector. Then, given n i.i.d. observations of $(Y_i^*, R_i, \mathbf{X}_i)$, the *inverse probability–weighted estimator* for $\mathrm{E}[Y_i]$ is

$$\hat{\mathrm{E}}_{IPW}[Y_i] = \frac{1}{n} \sum_{i=1}^{n} \frac{Y_i^* R_i}{\hat{p}_R(\mathbf{X}_i)}.$$

The earliest estimator of this kind was derived for the case of survey sampling with known response probabilities (Horvitz and Thompson 1952). The logic for IPW estimators is intuitively the same as in Example 6.2.2 (*Survey Reweighting*). Suppose that some units are unlikely to offer a response, and so they have small propensity scores. As a result, these types of units are under-represented in the observable data; accordingly, we would want to give the units that we *do* see greater weight. In the case where there is a discrete and finite number of values for $\mathbf{X}_i$, the IPW estimator is logically equivalent to the plug-in estimator from Section 6.2.1 (*Plug-In Estimation*).

The IPW estimator has high variability (that is, its standard error is large) with small samples. An alternative that performs better in practice is a "ratio estimator" proposed by Hájek (1971), known as the stabilized IPW estimator.

Definition 6.2.8. *Stabilized IPW Estimator for Missing Data*
Let Y_i and R_i be random variables with $\text{Supp}[R_i] = \{0,1\}$. Let $Y_i^* = Y_i R_i + (-99)(1 - R_i)$ and let $\mathbf{X}_i$ be a random vector. Then, given n i.i.d. observations of $(Y_i^*, R_i, \mathbf{X}_i)$, the *stabilized IPW estimator* for $\text{E}[Y_i]$ is

$$\hat{\text{E}}_{SIPW}[Y_i] = \frac{\frac{1}{n}\sum_{i=1}^{n}\frac{Y_i R_i}{\hat{p}_R(\mathbf{X}_i)}}{\frac{1}{n}\sum_{i=1}^{n}\frac{R_i}{\hat{p}_R(\mathbf{X}_i)}}.$$

When $\hat{p}_R(\mathbf{X}_i)$ converges (in an appropriate functional sense) to $p_R(\mathbf{X}_i)$, then the denominator of the fraction will converge in probability to 1. To see this, note that with the true propensity score, $\text{E}[\frac{R_i}{p_R(\mathbf{X}_i)}] = 1$. However, this normalization provides benefits in estimation. In the case where we draw an unusually large number of units where $p_R(\mathbf{X}_i)$ is large or small, the stabilized IPW estimator's denominators adjust accordingly. Because the stabilized IPW estimator accounts for this between-sample variation in $\sum_{i=1}^{n}\frac{1}{p_R(\mathbf{X}_i)}$, it typically confers efficiency gains over the IPW estimator in practice. Valid asymptotic inference for IPW estimators can be achieved under strong ignorability, proper specification of $\hat{p}_R(\mathbf{X}_i)$, and the usual plug-in regularity conditions via the bootstrap, re-estimating the propensity scores in each bootstrap sample.

6.2.6 Doubly Robust Estimators [7.2.7]

We are not forced to decide between regression estimators and weighting estimators; instead, we can use both using a *doubly robust (DR)* estimator. Under MAR, the DR estimator yields consistent estimates when *either* the regression specification *or* the propensity score specification is correct. Before we state this result, we note an important population result.

Theorem 6.2.9. *Double Robustness Theorem for Missing Data*
Let Y_i and R_i be random variables with $\text{Supp}[R_i] = \{0, 1\}$. Let $Y_i^* = Y_i R_i + (-99)(1 - R_i)$ and let $\mathbf{X}_i$ be a random vector. Let $\tilde{\text{E}}[Y_i | R_i = 1, \mathbf{X}_i = \mathbf{x}]$ be an approximation of the CEF evaluated at $R_i = 1$ and $\mathbf{X}_i = \mathbf{x}$, and let $\tilde{p}_R(\mathbf{X}_i)$ be an approximation of the propensity score. If MAR holds and if either

(i) $\tilde{\text{E}}[Y_i^* | R_i = 1, \mathbf{X}_i = \mathbf{x}] = \text{E}[Y_i^* | R_i = 1, \mathbf{X}_i = \mathbf{x}], \forall \mathbf{x} \in \text{Supp}[\mathbf{X}_i]$, and $\exists \epsilon > 0$ such that $\epsilon < \tilde{p}_R(\mathbf{x}) < 1 - \epsilon$,

or

(ii) $\tilde{p}_R(\mathbf{x}) = p_R(\mathbf{x}), \forall \mathbf{x} \in \text{Supp}[\mathbf{X}_i]$,

then

$$\text{E}[Y_i] = \text{E}\left[\tilde{\text{E}}[Y_i^* | R_i = 1, \mathbf{X}_i] + \frac{R_i\left(Y_i^* - \tilde{\text{E}}[Y_i^* | R_i = 1, \mathbf{X}_i]\right)}{\tilde{p}_R(\mathbf{X}_i)}\right].$$

Proof: To consider case (i), suppose that $\tilde{\text{E}}[Y_i^* | R_i = 1, \mathbf{X}_i = \mathbf{x}] = \text{E}[Y_i^* | R_i = 1, \mathbf{X}_i = \mathbf{x}], \forall \mathbf{x} \in \text{Supp}[\mathbf{X}_i]$. Then we have

$$\begin{aligned}
&\text{E}\left[\tilde{\text{E}}[Y_i^* | R_i = 1, \mathbf{X}_i] + \frac{R_i\left(Y_i^* - \tilde{\text{E}}[Y_i^* | R_i = 1, \mathbf{X}_i]\right)}{\tilde{p}_R(\mathbf{X}_i)}\right] \\
&\quad = \text{E}\left[\text{E}[Y_i^* | R_i = 1, \mathbf{X}_i] + \frac{R_i\left(Y_i^* - \text{E}[Y_i^* | R_i = 1, \mathbf{X}_i]\right)}{\tilde{p}_R(\mathbf{X}_i)}\right] \\
&\quad = \text{E}\big[\text{E}[Y_i^* | R_i = 1, \mathbf{X}_i]\big] + \text{E}\left[\frac{R_i Y_i^*}{\tilde{p}_R(\mathbf{X}_i)}\right] - \text{E}\left[\frac{R_i \text{E}[Y_i^* | R_i = 1, \mathbf{X}_i]}{\tilde{p}_R(\mathbf{X}_i)}\right] \\
&\quad = \text{E}\big[\text{E}[Y_i^* | R_i = 1, \mathbf{X}_i]\big] + \text{E}\left[\frac{R_i \text{E}[Y_i^* | R_i = 1, \mathbf{X}_i]}{\tilde{p}_R(\mathbf{X}_i)}\right] \\
&\qquad - \text{E}\left[\frac{R_i \text{E}[Y_i^* | R_i = 1, \mathbf{X}_i]}{\tilde{p}_R(\mathbf{X}_i)}\right] \\
&\quad = \text{E}\big[\text{E}[Y_i^* | R_i = 1, \mathbf{X}_i]\big] \\
&\quad = \text{E}[Y_i],
\end{aligned}$$

where the third equality follows from the Law of Iterated Expectations and the fifth follows from MAR (see Theorem 6.1.9).

To consider case (ii), suppose instead that $\tilde{p}_R(\mathbf{x}) = p_R(\mathbf{x}), \forall \mathbf{x} \in \text{Supp}[\mathbf{X}_i]$. Then

$$\begin{aligned}
&\text{E}\left[\tilde{\text{E}}[Y_i^*|R_i = 1, \mathbf{X}_i] + \frac{R_i\left(Y_i^* - \tilde{\text{E}}[Y_i^*|R_i = 1, \mathbf{X}_i]\right)}{\tilde{p}_R(\mathbf{X}_i)}\right] \\
&\quad = \text{E}\left[\tilde{\text{E}}[Y_i^*|R_i = 1, \mathbf{X}_i] + \frac{R_i\left(Y_i^* - \tilde{\text{E}}[Y_i^*|R_i = 1, \mathbf{X}_i]\right)}{p_R(\mathbf{X}_i)}\right] \\
&\quad = \text{E}\left[\tilde{\text{E}}[Y_i^*|R_i = 1, \mathbf{X}_i]\right] + \text{E}\left[\frac{R_i Y_i^*}{p_R(\mathbf{X}_i)}\right] - \text{E}\left[\frac{R_i\tilde{\text{E}}[Y_i^*|R_i = 1, \mathbf{X}_i]}{p_R(\mathbf{X}_i)}\right] \\
&\quad = \text{E}\left[\tilde{\text{E}}[Y_i^*|R_i = 1, \mathbf{X}_i]\right] + \text{E}\left[\frac{R_i Y_i^*}{p_R(\mathbf{X}_i)}\right] - \text{E}\left[\tilde{\text{E}}[Y_i^*|R_i = 1, \mathbf{X}_i]\right] \\
&\quad = \text{E}\left[\frac{R_i Y_i^*}{p_R(\mathbf{X}_i)}\right] \\
&\quad = \text{E}[Y_i]. \quad \square
\end{aligned}$$

The Double Robustness Theorem establishes that if either the approximation of the CEF or the approximation of the response propensity function are exactly correct, then we can write the expected value of the full (only partially observable) data in terms of simple expected values of the observable data and the approximations. This result motivates a plug-in estimator, obtained by replacing expected values with sample means, $\tilde{\text{E}}[Y_i|R_i = 1, \mathbf{X}_i = \mathbf{x}]$ with some estimate $\hat{\text{E}}[Y_i|R_i = 1, \mathbf{X}_i = \mathbf{x}]$, and $\tilde{p}_R(\mathbf{X}_i)$ with some estimate $\hat{p}_R(\mathbf{X}_i)$.

Definition 6.2.10. *Doubly Robust (DR) Estimator for Missing Data*
Let Y_i and R_i be random variables with $\text{Supp}[R_i] = \{0, 1\}$. Let $Y_i^* = Y_i R_i + (-99)(1 - R_i)$ and let $\mathbf{X}_i$ be a random vector. Then, given n i.i.d. observations of $(Y_i^*, R_i, \mathbf{X}_i)$, the *doubly robust estimator* is

$$\hat{\text{E}}_{DR}[Y_i] = \frac{1}{n}\sum_{i=1}^{n} \hat{\text{E}}[Y_i^*|R_i = 1, \mathbf{X}_i] + \frac{1}{n}\sum_{i=1}^{n} \frac{R_i\left(Y_i^* - \hat{\text{E}}[Y_i^*|R_i = 1, \mathbf{X}_i]\right)}{\hat{p}_R(\mathbf{X}_i)},$$

where $\hat{\text{E}}[Y_i^*|R_i = 1, \mathbf{X}_i]$ is an estimator for $\text{E}[Y_i^*|R_i = 1, \mathbf{X}_i]$, and $\hat{p}_R(\mathbf{X}_i)$ is an estimator for $p_R(\mathbf{X}_i)$.

The DR estimator can be decomposed into two elements. The first term, $\frac{1}{n}\sum_{i=1}^{n} \hat{\text{E}}[Y_i|R_i = 1, \mathbf{X}_i]$, is a standard regression estimator from Section 6.2.2

(*Regression Estimation*). The second term, $\frac{1}{n}\sum_{i=1}^{n}\frac{R_i(Y_i-\hat{E}[Y_i|R_i=1,\mathbf{X}_i])}{\hat{p}_R(\mathbf{X}_i)}$, is an IPW estimator correcting for any unusual deviations in the actual data from the regression estimate. As a plug-in estimator, if the conditions for Theorem 6.2.9 and the usual plug-in regularity conditions hold, the DR estimator can be used in the usual manner, with the bootstrap available for inference. Insofar as the MAR assumption can be believed, the DR estimator provides a sensible and flexible approach that combines the virtues of regression and IPW approaches to estimation.

6.3 APPLICATION: ESTIMATING THE CROSS-NATIONAL AVERAGE OF CLEAN ENERGY USE

We now consider an application, again using the Quality of Governance data (Teorell et al. 2016). Suppose we are interested in the average rate of use of alternative and nuclear energy at the country level. Alternative and nuclear energy use is measured as the percentage of total energy production in a country generated from non–carbon dioxide emitting sources, including, but not limited to, nuclear, wind, hydroelectric, geothermal, and solar power. However, of the 184 countries in the dataset, 50 countries are missing data on this variable. Our goal in this application is to compute estimates of the average using the identifying assumptions and methods detailed in this chapter.

We assume that our observed data are i.i.d. draws of (Y_i^*, R_i), where Y_i^* is equal to country i's percentage use of alternative and nuclear energy if observed and -99 if not observed, and R_i is an indicator for whether country i's rate of use of alternative and nuclear energy is observed. Our goal is to estimate $E[Y_i]$. We begin with the most credible approach: estimating sharp bounds, as discussed in Section 6.1.1 (*Bounds*). Since percentages are naturally bounded, the lowest and highest possible values for Y_i are 0 and 100, respectively. To estimate lower and upper bounds, we use the usual plug-in estimator, and compute standard errors for these quantities using the bootstrap. Without making further assumptions, our estimated bounds are consistent for the narrowest possible bounds on $E[Y_i]$ given the observable data (Y_i^*, R_i). These bounds are quite wide, leaving us with a large range of possibilities: our estimates imply that the true value of $E[Y_i]$ is likely to be somewhere between 7.110 and 34.283. Nevertheless, these estimates are not completely uninformative: accounting for sampling variability, a 95% confidence interval computed using our lower bound estimate excludes all values below 5.109, suggesting that we can be quite confident that the cross-national average rate of clean energy use is above 5%.

We can achieve point identification of $E[Y_i]$ under stronger assumptions, at the cost of reduced credibility. The simplest such assumption is MCAR—assuming that the population distribution of outcomes for countries for which we have data is the same as the population distribution of outcomes for countries for which we do not have data: $Y_i \perp\!\!\!\perp R_i$. This additional assumption gives us point identification, and yields a natural plug-in estimator: we take the sample mean for countries with observed outcomes, so that the MCAR plug-in estimator, $\hat{E}[Y_i] = \hat{E}[Y_i^* | R_i = 1] = 9.762$, and an associated 95% confidence interval is $(7.157, 12.367)$. However, the MCAR assumption may not be credible in this setting. The types of countries with observed values for clean energy use may differ systematically from the types of countries with missing values. For example, we might think that more developed countries would have both higher rates of clean energy use as well as better reporting standards. For this reason, we now turn to using covariates to estimate $E[Y_i]$ under more reasonable assumptions.

We now assume that the data are i.i.d. draws of $(Y_i^*, R_i, \mathbf{X}_i)$, where $\mathbf{X}_i$ is a vector of covariates. In this setting, we have in $\mathbf{X}_i$ the infant mortality rate, urban population, population with electricity, an indicator denoting whether the country is classified as a democracy, population growth rate, GDP/capita, Internet use, pollution levels (as measured by particulate matter), educational attainment for women ages 15–24, and access to clean water.[14] We could now assume MAR with respect to $\mathbf{X}_i$. This implies that, conditional on the values of the observed explanatory variables in $\mathbf{X}$, the distributions of outcomes for countries for which we have response data are exactly the same as the distribution of outcomes for countries for which we do not have response data: $Y_i \perp\!\!\!\perp R_i | \mathbf{X}_i$. While we might think that the estimates obtained by explicitly accounting for the observed explanatory variables are a better approximation of the truth, there is no such guarantee. For example, suppose that countries will only report their clean energy usage if it crosses some country-specific threshold unobservable to us. Then our estimates of $E[Y_i]$ assuming MAR will typically overestimate energy usage, and no conditioning strategy that fails to account for this (unobservable) threshold can be guaranteed to recover the truth.

That being said, if we assume MAR, we have a variety of estimators available to us. We first use two variants of regression estimation to

14 Infant mortality rate is measured as the number of infants who died before reaching one year of age per 1,000 live births in a given year; urban population is measured as the percentage of the population living in urban areas as defined by national statistical offices; population with electricity is measured as the percentage of the population with access to electricity; the democracy variable is coded as one if the country is a democracy and zero otherwise; population growth rate is measured as the annual population growth in percentage points; GDP/capita is measured as gross domestic product in current U.S. dollars divided by mid-year population; Internet use is measured as the number of individuals who have used the Internet in the last 12 months; particulate matter is measured as population-weighted three-year average exposure to fine particulate matter ($PM_{2.5}$); educational attainment for young women is measured as the average years of education for women ages 15–24; and access to clean water is measured as the percentage of the population with access to a source for clean drinking water. For further details, please refer to the Quality of Governance Standard Data codebook (Teorell et al. 2016).

TABLE 6.3.1. *Estimates of the Cross-National Average of Clean Energy Usage with Missing Data*

	Estimate	Bootstrap SE
Lower Bound Plug-In	7.110	1.021
Upper Bound Plug-In	34.283	3.128
MCAR Plug-In	9.762	1.329
OLS (Linear)	8.997	1.203
OLS (Polynomial)	8.084	1.260
Hot Deck Imputation	8.538	1.204
IPW	8.361	1.111
Stabilized IPW	8.737	1.154
Doubly Robust (Linear)	8.575	1.151
Doubly Robust (Polynomial)	8.716	1.187

impute missing responses. As we might expect, the first regression uses OLS under the working assumption that the CEF of the observed data is linear, $\mathrm{E}[Y_i^*|R_i, \mathbf{X}_i] \approx \beta_0 + \mathbf{X}_i\boldsymbol{\beta}$. The resulting estimate, denoted OLS (linear), is $\hat{\mathrm{E}}[Y_i] = 8.997$, somewhat lower than the MCAR plug-in estimate. We also use a more flexible specification, with $\mathrm{E}[Y_i^*|R_i, \mathbf{X}_i] \approx \beta_0 + \mathbf{X}_i\boldsymbol{\beta} + \mathbf{X}_{[2]i}\boldsymbol{\beta}_2$, where $\mathbf{X}_{[2]i}$ is a vector consisting of the squared values of each element $\mathbf{X}_i$. Estimating $\mathrm{E}[Y_i^*|R_i, \mathbf{X}_i]$ with OLS, we compute the OLS (polynomial) estimate $\hat{\mathrm{E}}[Y_i] = 8.084$, again, lower than the MCAR-based estimate.

In order to use the propensity score-based estimators, we need to first estimate the propensity scores, $p_R(\mathbf{X}_i) = \Pr[R_i = 1|\mathbf{X}_i]$. Doing so is not as simple as using the regression-based approaches, as we would like to ensure that $p_R(\mathbf{X}_i)$ obeys the natural constraints given on probabilities, namely that it lies in the unit interval. To do so, we impose as a working assumption that $p_R(\mathbf{X}_i) \approx \frac{e^{\mathbf{X}_i\Gamma}}{(1+e^{\mathbf{X}_i\Gamma})}$, or a *logit* binary choice model (see Section 5.1.2, *Binary Choice Model*, for more details). We estimate each $\hat{p}_R(\mathbf{X}_i)$ using maximum likelihood (ML) estimation (see Section 5.2, *Maximum Likelihood Estimation*). Our estimate using one-to-one, nearest-neighbor hot deck imputation based on the propensity score largely agrees with that of the regression estimates, with $\hat{\mathrm{E}}[Y_i] = 8.538$.[15]

15 The bootstrap may not work as a method for computing valid confidence intervals for hot deck imputation since the bias of the estimator may converge slowly (see, e.g., Abadie and Imbens 2008), but the bootstrap standard errors are likely to adequately characterize sampling variability.

We now turn to the IPW and DR estimators.[16] In this setting, we estimate that the IPW and DR estimators are the most precise of the MAR-based estimates, with bootstrap standard errors lower than those of the pure imputation-based approaches. The IPW estimator yields an estimate of $\hat{\mathrm{E}}[Y_i] = 8.361$, while the stabilized IPW estimator yields an estimate of $\hat{\mathrm{E}}[Y_i] = 8.737$. We implement two variants of the DR estimator: one using the OLS (linear) specification for imputation, yielding an estimate $\hat{\mathrm{E}}[Y_i] = 8.575$, and one using the OLS (polynomial) specification for imputation, yielding an estimate $\hat{\mathrm{E}}[Y_i] = 8.716$.

Table 6.3.1 summarizes these estimates. All our MAR-based estimates roughly agree, lying between 8 and 9 percent, with similar levels of uncertainty across estimates. Regardless of the specification, our MAR-based estimates (i) as expected, lie within the estimated bounds and (ii) are lower than the MCAR-based estimator. If we were to believe the MAR assumption, this would imply that countries with missing outcome data are, on average, less likely to use clean energy sources than are countries for which data are available. This finding, however, depends crucially on the assumption of MAR. And MAR remains unverifable, with no clear theoretical heuristic for ascertaining its validity in this setting. The agnostic analyst must interpret these estimates with appropriate skepticism.

6.4 FURTHER READINGS

Tsiatis (2006) provides a now-canonical book-length treatment of missing data, and links it to semiparametric theory elegantly—the book is strongly recommended. For discussions of partial identification of distributional features with missing data (and other partially revealed models), we strongly recommend Manski (2003) and Manski (2013) as comprehensive books; Imbens (2013) provides a valuable critical review of the latter. Rosenbaum (1987) provides an excellent discussion of the properties of IPW-style estimators. Kang and Schafer (2007) provides an informative review piece on the properties and history of doubly robust estimators. Van der Laan and Robins (2003) provide a highly technical book-length treatment of doubly robust estimation, building on earlier work from Robins and coauthors; e.g., Robins, Rotnitzky, and Zhao (1995) and Robins (1999). Bang and Robins (2005) offers an elegant and moderately technical article-length treatment of doubly robust estimation.

16 As discussed in Section 7.3.2, we Winsorize our propensity score estimates to lie within $[0.01, 1]$.

7

Causal Inference

Fortunate is one who is able to know the causes of things.

—VIRGIL

What is causal inference? Recall that a feature of a probability distribution is identified if it can be inferred given full knowledge of the distribution of observables. Causal identification is just identification of any feature of a distribution that can be interpreted as a causal effect. Causal inference, then, is the process of estimating these quantities from data.[1]

Major empirical debates in the social and health sciences often revolve around causal questions. Examples abound: Does smoking cause lung cancer, and if so, how much might we expect smoking cessation to increase longevity? Do cash transfers to the poor reduce labor supply and, if so, by how much? All else equal, how much does a job applicant's reported racial or gender identity affect the probability of receiving an interview? These questions have sparked considerable controversy in their respective fields. One reason that these and similar questions do, in fact, yield debates is that even causal questions of these types cannot be answered without making assumptions external to the statistical model; controversies cannot be resolved via statistical tools alone.

In this chapter, we discuss the kinds of assumptions necessary to answer causal questions through statistical models. We show that inferences about causal questions—causal inferences—rest on a fundamental identification challenge: causal questions can be viewed as an attempt to make a comparison between two or more hypothetical states of the world, yet we can only ever observe one. In order to proceed, we must be willing to make assumptions about quantities that are not observed by the researcher. This task

1 In this book, we have generally used the term "inference" to refer specifically to the quantification of uncertainty. However, the term "causal inference" is commonly used in this broader sense, encompassing both estimation and inference, and we will adhere to this established convention.

can be shown to be separable from the statistical assumptions necessary to characterize observed data.

Readers will note that the structure and language of this chapter largely mirrors (often near-identically) that of Chapter 6. This is no accident, and as we proceed, we will show how the identification results and estimation procedures that we derived for missing data are easily translated to address questions of cause and effect. Again, to highlight the parallels across chapters, section numbers in brackets will reference the analogous section in Chapter 6.

7.1 IDENTIFICATION WITH POTENTIAL OUTCOMES [6.1]

We employ a model of *potential outcomes* (Splawa-Neyman, Dabrowska, and Speed 1923) known as the *Neyman–Rubin Causal Model (NRCM)*.[2] The NRCM is a powerful and flexible framework for describing claims of cause and effect. There are other formalizations of causality, but the NRCM is the most commonly used framework in political science, biostatistics, and many branches of applied econometrics.

Suppose that we want to know the effect of a medication on a patient's self-reported level of pain. The problem is that we cannot observe a personâĂŹs counterfactual outcome. If the patient takes the medication, we cannot know what they would have reported if they had not. If the patient does not take the medication, we cannot know what they would have reported if they had. This is known as the *Fundamental Problem of Causal Inference* (Holland 1986).

7.1.1 Framework

Suppose that we have a binary treatment D_i, so that $D_i = 1$ if unit i receives the treatment and $D_i = 0$ otherwise. Then the NRCM can be formalized as follows:

Definition 7.1.1. *Potential Outcomes Model*
For an outcome variable Y_i and binary treatment variable D_i, the *potential outcomes model* is

$$Y_i = \begin{cases} Y_i(0) & : \quad D_i = 0 \\ Y_i(1) & : \quad D_i = 1 \end{cases}$$

$$= Y_i(1) \cdot D_i + Y_i(0) \cdot (1 - D_i),$$

where $Y_i(0)$ denotes the potential outcome under control for unit i, and $Y_i(1)$ denotes the potential outcome under treatment for unit i.

2 Also sometimes referred to as the Rubin Causal Model.

Throughout this section, we will assume that the potential outcomes model holds. Note that the distribution of (Y_i, D_i) is observable, but the distribution of $(Y_i(0), Y_i(1))$ is not directly observable. Thus, this is an *identification* problem (see Definition 6.0.1). Potential outcomes $Y_i(d)$ (for $d \in \{0,1\}$) can be binary, discrete, continuous, etc., as long as $\text{Supp}[Y_i(d)] \subseteq \mathbb{R}$. The population values of $(Y_i(0), Y_i(1), D_i)$ can have any joint distribution (subject to perhaps mild regularity conditions for identification and estimation).

Analogously to the *stable outcome model* for missing data (Definition 6.1.1), the above equation embeds what is known as the *stable unit treatment value assumption*. Potential outcomes are assumed to be stable. No matter what, for every unit i, when $D_i = 1$, we observe $Y_i(1)$, and when $D_i = 0$, we observe $Y_i(0)$. This implies that (1) there are no unobserved multiple versions of the treatment or control—every unit i has a single outcome value $Y_i(1)$ that is observed when $D_i = 1$, and a single outcome value $Y_i(0)$ that is observed when $D_i = 0$; and (2) there is no interference between units—unit i's potential outcomes are not affected by whether or not any other unit j receives the treatment.[3]

The potential outcomes model allows us to define some natural quantities as targets of inquiry. One foundational quantity is the (unobservable) treatment effect associated with each unit.

Definition 7.1.2. *Unit-Level Treatment Effect*
Under the potential outcomes model, the *causal effect of treatment* for unit i is

$$\tau_i = Y_i(1) - Y_i(0).$$

Note that τ_i is a random variable that reflects the distribution of treatment effects in the population. Again, the Fundamental Problem of Causal Inference is that we can never observe τ_i directly, since we can never observe both $Y_i(0)$ and $Y_i(1)$ for a given unit i.[4]

Our primary inferential target will be the expected value of this distribution of treatment effects. This expected value is known as the *average treatment effect (ATE)*, also known as the average causal effect (ACE).

3 Violations of the stable unit treatment value assumption do not rule out interesting work. There are generalizations of the NRCM that imply that all our calculations will be meaningful even when the stable unit treatment value assumption does not hold, though the interpretation is somewhat more complex. See, e.g., Hudgens and Halloran (2008) for a discussion of how typical methods estimate regime-specific causal effects when there is interference between units.

4 It might seem like we could solve this problem by simply observing the potential outcomes sequentially: observe $Y_i(0)$, and then administer the treatment and observe $Y_i(1)$. However, this requires the assumption that unit i does not change over time or as a result of the act of measurement. This assumption may be justifiable in some laboratory experiments in the natural sciences where conditions can be precisely controlled, but it is rarely a safe assumption to make in the social or health sciences. We also might be interested in outcomes that can only be measured once, such as which candidate a voter votes for in a particular election.

Definition 7.1.3. *Average Treatment Effect*
Under the potential outcomes model, the *average treatment effect (ATE)* is $E[\tau_i]$.

Some texts refer to this quantity as the population average treatment effect (PATE), since we are assuming independent and identically distributed (i.i.d.) sampling from some population.[5] Before continuing, we note an important direct result about the ATE that will be central to our discussion in Section 7.1.4.

Theorem 7.1.4. *ATE Decomposition*
Under the potential outcomes model, the ATE can be written as

$$E[\tau_i] = E[Y_i(1) - Y_i(0)] = E[Y_i(1)] - E[Y_i(0)].$$

The proof follows immediately from linearity of expectations. This means that the ATE can be written simply as the difference between the average potential outcome in treatment and the average potential outcome in control.

There are other causal targets that researchers have in mind, including the *average treatment effect among the treated (ATT)* ($E[\tau_i | D_i = 1]$) or the *average treatment effect among the control subjects (ATC)* ($E[\tau_i | D_i = 0]$). These targets are often of policy interest—the ATT, for instance, corresponds to the average effect of treatment among the (potentially non-representative) subpopulation of subjects who actually receive treatment, thus speaking to the real-world effect of an existing treatment. In addition, the ATT and ATC can each be point identified under weaker assumptions than the ATE. We focus here on the ATE, though our calculations would generalize straightforwardly via conditioning on D_i. We will return to briefly discuss the ATT as an inferential target, as well as others, in Section 7.3.

7.1.2 Ties to Missing Data

We do *not* directly observe i.i.d. draws of $Y_i(0)$ or $Y_i(1)$, and we *never* observe τ_i for any unit i. (This is the Fundamental Problem of Causal Inference.) We only observe i.i.d. draws of the random vector (Y_i, D_i). So the question is: given full knowledge of the distribution of (Y_i, D_i), what assumptions yield what information about the distributions of $Y_i(0)$, $Y_i(1)$, and τ_i?

[5] There exists an alternative formulation of causal inference under the NRCM that does *not* require the assumption of i.i.d. sampling, known as *design-based inference*. In this book, we focus on causal inference in the i.i.d. sampling context, as it considerably eases exposition.

Causal inference under the NRCM is a missing data problem.[6] We only learn about $Y_i(1)$ for treated units and we only learn about $Y_i(0)$ for control units.

Example 7.1.5. *Causal Inference as a Missing Data Problem*
Suppose we had binary outcomes: $\text{Supp}[Y_i(0)] \subseteq \{0,1\}$ and $\text{Supp}[Y_i(1)] \subseteq \{0,1\}$, and therefore $\text{Supp}[Y_i] \subseteq \{0,1\}$. We might see the following data:

Unit	Y_i	D_i
1	1	1
2	1	0
3	1	1
4	0	1
5	1	1
6	0	0

Given the potential outcomes model, this implies

Unit	$Y_i(0)$	$Y_i(1)$	D_i
1	?	1	1
2	1	?	0
3	?	1	1
4	?	0	1
5	?	1	1
6	0	?	0

We want to learn about the distributions of $Y_i(0)$ and $Y_i(1)$. But we have a missing data problem. We can identify the joint distribution of (Y_i, D_i) values—with large n, we could learn about the distribution of (Y_i, D_i) to arbitrary precision. But even with large n, we need additional assumptions to learn about the distributions of $Y_i(0)$ and $Y_i(1)$. It is even harder to learn about τ_i.

Recognizing that the Fundamental Problem of Causal Inference is essentially a missing data problem helps us to understand the types of assumptions that we need in order to estimate causal effects. Causal inference under the NRCM is about coming up with ways of "solving" this missing data problem with further assumptions. The approaches that we discuss in this chapter are completely analogous to those we presented for missing data in Chapter 6. △

6 This insight is attributed to Rubin (1974), which is a major reason why we have the "R" in NRCM. The converse, however, is also true. Missing data problems can also be viewed as a causal inference problem, an insight attributable to Robins (1986). To see this, we need only recognize that we are asking a question about a potential outcome that we did not observe. Missing data questions, wedded to an assumption of stable outcomes in Section 6.1 (*Identification with Missing Data*), are questions about counterfactual worlds.

7.1.3 Bounds [6.1.1]

We can apply bounds to this problem. We only assume that potential outcomes are bounded: $\forall d \in \{0,1\}, \text{Supp}[Y_i(d)] \subseteq [a,b]$, for some $a \leq b$. How can we estimate bounds for $\text{E}[\tau_i]$? We can apply the same principles that we applied in the case of missing data, as demonstrated in the following example.

Example 7.1.6. *Bounding Treatment Effects*
In Example 7.1.5, outcomes are binary, so $\forall d \in \{0,1\}$, $\text{Supp}[Y_i(d)] \subseteq \{0,1\} \subseteq [0,1]$. For the treated units (those with $D_i = 1$), we observe $Y_i(1)$, but we only know that $0 \leq Y_i(0) \leq 1$. Conversely, for the control units (those with $D_i = 0$), we observe $Y_i(0)$, but we only know that $0 \leq Y_i(1) \leq 1$. We know that $\text{E}[\tau_i] = \text{E}[Y_i(1)] - \text{E}[Y_i(0)]$, so an upper bound is obtained by estimating an upper bound for $\text{E}[Y_i(1)]$ and a lower bound for $\text{E}[Y_i(0)]$. These are computed in the standard way, by plugging in one for the missing values of $Y_i(1)$ and zero for the missing values of $Y_i(0)$:

Unit	$Y_i(0)$	$Y_i(1)$	D_i
1	0	1	1
2	1	1	0
3	0	1	1
4	0	0	1
5	0	1	1
6	0	1	0

Then, using the sample mean as a plug-in estimator for the expected value, our estimate of an upper bound for $\text{E}[Y_i(1)]$ is $\frac{5}{6}$, and our estimate of a lower bound for $\text{E}[Y_i(0)]$ is $\frac{1}{6}$. Thus, our estimate of an upper bound for $\text{E}[\tau_i]$ is $\frac{5}{6} - \frac{1}{6} = \frac{4}{6}$.

Likewise, to estimate a lower bound for $\text{E}[\tau_i]$, we estimate a lower bound for $\text{E}[Y_i(1)]$ and an upper bound for $\text{E}[Y_i(0)]$:

Unit	$Y_i(0)$	$Y_i(1)$	D_i
1	1	1	1
2	1	0	0
3	1	1	1
4	1	0	1
5	1	1	1
6	0	0	0

Our estimated lower bound for $\text{E}[Y_i(1)]$ is $\frac{3}{6}$, and our estimated upper bound for $\text{E}[Y_i(0)]$ is $\frac{5}{6}$. Thus, our estimated lower bound for $\text{E}[\tau_i]$ is $\frac{3}{6} - \frac{5}{6} = -\frac{2}{6}$. $\triangle$

More generally, we can write down exact sharp bounds for $\text{E}[\tau_i]$ in terms of the joint distribution of (Y_i, D_i), which can, in theory, be estimated to arbitrary precision with large n.

Theorem 7.1.7. *Sharp Bounds for the ATE*
Let $Y_i(0)$, $Y_i(1)$, and D_i be random variables such that, $\forall d \in \{0,1\}, \text{Supp}[Y_i(d)] \subseteq [a,b]$, and $\text{Supp}[D_i] = \{0,1\}$. Let $Y_i = Y_i(1) \cdot D_i + Y_i(0) \cdot (1 - D_i)$ and $\tau_i = Y_i(1) - Y_i(0)$. Then

$$\begin{aligned}\text{E}[\tau_i] \in \Big[&\text{E}[Y_i|D_i = 1]\Pr[D_i = 1] + a\Pr[D_i = 0] \\ &- \big(\text{E}[Y_i|D_i = 0]\Pr[D_i = 0] + b\Pr[D_i = 1]\big), \\ &\text{E}[Y_i|D_i = 1]\Pr[D_i = 1] + b\Pr[D_i = 0] \\ &- \big(\text{E}[Y_i|D_i = 0]\Pr[D_i = 0] + a\Pr[D_i = 1]\big)\Big].\end{aligned}$$

Proof: Our proof follows from Theorem 6.1.3 (*Sharp Bounds for the Expected Value*).

By the Law of Iterated Expectations,

$$\text{E}\big[Y_i(1)\big] = \text{E}\big[Y_i(1)\,\big|\,D_i = 1\big]\Pr[D_i = 1] + \text{E}\big[Y_i(1)\,\big|\,D_i = 0\big]\Pr[D_i = 0].$$

Then, since $Y_i = Y_i(1) \cdot D_i + Y_i(0) \cdot (1 - D_i)$,

$$\begin{aligned}\text{E}[Y_i|D_i = 1] &= \text{E}\big[Y_i(1) \cdot D_i + Y_i(0) \cdot (1 - D_i)\,\big|\,D_i = 1\big] \\ &= \text{E}\big[Y_i(1) \cdot 1 + Y_i(0) \cdot 0\,\big|\,D_i = 1\big] \\ &= \text{E}\big[Y_i(1)\,\big|\,D_i = 1\big].\end{aligned}$$

Thus,

$$\text{E}\big[Y_i(1)\big] = \text{E}[Y_i|D_i = 1]\Pr[D_i = 1] + \text{E}\big[Y_i(1)\,\big|\,D_i = 0\big]\Pr[D_i = 0].$$

Since $\text{Supp}[Y_i(1)] \subseteq [a,b]$, $\text{E}[Y_i(1)|D_i = 0] \geq a$, and therefore

$$\begin{aligned}\text{E}\big[Y_i(1)\big] &= \text{E}[Y_i|D_i = 1]\Pr[D_i = 1] + \text{E}\big[Y_i(1)\,\big|\,D_i = 0\big]\Pr[D_i = 0] \\ &\geq \text{E}[Y_i|D_i = 1]\Pr[D_i = 1] + a\Pr[D_i = 0].\end{aligned}$$

Likewise, since $\text{Supp}[Y_i(1)] \subseteq [a,b]$, $\text{E}[Y_i(1)|D_i = 0] \leq b$, and therefore

$$\begin{aligned}\text{E}\big[Y_i(1)\big] &= \text{E}[Y_i|D_i = 1]\Pr[D_i = 1] + \text{E}\big[Y_i(1)\,\big|\,D_i = 0\big]\Pr[D_i = 0] \\ &\leq \text{E}[Y_i|D_i = 1]\Pr[D_i = 1] + b\Pr[D_i = 0].\end{aligned}$$

Thus,

$$\begin{aligned}\text{E}\big[Y_i(1)\big] \in \big[&\text{E}[Y_i|D_i = 1]\Pr[D_i = 1] + a\Pr[D_i = 0], \\ &\text{E}[Y_i|D_i = 1]\Pr[D_i = 1] + b\Pr[D_i = 0]\big].\end{aligned}$$

Following parallel steps to bound $\mathrm{E}[Y_i(0)]$, we get

$$\mathrm{E}\big[Y_i(0)\big] \in \big[\mathrm{E}[Y_i|D_i=0]\Pr[D_i=0]+a\Pr[D_i=1], \\ \mathrm{E}[Y_i|D_i=0]\Pr[D_i=0]+b\Pr[D_i=1]\big].$$

Again, by the Law of Iterated Expectations, and substituting in the results from above,

$$\begin{aligned}\mathrm{E}[\tau_i] &= \mathrm{E}\big[Y_i(1)-Y_i(0)\big] \\ &= \mathrm{E}\big[Y_i(1)\big]-\mathrm{E}\big[Y_i(0)\big] \\ &= \mathrm{E}[Y_i|D_i=1]\Pr[D_i=1]+\mathrm{E}\big[Y_i(1)\,\big|\,D_i=0\big]\Pr[D_i=0] \\ &\quad -\Big(\mathrm{E}[Y_i|D_i=0]\Pr[D_i=0]+\mathrm{E}\big[Y_i(0)\,\big|\,D_i=1\big]\Pr[D_i=1]\Big).\end{aligned}$$

Combining the bounds we found above, since $\mathrm{Supp}[Y_i(d)] \subseteq [a,b]$, $\mathrm{E}[Y_i(1)|D_i=0] \geq a$ and $\mathrm{E}[Y_i(0)|D_i=1] \leq b$. Therefore, we can put a lower bound on $\mathrm{E}[\tau_i]$:

$$\begin{aligned}\mathrm{E}[\tau_i] &= \mathrm{E}[Y_i|D_i=1]\Pr[D_i=1]+\mathrm{E}\big[Y_i(1)\,\big|\,D_i=0\big]\Pr[D_i=0] \\ &\quad -\Big(\mathrm{E}[Y_i|D_i=0]\Pr[D_i=0]+\mathrm{E}\big[Y_i(0)\,\big|\,D_i=1\big]\Pr[D_i=1]\Big) \\ &\geq \mathrm{E}[Y_i|D_i=1]\Pr[D_i=1]+a\Pr[D_i=0] \\ &\quad -\Big(\mathrm{E}[Y_i|D_i=0]\Pr[D_i=0]+b\Pr[D_i=1]\Big).\end{aligned}$$

Likewise, $\mathrm{E}[Y_i(1)|D_i=0] \leq b$, and $\mathrm{E}[Y_i(0)|D_i=1] \geq a$, and we can put an upper bound on $\mathrm{E}[\tau_i]$:

$$\begin{aligned}\mathrm{E}[\tau_i] &= \mathrm{E}[Y_i|D_i=1]\Pr[D_i=1]+\mathrm{E}\big[Y_i(1)\,\big|\,D_i=0\big]\Pr[D_i=0] \\ &\quad -\Big(\mathrm{E}[Y_i|D_i=0]\Pr[D_i=0]+\mathrm{E}\big[Y_i(0)\,\big|\,D_i=1\big]\Pr[D_i=1]\Big) \\ &\leq \mathrm{E}[Y_i|D_i=1]\Pr[D_i=1]+b\Pr[D_i=0] \\ &\quad -\Big(\mathrm{E}[Y_i|D_i=0]\Pr[D_i=0]+a\Pr[D_i=1]\Big).\end{aligned}$$

Thus,

$$\begin{aligned}\mathrm{E}[\tau_i] \in \Big[&\mathrm{E}[Y_i|D_i=1]\Pr[D_i=1]+a\Pr[D_i=0] \\ &\quad -\big(\mathrm{E}[Y_i|D_i=0]\Pr[D_i=0]+b\Pr[D_i=1]\big), \\ &\mathrm{E}[Y_i|D_i=1]\Pr[D_i=1]+b\Pr[D_i=0] \\ &\quad -\big(\mathrm{E}[Y_i|D_i=0]\Pr[D_i=0]+a\Pr[D_i=1]\big)\Big]. \quad \square\end{aligned}$$

One interesting feature of these bounds is that their width is always $(b - a)$, and does not depend on any other feature of the data. Our discussion following Theorem 6.1.3 noted that the bounds in the missing data case were proportional to the amount of missing data. In the causal inference setting, the amount of "missing data" in terms of potential outcomes is always the same, as we always observe only one per subject.

Estimation of these bounds again follows from the plug-in principle (Section 3.3) and is again unbiased and consistent.

Theorem 7.1.8. *Estimating Sharp Bounds for the ATE*
Let $Y_i(0)$, $Y_i(1)$, and D_i be random variables such that, $\forall d \in \{0,1\}, \text{Supp}[Y_i(d)] \subseteq [a,b]$, and $\text{Supp}[D_i] = \{0,1\}$. Let $Y_i = Y_i(1) \cdot D_i + Y_i(0) \cdot (1 - D_i)$ and $\tau_i = Y_i(1) - Y_i(0)$. Then, given n i.i.d. observations of (Y_i, D_i), the plug-in estimator

$$\frac{1}{n}\sum_{i=1}^{n}\left(Y_iD_i + a(1-D_i) - Y_i(1-D_i) - bD_i\right)$$

is unbiased and consistent for the lower bound for $\text{E}[\tau_i]$. Likewise, the plug-in estimator

$$\frac{1}{n}\sum_{i=1}^{n}\left(Y_iD_i + b(1-D_i) - Y_i(1-D_i) - aD_i\right)$$

is unbiased and consistent for the upper bound for $\text{E}[\tau_i]$.

Proof: Our proof follows directly from Theorem 6.1.4 (*Estimating Sharp Bounds for the Expected Value*). Let $\tau_i^L = Y_iD_i + a(1-D_i) - Y_i(1-D_i) - bD_i$, so that

$$\overline{\tau_i^L} = \frac{1}{n}\sum_{i=1}^{n}\left(Y_iD_i + a(1-D_i) - Y_i(1-D_i) - bD_i\right).$$

By Theorem 3.2.3 (*The Expected Value of the Sample Mean is the Population Mean*) and the Weak Law of Large Numbers (WLLN), $\overline{Y_i^L}$ is unbiased and consistent for $\text{E}[\tau_i^L]$, and by the Law of Iterated Expectations,

$$\begin{aligned}
\text{E}\left[\tau_i^L\right] &= \text{E}\left[\tau_i^L \mid D_i = 1\right]\Pr[D_i = 1] + \text{E}\left[\tau_i^L \mid D_i = 0\right]\Pr[D_i = 0] \\
&= \text{E}\left[Y_iD_i + a(1-D_i) - Y_i(1-D_i) - bD_i \,\middle|\, D_i = 1\right]\Pr[D_i = 1] \\
&\quad + \text{E}\left[Y_iD_i + a(1-D_i) - Y_i(1-D_i) - bD_i \,\middle|\, D_i = 0\right]\Pr[D_i = 0] \\
&= \text{E}\left[Y_i \cdot 1 + a \cdot 0 - Y_i \cdot 0 - b \cdot 1 \middle| D_i = 1\right]\Pr[D_i = 1] \\
&\quad + \text{E}\left[Y_i \cdot 0 + a \cdot 1 - Y_i \cdot 1 - b \cdot 0 \middle| D_i = 0\right]\Pr[D_i = 0]
\end{aligned}$$

$$= \mathrm{E}[Y_i - b \mid D_i = 1]\Pr[D_i = 1]$$
$$+ E[a - Y_i \mid D_i = 0]\Pr[D_i = 0]$$
$$= \mathrm{E}[Y_i \mid D_i = 1]\Pr[D_i = 1] - b\Pr[D_i = 1] + a\Pr[D_i = 0]$$
$$- E[Y_i \mid D_i = 0]\Pr[D_i = 0]$$
$$= \mathrm{E}[Y_i \mid D_i = 1]\Pr[D_i = 1] + a\Pr[D_i = 0]$$
$$- \big(E[Y_i \mid D_i = 0]\Pr[D_i = 0] + b\Pr[D_i = 1]\big).$$

Thus, $\overline{\tau_i^L}$ is unbiased and consistent for the lower bound of $\mathrm{E}[\tau_i]$, $\mathrm{E}[Y_i \mid D_i = 1]\Pr[D_i = 1] + a\Pr[D_i = 0] - (E[Y_i \mid D_i = 0]\Pr[D_i = 0] + b\Pr[D_i = 1])$.

Similarly, let $\tau_i^U = Y_i D_i + b(1 - D_i) - Y_i(1 - D_i) - aD_i$, so that

$$\overline{\tau_i^U} = \frac{1}{n}\sum_{i=1}^{n}\big(Y_i D_i + b(1 - D_i) - Y_i(x1 - D_i) - aD_i\big).$$

Then, by the same logic, it follows that $\overline{\tau_i^U}$ is unbiased and consistent for $\mathrm{E}[Y_i \mid D_i = 1]\Pr[D_i = 1] + b\Pr[D_i = 0] - (\mathrm{E}[Y_i \mid D_i = 0]\Pr[D_i = 0] + a\Pr[D_i = 1])$. □

Under the usual plug-in regularity conditions, asymptotically valid confidence intervals for each bound can be computed using the bootstrap.

Without adding assumptions, these bounds are tight, and therefore $\mathrm{E}[\tau_i]$ is only partially identified. We now ask: what type of assumptions do we need to achieve point identification of $\mathrm{E}[\tau_i]$? The answer is completely analogous to the case of missing data.

7.1.4 Random Assignment [6.1.2]

It is generally thought that one of the strongest nonparametric assumptions we could impose is *random assignment* of the treatment. This assumption is analogous to missing completely at random (MCAR).

Definition 7.1.9. *Random Assignment*
Let $Y_i(0)$, $Y_i(1)$, and D_i be random variables with $\mathrm{Supp}[D_i] = \{0, 1\}$. Let $Y_i = Y_i(1) \cdot D_i + Y_i(0) \cdot (1 - D_i)$. Then D_i is *randomly assigned* if the following conditions hold:

- $(Y_i(0), Y_i(1)) \perp\!\!\!\perp D_i$ (independence of potential outcomes and treatment).
- $0 < \Pr[D_i = 1] < 1$ (positivity).

Random assignment implies that the distribution of potential outcomes is exactly the same for the population of units that get treated and the population of units that do not. Merely observing whether or not a unit was assigned to treatment reveals nothing about its potential outcomes. Under this assumption, $\mathrm{E}[\tau_i]$ is point identified.

Theorem 7.1.10. *ATE under Random Assignment*
Let $Y_i(0)$, $Y_i(1)$, and D_i be random variables with $\mathrm{Supp}[D_i] = \{0, 1\}$. Let $Y_i = Y_i(1) \cdot D_i + Y_i(0) \cdot (1 - D_i)$ and $\tau_i = Y_i(1) - Y_i(0)$. Then, if D_i is randomly assigned,

$$\mathrm{E}[\tau_i] = \mathrm{E}[Y_i | D_i = 1] - \mathrm{E}[Y_i | D_i = 0].$$

Proof: By independence (see Theorem 2.2.25, *Implications of Independence, Part III*),

$$\mathrm{E}\big[Y_i(0)\big] = \mathrm{E}\big[Y_i(0) \,\big|\, D_i = 0\big],$$

and by the potential outcomes model,

$$\mathrm{E}\big[Y_i(0) \,\big|\, D_i = 0\big] = \mathrm{E}[Y_i | D_i = 0].$$

Thus,

$$\mathrm{E}\big[Y_i(0)\big] = \mathrm{E}[Y_i | D_i = 0],$$

and by the same logic,

$$\mathrm{E}\big[Y_i(1)\big] = \mathrm{E}\big[Y_i(1) \,\big|\, D_i = 1\big] = \mathrm{E}[Y_i | D_i = 1].$$

Thus,

$$\begin{aligned}\mathrm{E}[\tau_i] &= \mathrm{E}\big[Y_i(1) - Y_i(0)\big] \\ &= \mathrm{E}\big[Y_i(1)\big] - \mathrm{E}\big[Y_i(0)\big] \\ &= \mathrm{E}[Y_i | D_i = 1] - \mathrm{E}[Y_i | D_i = 0]. \quad \square\end{aligned}$$

Under random assignment, the plug-in estimator for the ATE is just the difference of these two sample means, which we call the *difference-in-means estimator*:

$$\hat{\mathrm{E}}_{DM}[\tau_i] = \hat{\mathrm{E}}\big[Y_i(1)\big] - \hat{\mathrm{E}}\big[Y_i(0)\big] = \frac{\sum_{i=1}^{n} Y_i D_i}{\sum_{i=1}^{n} D_i} - \frac{\sum_{i=1}^{n} Y_i (1 - D_i)}{\sum_{i=1}^{n} (1 - D_i)}.$$

Much like MCAR for missing data, we can think of random assignment as allowing us, given large enough n, to impute the expected value of the unobserved potential outcomes using sample means. The following example illustrates this concept.

Example 7.1.11. *Imputation under Random Assignment*
We again consider the setting of Example 7.1.5. We have:

Unit	$Y_i(0)$	$Y_i(1)$	D_i
1	?	1	1
2	1	?	0
3	?	1	1
4	?	0	1
5	?	1	1
6	0	?	0

Assuming random assignment, $\text{E}[Y_i(1)|D_i = 0] = \text{E}[Y_i(1)]$ and $\text{E}[Y_i(0)|D_i = 1] = \text{E}[Y_i(0)]$, which we can estimate with sample means. This yields the following imputation with plug-in estimates:

Unit	$Y_i(0)$	$Y_i(1)$	D_i
1	$\hat{\text{E}}[Y_i(0)] = \frac{1}{2}$	1	1
2	1	$\hat{\text{E}}[Y_i(1)] = \frac{3}{4}$	0
3	$\hat{\text{E}}[Y_i(0)] = \frac{1}{2}$	1	1
4	$\hat{\text{E}}[Y_i(0)] = \frac{1}{2}$	0	1
5	$\hat{\text{E}}[Y_i(0)] = \frac{1}{2}$	1	1
6	0	$\hat{\text{E}}[Y_i(1)] = \frac{3}{4}$	0

Then the sample means of $Y_i(1)$ and $Y_i(0)$ with the missing values imputed are $\frac{3}{4}$ and $\frac{1}{2}$, respectively, and so our plug-in estimate of $\text{E}[\tau_i]$ is again $\frac{3}{4} - \frac{1}{2} = \frac{1}{4}$. As with MCAR, under random assignment, imputation is a redundant extra step—we are just using $\hat{\text{E}}[Y_i(1)]$ and $\hat{\text{E}}[Y_i(0)]$ to impute the missing values in order to get $\hat{\text{E}}[Y_i(1)]$ and $\hat{\text{E}}[Y_i(0)]$ again—but this way of thinking about estimating expected potential outcomes will become useful as we proceed. △

Even under random assignment, the only meaningful feature of τ_i that we can point identify is $\text{E}[\tau_i]$. This is because expectations are linear (Theorem 2.1.9), so we can separate $\text{E}[Y_i(1) - Y_i(0)]$ into $\text{E}[Y_i(1)] - \text{E}[Y_i(0)]$. It is not generally the case that, for an operator A, $A[Y_i(1) - Y_i(0)] = A[Y_i(1)] - A[Y_i(0)]$. The difference in medians, for instance, is not generally equal to the median difference, so we cannot identify the median treatment effect under random assignment without further assumptions. This is likewise the case for $\text{V}[\tau_i]$ and for the cumulative distribution function (CDF) of τ_i. Although the (marginal) distributions of $Y_i(1)$ and $Y_i(0)$ are identified by random assignment, their *joint* distribution, and thus the distribution of their difference, is not.

Random assignment, or a variant thereof, allows us to separate correlation from causation. Random assignment is *not* a given. Consider the following cases, and think about why random assignment would be unlikely to hold:

Unit	Treatment	Outcome
Country	WTO Membership	GNI per Capita
Registered Voter	Voter Turnout Phone Call	Voting
City	Needle Exchange Program	HIV Prevalence

In fact, if we erroneously assume random assignment and take the difference in expected values between treated units and control units, the result can be decomposed as follows:

$$\begin{aligned}
\mathrm{E}[Y_i|D_i=1]-\mathrm{E}[Y_i|D_i=0] &= \mathrm{E}\big[Y_i(1)\,\big|\,D_i=1\big]-\mathrm{E}\big[Y_i(0)\,\big|\,D_i=0\big] \\
&= \mathrm{E}\big[\tau_i+Y_i(0)\,\big|\,D_i=1\big]-\mathrm{E}\big[Y_i(0)\,\big|\,D_i=0\big] \\
&= \mathrm{E}[\tau_i|D_i=1] \\
&\quad +\mathrm{E}\big[Y_i(0)\,\big|\,D_i=1\big]-\mathrm{E}\big[Y_i(0)\,\big|\,D_i=0\big],
\end{aligned}$$

where $\mathrm{E}[\tau_i|D_i=1]$ is the *average treatment effect among the treated*, and $\mathrm{E}[Y_i(0)|D_i=1]-\mathrm{E}[Y_i(0)|D_i=0]$ is selection bias.

7.1.5 Ignorability [6.1.3]

If we have additional information on each unit, we can achieve point identification of the ATE under an alternative assumption to random assignment. This assumption is known as *strong ignorability*.[7]

Definition 7.1.12. *Strong Ignorability*
Let $Y_i(0)$, $Y_i(1)$, and D_i be random variables with $\mathrm{Supp}[D_i]=\{0,1\}$. Let $Y_i=Y_i(1)\cdot D_i+Y_i(0)\cdot(1-D_i)$. Then D_i is *strongly ignorable* conditional on $\mathbf{X}_i$ if the following conditions hold:

- $(Y_i(0),Y_i(1))\perp\!\!\!\perp D_i|\mathbf{X}_i$ (conditional independence assumption).
- $\exists\epsilon>0$ such that $\epsilon<\Pr[D_i=1|\mathbf{X}_i]<1-\epsilon$ (positivity).

(We are still assuming that treatment is binary. We will show how this assumption can be relaxed in Section 7.1.8, *Generalizing Beyond Binary Treatments*.)

[7] Strong ignorability is named as such because it imposes a joint independence assumption $(Y_i(0),Y_i(1))\perp\!\!\!\perp D_i|\mathbf{X}_i$. (Our definition of random assignment also invokes a joint independence assumption.) Weak ignorability only requires that $Y_i(d)\perp\!\!\!\perp D_i|\mathbf{X}_i,\forall d\in\{0,1\}$. In theory, all our results could be obtained under weak ignorability, but the distinction is only known to be of practical relevance when considering questions of complex counterfactuals (Richardson and Robins mimeo.).

Strong ignorability is to random assignment what missing at random (MAR) is to MCAR. It is random assignment *conditional on covariates*. The conditional independence assumption states that, among units with the same measured characteristics, the types that receive the treatment and the types that do not are exactly the same in terms of their distribution of potential outcomes.

For example, if we measured age and gender, we could say that, "for people who are forty years old and male, the conditional independence assumption implies that there are no systematic differences in potential outcomes between those who get the treatment and those who do not. But we still allow for the possibility that forty-year-olds may be more or less likely to get the treatment than fifty-year-olds." In other words, the conditional independence assumption implies that, after accounting for observable background characteristics, knowing whether or not a unit received treatment provides no additional information about a unit's potential outcomes. This assumption is not to be taken lightly. All the concerns that we would have about the plausibility of random assignment still remain, except the burden has simply been moved to the appropriate set of *conditioning variables*. In general, we recommend only invoking strong ignorability when justifiable by substantive knowledge. Our application (Section 7.5) considers one such case.

Like random assignment, strong ignorability allows us to point identify $\mathrm{E}[Y_i(0)]$, $\mathrm{E}[Y_i(1)]$, and $\mathrm{E}[\tau_i]$.

Theorem 7.1.13. *ATE under Strong Ignorability*
Let $Y_i(0)$, $Y_i(1)$, and D_i be random variables with $\mathrm{Supp}[D_i] = \{0,1\}$. Let $Y_i = Y_i(1) \cdot D_i + Y_i(0) \cdot (1 - D_i)$ and $\tau_i = Y_i(1) - Y_i(0)$, and let $\mathbf{X}_i$ be a discrete random vector.[8] Then, if D_i is strongly ignorable conditional on $\mathbf{X}_i$,

$$\mathrm{E}[\tau_i] = \sum_{\mathbf{x}} \mathrm{E}[Y_i | D_i = 1, \mathbf{X}_i = \mathbf{x}] \Pr[\mathbf{X}_i = \mathbf{x}] - \sum_{\mathbf{x}} \mathrm{E}[Y_i | D_i = 0, \mathbf{X}_i = \mathbf{x}] \Pr[\mathbf{X}_i = \mathbf{x}].$$

Proof: By the Law of Iterated Expectations,

$$\mathrm{E}\big[Y_i(0)\big] = \mathrm{E}\Big[\mathrm{E}\big[Y_i(0) \,\big|\, \mathbf{X}_i\big]\Big] = \sum_{\mathbf{x}} \mathrm{E}\big[Y_i(0) \,\big|\, \mathbf{X}_i = \mathbf{x}\big] \Pr[\mathbf{X}_i = \mathbf{x}],$$

and by strong ignorability (and the potential outcomes model),

$$\mathrm{E}\big[Y_i(0) \,\big|\, \mathbf{X}_i\big] = \mathrm{E}\big[Y_i(0) \,\big|\, D_i = 0, \mathbf{X}_i\big] = \mathrm{E}[Y_i | D_i = 0, \mathbf{X}_i].$$

8 We assume here that $\mathbf{X}_i$ is discrete to ease exposition. This assumption is not necessary, but it lets us work with PMFs instead of PDFs. The continuous case is analogous. Recall that we are writing $\sum_{\mathbf{x}}$ as a shorthand for $\sum_{\mathbf{x} \in \mathrm{Supp}[\mathbf{X}_i]}$.

Thus,

$$\mathrm{E}\big[Y_i(0)\big] = \sum_{\mathbf{x}} \mathrm{E}[Y_i | D_i = 0, \mathbf{X}_i = \mathbf{x}] \Pr[\mathbf{X}_i = \mathbf{x}],$$

and by the same logic,

$$\mathrm{E}\big[Y_i(1)\big] = \sum_{\mathbf{x}} \mathrm{E}[Y_i | D_i = 1, \mathbf{X}_i = \mathbf{x}] \Pr[\mathbf{X}_i = \mathbf{x}].$$

Thus,

$$\begin{aligned}\mathrm{E}[\tau_i] &= \mathrm{E}\big[Y_i(1)\big] - \mathrm{E}\big[Y_i(0)\big] \\ &= \sum_{\mathbf{x}} \mathrm{E}[Y_i | D_i = 1, \mathbf{X}_i = \mathbf{x}] \Pr[\mathbf{X}_i = \mathbf{x}] \\ &\quad - \sum_{\mathbf{x}} \mathrm{E}[Y_i | D_i = 0, \mathbf{X}_i = \mathbf{x}] \Pr[\mathbf{X}_i = \mathbf{x}]. \quad \square\end{aligned}$$

Since we can observe the random vector $(Y_i, D_i, \mathbf{X}_i)$, we can point identify $\mathrm{E}[Y_i | D_i = 1, \mathbf{X}_i = \mathbf{x}]$, $\mathrm{E}[Y_i | D_i = 0, \mathbf{X}_i = \mathbf{x}]$, and $\Pr[\mathbf{X}_i = \mathbf{x}]$. Thus, under ignorability, $\mathrm{E}[\tau_i]$ is point identified.

Furthermore, for every $\mathbf{x} \in \mathrm{Supp}[\mathbf{X}_i]$, the *conditional ATE* given $\mathbf{X}_i = \mathbf{x}$ is point identified.

Theorem 7.1.14. *Conditional ATE under Strong Ignorability*
Let $Y_i(0)$, $Y_i(1)$, and D_i be random variables with $\mathrm{Supp}[D_i] = \{0, 1\}$. Let $Y_i = Y_i(1) \cdot D_i + Y_i(0) \cdot (1 - D_i)$ and $\tau_i = Y_i(1) - Y_i(0)$, and let $\mathbf{X}_i$ be a random vector. Then, if D_i is strongly ignorable conditional on $\mathbf{X}_i$,

$$\mathrm{E}[\tau_i | \mathbf{X}_i] = \mathrm{E}[Y_i | D_i = 1, \mathbf{X}_i] - \mathrm{E}[Y_i | D_i = 0, \mathbf{X}_i].$$

Proof: As in the second and third lines of the proof of Theorem 7.1.13, we have

$$\mathrm{E}\big[Y_i(0) \,\big|\, \mathbf{X}_i\big] = \mathrm{E}\big[Y_i(0) \,\big|\, D_i = 0, \mathbf{X}_i\big] = \mathrm{E}[Y_i | D_i = 0, \mathbf{X}_i]$$

and

$$\mathrm{E}\big[Y_i(1) \,\big|\, \mathbf{X}_i\big] = \mathrm{E}\big[Y_i(1) \,\big|\, D_i = 1, \mathbf{X}_i\big] = \mathrm{E}[Y_i | D_i = 1, \mathbf{X}_i].$$

Thus, by linearity of conditional expectations,

$$\begin{aligned}\mathrm{E}[\tau_i | \mathbf{X}_i] &= \mathrm{E}\big[Y_i(1) - Y_i(0) \,\big|\, \mathbf{X}_i\big] \\ &= \mathrm{E}\big[Y_i(1) \,\big|\, \mathbf{X}_i\big] - \mathrm{E}\big[Y_i(0) \,\big|\, \mathbf{X}_i\big] \\ &= \mathrm{E}\big[Y_i | D_i = 1, \mathbf{X}_i\big] - \mathrm{E}\big[Y_i | D_i = 0, \mathbf{X}_i\big]. \quad \square\end{aligned}$$

Note that applying the Law of Iterated Expectations to this result yields the same identification result for the ATE under ignorability as stated in Theorem 7.1.13 (*The ATE under Strong Ignorability*):

$$\begin{aligned}
\mathrm{E}[\tau_i] &= \mathrm{E}\big[\mathrm{E}[\tau_i|\mathbf{X}_i]\big] \\
&= \sum_{\mathbf{x}} \mathrm{E}[\tau_i|\mathbf{X}_i = \mathbf{x}]\,\Pr[\mathbf{X}_i = \mathbf{x}] \\
&= \sum_{\mathbf{x}} \big(\mathrm{E}[Y_i|D_i = 1, \mathbf{X}_i = \mathbf{x}] - \mathrm{E}[Y_i|D_i = 0, \mathbf{X}_i = \mathbf{x}]\big)\Pr[\mathbf{X}_i = \mathbf{x}] \\
&= \sum_{\mathbf{x}} \mathrm{E}[Y_i|D_i = 1, \mathbf{X}_i = \mathbf{x}]\,\Pr[\mathbf{X}_i = \mathbf{x}] \\
&\quad - \sum_{\mathbf{x}} \mathrm{E}[Y_i|D_i = 0, \mathbf{X}_i = \mathbf{x}]\,\Pr[\mathbf{X}_i = \mathbf{x}].
\end{aligned}$$

When both random assignment and strong ignorability with respect to a set of covariates hold, we will typically prefer to invoke strong ignorability. One key reason for this is that we can then investigate conditional ATEs, whereas we cannot with only random assignment.[9] However, random assignment does not generally imply strong ignorability with respect to a set of covariates. In Section 7.1.7, we will discuss a case where random assignment holds, but strong ignorability with respect to a *post-treatment variable* does not.

7.1.6 The Role of the Propensity Score for Causal Inference [6.1.4]

For binary treatments, if strong ignorability holds, then instead of directly conditioning on all the covariates, it suffices to condition on a summary measure of treatment and the covariates.[10] This summary measure is the *propensity score*, which corresponds to the value of the *treatment propensity function* as applied to a unit's covariate values.

Definition 7.1.15. *Treatment Propensity Function*
Let $Y_i(0)$, $Y_i(1)$, and D_i be random variables with $\mathrm{Supp}[D_i] = \{0, 1\}$. Let $Y_i = Y_i(1) \cdot D_i + Y_i(0) \cdot (1 - D_i)$. Then the *treatment propensity function* is

$$p_D(\mathbf{x}) = \Pr[D_i = 1|\mathbf{X}_i = \mathbf{x}], \forall \mathbf{x} \in \mathrm{Supp}[\mathbf{X}_i].$$

The random variable $p_D(\mathbf{X}_i)$ is also known as the propensity score for unit i; it is conceptually identical to the propensity score in missing data.

9 Another reason is that we can typically estimate causal effects more efficiently by using information on covariates. Such practice is known as *regression adjustment*; see Schochet (2010), Pitkin et al. (mimeo.), and Wager et al. (2016) for discussions.

10 This insight is attributed to Rosenbaum and Rubin (1983).

Again, the propensity score is the conditional probability of treatment given the covariates, or the CEF of D_i with respect to $\mathbf{X}_i$ evaluated at $\mathbf{x}$. The propensity score for any given covariate profile is a function of the covariates: if we know that $\mathbf{X}_i = \mathbf{x}$, and we know the full joint distribution of $(D_i, \mathbf{X}_i)$, then we know $\Pr[D_i = 1 | \mathbf{X}_i = \mathbf{x}]$.

The following theorem states the key properties of the propensity score under strong ignorability.

Theorem 7.1.16. *Strong Ignorability and the Propensity Score*
Let $Y_i(0)$, $Y_i(1)$, and D_i be random variables with $\text{Supp}[D_i] = \{0,1\}$. Let $Y_i = Y_i(1) \cdot D_i + Y_i(0) \cdot (1 - D_i)$ and $\tau_i = Y_i(1) - Y_i(0)$, and let $\mathbf{X}_i$ be a random vector. Then, if D_i is strongly ignorable conditional on $\mathbf{X}_i$,

- $D_i \perp\!\!\!\perp \mathbf{X}_i | p_D(\mathbf{X}_i)$. (Balance conditional on $p_D(\mathbf{X}_i)$)
- $(Y_i(0), Y_i(1)) \perp\!\!\!\perp D_i | p_D(\mathbf{X}_i)$. (Conditional independence with respect to $p_D(\mathbf{X}_i)$)
- $\exists \epsilon > 0$ such that $\epsilon < \Pr[D_i = 1 | p_D(\mathbf{X}_i)] < 1 - \epsilon$. (Positivity conditional on $p_D(\mathbf{X}_i)$)

Proof: We will again prove the first two properties and omit a proof of the third; the proof follows nearly identically from Theorem 6.1.12 (*Ignorability and the Propensity Score*).
Balance: Since D_i is binary, its distribution is fully governed by its expected value (Example 5.1.2), so

$$D_i \perp\!\!\!\perp \mathbf{X}_i | p_D(\mathbf{X}_i) \iff \text{E}\big[D_i \big| \mathbf{X}_i, p_D(\mathbf{X}_i)\big] = \text{E}\big[D_i \big| p_D(\mathbf{X}_i)\big].$$

Since conditioning on a function of $\mathbf{X}_i$ provides no additional information when we have already conditioned on $\mathbf{X}_i$,

$$\text{E}\big[D_i \big| \mathbf{X}_i, p_D(\mathbf{X}_i)\big] = \text{E}[D_i | \mathbf{X}_i] = p_D(\mathbf{X}_i),$$

and by the Law of Iterated Expectations,

$$\text{E}\big[D_i \big| p_D(\mathbf{X}_i)\big] = \text{E}\big[\text{E}[D_i | \mathbf{X}_i] \big| p_D(\mathbf{X}_i)\big] = \text{E}\big[p_D(\mathbf{X}_i) \big| p_D(\mathbf{X}_i)\big] = p_D(\mathbf{X}_i).$$

Therefore,

$$\text{E}\big[D_i \big| \mathbf{X}_i, p_D(\mathbf{X}_i)\big] = p_D(\mathbf{X}_i) = \text{E}\big[D_i \big| p_D(\mathbf{X}_i)\big],$$

and thus $D_i \perp\!\!\!\perp \mathbf{X}_i | p_D(\mathbf{X}_i)$.

Conditional independence: Since D_i is binary,

$$D_i \perp\!\!\!\perp \big(Y_i(0), Y_i(1)\big) \big| p_D(\mathbf{X}_i) \iff \text{E}\Big[D_i \Big| \big(Y_i(0), Y_i(1)\big), p_D(\mathbf{X}_i)\Big] = \text{E}\big[D_i \big| p_D(\mathbf{X}_i)\big].$$

By the Law of Iterated Expectations,

$$\begin{aligned}
&\mathrm{E}\Big[D_i \,\Big|\, \big(Y_i(0), Y_i(1)\big), p_D(\mathbf{X}_i)\Big] \\
&\quad = \mathrm{E}\Bigg[\mathrm{E}\Big[D_i \,\Big|\, \big(Y_i(0), Y_i(1)\big), \mathbf{X}_i\Big] \,\Bigg|\, \big(Y_i(0), Y_i(1)\big), p_D(\mathbf{X}_i)\Bigg],
\end{aligned}$$

and by strong ignorability,

$$\mathrm{E}\Big[D_i \,\Big|\, \big(Y_i(0), Y_i(1)\big), \mathbf{X}_i\Big] = \mathrm{E}[D_i | \mathbf{X}_i] = p_D(\mathbf{X}_i).$$

So, by substitution,

$$\begin{aligned}
\mathrm{E}\Big[D_i \,\Big|\, \big(Y_i(0), Y_i(1)\big), p_D(\mathbf{X}_i)\Big] &= \mathrm{E}\Big[p_D(\mathbf{X}_i) \,\Big|\, \big(Y_i(0), Y_i(1)\big), p_D(\mathbf{X}_i)\Big] \\
&= p_D(\mathbf{X}_i) \\
&= \mathrm{E}\big[D_i \,|\, p_D(\mathbf{X}_i)\big],
\end{aligned}$$

and thus $D_i \perp\!\!\!\perp (Y_i(0), Y_i(1)) | p_D(\mathbf{X}_i)$. □

Again, Theorem 7.1.16 says that conditioning on the propensity score is equivalent to conditioning on all the covariates. This implies that if D_i is strongly ignorable conditional on $\mathbf{X}_i$, then D_i is also strongly ignorable conditional on the propensity score $p_D(\mathbf{X}_i)$.

It is important to note that balance on $\mathbf{X}_i$ is a *consequence* of conditioning on the propensity score. That is, after conditioning on the propensity score, the conditional distribution of covariates for treated units will be the same as the conditional distribution of covariates for control units.[11] In the context of observational studies, a *balance test* (a statistical test of equality of covariate distributions) merely tests the null hypothesis that we have successfully conditioned on the propensity score. If the distributions of covariates, conditional on the propensity score, for treated units and control units are significantly different, then we have done something wrong. However, balance does *not* imply that strong ignorability holds. Balance on observable characteristics does not imply balance on unobservable characteristics. Without further assumptions, there exists no general test of strong ignorability.

7.1.7 Post-Treatment Variables

In many circumstances (such as a randomized experiment), random assignment implies strong ignorability with respect to covariates. But this need not be the

11 A reminder: this is not a statement about any given sample, but rather a feature of the population from which sampled units are drawn.

case: random assignment does not generally imply strong ignorability. That is, it is possible that

- $(Y_i(0), Y_i(1)) \perp\!\!\!\perp D_i$, but
- $(Y_i(0), Y_i(1)) \not\perp\!\!\!\perp D_i | X_i$.

The classic case of this is when X_i is *post-treatment*, and therefore can be affected by treatment. If D_i has a *causal effect* on X_i, then controlling for X_i can cause inconsistency, as the following example illustrates.

Example 7.1.17. *Conditioning on Post-Treatment Variables*
Suppose that the joint distribution of potential outcomes and treatment is

$$f\big(Y_i(0), Y_i(1), X_i(1), X_i(0), D_i\big)$$
$$= \begin{cases} \frac{1}{6} & : \ Y_i(0) = 0, Y_i(1) = 0, X_i(1) = 0, X_i(0) = 0, D_i = 0 \\ \frac{1}{6} & : \ Y_i(0) = 1, Y_i(1) = 1, X_i(1) = 1, X_i(0) = 0, D_i = 0 \\ \frac{1}{6} & : \ Y_i(0) = 1, Y_i(1) = 1, X_i(1) = 1, X_i(0) = 1, D_i = 0 \\ \frac{1}{6} & : \ Y_i(0) = 0, Y_i(1) = 0, X_i(1) = 0, X_i(0) = 0, D_i = 1 \\ \frac{1}{6} & : \ Y_i(0) = 1, Y_i(1) = 1, X_i(1) = 1, X_i(0) = 0, D_i = 1 \\ \frac{1}{6} & : \ Y_i(0) = 1, Y_i(1) = 1, X_i(1) = 1, X_i(0) = 1, D_i = 1 \\ 0 & : \ \text{otherwise,} \end{cases}$$

where $X_i = X_i(1)D_i + X_i(0)(1 - D_i)$. In this case, we have

- random assignment of D_i with respect to all potential outcomes: $(Y_i(0), Y_i(1), X_i(1), X_i(0)) \perp\!\!\!\perp D_i$,
- no effect of D_i on Y_i whatsoever: $Y_i(1) = Y_i(0)$ always, and
- an effect of D_i on X_i.

The distribution of observables is

$$f(Y_i, X_i, D_i) = \begin{cases} \frac{1}{6} & : \ Y_i = 0, X_i = 0, D_i = 0 \\ \frac{1}{6} & : \ Y_i = 1, X_i = 0, D_i = 0 \\ \frac{1}{6} & : \ Y_i = 1, X_i = 1, D_i = 0 \\ \frac{1}{6} & : \ Y_i = 0, X_i = 0, D_i = 1 \\ \frac{1}{6} & : \ Y_i = 1, X_i = 1, D_i = 1 \\ \frac{1}{6} & : \ Y_i = 1, X_i = 1, D_i = 1 \\ 0 & : \ \text{otherwise.} \end{cases}$$

Plugging into Definition 7.1.13 (*The ATE under Strong Ignorability*), we have

$$\sum_{\mathbf{x}} \mathrm{E}[Y_i | D_i = 1, \mathbf{X}_i = \mathbf{x}] \Pr[\mathbf{X}_i = \mathbf{x}] - \sum_{\mathbf{x}} \mathrm{E}[Y_i | D_i = 0, \mathbf{X}_i = \mathbf{x}] \Pr[\mathbf{X}_i = \mathbf{x}] = -\frac{1}{4}.$$

But we know that $\mathrm{E}[\tau_i] = 0$. Therefore conditioning on a post-treatment variable can undo even random assignment. △

It is generally a risky endeavor to condition on post-treatment variables, and doing so requires justifications that cannot generally be ensured even by experimental design. Note that "mediation analysis" is logically equivalent to conditioning on a post-treatment variable. Mediation analysis requires strong assumptions beyond those discussed in this chapter, and cannot be justified by random assignment of D_i alone.

7.1.8 Generalizing Beyond Binary Treatments

We have only discussed causal identification for binary treatments, where each unit either receives the treatment ($D_i = 1$) or does not ($D_i = 0$). But suppose we want to consider the causal effects of multivalued or continuous treatments, such as the effects of various amounts of cash transfers on hours worked. In this section, we demonstrate that we can generalize the NRCM to accommodate such cases. Let D_i now be any random variable.

Definition 7.1.18. *Generalized Potential Outcomes Model*
For an outcome variable Y_i and a treatment variable D_i, the *generalized potential outcomes model* is

$$Y_i = \Big\{ Y_i(d) : D_i = d, \forall d \in \mathrm{Supp}[D_i],$$

where $Y_i(d)$ denotes the potential outcome when unit i receives treatment level d.

The generalized potential outcomes models states that, for every possible value of $d \in \mathrm{Supp}[D_i]$, each unit i has a corresponding (stable) potential outcome $Y_i(d)$, which is observed when D_i takes on that value. When D_i is binary, this generalization reduces to the original binary potential outcomes model.

Causal effects are then defined as differences in potential outcomes for different treatment levels. For any $d, d' \in \mathrm{Supp}[D_i]$, the causal effect of moving from d to d' is

$$\tau_i(d, d') = Y_i(d') - Y_i(d).$$

The key identification assumptions and results are all completely analogous to those we have derived for binary treatments. For example, strong ignorability would entail that

$$\big(Y_i(d)\big)_{d \in \mathrm{Supp}[D_i]} \perp\!\!\!\perp D_i | \mathbf{X}_i. \text{ (Conditional independence assumption)}$$

We will gloss over the requisite positivity assumption, since it is considerably more opaque in the generalized setting, but it basically ensures the identifiability of all salient expected values. Theorem 7.1.13 (*The ATE under Strong Ignorability*) then generalizes as follows: under strong ignorability with discrete $\mathbf{X}_i$, for any $d, d' \in \text{Supp}[D_i]$, the ATE of moving from d to d' is

$$\text{E}\big[\tau_i(d,d')\big] = \sum_{\mathbf{x}} \text{E}[Y_i \mid D_i = d', \mathbf{X}_i = \mathbf{x}]\Pr[\mathbf{X}_i = \mathbf{x}] - \sum_{\mathbf{x}} \text{E}[Y_i \mid D_i = d, \mathbf{X}_i = \mathbf{x}]\Pr[\mathbf{X}_i = \mathbf{x}].$$

The proof is completely analogous to the proof of Theorem 7.1.13. Since we can observe the random vector $(Y_i, D_i, \mathbf{X}_i)$, we can point identify $\text{E}[Y_i|D_i = d', \mathbf{X}_i = \mathbf{x}]$, $\text{E}[Y_i|D_i = d, \mathbf{X}_i = \mathbf{x}]$, and $\Pr[\mathbf{X}_i = \mathbf{x}]$. Thus, under ignorability, for any $d, d' \in \text{Supp}[D_i]$, $\text{E}[\tau_i(d,d')]$ is point identified. Likewise, the generalization of Theorem 7.1.14 (*The Conditional ATE under Strong Ignorability*) is: under strong ignorability, for any $d, d' \in \text{Supp}[D_i]$, the conditional average causal effect given $\mathbf{X}_i$ of moving from d to d' is

$$\text{E}\big[\tau_i(d,d') \,\big|\, \mathbf{X}_i\big] = \text{E}[Y_i \mid D_i = d', \mathbf{X}_i] - \text{E}[Y_i \mid D_i = d, \mathbf{X}_i].$$

Again, the proof is completely analogous to the proof of Theorem 7.1.14. Thus, under ignorability, for any $d, d' \in \text{Supp}[D_i]$ and any $\mathbf{x} \in \text{Supp}[\mathbf{X}_i]$, $\text{E}[\tau_i(d,d')|\mathbf{X}_i = \mathbf{x}]$ is point identified. The Law of Iterated Expectations then implies that for any $d, d' \in \text{Supp}[D_i]$, $\text{E}[\tau_i(d,d')]$ is also point identified under ignorability, as stated above.

Given the many possible causal contrasts that we could make (d and d' are arbitrary), we might ask how to summarize the causal relationship between D_i and Y_i. The most natural summary relates back to the average partial derivative (Definition 4.3.6). If we assume that $Y_i(d)$ is differentiable with respect to d, then the following definition allows us to derive a concise measure.

Definition 7.1.19. *Average Marginal Causal Effect*
The *average marginal causal effect* of D_i is

$$AMCE = \text{E}\left[\frac{\partial \text{E}[Y_i(D_i) \mid D_i, \mathbf{X}_i]}{\partial D_i}\right].$$

The Average Marginal Causal Effect is very simple to interpret: averaging over the entire distribution of D_i and $\mathbf{X}_i$, how much would we expect a small change in D_i to affect Y_i? Furthermore, under the conditional independence assumption, the CEF is causal, hence

$$AMCE = APD_{D_i} = \text{E}\left[\frac{\partial \text{E}[Y_i \mid D_i, \mathbf{X}_i]}{\partial D_i}\right].$$

In other words, under strong ignorability, the average partial derivative with respect to D_i is the average marginal causal effect of D_i. In the following section, where we consider estimation, we will not give further consideration to this generalized potential outcomes model. Generalizations to our results will largely carry through, albeit with more complexity, including working with treatment density functions instead of propensity scores.

7.2 ESTIMATION OF CAUSAL EFFECTS UNDER IGNORABILITY [6.2]

We have shown that, under random assignment, estimating $\mathrm{E}[\tau_i]$ is straightforward: the plug-in estimator is just the difference-in-means estimator. Under strong ignorability, estimation can become much more complex. In this section, we discuss several ways to implement the strong ignorability assumption to obtain estimates of the ATE.

7.2.1 Plug-In Estimation [6.2.1]

If we have discrete covariates, then under the strong ignorability assumption, we can again estimate $\mathrm{E}[\tau_i]$ with a simple plug-in estimator. Recall from Theorem 7.1.13 that, if $\mathbf{X}_i$ is discrete,

$$\begin{aligned}\mathrm{E}[\tau_i] &= \sum_{\mathbf{x}} \mathrm{E}[Y_i \mid D_i = 1, \mathbf{X}_i = \mathbf{x}] \Pr[\mathbf{X}_i = \mathbf{x}] \\ &\quad - \sum_{\mathbf{x}} \mathrm{E}[Y_i \mid D_i = 0, \mathbf{X}_i = \mathbf{x}] \Pr[\mathbf{X}_i = \mathbf{x}] \\ &= \sum_{\mathbf{x}} \big(\mathrm{E}[Y_i \mid D_i = 1, \mathbf{X}_i = \mathbf{x}] - \mathrm{E}[Y_i \mid D_i = 0, \mathbf{X}_i = \mathbf{x}]\big) \Pr[\mathbf{X}_i = \mathbf{x}].\end{aligned}$$

So the plug-in estimator is

$$\begin{aligned}\hat{\mathrm{E}}[\tau_i] &= \sum_{\mathbf{x} \in \widehat{\mathrm{Supp}}[\mathbf{X}_i]} \Big(\hat{\mathrm{E}}[Y_i \mid D_i = 1, \mathbf{X}_i = \mathbf{x}] - \hat{\mathrm{E}}[Y_i \mid D_i = 0, \mathbf{X}_i = \mathbf{x}]\Big) \widehat{\Pr}[\mathbf{X}_i = \mathbf{x}] \\ &= \sum_{\mathbf{x} \in \widehat{\mathrm{Supp}}[\mathbf{X}_i]} \left(\frac{\sum_{i=1}^n Y_i D_i \cdot \mathrm{I}(\mathbf{X}_i = \mathbf{x})}{\sum_{i=1}^n D_i \cdot \mathrm{I}(\mathbf{X}_i = \mathbf{x})} - \frac{\sum_{i=1}^n Y_i (1 - D_i) \cdot \mathrm{I}(\mathbf{X}_i = \mathbf{x})}{\sum_{i=1}^n (1 - D_i) \cdot \mathrm{I}(\mathbf{X}_i = \mathbf{x})} \right) \\ &\quad \cdot \frac{\sum_{i=1}^n \mathrm{I}(\mathbf{X}_i = \mathbf{x})}{n},\end{aligned}$$

where $\mathrm{I}(\cdot)$ is the indicator function and $\widehat{\mathrm{Supp}}[\mathbf{X}_i]$ is the set of all observed values of $\mathbf{X}_i$.[12] This estimator is sometimes known as the post-stratification estimator for causal inference, which is named after its analog in the context

12 This requires that we have at least one treated unit and one control unit with $\mathbf{X}_i = \mathbf{x}$ for every covariate profile $\mathbf{x} \in \widehat{\mathrm{Supp}}[\mathbf{X}_i]$, otherwise we will have a zero in the denominator. See Footnote 15.

of missing data. It can be seen as a weighted average of the difference-in-means estimators for units with the same covariate values, where the weights are the observed frequencies of those covariate profiles.

Example 7.2.1. *Plug-In Estimation of the ATE*
We return to Example 7.1.5 (*Causal Inference as a Missing Data Problem*), but now assume that we also observe a binary covariate X_i for every unit:

Unit	$Y_i(0)$	$Y_i(1)$	D_i	X_i
1	?	1	1	1
2	1	?	0	0
3	?	1	1	0
4	?	0	1	1
5	?	1	1	1
6	0	?	0	1

The above plug-in estimator assuming ignorability yields the estimate

$$\begin{aligned}\hat{\mathrm{E}}[\tau_i] &= \Big(\hat{\mathrm{E}}[Y_i|D_i=1,X_i=0]-\hat{\mathrm{E}}[Y_i|D_i=0,X_i=0]\Big)\widehat{\Pr}[X_i=0] \\ &\quad+\Big(\hat{\mathrm{E}}[Y_i|D_i=1,X_i=1]-\hat{\mathrm{E}}[Y_i|D_i=0,X_i=1]\Big)\widehat{\Pr}[X_i=1] \\ &= (1-1)\cdot\frac{2}{6}+\left(\frac{2}{3}-0\right)\cdot\frac{4}{6} \\ &= \frac{4}{9}.\end{aligned}$$

Note that this estimate differs from the random assignment-based estimate of $\frac{1}{4}$.

Like random assignment, we can think of strong ignorability as allowing us to impute the unobserved potential outcomes, only now we impute the missing potential outcome for each unit using the sample mean of units in the other treatment condition *with the same covariate values*. In Example 7.1.5, this yields

Unit	$Y_i(0)$	$Y_i(1)$	D_i	X_i
1	$\hat{\mathrm{E}}[Y_i(0)\|X_i=1]=0$	1	1	1
2	1	$\hat{\mathrm{E}}[Y_i(1)\|X_i=0]=1$	0	0
3	$\hat{\mathrm{E}}[Y_i(0)\|X_i=0]=1$	1	1	0
4	$\hat{\mathrm{E}}[Y_i(0)\|X_i=1]=0$	0	1	1
5	$\hat{\mathrm{E}}[Y_i(0)\|X_i=1]=0$	1	1	1
6	0	$\hat{\mathrm{E}}[Y_i(1)\|X_i=1]=\frac{2}{3}$	0	1

Then the sample means of $Y_i(1)$ and $Y_i(0)$ with the missing values imputed are $\frac{7}{9}$ and $\frac{1}{3}$, respectively, and so our estimate of $\mathrm{E}[\tau_i]$ is again $\frac{7}{9}-\frac{1}{3}=\frac{4}{9}$. △

Plug-in estimation of this type works when we have only a small number of possible covariate values. In such cases, the estimator is consistent under the usual plug-in regularity conditions. When we have many covariates, or continuous covariates, simple plug-in estimation generally is not feasible. In the remainder of this chapter, we discuss some other ways of estimating the ATE under strong ignorability.

7.2.2 Regression Estimation [6.2.2]

Recall Theorem 7.1.14: under strong ignorability, the conditional ATE given $\mathbf{X}_i$ is point identified as

$$\mathrm{E}[\tau_i|\mathbf{X}_i] = \mathrm{E}[Y_i|D_i = 1, \mathbf{X}_i] - \mathrm{E}[Y_i|D_i = 0, \mathbf{X}_i].$$

Under strong ignorability, the difference between $\mathrm{E}[Y_i|D_i = 1, \mathbf{X}_i]$ and $\mathrm{E}[Y_i|D_i = 0, \mathbf{X}_i]$ is equivalent to a causal effect. But notice that $\mathrm{E}[Y_i|D_i, \mathbf{X}_i]$ is a conditional expectation function (CEF). When strong ignorability holds, some features of the CEF of Y_i are imbued with a causal interpretation.

We have a readily available tool for estimating the CEF: ordinary least squares (OLS) regression consistently estimates the best linear predictor (BLP) of the CEF—where "best" means minimum mean squared error (MSE). Suppose we assumed that, at least to a first approximation,

$$\mathrm{E}[Y_i|D_i, \mathbf{X}_i] = \beta_0 + \beta_1 D_i + \mathbf{X}_i\boldsymbol{\beta}.$$

Then

$$\begin{aligned}\mathrm{E}[\tau_i|\mathbf{X}_i] &= \mathrm{E}[Y_i|D_i = 1, \mathbf{X}_i] - \mathrm{E}[Y_i|D_i = 0, \mathbf{X}_i] \\ &= \beta_0 + \beta_1 \cdot 1 + \mathbf{X}_i\boldsymbol{\beta} - \left(\beta_0 + \beta_1 \cdot 0 + \mathbf{X}_i\boldsymbol{\beta}\right) \\ &= \beta_1,\end{aligned}$$

so we can estimate the conditional ATE given $\mathbf{X}_i$ using the OLS coefficient estimate $\hat{\beta}_1$:

$$\hat{\mathrm{E}}[\tau_i|\mathbf{X}_i] = \hat{\beta}_1.$$

Then, by the Law of Iterated Expectations,

$$\begin{aligned}\mathrm{E}[\tau_i] &= \sum_{\mathbf{x}} \mathrm{E}[\tau_i|\mathbf{X}_i = \mathbf{x}] \Pr[\mathbf{X}_i = \mathbf{x}] \\ &= \sum_{\mathbf{x}} \beta_1 \Pr[\mathbf{X}_i = \mathbf{x}] \\ &= \beta_1 \sum_{\mathbf{x}} \Pr[\mathbf{X}_i = \mathbf{x}] \\ &= \beta_1 \cdot 1 \\ &= \beta_1,\end{aligned}$$

so we can likewise estimate the ATE with $\hat{\mathrm{E}}[\tau_i] = \hat{\beta}_1$. Thus, insofar as $\mathrm{E}[Y_i|D_i, \mathbf{X}_i] \approx \beta_0 + \beta_1 D_i + \mathbf{X}_i\boldsymbol{\beta}$, we can interpret $\hat{\beta}_1$ as a good approximation of the ATE. This is illustrated in the following example.

Example 7.2.2. *Causal Inference with OLS Regression*
Suppose we had the following data:

Unit	$Y_i(0)$	$Y_i(1)$	D_i	$X_{[1]i}$	$X_{[2]i}$
1	?	2	1	1	7
2	5	?	0	8	2
3	?	3	1	10	3
4	?	10	1	3	1
5	?	2	1	5	2
6	0	?	0	7	0

We want to fill in all the missing values with $\hat{\text{E}}[Y_i|D_i=d, X_{[1]i}=x_{[1]}, X_{[2]i}=x_{[2]}]$. We can see how we could do this using regression. We will start by assuming that, at least to a first approximation,

$$\text{E}[Y_i|D_i, X_{[1]i}, X_{[2]i}] = \beta_0 + \beta_1 D_i + \beta_2 X_{[1]i} + \beta_3 X_{[2]i}.$$

Then we could estimate the coefficients with OLS and use the resulting equation to impute the missing values:

Unit	$Y_i(0)$	$Y_i(1)$	D_i	$X_{[1]i}$	$X_{[2]i}$
1	$\hat{\beta}_0+\hat{\beta}_1\cdot 0+\hat{\beta}_2\cdot 1+\hat{\beta}_3\cdot 7$	2	1	1	7
2	5	$\hat{\beta}_0+\hat{\beta}_1\cdot 1+\hat{\beta}_2\cdot 8+\hat{\beta}_3\cdot 2$	0	8	2
3	$\hat{\beta}_0+\hat{\beta}_1\cdot 0+\hat{\beta}_2\cdot 9+\hat{\beta}_3\cdot 3$	3	1	9	3
4	$\hat{\beta}_0+\hat{\beta}_1\cdot 0+\hat{\beta}_2\cdot 3+\hat{\beta}_3\cdot 1$	10	1	3	1
5	$\hat{\beta}_0+\hat{\beta}_1\cdot 0+\hat{\beta}_2\cdot 5+\hat{\beta}_3\cdot 2$	2	1	5	2
6	0	$\hat{\beta}_0+\hat{\beta}_1\cdot 1+\hat{\beta}_2\cdot 7+\hat{\beta}_3\cdot 0$	0	7	0

(Remember: these are just expectations for units with the same covariate values; we cannot actually fill in the missing potential outcomes.) Equivalently, we could instead impute all the potential outcomes, which will yield the same estimate for $\text{E}[\tau_i]$ and is more straightforward to implement:

Unit	$Y_i(0)$	$Y_i(1)$	D_i	$X_{[1]i}$	$X_{[2]i}$
1	$\hat{\beta}_0+\hat{\beta}_1\cdot 0+\hat{\beta}_2\cdot 1+\hat{\beta}_3\cdot 7$	$\hat{\beta}_0+\hat{\beta}_1\cdot 1+\hat{\beta}_2\cdot 1+\hat{\beta}_3\cdot 7$	1	1	7
2	$\hat{\beta}_0+\hat{\beta}_1\cdot 0+\hat{\beta}_2\cdot 8+\hat{\beta}_3\cdot 2$	$\hat{\beta}_0+\hat{\beta}_1\cdot 1+\hat{\beta}_2\cdot 8+\hat{\beta}_3\cdot 2$	0	8	2
3	$\hat{\beta}_0+\hat{\beta}_1\cdot 0+\hat{\beta}_2\cdot 9+\hat{\beta}_3\cdot 3$	$\hat{\beta}_0+\hat{\beta}_1\cdot 1+\hat{\beta}_2\cdot 9+\hat{\beta}_3\cdot 3$	1	9	3
4	$\hat{\beta}_0+\hat{\beta}_1\cdot 0+\hat{\beta}_2\cdot 3+\hat{\beta}_3\cdot 1$	$\hat{\beta}_0+\hat{\beta}_1\cdot 1+\hat{\beta}_2\cdot 3+\hat{\beta}_3\cdot 1$	1	3	1
5	$\hat{\beta}_0+\hat{\beta}_1\cdot 0+\hat{\beta}_2\cdot 5+\hat{\beta}_3\cdot 2$	$\hat{\beta}_0+\hat{\beta}_1\cdot 1+\hat{\beta}_2\cdot 5+\hat{\beta}_3\cdot 2$	1	5	2
6	$\hat{\beta}_0+\hat{\beta}_1\cdot 0+\hat{\beta}_2\cdot 7+\hat{\beta}_3\cdot 0$	$\hat{\beta}_0+\hat{\beta}_1\cdot 1+\hat{\beta}_2\cdot 7+\hat{\beta}_3\cdot 0$	0	7	0

In either case, the estimate of $\text{E}[\tau_i]$ is just the difference-in-means estimator with the imputed values. This estimator would be consistent if ignorability held and if the functional form of the CEF were in fact $\text{E}[Y_i|D_i, X_{[1]i}, X_{[2]i}] = \beta_0 + \beta_1 D_i + \beta_2 X_{[1]i} + \beta_3 X_{[2]i}$. In the case without interactions or polynomials, the resulting estimate of $\text{E}[\tau_i]$ is just $\hat{\beta}_1$. △

When n is small, we are likely to want to fit a simple linear approximation to avoid overfitting (Section 4.3.2). Our data are too micronumerous to fit a more complicated model. In larger samples, we could use polynomials, interactions or any other way of accounting for nonlinearity discussed in Section 4.3. One particularly common approach—closely mirroring the approach from missing data—is to fit separate (or *unpooled*) regression models across the treatment and control groups. This specification is logically equivalent to running a single regression model with D_i interacted with all elements of $\mathbf{X}_i$, and yields consistent estimates when $\text{E}[Y_i|D_i = d, \mathbf{X}_i] = \beta_{d0} + \mathbf{X}_i\boldsymbol{\beta}_d$, $\forall d \in \{0,1\}$.

In general, to quickly produce an estimate of the ATE following regression estimation, it is easiest to take predicted values for all potential outcomes and then take the difference in means. The logic of this procedure is clear from the plug-in principle:

$$\text{E}[\tau_i] = \text{E}[Y_i(1)] - \text{E}[Y_i(0)] = \text{E}\big[\text{E}[Y_i|D_i = 1, \mathbf{X}_i]\big] - \text{E}\big[\text{E}[Y_i|D_i = 0, \mathbf{X}_i]\big],$$

for which a natural plug-in estimator is the difference in means of predicted values. We refer to this estimator as the regression estimator for causal inference.

Definition 7.2.3. *Regression Estimator for Causal Inference*
Let $Y_i(0)$, $Y_i(1)$, and D_i be random variables with $\text{Supp}[D_i] = \{0,1\}$. Let $Y_i = Y_i(1) \cdot D_i + Y_i(0) \cdot (1 - D_i)$ and $\tau_i = Y_i(1) - Y_i(0)$, and let $\mathbf{X}_i$ be a random vector. Then, given n i.i.d. observations of $(Y_i, D_i, \mathbf{X}_i)$, the *regression estimator* for $\text{E}[\tau_i]$ is

$$\begin{aligned}\hat{\text{E}}_R[\tau_i] &= \hat{\text{E}}\big[Y_i(1)\big] - \hat{\text{E}}\big[Y_i(0)\big] \\ &= \frac{1}{n}\sum_{i=1}^{n} \hat{\text{E}}[Y_i|D_i = 1, \mathbf{X}_i] - \frac{1}{n}\sum_{i=1}^{n} \hat{\text{E}}[Y_i|D_i = 0, \mathbf{X}_i],\end{aligned}$$

where $\hat{\text{E}}[Y_i|D_i = d, \mathbf{X}_i = \mathbf{x}]$ is an estimator of the CEF.

As the regression estimator is a plug-in estimator, we have a good sense of its theoretical properties: the estimator will behave well when the CEF is well characterized by the specification of the regression and the usual plug-in regularity conditions hold.

In this section, we have established conditions for using regression to obtain principled estimates of causal relationships. This result is at the heart of the difference between our approach to causal inference and the standard treatment in econometrics and statistical modeling. We have established a basis for causal inference with regression *without*

- making any assumptions about an error distribution (such as homoskedasticity and normality),
- assuming linearity (except as an approximation that can be made arbitrarily flexible), or
- discussing "exogeneity," "endogeneity," "omitted variables bias," or "errors uncorrelated with regressors."

We have invoked a *substantive* assumption about the relationship between potential outcomes and treatment. This assumption is strong, but we need not conflate this essential identification assumption with the details of statistical specification.

7.2.3 Maximum Likelihood Plug-In Estimation of Causal Effects

Using the tools developed in Section 5.2.4 (*Plug-In Estimation and Conditional Expectation Functions*), it is possible to directly wed the causal identification assumptions here to the parametric models discussed in Chapter 5. Suppose that we have strong ignorability and further suppose that we have a parametric model that is true: $g(y,(d,\mathbf{x}),\boldsymbol{\theta}) = f_{Y_i|(D_i,\mathbf{X}_i)}(y|(d,\mathbf{x}))$. Then it is the case that all average potential outcomes over the support of D_i are point identified, and can be written in terms of the parametric model. The average potential outcome when $D_i = d$ is

$$\begin{aligned} \mathrm{E}\big[Y_i(d)\big] &= \int_{-\infty}^{\infty} \mathrm{E}[Y_i|D_i = d, \mathbf{X}_i = \mathbf{x}] f_{\mathbf{X}_i}(\mathbf{x}) d\mathbf{x} \\ &= \int_{-\infty}^{\infty} \left(\int_{-\infty}^{\infty} y g\big(y,(d,\mathbf{x}),\boldsymbol{\theta}\big) dy \right) f_{\mathbf{X}_i}(\mathbf{x}) d\mathbf{x}, \end{aligned}$$

where the first equality holds due to ignorability, and the second holds due to proper specification of the parametric model.

Recall that Definition 7.2.3 (*Regression Estimator for Causal Inference*) does not exclude estimates of the CEF produced by other means. Thus, combining Definition 5.2.10 (*Maximum Likelihood Plug-In Estimator*) and Definition 7.2.3, we can see that the maximum likelihood plug-in estimator for $\mathrm{E}[Y_i(d)]$ is computed by substituting $\hat{\boldsymbol{\theta}}_{ML}$ for $\boldsymbol{\theta}$ and replacing the expected value with respect to $\mathbf{X}_i$ with a sample mean:

$$\hat{\mathrm{E}}\big[Y_i(d)\big] = \frac{1}{n}\sum_{i=1}^{n}\left(\int_{-\infty}^{\infty} y g\big(y,(d,\mathbf{x}),\hat{\boldsymbol{\theta}}_{ML}\big) dy \right).$$

The ML plug-in estimator for $\mathrm{E}[\tau_i]$ is therefore given by

$$\hat{\mathrm{E}}_{ML}[\tau_i] = \frac{1}{n}\sum_{i=1}^{n}\left(\int_{-\infty}^{\infty} yg\big(y,(1,\mathbf{X}_i),\hat{\boldsymbol{\theta}}_{ML}\big)dy - \int_{-\infty}^{\infty} yg\big(y,(0,\mathbf{X}_i),\hat{\boldsymbol{\theta}}_{ML}\big)dy\right).$$

If the parametric model is correct, and the usual plug-in regularity conditions hold, maximum likelihood plug-in estimation works as usual here.

7.2.4 Matching [6.2.3]

The most common, but certainly not only, propensity score-based method for causal inference is *propensity score matching*, an estimator analogous to hot-deck imputation. There are many types of matching, but we will discuss just one type: one-to-one, nearest-neighbor, with-replacement, propensity score matching. For the moment, we will ignore the need to estimate propensity scores and assume that they are known. (We consider estimation of propensity scores in the following section.)

Example 7.2.4. *Propensity Score Matching*
Suppose we had the following data:

Unit	$Y_i(0)$	$Y_i(1)$	D_i	$X_{[1]i}$	$X_{[2]i}$	$p_D(\mathbf{X}_i)$
1	?	2	1	1	7	0.33
2	5	?	0	8	2	0.14
3	?	3	1	10	3	0.73
4	?	10	1	3	1	0.35
5	?	2	1	5	2	0.78
6	0	?	0	7	0	0.70

Assume that strong ignorability holds and that our goal is to estimate $\mathrm{E}[\tau_i]$. By Theorem 7.1.16 (*Strong Ignorability and the Propensity Score*), strong ignorability and the potential outcomes model imply that

$$\begin{aligned}\mathrm{E}\big[Y_i(0)\,\big|\,D_i=1,p_D(\mathbf{X}_i)\big] &= \mathrm{E}\big[Y_i(0)\,\big|\,D_i=0,p_D(\mathbf{X}_i)\big]\\ &= \mathrm{E}\big[Y_i\,\big|\,D_i=0,p_D(\mathbf{X}_i)\big]\end{aligned}$$

and

$$\begin{aligned}\mathrm{E}\big[Y_i(1)\,\big|\,D_i=0,p_D(\mathbf{X}_i)\big] &= \mathrm{E}\big[Y_i(1)\,\big|\,D_i=1,p_D(\mathbf{X}_i)\big]\\ &= \mathrm{E}\big[Y_i\,\big|\,D_i=1,p_D(\mathbf{X}_i)\big],\end{aligned}$$

so we can impute the missing potential outcomes with estimates of $\mathrm{E}[Y_i|D_i = d,p_D(\mathbf{X}_i)]$:

Unit	$Y_i(0)$	$Y_i(1)$	D_i	$X_{[1]i}$	$X_{[2]i}$	$p_D(\mathbf{X}_i)$
1	$\hat{\text{E}}[Y_i \mid D_i = 0, p_D(\mathbf{X}_i) = 0.33]$	2	1	1	7	0.33
2	5	$\hat{\text{E}}[Y_i \mid D_i = 1, p_D(\mathbf{X}_i) = 0.14]$	0	8	2	0.14
3	$\hat{\text{E}}[Y_i \mid D_i = 0, p_D(\mathbf{X}_i) = 0.73]$	3	1	10	3	0.73
4	$\hat{\text{E}}[Y_i \mid D_i = 0, p_D(\mathbf{X}_i) = 0.35]$	10	1	3	1	0.35
5	$\hat{\text{E}}[Y_i \mid D_i = 0, p_D(\mathbf{X}_i) = 0.78]$	2	1	5	2	0.78
6	0	$\hat{\text{E}}[Y_i \mid D_i = 1, p_D(\mathbf{X}_i) = 0.70]$	0	7	0	0.70

Then, if our estimator of $\text{E}[Y_i \mid D_i = d, p_D(\mathbf{X}_i) = p_D(\mathbf{x})]$ is consistent, the difference in means with the missing potential outcomes imputed will be a consistent estimator of the ATE.

There are many imputation-type estimators for causal inference that exploit ignorability. (Regression is itself an imputation estimator.) The procedure for (one-to-one, nearest-neighbor) matching is perhaps the simplest possible: for each treated unit, find the control unit that is closest on $p_D(\mathbf{X}_i)$ and use that unit's outcome to fill in the missing control potential outcome for the treated unit. Likewise, for each control unit, find the treated unit that is closest on $p_D(\mathbf{X}_i)$ and use that unit's outcome to fill in the missing treatment potential outcome for the control unit.

In this example, this yields

Unit	$Y_i(0)$	$Y_i(1)$	D_i	$X_{[1]i}$	$X_{[2]i}$	$p_D(\mathbf{X}_i)$
1	5	2	1	1	7	0.33
2	5	2	0	8	2	0.14
3	0	3	1	10	3	0.73
4	5	10	1	3	1	0.35
5	0	2	1	5	2	0.78
6	0	3	0	7	0	0.70

So the matching estimate of $\text{E}[\tau_i]$ is $\frac{22}{6} - \frac{15}{6} = \frac{7}{6} \approx 1.17$. △

All matching estimators are based on some variant of this logic. Some versions match on some other summary metric of $\mathbf{X}_i$. Some do one-to-k matching. Some choose observations to empirically maximize a measure of the balance of the matched groups. Some even choose, whenever possible, observations that *exactly* match on all covariates—though of course this requires, at minimum, that $\mathbf{X}_i$ be discrete.

Why is one-to-one, nearest-neighbor matching not such a great idea, even when we assume strong ignorability? Why would we not want to just use the outcome for the closest unit in the other treatment condition to estimate a missing potential outcome? Intuitively, matching only uses a small amount of the information available to impute the missing potential outcomes. In the above example, we used $Y_1(1) = 2$ to impute $Y_2(1)$ because $P_1 = 0.33$ is closest to $P_2 = 0.14$. But $P_4 = 0.35$ is almost as close to P_1, so $Y_4(1) = 10$ probably also gives us some information about $E[Y_i(1)|p_D(\mathbf{X}_i) = 0.14]$. So why would we ignore $Y_4(1)$ entirely and just use $Y_1(1)$ as our guess for $Y_2(1)$?

The problems with this method are exacerbated when the treatment propensity function is unknown. In the following section, we consider estimation of propensity scores. However, matching estimators are *not* plug-in estimators, and so their properties do not operate quite as expected. For example, even if we have a consistent estimator of $p_D(\mathbf{X}_i)$, matching with estimated propensity scores is not generally root-n consistent—the bias (and therefore MSE) of the estimator shrinks "too slowly" as n grows large—and, thus, the usual methods for constructing confidence intervals, *including the bootstrap*, do not generally work.[13]

7.2.5 Maximum Likelihood Plug-In Estimation of Propensity Scores [6.2.4]

Estimation of propensity scores is unchanged from missing data. We reiterate the discussion here. Recall from Definition 7.1.15 that the propensity score $p_D(\mathbf{x}) = \Pr[D_i = 1|\mathbf{X}_i = \mathbf{x}]$, and, from Example 2.1.3, that $\Pr[D_i = 1|\mathbf{X}_i = \mathbf{x}] = E[D_i|\mathbf{X}_i = \mathbf{x}]$. Therefore, estimating the treatment propensity function is equivalent to estimating the CEF of D_i with respect to $\mathbf{X}_i$. Just as with missing data, this is a case where OLS would not be suitable for estimating an unknown CEF. A linear approximation could predict propensity score estimates that are greater than one or less than zero. A natural path forward lies with a binary choice model (Section 5.1.2) that respects the constraints on the distribution of D_i.

Suppose now that we have a binary choice model for treatment with mean function h. If this model is true, then following Section 5.2.4, we can use a ML estimator for the propensity score, $\hat{p}_D(\mathbf{x}) = h(\mathbf{x}\hat{\boldsymbol{\beta}}_{ML})$. If the binary choice model is true, then, under the usual plug-in regularity conditions, $\hat{p}_D(\mathbf{x})$ will be consistent for $p_D(\mathbf{x})$. As with missing data, if the model is not true, then our propensity score estimates will only be as good as our approximation permits. Again, with large n, we can use polynomials, interactions, mixture models, or other relaxations of the model in order to obtain a better approximation. Regardless of the exact specification, we will assume as we proceed that we are using an ML plug-in estimate from a binary choice model, $\hat{p}_D(\mathbf{x})$, for our plug-in estimates, though our results do not depend on this.

7.2.6 Weighting Estimators [6.2.5]

Matching is not the only way to use the propensity score to estimate $E[\tau_i]$. Much as they do in the case of missing data, inverse probability–weighted (IPW) estimators provide one such method. Before we can describe these estimators, we first establish an important population result. Transforming

13 See, e.g., Abadie and Imbens (2008).

the outcomes by weighting by $\frac{1}{p_D(\mathbf{X}_i)}$ (if in treatment) or $\frac{1}{1-p_D(\mathbf{X}_i)}$ (if in control) allows us to write the ATE as a simple expected value.

Theorem 7.2.5. *Reweighting under Strong Ignorability*
Let $Y_i(0)$, $Y_i(1)$, and D_i be random variables with $\text{Supp}[D_i] = \{0,1\}$. Let $Y_i = Y_i(1) \cdot D_i + Y_i(0) \cdot (1 - D_i)$ and $\tau_i = Y_i(1) - Y_i(0)$, and let $\mathbf{X}_i$ be a random vector. Then, if D_i is strongly ignorable conditional on $\mathbf{X}_i$,

$$\text{E}[\tau_i] = \text{E}\left[\frac{Y_i D_i}{p_D(\mathbf{X}_i)} - \frac{Y_i(1-D_i)}{1-p_D(\mathbf{X}_i)}\right].$$

Proof: By definition,

$$\text{E}\left[\frac{Y_i D_i}{p_D(\mathbf{X}_i)}\middle|\mathbf{X}_i\right] = \text{E}\left[Y_i \cdot \frac{D_i}{\Pr[D_i = 1|\mathbf{X}_i]}\middle|\mathbf{X}_i\right],$$

and by the potential outcomes model,

$$\text{E}\left[Y_i \cdot \frac{D_i}{\Pr[D_i = 1|\mathbf{X}_i]}\middle|\mathbf{X}_i\right] = \text{E}\left[Y_i(1) \cdot \frac{D_i}{\Pr[D_i = 1|\mathbf{X}_i]}\middle|\mathbf{X}_i\right].$$

Then, since strong ignorability holds, $Y_i(1) \perp\!\!\!\perp D_i|\mathbf{X}_i$, so

$$\begin{aligned}
\text{E}\left[Y_i(1) \cdot \frac{D_i}{\Pr[D_i = 1|\mathbf{X}_i]}\middle|\mathbf{X}_i\right] &= \text{E}\big[Y_i(1)\big|\mathbf{X}_i\big] \cdot \text{E}\left[\frac{D_i}{\Pr[D_i = 1|\mathbf{X}_i]}\middle|\mathbf{X}_i\right] \\
&= \text{E}\big[Y_i(1)\big|\mathbf{X}_i\big] \cdot \frac{\text{E}[D_i|\mathbf{X}_i]}{\Pr[D_i = 1|\mathbf{X}_i]} \\
&= \text{E}\big[Y_i(1)\big|\mathbf{X}_i\big] \cdot \frac{\Pr[D_i = 1|\mathbf{X}_i]}{\Pr[D_i = 1|\mathbf{X}_i]} \\
&= \text{E}\big[Y_i(1)\big|\mathbf{X}_i\big].
\end{aligned}$$

Thus,

$$\text{E}\left[\frac{Y_i D_i}{p_D(\mathbf{X}_i)}\middle|\mathbf{X}_i\right] = \text{E}\big[Y_i(1)\big|\mathbf{X}_i\big].$$

So, by the Law of Iterated Expectations,

$$\text{E}\big[Y_i(1)\big] = \text{E}\Big[\text{E}\big[Y_i(1)\big|\mathbf{X}_i\big]\Big] = \text{E}\left[\text{E}\left[\frac{Y_i D_i}{p_D(\mathbf{X}_i)}\middle|\mathbf{X}_i\right]\right] = \text{E}\left[\frac{Y_i D_i}{p_D(\mathbf{X}_i)}\right],$$

and by the same logic,

$$\text{E}\big[Y_i(0)\big] = \text{E}\Big[\text{E}\big[Y_i(0)\big|\mathbf{X}_i\big]\Big] = \text{E}\left[\text{E}\left[\frac{Y_i(1-D_i)}{1-p_D(\mathbf{X}_i)}\middle|\mathbf{X}_i\right]\right] = \text{E}\left[\frac{Y_i(1-D_i)}{1-p_D(\mathbf{X}_i)}\right].$$

Thus, by linearity of expectations,

$$\begin{aligned} \mathrm{E}[\tau_i] &= \mathrm{E}\big[Y_i(1) - Y_i(0)\big] \\ &= \mathrm{E}\big[Y_i(1)\big] - \mathrm{E}\big[Y_i(0)\big] \\ &= \mathrm{E}\left[\frac{Y_i D_i}{p_D(\mathbf{X}_i)}\right] - \mathrm{E}\left[\frac{Y_i(1-D_i)}{1-p_D(\mathbf{X}_i)}\right] \\ &= \mathrm{E}\left[\frac{Y_i D_i}{p_D(\mathbf{X}_i)} - \frac{Y_i(1-D_i)}{1-p_D(\mathbf{X}_i)}\right]. \quad \square \end{aligned}$$

The IPW estimator is again a plug-in estimator: we replace $p_D(\mathbf{X}_i)$ with an estimate thereof, $\hat{p}_D(\mathbf{X}_i)$ (as in the previous section), and substitute sample means for expected values.

Definition 7.2.6. *Inverse Probability–Weighted (IPW) Estimator for Causal Inference*
Let $Y_i(0)$, $Y_i(1)$, and D_i be random variables with $\text{Supp}[D_i] = \{0,1\}$. Let $Y_i = Y_i(1) \cdot D_i + Y_i(0) \cdot (1 - D_i)$ and $\tau_i = Y_i(1) - Y_i(0)$, and let $\mathbf{X}_i$ be a random vector. Then, given n i.i.d. observations of $(Y_i, D_i, \mathbf{X}_i)$, the *inverse probability–weighted estimator* for $\mathrm{E}[\tau_i]$ is

$$\hat{\mathrm{E}}_{IPW}[\tau_i] = \frac{1}{n}\sum_{i=1}^{n}\left(\frac{Y_i D_i}{\hat{p}_D(\mathbf{X}_i)} - \frac{Y_i(1-D_i)}{1-\hat{p}_D(\mathbf{X}_i)}\right).$$

The IPW estimator weights every treated unit's outcome by the inverse of its probability of being in treatment and every control unit's outcome by the inverse of its probability of being in control, and then takes the difference in means (with missing potential outcomes effectively set equal to zero).

The logic behind IPW estimators for causal inference is the same as for missing data. Suppose that some units are very unlikely to be assigned to treatment, so they have small propensity scores. These units are likely to be underrepresented in the treatment group and overrepresented in the control group, so we want to up-weight them when they are in treatment and down-weight them when they are in control. The reverse goes for units that are unlikely to be assigned to control: we want to up-weight them when they are in control and down-weight them when they are in treatment. In the case where we have a discrete and finite number of values for $\mathbf{X}_i$, the IPW estimator is logically equivalent to the plug-in estimator from Section 7.2.1 (*Plug-In Estimation*).

The IPW estimator has high variability (that is, its standard error is large) with small samples. An alternative that performs better in practice is the causal inference version of the stabilized IPW estimator.

Definition 7.2.7. *Stabilized IPW Estimator for Causal Inference*
Let $Y_i(0)$, $Y_i(1)$, and D_i be random variables with $\text{Supp}[D_i] = \{0,1\}$. Let $Y_i = Y_i(1) \cdot D_i + Y_i(0) \cdot (1 - D_i)$ and $\tau_i = Y_i(1) - Y_i(0)$, and let $\mathbf{X}_i$ be a random vector. Then, given n i.i.d. observations of $(Y_i, D_i, \mathbf{X}_i)$, the *stabilized IPW estimator* for $\text{E}[\tau_i]$ is

$$\hat{\text{E}}_{SIPW}[\tau_i] = \frac{\frac{1}{n}\sum_{i=1}^{n} \frac{Y_i D_i}{\hat{p}_D(\mathbf{X}_i)}}{\frac{1}{n}\sum_{i=1}^{n} \frac{D_i}{\hat{p}_D(\mathbf{X}_i)}} - \frac{\frac{1}{n}\sum_{i=1}^{n} \frac{Y_i(1-D_i)}{1-\hat{p}_D(\mathbf{X}_i)}}{\frac{1}{n}\sum_{i=1}^{n} \frac{1-D_i}{1-\hat{p}_D(\mathbf{X}_i)}}.$$

When $\hat{p}_D(\mathbf{X}_i)$ converges (in an appropriate functional sense) to $p_D(\mathbf{X}_i)$, then the denominator of each fraction will converge in probability to one. To see this, note that, with the true propensity score, $\text{E}[\frac{D_i}{p_D(\mathbf{X}_i)}] = \text{E}[\frac{1-D_i}{1-p_D(\mathbf{X}_i)}] = 1$. However, this normalization provides benefits in estimation. In the case where we draw an unusually large number of units where $p_D(\mathbf{X}_i)$ is large or small, the stabilized IPW estimator's denominators adjust accordingly. Because the stabilized IPW estimator accounts for this between-sample variation in $\sum_{i=1}^{n} \frac{1}{p_D(\mathbf{X}_i)}$ and $\sum_{i=1}^{n} \frac{1}{1-p_D(\mathbf{X}_i)}$, it typically confers efficiency gains over the IPW estimator in practice. Valid asymptotic inference for IPW estimators can be achieved under strong ignorability, proper specification of $\hat{p}_D(\mathbf{X}_i)$, and the usual plug-in regularity conditions via the bootstrap, re-estimating the propensity scores in each bootstrap sample.

7.2.7 Doubly Robust Estimators [6.2.6]

Finally, as with missing data, it is also possible to combine regression with weighting specifications using a doubly robust (DR) estimator. All our results from the case of missing data carry through naturally. Under strong ignorability, these approaches yield consistent estimates when either the regression specification or the propensity score specification is correct. Before we state this result, we note an important population result.

Theorem 7.2.8. *Double Robustness Theorem for Causal Inference*
Let $Y_i(0)$, $Y_i(1)$, and D_i be random variables with $\text{Supp}[D_i] = \{0,1\}$. Let $Y_i = Y_i(1) \cdot D_i + Y_i(0) \cdot (1 - D_i)$ and $\tau_i = Y_i(1) - Y_i(0)$, and let $\mathbf{X}_i$ be a random vector. Let $\tilde{\text{E}}[Y_i|D_i = d, \mathbf{X}_i = \mathbf{x}]$ be an approximation of the CEF evaluated at $D_i = d$ and $\mathbf{X}_i = \mathbf{x}$, and let $\tilde{p}_D(\mathbf{X}_i)$ be an approximation of the propensity score. If strong ignorability holds and if either

(i) $\tilde{E}[Y_i|D_i = d, \mathbf{X}_i = \mathbf{x}] = E[Y_i|D_i = d, \mathbf{X}_i = \mathbf{x}], \forall d \in \{0,1\}, \mathbf{x} \in \text{Supp}[\mathbf{X}_i]$, and $\exists \epsilon > 0$ such that $\epsilon < \tilde{p}_D(\mathbf{x}) < 1 - \epsilon$,

or

(ii) $\tilde{p}_D(\mathbf{x}) = p_D(\mathbf{x}), \forall \mathbf{x} \in \text{Supp}[\mathbf{X}_i]$,

then

$$E[\tau_i] = E\left[\tilde{E}[Y_i|D_i = 1, \mathbf{X}_i] + \frac{D_i\left(Y_i - \tilde{E}[Y_i|D_i = 1, \mathbf{X}_i]\right)}{\tilde{p}_D(\mathbf{X}_i)} - \tilde{E}[Y_i|D_i = 0, \mathbf{X}_i] - \frac{(1 - D_i)\left(Y_i - \tilde{E}[Y_i|D_i = 0, \mathbf{X}_i]\right)}{1 - \tilde{p}_D(\mathbf{X}_i)}\right].$$

Proof: We will show that

$$E\left[Y_i(1)\right] = E\left[\tilde{E}[Y_i|D_i = 1, \mathbf{X}_i] + \frac{D_i\left(Y_i - \tilde{E}[Y_i|D_i = 1, \mathbf{X}_i]\right)}{\tilde{p}_D(\mathbf{X}_i)}\right].$$

To consider case (i), suppose that $\tilde{E}[Y_i|D_i = d, \mathbf{X}_i = \mathbf{x}] = E[Y_i|D_i = d, \mathbf{X}_i = \mathbf{x}], \forall d \in \{0,1\}, \mathbf{x} \in \text{Supp}[\mathbf{X}_i]$. Then we have

$$\begin{aligned}
&E\left[\tilde{E}[Y_i|D_i = 1, \mathbf{X}_i] + \frac{D_i\left(Y_i - \tilde{E}[Y_i|D_i = 1, \mathbf{X}_i]\right)}{\tilde{p}_D(\mathbf{X}_i)}\right] \\
&\quad = E\left[E[Y_i|D_i = 1, \mathbf{X}_i] + \frac{D_i\left(Y_i - E[Y_i|D_i = 1, \mathbf{X}_i]\right)}{\tilde{p}_D(\mathbf{X}_i)}\right] \\
&\quad = E\left[E[Y_i|D_i = 1, \mathbf{X}_i]\right] + E\left[\frac{D_i Y_i}{\tilde{p}_D(\mathbf{X}_i)}\right] - E\left[\frac{D_i E[Y_i|D_i = 1, \mathbf{X}_i]}{\tilde{p}_D(\mathbf{X}_i)}\right] \\
&\quad = E\left[E[Y_i|D_i = 1, \mathbf{X}_i]\right] + E\left[\frac{D_i E[Y_i|D_i = 1, \mathbf{X}_i]}{\tilde{p}_D(\mathbf{X}_i)}\right] \\
&\qquad - E\left[\frac{D_i E[Y_i|D_i = 1, \mathbf{X}_i]}{\tilde{p}_D(\mathbf{X}_i)}\right] \\
&\quad = E\left[E[Y_i|D_i = 1, \mathbf{X}_i]\right] \\
&\quad = E\left[Y_i(1)\right],
\end{aligned}$$

where the third equality follows from the Law of Iterated Expectations and the fifth follows from strong ignorability (see Theorem 7.1.13).

To consider case (ii), suppose instead that $\tilde{p}_D(\mathbf{x}) = p_D(\mathbf{x}), \forall \mathbf{x} \in \text{Supp}[\mathbf{X}_i]$. Then

$$\begin{aligned}
&\mathrm{E}\left[\tilde{\mathrm{E}}[Y_i|D_i=1,\mathbf{X}_i] + \frac{D_i\big(Y_i - \tilde{\mathrm{E}}[Y_i|D_i=1,\mathbf{X}_i]\big)}{\tilde{p}_D(\mathbf{X}_i)}\right] \\
&\quad = \mathrm{E}\left[\tilde{\mathrm{E}}[Y_i|D_i=1,\mathbf{X}_i] + \frac{D_i\big(Y_i - \tilde{\mathrm{E}}[Y_i|D_i=1,\mathbf{X}_i]\big)}{p_D(\mathbf{X}_i)}\right] \\
&\quad = \mathrm{E}\Big[\tilde{\mathrm{E}}[Y_i|D_i=1,\mathbf{X}_i]\Big] + \mathrm{E}\left[\frac{D_iY_i}{p_D(\mathbf{X}_i)}\right] - \mathrm{E}\left[\frac{D_i\tilde{\mathrm{E}}[Y_i|D_i=1,\mathbf{X}_i]}{p_D(\mathbf{X}_i)}\right] \\
&\quad = \mathrm{E}\Big[\tilde{\mathrm{E}}[Y_i|D_i=1,\mathbf{X}_i]\Big] + \mathrm{E}\left[\frac{D_iY_i}{p_D(\mathbf{X}_i)}\right] - \mathrm{E}\Big[\tilde{\mathrm{E}}[Y_i|D_i=1,\mathbf{X}_i]\Big] \\
&\quad = \mathrm{E}\left[\frac{D_iY_i}{p_D(\mathbf{X}_i)}\right] \\
&\quad = \mathrm{E}\big[Y_i(1)\big].
\end{aligned}$$

All results carry through analogously to $\mathrm{E}[Y_i(0)]$, and linearity of expectations completes the result. □

As with missing data, the Double Robustness Theorem establishes that if either the approximation of the CEF or the approximation of the treatment propensity function are exactly correct, then we can write the average treatment effect in terms of simple expected values of the observable data and the approximations. This result motivates a plug-in estimator, obtained by replacing expected values with sample means, $\tilde{\mathrm{E}}[Y_i|D_i=d,\mathbf{X}_i=\mathbf{x}]$ with some estimate $\hat{\mathrm{E}}[Y_i|D_i=d,\mathbf{X}_i=\mathbf{x}]$, and $\tilde{p}_D(\mathbf{X}_i)$ with some estimate $\hat{p}_D(\mathbf{X}_i)$.

Definition 7.2.9. *Doubly Robust (DR) Estimator for Causal Inference*
Let $Y_i(0)$, $Y_i(1)$, and D_i be random variables with $\text{Supp}[D_i] = \{0,1\}$. Let $Y_i = Y_i(1) \cdot D_i + Y_i(0) \cdot (1 - D_i)$ and $\tau_i = Y_i(1) - Y_i(0)$, and let $\mathbf{X}_i$ be a random vector. Then, given n i.i.d. observations of $(Y_i, D_i, \mathbf{X}_i)$, the *doubly robust estimator* is

$$\begin{aligned}
\hat{\mathrm{E}}_{DR}[\tau_i] = {} & \frac{1}{n}\sum_{i=1}^{n}\hat{\mathrm{E}}[Y_i|D_i=1,\mathbf{X}_i] + \frac{1}{n}\sum_{i=1}^{n}\frac{D_i\big(Y_i - \hat{\mathrm{E}}[Y_i|D_i=1,\mathbf{X}_i]\big)}{\hat{p}_D(\mathbf{X}_i)} \\
& - \frac{1}{n}\sum_{i=1}^{n}\hat{\mathrm{E}}[Y_i|D_i=0,\mathbf{X}_i] - \frac{1}{n}\sum_{i=1}^{n}\frac{(1-D_i)\big(Y_i - \hat{\mathrm{E}}[Y_i|D_i=0,\mathbf{X}_i]\big)}{1-\hat{p}_D(\mathbf{X}_i)},
\end{aligned}$$

where, $\forall d \in \{0,1\}$, $\hat{\mathrm{E}}[Y_i|D_i=d,\mathbf{X}_i]$ is an estimator for $\mathrm{E}[Y_i|D_i=d,\mathbf{X}_i]$, and $\hat{p}_D(\mathbf{X}_i)$ is an estimator for $p_D(\mathbf{X}_i)$.

The DR estimator can be decomposed much as in the case of missing data. The first term, $\frac{1}{n}\sum_{i=1}^{n}\hat{\mathrm{E}}[Y_i|D_i = 1, \mathbf{X}_i]$, is a standard regression estimator from Section 7.2.2 (*Regression Estimation*). The second term, $\frac{1}{n}\sum_{i=1}^{n}\frac{D_i(Y_i-\hat{\mathrm{E}}[Y_i|D_i=1,\mathbf{X}_i])}{\hat{p}_D(\mathbf{X}_i)}$, is an IPW estimator correcting for any unusual deviations in the actual data from the regression estimate. Analogous calculations carry through the latter two sums. As a plug-in estimator, if the conditions for Theorem 7.2.8 and the usual plug-in regularity conditions hold, the DR estimator can be used in the usual manner, with the bootstrap available for inference. The DR estimator often provides a practical solution to the statistical problems posed by implementing the strong ignorability assumption.

7.2.8 Placebo Testing

Readers may ask: are there any ways to *test* strong ignorability? The answer is a (somewhat qualified) no: although some assumptions can be tested, the conditional independence assumption cannot directly be tested. Because of the Fundamental Problem of Causal Inference, we can *never* observe whether the distributions of potential outcomes for treated units are different from those of control units (conditional on covariates).

However, depending on the substance of the study in question, it is sometimes possible to present statistical evidence that may strengthen the credibility of the research design. Suppose that we have an additional set of *placebo* (or *negative control*) variables $\mathbf{W}_i$ that we do not think we need to condition on and that are not causally affected by the treatment assignment.

Then we can test the null hypothesis that

$$\mathbf{W}_i \perp\!\!\!\perp D_i | \mathbf{X}_i.$$

This is known as a *placebo test.*[14] One simple way to implement this is by performing an F-test. An F-test compares a regression of D_i on $\mathbf{W}_i$ and $\mathbf{X}_i$ with a regression of D_i on $\mathbf{X}_i$ alone, and asks: does adding $\mathbf{W}_i$ to the regression explain more of the remaining variation in D_i than we would expect by chance? If so, then we can reject the null hypothesis that $\mathbf{W}_i$ is independent of D_i conditional on $\mathbf{X}_i$.

Substantively, we may not be willing to believe that $(Y_i(0), Y_i(1)) \perp\!\!\!\perp D_i|\mathbf{X}_i$ holds if it is statistically unlikely that $\mathbf{W}_i \perp\!\!\!\perp D_i|\mathbf{X}_i$ holds. That is, if we can show that, even conditional on $\mathbf{X}_i$, treated units are systematically different from control units in at least some ways, then we should worry that they might also be systematically different in terms of their potential outcomes. In

14 Placebo tests of this type should not be confused with balance tests after matching or inverse probability weighting. Balance tests are used to assess whether or not we have successfully implemented the matching or weighting algorithm. By Theorem 7.1.16 (*Strong Ignorability and the Propensity Score*), if we have the right propensity score specification, we know that the "balancing property" ensures that we will have statistical independence of D_i and $\mathbf{X}_i$.

such cases, imbalance on $\mathbf{W}_i$ provides valuable evidence about the validity of our identifying assumptions.

7.3 OVERLAP AND POSITIVITY

In the previous section, we discussed placebo tests designed to assess the plausibility of the conditional independence assumption, $(Y_i(0), Y_i(1)) \perp\!\!\!\perp D_i|\mathbf{X}_i$. Another important issue arises relating to the positivity assumption, $\exists\epsilon > 0$ such that $\epsilon < p_D(\mathbf{X}_i) < 1-\epsilon$. In this section, we consider the consequences of the positivity assumption not holding; for instance, what if $\exists\mathbf{x} \in \text{Supp}[\mathbf{X}_i]$ such that $p_D(\mathbf{x}) = 0$ or $p_D(\mathbf{x}) = 1$.[15]

In practice, even if the positivity assumption holds, but $\exists\mathbf{x} \in \text{Supp}[\mathbf{X}_i]$ such that $p_D(\mathbf{x})$ is near zero or one, then difficulties in estimation may ensue. Both of these issues are tied to the idea of "overlap" in the distributions of $\mathbf{X}_i$ across treatment and control arms. We proceed by illustrating that a failure of the positivity assumption logically implies incomplete (or "limited") overlap in the population of interest. When the positivity assumption fails, then the distributions of $\mathbf{X}_i$ for treated and control units have regions with positive probability that do not completely overlap with one another. This notion of overlap is formalized in the following definition.

Definition 7.3.1. *Complete Population Overlap*
Let D_i be a random variable with $\text{Supp}[D_i] = \{0,1\}$, and let $\mathbf{X}_i$ be a random vector. Then D_i has *complete population overlap* with respect to $\mathbf{X}_i$ if

$$\text{Supp}[\mathbf{X}_i|D_i = 1] = \text{Supp}[\mathbf{X}_i|D_i = 0].$$

Overlap simply implies that, if there exists a covariate value in the treatment group with positive (conditional) density, then that covariate value also has positive density conditional on being the control group, and vice versa. We now state our primary result in this section, which establishes that positivity and overlap are tightly connected.

Theorem 7.3.2. *Positivity Implies Complete Population Overlap*
Let D_i be a random variable with $\text{Supp}[D_i] = \{0,1\}$, and let $\mathbf{X}_i$ be a random vector. If $\exists\epsilon > 0$ such that $\epsilon < p_D(\mathbf{X}_i) < 1-\epsilon$, then D_i has complete population overlap with respect to $\mathbf{X}_i$.

Furthermore, the converse of this claim (that population overlap implies positivity) can almost be stated here, but requires some measure-theoretic

15 In the analogous problem of missing data, we might worry that $\exists\mathbf{x} \in \text{Supp}[\mathbf{X}_i]$ such that $p_R(\mathbf{x}) = 0$. Our results in this section apply analogously to Chapter 6.

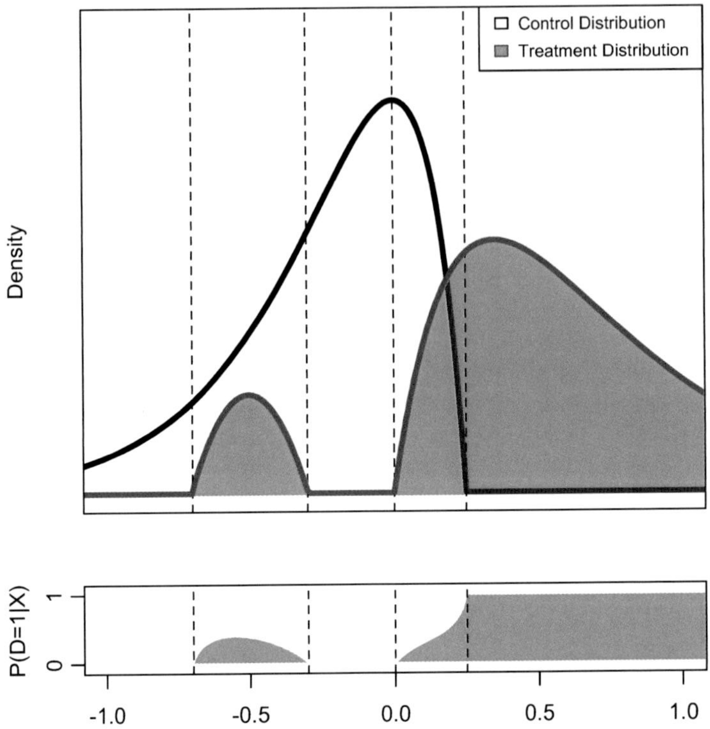

FIGURE 7.3.1. *Limited Population Overlap Illustration*

conditions on support. We omit the formal proof, but provide an illustrative example in the case of a single covariate.

Example 7.3.3. *Limited Population Overlap*
The upper part of Figure 7.3.1 graphs the probability density functions of a single covariate X_i conditional on $D_i = 1$ (in red) and $D_i = 0$ (in black); population overlap fails to hold in the ranges of X_i where one of the conditional densities is positive but the other is zero. The lower part of the figure graphs the propensity score $p_D(X_i) = \Pr[D_i = 1|X_i]$; positivity fails to hold in the ranges of X_i where the propensity score is zero or one. Note that the failures of overlap and positivity occur in exactly the same regions: in the upper range of X_i, where there are treated units but no control units, the propensity score must equal one, and in the ranges where there are control units but no treated units, the propensity score must equal zero. $\triangle$

When overlap fails to hold, there are values of $\mathbf{X}_i$ where the conditional independence assumption is not sufficient for identification of $\mathrm{E}[Y_i(1) - Y_i(0)|\mathbf{X}_i]$, since either all such units are treated or all such units are untreated. Therefore, the population average treatment effect $\mathrm{E}[Y_i(1) - Y_i(0)]$ is not identified without additional assumptions. Approaches to causal inference in this situation include bounding exercises, extrapolation from other regions of the data, and changing the target population. We next consider the latter of these approaches, which can often be done agnostically while retaining practical applicability.

7.3.1 Changing the Target Population

A problem of limited overlap is not just mechanical, but rather may also reflect a more fundamental problem. For instance, we may be interested in the question of the effects of Medicare takeup on a given health outcome; but how might we consider the impact of Medicare takeup for non-Americans—or, on non-seniors, for that matter? Would it make sense to talk about the treatment effects of Medicare takeup for such populations? The fact that zero non-Americans and zero non-seniors take up Medicare may lead us to question whether some queries even admit meaningful answers. In such circumstances, and even in less straightforward cases, the researcher may wish to consider examining an alternative population that features variation in treatment assignments along all salient dimensions.

We could even define alternative populations from the population under study, and condition on the types of observations that have some probability of having variation in $\mathbf{X}_i$. In such cases, it might make sense to restrict our attention to, say, $\mathrm{E}[Y_i(d) | \epsilon < p_D(\mathbf{X}_i) < 1 - \epsilon]$, for some researcher-specified value of $\epsilon \in (0, .5)$. As long as $\Pr[\epsilon < p_D(\mathbf{X}_i) < 1 - \epsilon] > 0$, positivity holds by definition for this subpopulation. We might also choose an estimand that weights members of the population by some function of the propensity score. For example, the estimand $\mathrm{E}[p_D(\mathbf{X}_i)\tau_i]$, which weights by the propensity score itself, is equivalent to the *average treatment effect on the treated (ATT)*, $\mathrm{E}[\tau_i | D_i = 1]$. The ATT is nonparametrically identified under the CIA and a weaker positivity assumption, $p_D(\mathbf{X}_i) < \epsilon < 1$. In the case of the Medicare example, the ATT would correspond to the average effect of Medicare takeup among those who took up Medicare. Other targets are also possible. Angrist and Krueger (1999) demonstrates that a regression of Y_i on D_i and $p_D(\mathbf{X}_i)$ recovers a weighted average treatment effect with weights $p_D(\mathbf{X}_i)(1 - p_D(\mathbf{X}_i))$. Thus, if the usual plug-in regularity conditions hold, the treatment propensity function is known (or can be estimated consistently), and the CIA holds, then regression will consistently estimate the average treatment effect for a reweighted population. Such actions resolve technical issues of positivity, but perhaps introduce nuance in the interpretation that is not immediately evident to the researcher (Crump et al. 2006).

7.3.2 Empirical Overlap, Micronumerosity, and Weighting Estimators

As usual, our final topic is data. If we could know whether or not positivity held, we could adjust our target accordingly. But in finite samples, it might

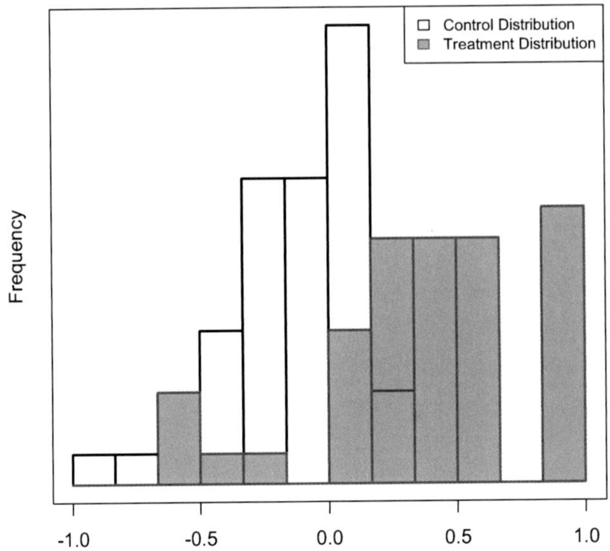

FIGURE 7.3.2. *Empirical Overlap Illustration*

be difficult to distinguish between a failure of the positivity assumption or just not having enough data. We will show that this problem is again one of micronumerosity. To see this, we consider the empirical analog to the example in Section 7.3.

Example 7.3.4. *Limited Empirical Overlap*
Our data here are a random sample from the distribution illustrated in Figure 7.3.1, and we have presented a histogram in Figure 7.3.2 that represents the observed distributions of X_i in the treatment group and the control group. Consider the region where $X_i < -0.67$. Our sample has some control units but no treated units in this range. From the observed data alone, we cannot tell whether the problem is a failure of positivity or just micronumerosity (in which case we would expect to eventually see some treated units with $X_i < -0.67$ if we increased the sample size). But either way, if additional data collection is not an option, then the lack of empirical overlap in certain regions (such as $X_i < -0.67$ and $X_i > 0.33$) implies that we cannot rely on the conditional independence assumption alone for estimation of the population average treatment effect; such endeavors must lean on other approximating assumptions. △

These concerns can be fundamental unless we are willing to impose more structure on the problem. Suppose, for example, that we have a propensity score model that we believe to be accurate. Then we can use it to change the target population, either by trimming based on the empirical values, or, more generally, by selecting an alternative target population through reweighting. This might have good properties, particularly if the researcher is skeptical about the validity of the positivity assumption for their target population.

If the substance of the problem necessitates inference on the full population, and we believe that positivity does in fact hold, then a failure of empirical overlap is simply a case of micronumerosity. In order to estimate the ATE when n is small and overlap is limited, we may have to use an estimator that relies on a restrictive specification (such as linearity of the CEF). Ultimately, however, our best hope for obtaining a good approximation of the ATE lies in the collection of more data. To fully appreciate this tie to micronumerosity, we can note that propensity scores near zero or one have extremely negative consequences for the behavior of the IPW estimator,

$$\hat{\mathrm{E}}_{IPW}[\tau_i] = \frac{1}{n}\sum_{i=1}^{n}\left(\frac{Y_i D_i}{p_D(\mathbf{X}_i)} - \frac{Y_i(1-D_i)}{1-p_D(\mathbf{X}_i)}\right).$$

Intuitively, when $p_D(\mathbf{X}_i)$ is near zero or one, we can see that extremely low or extremely high values can be obtained if we happen to have a "chance" draw of one or more units with extremely large IPW weights. (The stabilized IPW and DR estimators do much to control these problems, but nevertheless the disproportionate influence that observations with high IPW weights will have increases the variability of our estimators.) The problem can be exacerbated in small samples when the propensity scores are estimated, leading to an additional way in which the IPW weights might become very large. This motivates a practice known as *Winsorization*, which is the practice that we have used and will be using in our applications for our weighting-type estimators, including DR estimators.[16]

Definition 7.3.5. *Winsorized (Treatment) Propensity Score*
Suppose we have a (treatment) propensity score estimate $\hat{p}_D(\mathbf{x})$ for some $\mathbf{x}$. Then, given a *Winsorization* $\epsilon \in (0,.5)$, the associated *Winsorized estimate* is

$$\hat{p}_{D,W}(\mathbf{x}) = \begin{cases} 1-\epsilon & : \hat{p}_D(\mathbf{x}) \geq 1-\epsilon \\ \hat{p}_D(\mathbf{x}) & : \epsilon < \hat{p}_D(\mathbf{x}) < 1-\epsilon \\ \epsilon & : \hat{p}_D(\mathbf{x}) \leq \epsilon. \end{cases}$$

For example, if we set $\epsilon = 0.01$, then our propensity score estimates are constrained to lie in $[0.01, 0.99]$. Winsorization thus controls the sampling variance of our weighting estimators, as it prevents chance events from wildly

[16] In the case of missing data, we only need to Winsorize so that the Winsorized estimate $\hat{p}_{R,W}$ is constrained to be above ϵ.

distorting the distribution of our estimator. But just as in sieve estimation, we need not take ϵ as fixed. As data permit, we can admit estimated propensity scores that increasingly tend toward zero or one. If positivity does indeed hold, then Winsorization will become an exceedingly rare event as n grows large.

7.4 FURTHER EXTENSIONS

We note that our treatment of causal inference is incomplete with respect to the myriad ways that point identification of causal parameters can be achieved. At their core, however, most such approaches for causal inference rely on an assumption resembling ignorability. We consider some examples. Instrumental variable strategies typically require an ignorable *instrument*, which is a variable that affects the outcome only through the channel of one particular treatment. Regression discontinuity designs typically require an assumption closely resembling ignorability at a single point in some *forcing variable* that determines whether or not a unit is treated. Approaches that attempt to use panel (longitudinal) data to achieve point identification usually depend on some type of ignorability assumption, though there are many that can be invoked: ignorability conditional on unit (*fixed effects* estimation), ignorability conditional on behavior and treatments in prior periods (*sequential ignorability*), or an assumption that treatment is ignorable with respect to trends in potential outcomes (*difference-in-difference* estimation).

The key ideas expressed in this chapter are readily extendable to most identification strategies commonly used in the social and health sciences. As usual, regression, weighting, or DR estimators can be used to implement these assumptions. There is no magic in achieving causal inference; there is simply the union of substantive assumptions and statistical approximation. Sometimes these approaches are sufficient to achieve consistent point estimates of the quantities of interest, but a healthy dose of agnosticism goes a long way.

7.5 APPLICATION: THE EFFECT OF GENDER ON SWISS CITIZENSHIP APPROVAL VOTES

We consider an application using data from Hainmueller and Hangartner (2013). Hainmueller and Hangartner examine Swiss municipalities where naturalization requests were decided at the municipality level by referendum. Voters in these municipalities received leaflets with detailed descriptions of immigrant applicants, and then cast secret ballots to vote "yes" or "no" on each individual's request. Applicants receiving a majority of "yes" votes were approved for citizenship. This dataset covers 2,419 naturalization referenda held between 1977 and 2003 in forty-four Swiss municipalities, so $n = 2{,}419$.[17]

[17] The original dataset contained 2,429 observations; we exclude from analysis 10 observations for which the age of the applicant was unknown. As all 10 of these observations were

The outcome of interest is percentage of "no" votes on the referendum, and we examine whether gender has a causal effect on the percentage of "no" votes. Gender is coded as one if male and zero if female. Of the 2,419 applicants, 1,640 identified as male and 779 as female.[18] Covariates are region of origin, age, years since arrival, education, unemployment period, refugee status, marriage status, language, level of integration, number of applications, attractiveness in photograph, skill of labor, and decade of evaluation.[19] We assume the data are i.i.d. draws of $(Y_i, D_i, \mathbf{X}_i)$, where Y_i denotes percentage of "no" votes on an applicant's referendum, D_i is a binary variable for gender, and $\mathbf{X}_i$ is the covariate matrix. Our goal is to estimate the effect that the described gender of the applicant has on the outcome.

The counterfactual interpretation is interesting here, and interpreting the potential outcomes model—$Y_i = Y_i(1) \cdot D_i + Y_i(0) \cdot (1 - D_i)$—relies on substantive judgment. Gender is not typically a trait that can easily be viewed as causal—it is embedded deeply in identity, and its meaning is complex. However, we can identify a very particular form of counterfactual: what if the applicant description had been *exactly* the same, except the gender of the applicant had been switched? This setting resembles experiments where researchers send out otherwise identical job or housing applications for evaluation, but experimentally manipulate the gender (see, e.g., Moss-Racusin et al. 2012). Here, the presented gender is not experimentally manipulated, but our potential outcome interpretation remains the same. Thus, when we define potential

male applicants, simple plug-in type estimates fail in this setting: our plug-in estimate of the propensity score will be one for all such subjects.

18 No applicants identified with a non-binary gender.

19 Region of origin reports the country or region the applicant has come from: Northern and Western Europe, Southern Europe, Central and Eastern Europe, the former Yugoslavia, Turkey, Asian countries, and other non-European countries. Age is recorded as one for only one of the following indicators, and zero otherwise: if the applicant is 21–40 years old, 41–60 years old, and over 60 years old. Years since arrival is recorded as number of years from the applicant's arrival in Switzerland to time of application, divided by 10. Education is measured as the number of years of formal education. Unemployment period is coded as one if the description of the applicant mentions any period of unemployment and zero otherwise. Refugee status is coded as one if the applicant entered Switzerland as a refugee and zero otherwise. Marriage status is coded as one if the applicant is married and zero otherwise. Language measures the applicant's Swiss German skills, as reported on the leaflet, as "excellent," "good," "sufficient," or "insufficient." Level of integration is reported under several variables based on how applicants were described to voters: "assimilated" is coded as quasi-continuous with scores between 0 and 2; "integrated" is coded as quasi-continuous with scores between 0 and 2; and "adjusted," "indistinguishable from a Swiss citizen," and "familiar with Swiss customs and traditions" are all coded as binary variables. Number of applications measures the number of times the applicant has applied for naturalization. Attractiveness in photograph was coded by Hainmueller and Hangartner's research assistants as "attractive" or "average." Skill of labor aggregates ISCO-88 codes, coding the first two groups as highly skilled, groups three to five as medium skilled, and the rest as low skilled. Decade of evaluation reports the decade of the referendum. Missing covariate values are addressed with indicator variables in analysis.

outcomes, $Y_i(0)$ refers to the "no" vote share we would (or did) observe had the applicant description been exactly as it was, but with the gender identified as female; and $Y_i(1)$ refers to the "no" vote share we would (or did) observe had the applicant description been exactly as it was, but with the gender identified as male.

Assuming the potential outcomes model—and the fact that vote shares are bounded between 0 and 100%—we can compute bounds on the average potential outcome $\mathrm{E}[Y_i(0)]$, that is, the average "no" vote share had each application had a female-identified applicant. We can of course also compute bounds on the ATE $\mathrm{E}[\tau_i] = \mathrm{E}[Y_i(1) - Y_i(0)]$, that is, the ATE of switching each application from female-identified to male-identified, all else equal. The bounds in this setting are quite wide, to the point of being largely uninformative. Even without accounting for uncertainty, our point estimates imply that the effect of gender could be anywhere between -54.156 and 45.844 percentage points. Without further assumptions, this is the best we can do.

We turn now to assumptions that allow us to point identify average potential outcomes and treatment effects. In this setting, the random assignment assumption is unlikely. There are many reasons to expect that the applications of men may differ from the applications of women in ways that would affect the judgments of voters, and thus $(Y_i(0), Y_i(1)) \not\perp\!\!\!\perp D_i$. For example, men and women may have different education levels, marital statuses, or employment statuses, perhaps due to long-term structural or cultural influences. If we were to assume random assignment and use the plug-in estimator (difference-in-means), we have a point estimate of $\hat{\mathrm{E}}[\tau_i] = 1.335$, with a two-tailed p-value (against the null hypothesis that $\mathrm{E}[\tau_i] = 0$) of 0.051—very nearly reaching the conventional significance level of $p = 0.05$.

The fact that random assignment is unlikely to hold does not mean that all hope is lost. This is a setting where the ignorability assumption, implying $(Y_i(0), Y_i(1)) \perp\!\!\!\perp D_i | \mathbf{X}_i$, is quite plausible. As long as voters do not directly know the applicant, the applicant description contains *all* of the information available to voters. Assuming that the researchers' coding of the applicant descriptions—that is, the variables in $\mathbf{X}_i$—does indeed account for all the information presented to the voters, then, *by definition*, D_i must be conditionally independent of potential outcomes.

If we assume ignorability, then we again have a variety of estimators available. We begin by using two variants of regression estimation to impute missing potential outcomes. The first, OLS (linear), uses OLS under the working assumption that the CEF of the observed data is linear in D_i and $\mathbf{X}_i$: $\mathrm{E}[Y_i | D_i, \mathbf{X}_i] \approx \beta_0 + \beta_1 D_i + \mathbf{X}_i \boldsymbol{\beta}$. The second, OLS (unpooled), fits separate regression models to be fitted for male and female applicants: $\mathrm{E}[Y_i | D_i = d, \mathbf{X}_i] \approx \beta_{d0} + \mathbf{X}_i \boldsymbol{\beta}_d$, $\forall d \in \{0, 1\}$. The estimated ATEs from these two specifications largely agree in direction and magnitude, yielding respective ATE estimates of 0.706 and 1.146. We see that conditioning on $\mathbf{X}_i$ has reduced the magnitude of our estimated effect, and the estimates are no longer near traditional levels of statistical significance, as the p-value against the null hypothesis of zero ATE is 0.165.

Again, in order to use the propensity score-based estimators, we need to first estimate the propensity score, $p_D(\mathbf{X}_i) = \Pr[D_i = 1 | \mathbf{X}_i]$. Again, we will impose the working assumption that $\Pr[D_i = 1 | X_i] \approx \frac{e^{\mathbf{X}_i \Gamma}}{(1+e^{\mathbf{X}_i \Gamma})}$ and use maximum likelihood (ML) estimation to estimate each $\hat{p}_D(\mathbf{X}_i)$. (See Sections 5.1.2, *Binary Choice Model* and 5.2, *Maximum Likelihood Estimation.*) Immediately, we see that one-to-one, nearest-neighbor matching appears to perform abysmally. We estimate that its standard error is nearly 4 times as large as that associated with the OLS (linear) specification, and the associated point estimate of $\mathrm{E}[\tau_i]$ is half again as large as the random assignment plug-in estimator.[20] This is likely to be attributable to the pathologies of matching-type estimators discussed in Section 7.2.4 (*Matching*).

We turn now to the IPW and DR estimators.[21] The IPW estimator has markedly bad performance, with the second-largest estimated standard error, and an estimate of $\mathrm{E}[\tau_i]$ nearly three times as large as the random assignment plug-in estimator. The stabilized IPW estimator, on the other hand, yields the smallest of our estimated treatment effects, with $\hat{\mathrm{E}}[\tau_i] = 0.316$. The fact that the IPW estimates are in such disagreement with the other estimates and with each other may suggest some misspecification of the propensity score model. For the DR estimator, we combine the OLS (unpooled) specification for imputation with the propensity score specification for the IPW estimators.[22] The DR estimator largely agrees with the OLS-based imputation estimate, albeit with some loss of precision, perhaps attributable to potential propensity score misspecification.

Table 7.5.1 summarizes these estimates. With the exception of the (potentially pathological) matching and IPW estimators, the ignorability-based estimates reflect a downward adjustment from the random assignment–based plug-in estimate. (The OLS specifications largely agree with their more technical cousin: the DR estimator.) If we accept the ignorability assumption, then, substantively, this suggests that men have traits that are, on average, less desirable to the voting public. After conditioning on their observable differences from women, we find no estimated effect of gender that approaches traditional levels of statistical significance, though our estimates still suggest that—all

20 As with hot deck imputation, the bootstrap may not work as a method for computing valid confidence intervals for matching estimators since the bias of the estimator may converge very slowly (see, e.g., Abadie and Imbens 2008), but the bootstrap standard errors are likely to adequately characterize sampling variability.

21 As discussed in Section 7.3.2, we Winsorize our propensity score estimates to lie within [0.01, 0.99].

22 It is standard practice for DR estimators to rely on unpooled regression fits across treatment arms for imputation.

TABLE 7.5.1. *Estimates for Effect of Gender on Percentage "No" Votes*

Estimator	Target	Estimate	SE
Lower Bound Plug-In	$\text{E}[Y_i(0)]$	11.523	0.388
	$\text{E}[\tau_i]$	−54.156	0.429
Upper Bound Plug-In	$\text{E}[Y_i(0)]$	79.319	0.657
	$\text{E}[\tau_i]$	45.844	0.429
Random Assignment	$\text{E}[Y_i(0)]$	35.780	0.557
	$\text{E}[\tau_i]$	1.335	0.685
OLS (Linear)	$\text{E}[Y_i(0)]$	36.206	0.487
	$\text{E}[\tau_i]$	0.706	0.508
OLS (Unpooled)	$\text{E}[Y_i(0)]$	35.700	0.649
	$\text{E}[\tau_i]$	1.146	0.646
Matching	$\text{E}[Y_i(0)]$	34.732	1.951
	$\text{E}[\tau_i]$	2.009	1.988
IPW	$\text{E}[Y_i(0)]$	33.690	0.997
	$\text{E}[\tau_i]$	3.731	1.088
Stabilized IPW	$\text{E}[Y_i(0)]$	36.638	0.756
	$\text{E}[\tau_i]$	0.316	0.753
Doubly Robust	$\text{E}[Y_i(0)]$	35.676	0.701
	$\text{E}[\tau_i]$	1.187	0.709

Estimates are of average potential outcome for female applicants ($\text{E}[Y(0)]$) and ATE of male identification ($\text{E}[\tau]$) with respect to "no" vote share in referenda on approving Swiss citizenship applications (Hainmueller and Hangartner 2013).

else equal—being male decreases voter support for one's immigration application. Together, our results highlight how a clever observational study can shed light on well-defined causal quantities and illustrate the importance of wedding credible identifying assumptions to sensible estimation strategies.

7.6 FURTHER READINGS

As might be expected given the parallel structures of Chapter 6 and Chapter 7, the readings from Chapter 6 remain highly relevant here. Angrist and Pischke (2009), Morgan and Winship (2014), and Hernan and Robins (in press) provide the most natural extensions from our materials here and are highly recommended; they discuss practical strategies for obtaining point identification for causal quantities. Angrist and Krueger (1999) contains an excellent and highly practical article covering of many of the same materials as Angrist and Pischke (2009). Manski (1990) provides a now-canonical derivation of the bounds that we discussed in Section 7.1.3, along with assumptions that may reduce the width of these bounds. VanderWeele (2015) provides a book-length discussion of strategies for identification of complex counterfactual quantities, including mediation effects and spillover effects. Rubin (2006) provides a book-length discussion of matching-based methods. There are also three review articles on developments in causal inference that we recommend: the first two are Imbens and Wooldridge (2009) and Athey and Imbens (mimeo.), which each discuss causal identification strategies and associated estimators. But perhaps most importantly, Richardson and Rotnitzky (2014) contains an excellent review of the enormously influential and wide-ranging body of work by James Robins. We cannot recommend this review article highly enough for those seeking a starting point to explore more advanced topics in causal inference, particularly with respect to longitudinal data.

As with Chapter 6, we did not consider design-based approaches to causal inference. One strain of this research, Fisherian randomization inference, focuses on testing sharp null hypotheses (that is, hypotheses where the causal effect for every unit is hypothesized, rather than just average treatment effects) and constructing confidence intervals accordingly. This approach has excellent book-length treatments in Rosenbaum (2002) and in the more introductory Rosenbaum (2010). Another type of design-based research follows from Splawa-Neyman, Dabrowska, and Speed (1923), wherein the inferential targets are average treatment effects defined on finite populations. This line of research was repopularized by Robins (1988), Reichardt and Gollob (1999), Freedman (2008a), and Freedman (2008b). We strongly recommend these articles, along with the extraordinarily clear and elegant response to Freedman given by Lin (2013). We further recommend Aronow and Samii (in press), which provides a generalization of this framework for generic experimental designs and permits some forms of interference between units. Imbens and Rubin (2011) is a valuable textbook that includes a significant focus on Neyman-style design-based causal inference.

Finally, we reiterate that while we did not consider graph-based approaches for identification of causal quantities in this book, we view the topic as highly important. Pearl (2000) provides the canonical treatment of directed acyclic graphs, the most common class of nonparametric graph-based causal models. Morgan and Winship (2014) includes a clear and practical exposition of the use of directed acyclic graphs for identification of causal quantities. Richardson and Robins (mimeo.) develops a generalization of directed acyclic graphs (single world intervention graphs) that provides a clear unification of graph-based and potential outcomes–based models; we recommend that readers interested in graph-based approaches to causality read it after internalizing the core ideas from Pearl (2000).

Glossary of Mathematical Notation

In this appendix, we provide a glossary of mathematical notation not defined in the text.

Notation	Definition and Usage
$\in$	*Set membership.* $s \in A$ (read "s is an element of A" or "s is in A") denotes that the object s (which could be a number, a vector, a set, etc.) is an element of the set A. For example, $2 \in \{1,2,4\}$. The negation of $\in$ is denoted by $\notin$; $s \notin A$ (read "s is not an element of A" or "s is not in A") denotes that the object s is *not* an element of the set A. For example, $3 \notin \{1,2,4\}$.
$\forall$	*For all.* Used to state that all elements of a particular set satisfy a given expression. For example, $\forall x \in \{1,2,3,4,5\}$, $2x \leq 10$. The set may be omitted if it is clear from context. For example, $\forall x$, $x+1 > x$ might mean that $x+1 > x$ is true for any real number x. Similarly, $\forall k > 1, f(k) = 0$ might mean that $f(k) = 0$ is true for any integer k that is greater than one. Usually, when defining a function, we will include a "for all" statement after the equation to denote the domain of the function. For example, $g(x) = \sqrt{x}, \forall x \geq 0$.
$\exists$	*There exists.* Used to state that there is *at least one* element of a particular set that satisfies a given expression. For example, $\exists x \in \{1,2,3,4,5\}$ such that $x^2 = 16$. As with $\forall$, the set may be omitted if it is clear from context. For example, $\exists x > 0$ such that $x^2 - 3x - 1 = 0$.

$\iff$	*If and only if.* Denotes that two statements are logically equivalent; each implies the other. Sometimes written as "iff." For example, $2x = 10 \iff x = 5$.
$\square$	*Quod erat demonstrandum (QED).* Latin for "that which was to be demonstrated." This denotes that a proof is complete.
$\triangle$	*End of example.* This nonstandard notation allows us to clearly delineate where an example ends.
$\subseteq$	*Subset.* $A \subseteq B$ (read "A is a subset of B") means that the set B contains every element in the set A. Formally, $A \subseteq B \iff \forall s \in A, s \in B$. For example, $\{2,3,5\} \subseteq \{1,2,3,4,5\}$. Note that $A = B \iff A \subseteq B$ and $B \subseteq A$.
$\emptyset$	The *empty set.* The set containing no elements. Sometimes written as $\{\}$.
A^C	The *complement* of a set. When all sets under consideration are subsets of some *universal set* U, the complement of a set A is the set of all elements in U that are not in A. Formally, $A^C = \{s \in U : s \notin A\}$.
$\cup$	The *union* of sets. $A \cup B$ (read "A union B") denotes the set containing all elements that are in *either A or B* (or both). Formally, $A \cup B = \{s : s \in A \text{ or } s \in B\}$. For example, $\{1,2,5\} \cup \{2,3\} = \{1,2,3,5\}$. Union is associative, so for multiple unions parentheses can be omitted without ambiguity. For example, $(A \cup B) \cup C = A \cup (B \cup C) = A \cup B \cup C$.
$\cap$	The *intersection* of sets. $A \cap B$ (read "A intersect B") denotes the set containing all elements that are in *both A and B*. Formally, $A \cap B = \{s : s \in A \text{ and } s \in B\}$. For example, $\{1,2,5,6\} \cap \{2,3,6\} = \{2,6\}$. Intersection is associative, so for multiple intersections parentheses can be omitted without ambiguity. For example, $(A \cap B) \cap C = A \cap (B \cap C) = A \cap B \cap C$.
$\setminus$	*Set subtraction.* $A \setminus B$ (read "A set-minus B") denotes the set that contains all the elements in A *except* any that are also in B. Formally, $A \setminus B = \{s \in A : s \notin B\}$. $A \setminus B$ is called the *relative complement* of B in A, since $A \setminus B = A \cup B^C$.
$\mathcal{P}(A)$	The *power set* of A, that is, the set of all subsets of A. For example, $\mathcal{P}(\{1,2,3\}) = \{\emptyset, \{1\}, \{2\}, \{3\}, \{1,2\}, \{2,3\}, \{1,3\}, \{1,2,3\}\}$.

$\lvert A \rvert$	The *cardinality* (or *size*) of a set. For finite sets, the cardinality is the number of elements in the set. For example, $\lvert\{1,2,3,5,6,8\}\rvert = 6$.
$\mathbb{N}$	The set of all *natural numbers*, that is, positive integers: $\mathbb{N} = \{1,2,3,\ldots\}$. Note that while some texts include zero in $\mathbb{N}$, we do not.
$\mathbb{Z}$	The set of all *integers*: $\mathbb{Z} = \{\ldots,-3,-2,-1,0,1,2,3,\ldots\}$. (The letter "Z" here stands for *Zahlen*, German for "numbers.")
$\mathbb{R}$	The set of all *real numbers*. In classical mathematics, there are many ways of rigorously defining the real numbers, but for our purposes it suffices to say that the real numbers are all the points on a continuous number line.
$\mathbb{R}^n$	The *real coordinate space* of dimension n, that is, the set of all *vectors* of length n with real entries. Formally, $\mathbb{R}^n = \{(x_1,x_2,\ldots,x_n) : x_i \in \mathbb{R}, \forall i \in \{1,2,\ldots,n\}\}$. $\mathbb{N}^n$, $\mathbb{Z}^n$, etc. are defined analogously.
$f : S \to T$	A *function* f from S to T. The set S is the *domain* of f, the set of all values s for which $f(s)$ is defined. The set T is the *codomain* of f, a set that contains all possible values of $f(s)$. Formally, $\forall s \in S$, $f(s) \in T$.
$f(A)$	The *image* of the set A under the function f, that is, the set of all values the function f can take on when applied to an element of A. Formally, for a function $f : S \to T$ and a set $A \subseteq S$, $f(A) = \{t \in T : \exists a \in A \text{ such that } f(a) = t\}$. Note that $f(S)$ is the *range* of f.
$g \circ f$	The *composition* of two functions. For functions $f : S \to T$ and $g : U \to V$, where $f(S) \subseteq U \subseteq T$, $g \circ f : S \to V$ is the function that first applies f and then applies g to its output: $\forall s \in S$, $(g \circ f)(s) = g(f(s))$.
$\sum$	*Summation* of a sequence. For example, $$\sum_{i=1}^{5} i^2 = 1^2 + 2^2 + 3^2 + 4^2 + 5^2 = 55.$$
$\prod$	*Product* of a sequence. For example, $$\prod_{i=1}^{6} (i+1) = (1+1)(2+1)(3+1)(4+1)(5+1)(6+1) = 5{,}040.$$

$\arg\max$	The value, among all values in a particular set, that maximizes the given expression. For example, $\arg\max_{x\in\mathbb{R}}(-x^2-2x+3)=-1$, as $-x^2-2x+3$ attains its maximum value at $x=-1$. Our use of $\arg\max$ assumes that there exists a unique maximum. More generally, $\arg\max$ denotes the set of values at which the maximum is attained.
$\arg\min$	The value, among all values in a particular set, that minimizes the given expression. For example, $\arg\min_{x\in\mathbb{R}}(x^2-4x+1)=2$, as x^2-4x+1 attains its minimum value at $x=2$. Our use of $\arg\min$ assumes that there exists a unique minimum. More generally, $\arg\min$ refers to the set of values at which the minimum is attained.
$\mathbb{A}^T$	The *transpose* of a matrix. $\mathbb{A}^T$ denotes the matrix whose columns are the rows of $\mathbb{A}$. Sometimes written as $\mathbb{A}'$. For example, if $\mathbb{A}=\begin{pmatrix}1&2&3\\4&5&6\end{pmatrix}$, then $\mathbb{A}^T=\begin{pmatrix}1&4\\2&5\\3&6\end{pmatrix}$.
$\mathbb{A}^{-1}$	The *inverse* of a (square) matrix. If $\mathbb{A}$ is *invertible*, then $\mathbb{A}^{-1}$ denotes the matrix that, when multiplied by $\mathbb{A}$, yields the identity matrix of the appropriate dimensions: $\mathbb{A}\mathbb{A}^{-1}=\mathbb{A}^{-1}\mathbb{A}=\mathbb{I}=\begin{pmatrix}1&0&0&\cdots&0\\0&1&0&\cdots&0\\0&0&1&\cdots&0\\\vdots&\vdots&\vdots&\ddots&\vdots\\0&0&0&\cdots&1\end{pmatrix}$ For example, if $\mathbb{A}=\begin{pmatrix}2&1&1\\-5&-3&0\\1&1&-1\end{pmatrix}$, then $\mathbb{A}^{-1}=\begin{pmatrix}-3&-2&-3\\5&3&5\\2&1&1\end{pmatrix}$.

Glossary of Common Abbreviations

Commonly abbreviated terms are defined when first used in the text. We provide the unabbreviated terms here for reference.

Abbreviation	Term and Reference in Text
ATE	Average Treatment Effect; Section 7.1.1
BLP	Best Linear Predictor; Theorem 2.2.21
CDF	Cumulative Distribution Function; Definition 1.2.11
CEF	Conditional Expectation Function; Definition 2.2.15
CMT	Continuous Mapping Theorem; Theorem 3.2.7
DR	Doubly Robust; Section 6.2.6
i.i.d.	Independent and identically distributed; Definition 3.1.1
IPW	Inverse Probability–Weighted; Section 6.2.5
KL	Kullback–Leibler; Definition 5.2.7
MAR	Missing at Random; Definition 6.1.8
MCAR	Missing Completely at Random; Definition 6.1.5
ML	Maximum Likelihood; Section 5.2
MSE	Mean Squared Error; Section 2.1.3
NRCM	Neyman–Rubin Causal Model; within Section 7.1

OLS	Ordinary Least Squares; Definition 4.1.2
PDF	Probability Density Function; Definition 1.2.15
PMF	Probability Mass Function; Definition 1.2.5
WLLN	Weak Law of Large Numbers; Theorem 3.2.8

References

Abadie, Alberto and Guido W. Imbens. 2008. On the failure of the bootstrap for matching estimators. *Econometrica*. 76(6): 1537–1557.

Angrist, Joshua D. 2013. Pop Quiz. *Mostly Harmless Econometrics*. Posted November 28, 2013. www.mostlyharmlesseconometrics.com/2013/11/pop-quiz-2/

Angrist, Joshua D. and Guido W. Imbens. 2002. Comment on "Covariance adjustment in randomized experiments and observational studies" by P. R. Rosenbaum. *Statistical Science*. 17(3): 304–307.

Angrist, Joshua D. and Alan B. Krueger. 1999. Empirical strategies in labor economics. *Handbook of Labor Economics*. 3: 1277–1366.

Angrist, Joshua D. and Jörn-Steffen Pischke. 2009. *Mostly harmless econometrics: An empiricist's companion*. Princeton, NJ: Princeton University Press.

Aronow, Peter M. and Cyrus Samii. In press. Estimating average causal effects under general interference, with application to a social network experiment. *Annals of Applied Statistics*.

Athey, Susan and Guido W. Imbens. Working paper. The state of applied econometrics: Causality and policy evaluation.

Bang, Heejung and James M. Robins. 2005. Doubly robust estimation in missing data and causal inference models. *Biometrics*. 61: 962–972.

Belloni, Alexandre, Victor Chernozhukov, and Christian Hansen. 2014. High-dimensional methods and inference on structural and treatment effects. *Journal of Economic Perspectives*. (28)2, 2014: 29–50.

Billingsley, Patrick. 1995. *Probability and measure*, 3rd edn. Hoboken, NJ: John Wiley & Sons, Inc.

Blitzstein, Joseph K. and Jessica Hwang. 2014. *Introduction to probability*. Boca Raton, FL: CRC Press.

Buja, Andreas et al. Working paper. Models as approximations: A conspiracy of random regressors and model misspecification against classical inference in regression.

Cameron, A. Colin and Douglas L. Miller. 2015. A practitioner's guide to cluster-robust inference. *Journal of Human Resources*. 50(2): 317–372.

Cameron, A. Colin and Pravin K. Trivedi. 2005. *Microeconomics: Methods and applications*. New York, NY: Cambridge University Press.

Casella, George and Roger L. Berger. 2001. *Statistical inference*, 2nd edn. Pacific Grove, CA: Duxbury.

Chen, Xiaohong. 2007. Large sample sieve estimation of semi-nonparametric models. *Handbook of Econometrics*. 6: 5549–5632.

Cochran, William G. 1977. *Sampling techniques*, 3rd edn. New York, NY: John Wiley & Sons.

Crump, Richard K., V. Joseph Hotz, Guido W. Imbens, and Oscar Mitnik. 2006. Moving the goalposts: Addressing limited overlap in estimation of average treatment effects by changing the estimand. NBER Technical Working Paper No. 330.

Dasgupta, Anirban. 2008. *Asymptotic theory of statistics and probability*. New York, NY: Springer-Verlag New York.

Davidson, Russell and James G. MacKinnon. 2004. *Econometric theory and methods*, Vol. 5. New York, NY: Oxford University Press.

Davison, Anthony C. and David V. Hinkley. 1997. *Bootstrap methods and their application*. New York, NY: Cambridge University Press.

Diaconis, Persi, Sarah Holmes, and Richard Montgomery. 2007. Dynamical bias in the coin toss. *Society for Industrial and Applied Mathematics Review*. 49(2): 211–235.

Dubins, Lester E. and David A. Freedman. 1979. Exchangeable processes need not be mixtures of independent, identically distributed random variables. *Z. Wahrscheinlichkeitsth. verw. Gebiete*. 48: 115–132.

Efron, Bradley and Robert J. Tibshirani. 1994. *An introduction to the bootstrap*. Boca Raton, FL: CRC Press LLC.

Feller, William. 1968. *An introduction to probability theory and its applications*, 3rd edn., Vol. 1. New York, NY: John Wiley.

Freedman, David A. 2008a. On regression adjustments to experimental data. *Advances in Applied Mathematics*. 40: 180–193.

2008b. On regression adjustments in experiments with several treatments. *The Annals of Applied Statistics*. 2: 176–196.

2009. *Statistical models: Theory and practice*. New York, NY: Cambridge University Press.

Freedman, David A., Robert Pisani, and Roger A. Purves. 1998. *Statistics*, 3rd edn. New York, NY: Norton.

Freedman, David A. and Philip B. Stark. 2003. What is the chance of an earthquake? *NATO Science Series IV: Earth and Environmental Sciences*. 32: 201–213.

Goldberger, Arthur S. 1968. *Topics in regression analysis*. New York, NY: Macmillan.

1991. *A course in econometrics*. Cambridge, MA: Harvard University Press.

Greene, William H. 2012. *Econometric analysis*, 7th edn. New York, NY: Pearson.

Greenland, Sander et al. 2016. Statistical tests, P values, confidence intervals, and power: A guide to misinterpretations. 2016. *European Journal of Epidemiology*. 31(4): 337–350.

Hainmueller, Jens and Dominik Hangartner. 2013. Who gets a Swiss passport? A natural experiment in immigrant discrimination. *American Political Science Review*. 107(1): 159–187.

Hájek, Jaroslav. 1971. Comment on "An essay on the logical foundations of survey sampling, Part I." In Godambe, Vidyadhar P., and David A. Sprott (Eds.). *Foundations of Statistical Inference*. Toronto: Holt, Rinehart, and Winston.

Hansen, Bruce E. 2013. *Econometrics*. Unpublished manuscript, University of Wisconsin.

Hastie, Trevor, Robert Tibshirani, and Jerome Friedman. 2009. *The elements of statistical learning: Data mining, inference, and prediction*. New York, NY: Springer-Verlag New York.

Hayashi, Fumio. 2001. *Econometrics*. Princeton, NJ: Princeton University Press.

Hernan, Miguel and James M. Robins. In press. *Causal inference*. London: Chapman and Hall.

Holland, Paul W. 1986. Statistics and causal inference. *Journal of the American Statistical Association*. 81(396): 945–968.

Horvitz, Daniel G. and Donovan J. Thompson. 1952. A generalization of sampling without replacement from a finite universe. *Journal of the American Statistical Association*. 47: 663–684.

Hudgens, Michael G. and M. Elizabeth Halloran. 2008. Toward causal inference with interference. *Journal of the American Statistical Association*. 103(482): 832–842.

Imbens, Guido W. 2013. Book review feature: Public policy in an uncertain world: By Charles F. Manski. *The Economic Journal*. 123(August): F401–F411.

Imbens, Guido W. and Michel Kolesar. In press. Robust standard errors in small samples: Some practical advice. *The Review of Economics and Statistics*.

Imbens, Guido W. and Donald B. Rubin. 2011. *Causal inference in statistics and social sciences*. Unpublished manuscript. Harvard University.

Imbens, Guido W. and Jeffrey M. Wooldridge. 2009. Recent developments in the econometrics of program evaluation. *Journal of Economic Literature*. 47(1): 5–86.

James, Gareth et al. 2014. *An introduction to statistical learning with applicationsin R*. New York, NY: Springer Science+Business Media New York.

Kang, Joseph D. Y. and Joseph L. Schafer. 2007. Demystifying double robustness: A comparison of alternative strategies for estimating population means from incomplete data. *Statistical Science*. 22(4): 523–539.

Leeb, Hannes and Benedikt M. Pötscher. 2006. Can one estimate the conditional distribution of post-model-selection estimators? *Annals of Statistics*. 34(5): 2554–2591.

Lehmann, Erich L. 1999. *Elements of large-sample theory*. New York, NY: Springer-Verlag New York.

Lehmann, Erich L. and Joseph P. Romano. 2005. *Testing statistical hypotheses*, 3rd edn. New York, NY: Springer-Verlag New York.

Lin, Winston. 2013. Agnostic notes on regression adjustments to experimental data: Reexamining Freedman's critique. *The Annals of Applied Statistics*. 7(1): 295–318.

Manski, Charles F. 1988. *Analog estimation methods in econometrics*. New York, NY: Chapman & Hall.

1990. Nonparametric bounds on treatment effects. *American Economic Review*. 80(2): 319–323.

1999. *Identification problems in the social sciences*. Cambridge, MA: Harvard University Press.

2003. *Partial identification of probability distributions*. New York, NY: Springer-Verlag New York.

2013. *Public policy in an uncertain world: Analysis and decisions*. Cambridge, MA: Harvard University Press.

Morgan, Stephen L. and Christopher Winship. 2014. *Counterfactuals and causal inference*. New York, NY: Cambridge University Press.

Moss-Racusin, Corinne A., John F. Dovidio, Victoria L. Brescoll, Mark J. Graham, and Jo Handelsman. 2012. Science faculty's subtle gender biases favor male students. *PNAS*. 109(41): 16474–16479.

Newey, Whitney K. 1990. Semiparametric efficiency bounds. *Journal of Applied Economics*. 5(2): 99–135.

Pearl, Judea. 2000. *Causality: Models, reasoning, and inference*. New York, NY: Cambridge University Press.

Pitkin, Emil, Richard Berk, Lawrence Brown, Andreas Buja, Edward George, Kai Zhang, and Linda Zhao. Working paper. An asymptotically powerful test for the average treatment effect.

Pitman, Jim. 1993. *Probability*. New York, NY: Springer-Verlag New York.

Powell, James L. 2010. Asymptotics for least squares. Lecture Notes. Department of Economics. University of California, Berkeley. https://eml.berkeley.edu/~powell/e240b_sp10/alsnotes.pdf.

Reichardt, Charles S. and Harry F. Gollob. 1999. Justifying the use and increasing the power of a *t* test for a randomized experiment with a convenience sample. *Psychological Methods*. 4: 117.

Rice, John A. 2007. *Mathematical statistics and data analysis*, 3rd edn. Belmont, CA: Duxbury.

Richardson, Thomas S. and James M. Robins. Working paper. Single-world intervention graphs (SWIGs): A unification of the counterfactual and graphical approaches to causality. Working Paper Number 128. Center for the Statistics and the Social Sciences, University of Washington, Seattle.

Richardson, Thomas S. and Andrea Rotnitzky. 2014. Causal etiology of the research of James M. Robins. *Statistical Science*. 29(4): 259–284.

Riesbeck, Chris. N.d. Mathematician-physicist-engineer jokes. www.cs.northwestern.edu/~riesbeck/mathphyseng.html.

Robins, James M. 1986. A new approach to causal inference in mortality studies with a sustained exposure period? Application to control of the healthy worker survivor effect. Mathematical models in medicine: Diseases and epidemics. Part 2. *Mathematical Modelling*. 7: 1393–1512.

1988. Confidence intervals for causal parameters. *Statistics in Medicine*. 7(7): 773–785.

1999. Robust estimation in sequentially ignorable missing data and causal inference models. In *ASA Proceedings of the Section on Bayesian Statistical Science* 6–10. American Statistical Association, Alexandria, VA.

Robins, James M., Andrea Rotnitzky, and Lue Ping Zhao. 1995. Analysis of semiparametric regression models for repeated outcomes in the presence of missing data. *Journal of the American Statistical Association*. 90(429): 106–121.

Rosenbaum, Paul R. 1987. Model- based direct adjustment. *Journal of the American Statistical Association*. 82(398): 387–394.

2002. *Observational studies*, 2nd edn. New York, NY: Springer-Verlag New York.

2010. *Design of observational studies*. New York, NY: Springer-Verlag New York.

Rosenbaum, Paul R. and Donald B. Rubin. 1983. The central role of the propensity score in observational studies for causal effects. *Biometrika*. 70(1): 41–55.

Rubin, Donald B. 1974. Estimating causal effects of treatments in randomized and nonrandomized studies. *Journal of Educational Psychology*. 66(5): 688–701.
2006. *Matched sampling for causal effects*. New York, NY: Cambridge University Press.

Runge, Carl. 1901. Über empirische Funktionen und die Interpolation zwischen äquidistanten Ordinaten. *Zeitschrift für Mathematik und Physik*. 46: 224–243.

Särndal, Carl-Erik, Bengt Swensson, and Jan Wretman. 1992. *Model assisted survey sampling*. New York: Springer-Verlag New York.

Schochet, Peter Z. 2010. Is regression adjustment supported by the Neyman model for causal inference? *Journal of Statistical Planning and Inference*. 140: 246–259.

Silverman, Bernard W. 1986. *Density estimation for statistics and data analysis*. London; New York, NY: CRC Press.

Splawa-Neyman, Jerzy, Dorota M. Dabrowska, and Terence P. Speed. 1923. Reprint, 1990. On the application of probability theory to agricultural experiments: Essay on principles, section 9. *Statistical Science*. 5(4): 465–472.

Stefanski, Leonard A. and Dennis D. Boos. 2002. The calculus of M-estimation. *The American Statistician*. 56(1): 29–38.

Teorell, Jan et al. 2016. The Quality of Government standard dataset, version Jan 16. University of Gothenburg: The Quality of Government Institute. www.qog.pol.gu.se doi:10.18157/QoGStdJan16.

Thompson, M. E. 1997. *Theory of sample surveys*. London: Chapman and Hall.

Tibshirani, Robert. 1996. Regression shrinkage and selection via the lasso. *Journal of the Royal Statistical Society. Series B (Methodological)*. 58(1): 267–288.

Tsiatis, Anastasios. 2006. *Semiparametric theory and missing data*. New York, NY: Springer-Verlag New York.

Tsybakov, Alexandre B. 2009. *Introduction to nonparametric estimation*. New York, NY: Springer Science+Business Media, LLC.

Van der Laan, Mark J. and James M. Robins. 2003. *Unified methods for censored longitudinal data and causality*. New York, NY: Springer-Verlag New York.

Van der Laan, Mark J. and Sherri Rose. 2011. *Targeted learning: Causal inference for observational and experimental data*. New York, NY: Springer-Verlag New York.

VanderWeele, Tyler J. 2015. *Causal inference: Methods for mediation and interaction*. New York, NY: Oxford University Press.

Varian, Hal R. 2014. Big data: New tricks for econometrics. *Journal of Economic Perspectives*. 28(2): 3–28.

Wackerly, Dennis D., William Mendenhall III, and Richard L. Scheaffer. 2008. *Mathematical statistics with applications*, 7th edn. Belmont, CA: Thomson Brooks/Cole.

Wager, Stefan, Wenfei Du, Jonathan Taylor, and Robert J. Tibshirani. 2016. High-dimensional regression adjustments in randomized experiments. *Proceedings of the National Academy of Sciences*. 113(45): 12673–12678.

Wasserman, Larry. 2004. *All of statistics: A concise course in statistical inference*. New York, NY: Springer Science+Business Media, Inc.
2006. *All of nonparametric statistics*. New York, NY: Springer Science+Business Media, Inc.
2012. Lecture notes for 10-705/36-705 Intermediate Statistics.

Wooldridge, Jeffrey M. 2010. *Econometric analysis of cross section and panel data*, 2nd edn. Cambridge, MA: MIT Press.

Index

absolute convergence, 45n2, 55n7
Addition Rule, 9–10
almost sure convergence, 117n29
asymptotic estimation theory, 111–116
asymptotic mean squared error, 113
asymptotic normality, 112, 125
  of plug-in estimators, 120
asymptotic relative efficiency, 113
asymptotic standard error, 113
asymptotic unbiasedness, 112
atomic events, 6
average marginal causal effect, 255
average partial derivative, 166–168, 171, 255
average treatment effect (ATE), 237–238
  conditional, 249–250
  decomposition, 238
  plug-in estimation of, 256–257
  sharp bounds for, 240–243
  under random assignment, 245
  under strong ignorability, 248–249, 253, 255
average treatment effect among the treated (ATT), 238, 247, 273

balance, 218, 251–252
balance test, 252, 270n14
bandwidth, 121
Bayes' Rule, 11–12
  alternative form of, 13
Bayesian probability, 4n2
Bernoulli distribution, 19, 46, 58, 67, 70, 135, 182
  generalized, 180
Bernoulli random variable, *see* Bernoulli distribution
best linear predictor (BLP), 76–84
  and independence, 82–84
  and the CEF, 78–79
  coefficients of, 87
  estimating, 144–147
  multivariate case, 86–87
  properties of deviations from, 79, 87
  under nonlinearity, 81
bias, 103
binary choice model, 182–185, 226, 233, 264, 279
  CEF for, 183, 198
bivariate normal distribution, 66n13
bivariate relationships, 31–39
bootstrap, 130–132, 141–142, 153–154, 203, 234
bounds, *see* sharp bounds

cardinality, 7, 284
categorical distribution, 180
Cauchy–Schwarz Inequality, 63n12
causal inference, 235–281
  as a missing data problem, 238–239
  Double Robustness Theorem for, 267–269
  doubly robust estimator for, 267, 269–270
  propensity score for, 250–252
  regression estimator for, 260, 261
Central Limit Theorem (CLT)
  for cluster samples, 139
  for sample means, 108–110

Chebyshev's Inequality, 55, 105
for the sample mean, 98
classical linear model, 180–182
CEF for, 181, 198
maximum likelihood estimation of, 189–192
cluster average, 136–139
cluster sample mean, 136–137
sampling variance of, 137, 140
cluster samples, 135–141
CLT for, 139
estimation with, 136–139
inference with, 140–141
WLLN for, 138
collinearity, 132n43, 149
complement, 6, 22, 24, 283
complement rule, 8, 9
conditional average treatment effect, 249–250
under strong ignorability, 249
conditional expectation, 67–69
linearity of, 69, 249
multivariate case, 85
of a function of a random variable, 68
conditional expectation function (CEF), 69–76
and independence, 82–84
and the BLP, 78–79
for binary choice models, 183, 198
for the classical linear model, 181, 198
kernel plug-in estimation of, 124
multivariate case, 85
partial derivatives of, 165–168
polynomial approximation of, 158, 165n11, 169
properties of deviations from, 74–75
under MAR, 217
conditional independence assumption, 216, 248, 254, 255, 270–272, 274
conditional PDF, 37–38
multivariate case, 42
conditional PMF, 34
multivariate case, 42
conditional probability, 10–12, 67, 182
and independence, 14–15, 39
conditional variance, 68, 74
conditional variance function, 70, 85
confidence interval, 124–127, 134–135, 212, 231
asymptotic validity of, 125
for regression, 154
for the population mean, 127
normal approximation-based, 125, 128, 131, 133–135, 140
validity of, 124
confidence level, 124
consistency, 105
of maximum likelihood estimation, 193
of sampling variance and standard error estimators, 113
of the sample mean, 105
Continuous Mapping Theorem (CMT), 100, 107, 108, 110, 114, 116, 125–126, 140
continuous random variable, 24
event probabilities for, 25–27
convergence
absolute, 45n2, 55n7
almost sure, 117n29
in distribution, 108
in probability, 99–100
correlation, 62–63
and independence, 64–66
and linear dependence, 62
properties of, 63
covariance, 59–60
alternative formula for, 60
and independence, 64
properties of, 61–62
covariance matrix, 84
cumulative distribution function (CDF), 21–24, 101–102
empirical, 116–120
estimating, 102, 117
joint, 32–33, 40
properties of, 22

degenerate distribution, 47
difference-in-means estimator, 245, 256, 257, 259
discrete random variable, 18–21
event probabilities for, 21
distribution, 3–4, 20, 21
Double Robustness Theorem
for causal inference, 267–269
for missing data, 229–230
doubly robust (DR) estimator
for causal inference, 267, 269–270
for missing data, 228, 230
draw, 4

efficiency, *see* relative efficiency
elementary event, 6
empirical CDF, 116–117, 120
estimation theory, 96–116
asymptotic, 111–116
estimator, 103–105
bias of, 103
consistency of, 105

doubly robust, *see* doubly robust (DR) estimator
inverse probability–weighted (IPW), *see* inverse probability–weighted estimators
kernel density, 122
kernel plug-in, 123
lasso, 169–170, 174, 202
MSE of, 104–105
plug in, *see* plug-in estimator
post-stratification, 219, 256
regression, *see* regression
relative efficiency of, 105
sampling variance of, 104
sieve, 168–169
standard error of, 104
unbiased, 103
event, *see* random event
event space, 5–8
expectation, 45–50
conditional, 67–69
linearity of, 49–50
of a function of a random variable, 47
of a function of two random variables, 49
of a random vector, 48
of the sample mean, 97
properties of, 47–50
under MAR, 216
under MCAR, 213–215
expectation operator, 45, 47
expected value, *see* expectation
experiment, 4
explanatory variable, 79

finite population, 93–94
frequentist probability, 4
function of a random variable, 16–17
conditional expectation of, 68
equality of, 32, 70
expectation of, 47, 49, 68
functional, *see* statistical functional
Fundamental Problem of Causal Inference, 236–239, 270

geometric distribution, 19
Glivenko–Cantelli Theorem, 102n14, 117n27, 120n31

heteroskedasticity, 156
homoskedasticity, 155, 156, 261
hot deck imputation, 224–225, 233
hypothesis testing, 128–130

i.i.d., 91–92, 94–98
identification
with missing data, 208–219
with potential outcomes, 236–256
ignorability, *see* missing at random (MAR)
imputation
hot deck, 224–226, 233
under MAR, 220
under MCAR, 214–215
under random assignment, 246
under strong ignorability, 258
independence
CEFs and BLPs under, 82–84
conditional, 216, 248, 251, 254, 255, 270–272, 274
conditional probability and, 14–15, 39
correlation and, 64–66
covariance and, 59–60
implications of, 39, 64–65, 82
of events, 14
of random variables, 38–39
independent and identically distributed, *see* i.i.d.
inference, 124–135
with clustering, 140–141
with maximum likelihood estimation, 202–203
with regression, 151–156
interactions, 164–165
inverse probability–weighted (IPW) estimators, 226–228, 231, 234, 264, 266–267, 270, 275, 279
for causal inference, 266–267
for missing data, 227–228
stabilized, 228, 266–267

joint CDF, 32–33
multivariate case, 40
joint PDF, 36
multivariate case, 41
joint PMF, 32
multivariate case, 40
joint probability, 9–10
jointly continuous random variables, 36–38, 41, 42, 49, 50, 64–65, 67–69, 72–73, 85

kernel, 121
kernel density estimator, 121
kernel plug-in estimator, 123
Kolmogorov Axioms, 6–8, 20, 183
Kullback–Leibler Divergence, 195–196

lasso estimator, 169–170, 174, 202
Law of Iterated Expectations, 71–76, 155, 167, 198, 211, 212, 216, 218, 220, 227, 229, 241–243, 248, 250, 251, 258, 265, 268
Law of Total Probability, 12–13, 15, 33
Law of Total Variance, 73–75
leave-one-out cross-validation, 170, 174
likelihood function, 186, 189
linearity of expectations, 49–50
link function, 183n3
log-likelihood, 187–190, 192, 194, 202
logit model, 183–184, 233

M-estimators, 187n7
Manski bounds, *see* sharp bounds
marginal effect, 165
marginal PDF, 37
  multivariate case, 41–42
marginal PMF, 33–34
  multivariate case, 41–42
matching, 262–264
maximum likelihood (ML) estimation, 185–203, 233
  consistency of, 193
  inference with , 202–203
  logic of, 185–193
  of mixture models, 198–201
  of the classical linear model , 189–192
  of the probit model, 192–193
  penalized, 201–202
  plug-in estimator, 197–198
  under misspecification, 194
mean function, 183–184, 226, 264
mean squared error (MSE), 56–58
  alternative formula for, 57
  asymptotic, 113
  expected value minimizes, 57–58, 151
  of an estimator, 104
  root, 57
micronumerosity, 132–135, 149, 161, 162, 168, 274
missing at random (MAR), 215–217
  and the propensity score, 217–219
  CEF under, 217
  expected value under, 216
  imputation under, 220–221
  reweighting under, 226–227
missing completely at random (MCAR), 213–215
  expected value under, 213–214
  imputation under, 214–215
missing data, 208–219
  Double Robustness Theorem for, 230, 267
  doubly robust estimator for, 228, 230
  plug-in estimator for, 220–222
  propensity score for, 217–219
  regression estimator for, 224
  with binary outcomes, 209, 212, 214, 220, 222, 239
mixture model, 198–201
models, *see* parametric models
moments
  central, 51
  raw, 51
multicollinearity, *see* collinearity
multiplicative law for PDFs, 38
multiplicative law for PMFs, 35
Multiplicative Law of Probability, 10, 11, 13, 14, 35, 38
multivariate normal distribution, 152

negative control, *see* placebo testing
Newton–Raphson method, 191n11
Neyman–Rubin Causal Model (NRCM), 236, 239, 254
normal distribution, 55–56
  bivariate, 66n13
  mean and standard deviation of, 56
  properties of, 56
  standard, 28–30
null hypothesis, 128–130, 278

operator, 17, 45, 47, 67, 118
ordinary least squares (OLS) regression estimator, 145–146, *see also* regression
outcome, 4–5, *see also* potential outcomes model
overfitting, 161–164
overlap
  empirical, 273–276
  population, 271–273

p-value, 128–133, 140, 152, 154, 278, 279
parameter space, 179, 180, 183
parameter vector, 179, 182, 185
parametric models, 178–203
  as approximations, 203
  binary choice models, 182–185
  classical linear model, 180–182
  maximum likelihood estimation of, *see* maximum likelihood estimation
partial derivative at the average, 166–168, 171

partition, 12–13
penalized maximum likelihood estimation, 201–202
penalized regression, 169–170
penalty parameter, 169, 202
placebo testing, 270–271
plug-in estimator, 120
  asymptotic normality of, 120
  for the ATE under strong ignorability, 256–257
  for the expected value under MAR, 219–220
  maximum likelihood, 197–198
  plug-in sample variance as, 119
  regression as, 143–147
  regularity conditions, 120
  sample mean as, 118, 210, 240
plug-in principle, 116–124
plug-in sample variance, 105–108
  as plug-in estimator, 119
  properties of, 106
point identification, 207
polynomial approximation of the CEF, 158, 165n11, 169
population, 91, 95–96
  finite, 93–94
population mean, 93, 94, 97, 101, 103, 105, 106, 110, 115, 124, 127, 132, 133, 143, 151, 212, 214, 219, 224, 243
  confidence interval for, 127
  consistency of the sample mean for, 105
population regression function, 145
population variance, 94, 105, 116
positivity, 271–276
post-stratification estimator, 219, 256
post-treatment variables, 252–254
potential outcomes model, 236–239, 245, 248, 262, 265, 277, 278
  generalized, 254–256
probability density function (PDF), 24–25
  conditional, 37–38, 42
  joint, 36, 40
  marginal, 37, 42
  multiplicative law for, 38
  properties of, 25
probability limit, 99
probability mass function (PMF), 18–21
  conditional, 42
  joint, 32, 40
  marginal, 33–34, 41–42
  multiplicative law for, 35
  properties of, 20
probability measure, 6, 7
probability space, 6, 8
probit model, 183
  maximum likelihood estimation of , 192–193
propensity score
  for causal inference, 250–252
  for missing data, 217–219
  imputation with, 224–225
  MAR and, 217–219
  matching on, 262–264
  maximum likelihood plug-in estimation of, 225, 264
  strong ignorability and, 251–252
  Winsorization, 275
pseudopopulation, 95

random assignment, 244–247
  ATE under, 245
  imputation under, 246
random event, 4, 15
  independence of, 14
random generative process, 3–8, 14–16, 93
random sampling, 92–94
  finite population, 93–94
  with replacement, 94
  without replacement, 94
random variable, 15–31
  continuous, 24–30
  degenerate, 47, 108, 110, 113
  discrete, 18–21
  equality of, 31–32
  function of, 16
  independence of, 38–39
  independent and identically distributed, 91–92
  operator on, 17, 45
random vector, 39–40
  covariance matrix of, 84
  expectation of, 48
range, 16n15, 18, 284
realization, 4
regression, 143–151
  as plug-in estimator, 143–147
  bivariate case, 144–145
  classical standard errors for, 155–156
  confidence intervals for, 154
  estimator for causal inference, 258–261
  estimator for missing data, 222–224
  penalized, 169–170
  properties of residuals from, 149–151
  robust sampling variance estimator for, 153
  robust standard errors for, 152–154
  with matrix algebra, 147–151

regressor matrix, 147
relative efficiency, 105
  asymptotic, 113
residual, 147–149
response propensity function, 217, 225, 230
reweighting
  survey, 220–222
  under MAR, 226–227
  under strong ignorability, 265–266
root mean squared error, 57

sample mean
  as plug-in estimator, 118, 210, 240
  Chebyshev's Inequality for, 98–99
  consistency of, 105
  consistency of the standard error of, 115
  estimating the sampling variance of, 114
  expected value of, 97
  sampling variance of, 97–98
  standard error of, 115
  standardized, 109, 139
sample points, 5
sample space, 5
sample statistic, 96
sample variance
  plug-in, 105–107
  unbiased, 107
sampling, *see* random sampling
sampling variance, 104
  estimator of, 114–115
  of the cluster sample mean, 137, 140
  of the sample mean, 97–98
sandwich estimator, 153
sharp bounds, 209–213, 231, 240–244
  estimating, 211–212, 243–244
  for the ATE, 240–243
  for the expected value, 209–211
sieve estimator, 168–169
sigma field, 6n6
simple event, 6
Slutsky's Theorem, 109–110, 125, 126
stabilized IPW estimator
  for causal inference, 266–267
  for missing data, 228
stable outcomes model, 208
stable unit treatment value assumption, 237
standard deviation, 53
  of the normal distribution, 56
  properties of, 53–54
standard error, 104
  asymptotic, 113
  estimator of, 113–115
  of the regression estimator, *see* regression
  of the sample mean, 115
standard normal distribution, 28–30, 55
  expected value of, 46
standard uniform distribution, 28
standardized sample mean, 109, 139
statistical functional, 118
strong ignorability, 247–258, 261, 262
  and the propensity score, 250–252
  ATE under, 248–249, 253, 255
  conditional ATE under, 249
  imputation under, 257–258
  reweighting under, 265–266
superpopulation, 94
support, 30–31
survey reweighting, 221

t-statistic, 129
test statistic, 128n37
treatment effect, *see* unit-level treatment effect
treatment propensity function, 250, 264, 269, 273

unbiased sample variance, 107–108
  properties of, 108
unbiasedness, 103–105
  asymptotic, 112
uniform distribution, 28
unit-level treatment effect, 237

variance, 51–53
  alternative formula for, 52, 57
  conditional, 68
  population, 94, 105, 116
  properties of, 52–53
  sample, 105–108
  sampling, 104
variance rule, 60, 65
  multivariate, 84, 137

Weak Law of Large Numbers (WLLN), 99–102, 105, 107, 189, 193, 212, 243
  for cluster samples, 138
Weierstrass Approximation Theorem, 158
weighting estimator, 226–228, 264–267, 273–276
Winsorization, 275

Made in the USA
Las Vegas, NV
29 December 2023

83647154R00190